MW01196633

ALSO BY IAIN MacGREGOR

The Lighthouse of Stalingrad:
The Hidden Truth at the Heart of the Greatest Battle of World War II

Checkpoint Charlie:
The Cold War, the Berlin Wall, and the Most Dangerous Place on Earth

THE
HIROSHIMA
MEN

The Quest to Build the Atomic Bomb,
and the Fateful Decision to Use It

IAIN MacGREGOR

SCRIBNER
New York   Amsterdam/Antwerp   London   Toronto   Sydney/Melbourne   New Delhi

Scribner
An Imprint of Simon & Schuster, LLC
1230 Avenue of the Americas
New York, NY 10020

For more than 100 years, Simon & Schuster has championed authors and the stories they create. By respecting the copyright of an author's intellectual property, you enable Simon & Schuster and the author to continue publishing exceptional books for years to come. We thank you for supporting the author's copyright by purchasing an authorized edition of this book.

No amount of this book may be reproduced or stored in any format, nor may it be uploaded to any website, database, language-learning model, or other repository, retrieval, or artificial intelligence system without express permission. All rights reserved. Inquiries may be directed to Simon & Schuster, 1230 Avenue of the Americas, New York, NY 10020 or permissions@simonandschuster.com.

Copyright © 2025 by Iain MacGregor
Foreword copyright © 2025 by Kenji Shiga
Originally published in Great Britain in 2025 by Constable, an imprint of Little, Brown Book Group

All rights reserved, including the right to reproduce this book or portions thereof in any form whatsoever. For information, address Scribner Subsidiary Rights Department, 1230 Avenue of the Americas, New York, NY 10020.

First Scribner hardcover edition July 2025

SCRIBNER and design are trademarks of Simon & Schuster, LLC

Simon & Schuster strongly believes in freedom of expression and stands against censorship in all its forms. For more information, visit BooksBelong.com.

For information about special discounts for bulk purchases, please contact Simon & Schuster Special Sales at 1-866-506-1949 or business@simonandschuster.com.

The Simon & Schuster Speakers Bureau can bring authors to your live event. For more information or to book an event, contact the Simon & Schuster Speakers Bureau at 1-866-248-3049 or visit our website at www.simonspeakers.com.

Interior design by Lexy East

Manufactured in the United States of America

10 9 8 7 6 5 4 3 2 1

Library of Congress Cataloging-in-Publication Data has been applied for.

ISBN 978-1-6680-3804-8
ISBN 978-1-6680-3806-2 (ebook)

To Duncan, Lena, Miles, and Manuela

There is no power on earth that can
protect him from being bombed.
Whatever people may tell him, the bomber will
always get through; the only defence is offense,
which means that you have to kill more
women and children more quickly
than the enemy if you want to save yourselves.

STANLEY BALDWIN, BRITISH LORD PRESIDENT,
WORLD DISARMAMENT CONFERENCE, GENEVA, 1932

Contents

Chronology

1937

John Hersey starts apprenticeship as a journalist at *Time* magazine in New York City.

1938

December: German physicists Otto Hahn and Fritz Strassman discover nuclear fission.

1939

August 2: President Roosevelt receives the "Einstein Letter" warning of Nazi Germany's efforts to create an atomic weapon.
September 1: Nazi Germany invades Poland; World War II begins.
October 21: The first meeting of the Advisory Committee on Uranium is held in Washington, DC.

1940

June 27: The National Defense Research Committee (NDRC) is created to organize US scientific resources for war including research on the atom and the fission of uranium.

1941

February 24: Physicist Glenn Seaborg discovers plutonium.

December 7: Japan attacks United States Pacific Fleet at Pearl
    Harbor, in Hawaii.

December 8: The United States declares war on Japan.

December 11: The United States declares war on Germany and
    Italy (Germany and Italy had declared war on the United
    States first).

1942

January 19: President Roosevelt approves the creation of an atomic
    bomb.

April 18: Lieutenant Colonel James Doolittle leads B-25 bombers
    from the aircraft carrier USS *Hornet* for the first air raid against
    Japan.

May 8: Imperial Japanese forces complete conquest of the
    Philippines.

June 4–7: American naval victory at the Battle of Midway.

August 7: Campaign to capture Guadalcanal begins.

September 17: U.S. Army Brigadier General Leslie Groves (still a
    colonel until September 23) is appointed head of the Manhattan
    Engineer District.

September 19: Oak Ridge, Tennessee, chosen as site for uranium
    enrichment.

October: J. Robert Oppenheimer is selected to lead the Manhattan
    Project's secret weapons laboratory.

November 16: The Chicago Pile (CP-1), the world's first
    experimental nuclear reactor, begins construction at the
    University of Chicago.

November 25: Groves approves Oppenheimer's choice of Los
    Alamos to be the secret site for atomic bomb development and
    construction.

1943

January 14–23: The Casablanca Conference. Roosevelt vows to
    pursue the "unconditional surrender" of Japan.

January 16: Groves approves Hanford, Washington, as a secret site for plutonium production.

February: Major Paul Tibbets returns to the United States to begin training on the B-29.

August 17–24: Top secret summit between the US, Great Britain, and Canada at the First Quebec Conference, discussing invasion of Europe and development of an atomic bomb.

November 4: Oak Ridge's X-10 Graphite Reactor, the world's first full-scale reactor, reaches criticality.

1944

March: Japan reorganizes its home air defense against expected B-29 attacks.

April 4: The Twentieth Air Force is activated.

June: Operation Matterhorn—B-29s bombing Japan from mainland China.

June 6: Operation Overlord is launched, as Allied forces gain a foothold on the European continent in northern France.

June–November: Task Force 58 launches Operation Granite II to capture the Mariana and Palau Islands. It will establish B-29 air bases in Guam, Saipan, and Tinian.

September 1: Colonel Tibbets is secretly briefed on the Manhattan Project. He is selected to command the 509th Composite Group. Training begins at their new base in Wendover, Utah.

September 26: Hanford's "B" Reactor reaches criticality. It would reach full plutonium production power in February 1945.

October 20: Liberation of the Philippines by American forces of General Douglas MacArthur begins.

October 23–26: American naval victory at the Battle of Leyte Gulf, Philippines.

October–November: B-29s arrive on Saipan and Guam.

November 24: First B-29 mission against Japan launched from the Marianas.

December 27: North Field in Tinian operational for B-29s.

1945

January 21: Major General Curtis LeMay relieves Haywood Hansell of command of XXI Bomber Command.

February 4–11: President Roosevelt meets with Churchill and Stalin at the Yalta Conference.

February 19: US Marines invade Iwo Jima.

March 9–10: B-29 low-level incendiary raid on Tokyo.

March 23: US Marines capture Iwo Jima.

April 1: Okinawa invaded by US forces.

April 7: B-29 jamming of Japanese fire-control radars employed for the first time.

April 12: President Roosevelt dies. His successor, Harry S. Truman, first learns of the Manhattan Project's existence the next day.

May 8: "Victory in Europe" declared. John Hersey's novel *A Bell for Adano* wins the Pulitzer Prize.

May: 509th Composite Group moves to Tinian Air Base.

July 16: Successful atomic bomb test at the Trinity Site in New Mexico.

July 17–August 2: President Truman meets with Stalin and Churchill in Potsdam, Germany.

July 25: General Thomas T. Handy issues order to employ atomic bombs.

July 26: Truman issues the Potsdam Declaration, warning Japan of incomprehensible destruction if they do not surrender.

August 1: Most B-29s sent on combat missions against Japan in a single day. Of 836 B-29s launched, 784 hit targets in Japan.

August 6: Atomic attack by the *Enola Gay* on Hiroshima.

August 8: The Soviet Union declares war on Japan.

August 9: *Bockscar* drops an atomic bomb (Fat Man) on Nagasaki.

August 15: Japan surrenders.

September 2: Japan formally signs the "Instrument of Surrender" aboard the USS *Missouri*.

November 28: General Groves testifies to a US Senate Special Committee on the effects of radiation poisoning.

1946

May: John Hersey travels to Japan and spends three weeks in
Hiroshima interviewing survivors.

August 31: "Hiroshima" is published in *The New Yorker* magazine to
critical acclaim.

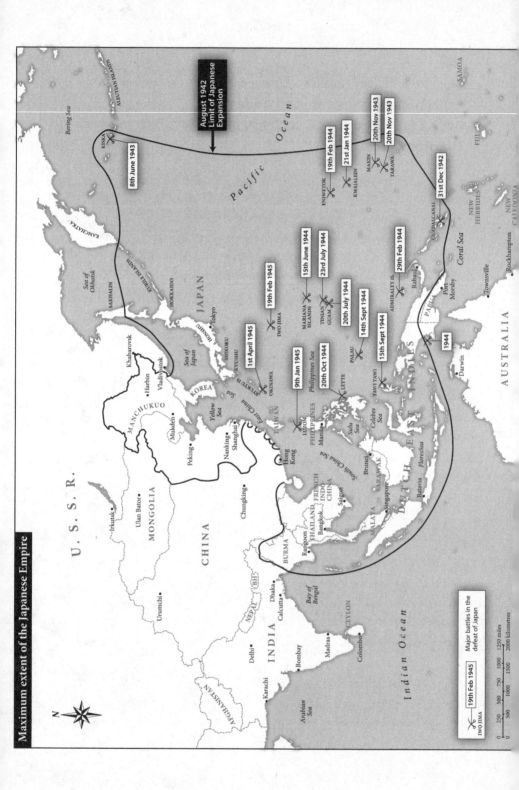

Maximum extent of the Japanese Empire

Foreword

At 8:15 a.m. on August 6, 1945, Hiroshima was instantly destroyed by a single atomic bomb. It is still unknown how many of the 350,000 people in Hiroshima were killed. The heat rays and blast from the bomb burned everything within a one-mile radius of the hypocenter and knocked down buildings. Radiation poisoned people from the inside, killing them. Those who barely survived spent their days in shacks built in the burnt-out area, suffering from ugly keloids (scars) on their skin burned by the heat rays and internal damage caused by the radiation. This was Hiroshima immediately after the bombing, when it was said that 'no grass or trees would grow for seventy-five years."

Ten years later, the streets of Hiroshima in my memory were no longer in ruins, but the scars left by the atomic bomb could still be seen in places. Keloids left on people's bodies never healed, and whenever I got onto a bus, I always saw people with them. My grandmother, who looked after me as a young child, was also covered with keloids all over her upper body and was unable to straighten her arms and fingers. By the mid-1960s, when she died, people with such keloids were no longer seen.

At the same time, the landscapes of the city that hinted at the atomic bombing were disappearing one after another. This was the beginning of Hiroshima's rebirth. In addition to people's steady dedicated efforts and support from home and abroad, the regeneration of Hiroshima was largely supported by the Hiroshima Peace Memorial City Construction Law. This special law aimed to revitalize Hiroshima as a Peace Memorial City symbolizing lasting peace, which led to full-scale state financial support and a strong push for the development of urban infrastructure.

The first project initiated was the Peace Memorial Park, which was constructed near the hypocenter. In the park, the Atomic Bomb Dome, the Cenotaph for the Atomic Bomb Victims, and the main building of the Peace Memorial Museum are located in a straight line along a single axis running through the park in a north–south direction. This axis is known as the "Peace Axis," and together with Peace Boulevard, which runs east–west directly across the southern end of the park, it remains the basis of urban planning in Hiroshima eighty years after the bombing and is a symbol of the rebirth of the city.

This narrative you are about to read will hopefully tell the story of how the world arrived at the nuclear age and the many dangers it still poses in the twenty-first century.

Kenji Shiga
Former director of the Hiroshima Peace Memorial Museum.

Prologue

Silence dominates the confined, stuffy room. A composed, elderly Japanese lady sits across from me. Her name is Michiko Kodama, and I have traveled halfway across the globe to interview her. A simple Formica table separates us, with our two coffee cups, my microphone, pad, and pen placed upon it. We are surrounded by boxes piled high, containing posters, leaflets, magazines, and badges of her organization.

We're sitting inside the nondescript offices of the Nihon Hidan-kyo,[1] the Confederation of A- & H-bomb Sufferers Organizations. Michiko is assistant secretary general, a picture of serenity in her royal navy suit. She indicates she is ready to start our interview. I'm momentarily surprised when she dictates her personal details for the recording and reveals she is eighty-seven years of age. Her jet-black hair and her elegant appearance and speech suggest she is younger.

As I begin the interview with formal greetings through my Japanese interpreter, her face comes to life, a warmth emanating from her gleaming smile and sparkling eyes. Those same eyes will soon dull and moisten as we discuss her memories of her childhood in Hiroshima, the city destroyed by a lone American bomber, high up in the crystal-blue sky, on the morning of August 6, 1945. The day that turned her world upside down and set in motion the end of the Greater East Asia War.[2]

Michiko tells me her ancient lineage is samurai but that by the twentieth century her family had modernized, taking up professional roles in banking and printing. She recalls details of her comfortable life growing up with two younger brothers and a father who ran printing businesses in and around Hiroshima Prefecture[3]—the vital military capital port of southwestern Honshu Island.[4] Both her parents' families were longtime residents of the city, going back decades. A quirk of fate would save her family from the atomic attack. American B-29 bombers were wreaking havoc across the country by the summer of 1945, their incendiary bombs having reduced up to sixty cities in the Home Islands to ashes. The traditional Japanese housing constructed of paper and wood proved to be the perfect kindling for the enemy's bombs to create firestorms killing tens of thousands of civilians. The cities that so far remained untouched, including Hiroshima, were ordered by the Tokyo government to create firebreaks to stall any more conflagrations.

Like thousands of other buildings in the city, Michiko's family house was demolished by military and volunteer teams.[5] Despite vociferous protests by many of the city's homeowners, the area's military commander, Field Marshal Shunroku Hata,[6] together with the governor of Hiroshima Prefecture, Genshin Takano, overruled civilian protests. Thousands had been forced to leave the city to find shelter elsewhere. Michiko's family now had to relocate two miles away from their main home, which unbeknownst to them now lay only six hundred yards from what would come to be known as Ground Zero.

Michiko would now have to attend a different school closer to her new home. Although she was too young to be drafted into the Volunteer Citizen Corps,[7] her sixteen-year-old cousin had been ordered to join. She was also not yet old enough to work in one of the hundreds of cellar factories, where students were busy constructing parts for military vehicles, or ordnance for rifles and artillery—a cottage industry that had developed all around Hiroshima in readiness for the expected American invasion. Her age would play a crucial part in Michiko surviving what was to come.

August 6 was a beautiful, warm, sunny morning as Michiko happily walked alongside her father to start her first day at Furuta Elementary National School among new teachers and classmates. The city bustled with life as thousands of workers traveled to their jobs via foot, bicycle, or one of the many streetcars and buses.[8] The center of the city's parks' manicured gardens were all bursting with an array of flowers and foliage, and the dozens of wooden teahouses along the riverbanks were already doing a roaring trade with the daily commuters and military personnel. As they made their way through the streets, Michiko gazed at the long lines of soldiers and students attached to ropes like a giant tug-of-war team, hoping to spot her cousin.

Over forty-three thousand troops were now stationed in and around Hiroshima, with more arriving daily as part of the buildup to defend the country from the expected invasion. The Imperial Navy still had various ships and boats in the harbor with major storage facilities and arsenals all along the coast. The Imperial Navy task force that had launched the war against the United States at Pearl Harbor on December 7, 1941, had embarked from these very docks. For all citizens living in and around the city, it was an inescapable fact that they were a military target for the enemy.

After perhaps thirty minutes, they reached Furuta School. Michiko's father waved goodbye and turned for home as she walked through the metal gates into a courtyard leading to a large, two-story wooden building, already bustling with life.

"I entered the classroom. I had a bag that my mother made for me. She was very good at sewing, though she didn't know anything about cooking. When I came into the room, I put my bag on the desk by the window. In those days, we had a disaster prevention cushion that we were supposed to wear to protect our heads. I was wondering if I should go to the playground first. Half of the school ground was free to use, but the other half was a field where potatoes were grown to help tackle the food shortage." [9]

As she studied her surroundings, she hoped her new classmates would eventually accept her as willingly as her old school friends, and worried at how her world had been turned upside down.

"Suddenly, I saw this glaring, bright light that came at me. I can't even fully describe what the light really looked like. It was a mixture of yellow, silver, orange. In no time after I wondered what it was, the wind blasted the windows of the room, sending sharp glass shards and wooden splinters flying everywhere. They stabbed desks, chairs, walls, floors, and other places. Without knowing what had happened, I ducked under the desk. I was able to cover my right shoulder by the desk, but not the left. I realized later that shards of glass were stuck on my left shoulder."

A new incredibly powerful weapon—which would later come to be known as Little Boy—had exploded nineteen hundred feet above Ground Zero[10] with the equivalent of fifteen thousand tons of TNT.[11] The heat and shock waves blasted across the city, as the temperature close to the epicenter reached several thousand degrees Celsius, almost as hot as the surface of the sun. Anything flammable burst into flame as the explosion caused hundreds of fires, which then conflagrated into an enormous firestorm, consuming everything within a mile radius. Steel building frames liquefied, the wooden teahouses and local buildings were simply reduced to ashes, while flying birds and animals burst into flames. Within minutes of the blast, nine out of ten people caught half a mile or less from the initial detonation were dead,[12] many of them suffering the evaporation of their internal organs, with eyes melting in sockets and skin disintegrating. In many cases nothing remained of them but their dark shadows where they had been standing or sitting down.

Situated over two miles from the epicenter of the blast, Michiko's school survived the initial blast, but in a city built on such flat terrain it meant the shock wave that followed had torn through with devastating effect. Traveling at over ten thousand feet per second, the heat wave smashed through brick and mortar, wood and steel with ease within a half mile, flattening practically everything in its path.

"In the [school] clinic, a teacher was treating students who had been badly cut by the glass shards and wood splinters. She helped pull the big pieces out. Everyone was covered in blood. Our health clinic had nothing significant in terms of medical equipment to treat children, no gauze, no bandages, and little sanitizer. That's all they had. Our teacher ripped the cotton curtains down to use for bandages. There were now several teachers who gathered from other classrooms. I don't remember any male teachers. Most of them were women, older ones, and even a pregnant one.

"The roof had been blasted off, and then the second-story ceiling came down. But the structural frame itself remained. The injured students who had received treatment went outside to make room for other students coming into the clinic. In the school ground there were air raid dugouts, where we were supposed to wait for our parents to come pick us up. But many didn't see their parents, so they were told to stay in the dugouts. I just moved there on my own, as I didn't have too many friends yet.

"Fortunately, my father hurriedly returned to find me and pick me up. He was relieved to see me but shocked at my appearance. With my injuries to my upper body, and to move quickly, he decided to carry me on his back. He intended to get home, but to get there we had to walk toward Ground Zero, which was the quickest route. That's when I witnessed a living hell.

"Amid the smoke, fires and debris being blown around by the fierce winds, I could make out burned, charcoal-colored people littering the ground. Many seemed lifeless. Others staggered in all directions: a mother who had a charcoal baby, a person who was trying to pop the eyes back into their sockets, or that's what it looked like to me. Of course, they couldn't see where they were going, with skin hanging down from severe burns, but some asked for help and for water, grabbing my father's arms and my legs. We shook them off as we passed by because there really wasn't anything we could do. I'm sure my father felt helpless, too. Every time someone reached out to us, he'd clutch me and hold me tighter. These images are burned into my memory.

"I saw this one young girl about my age whose clothes and half of her face were burned. She couldn't say anything, but her eyes were beseeching us. Our eyes locked. She was asking me, 'Water, water. Please help me.'

"I will never forget those eyes. I looked back at her as I clung from my father's shoulders and saw her fall to the ground. I so regretted that I couldn't even offer her a drop of water for the last time. It was excruciating. My senses soon became numb."

After what seemed like hours walking through the dystopian landscape that was now devoid of any familiar landmarks, Michiko and her father reached their home, or what was left of it. Thankfully her mother and younger brothers were still alive, but their new house had been severely damaged by the blast.

"Half of the tiled roof was gone, exposing the house to the sky. The overhanging balcony had protected the kitchen on the first floor, so that area was okay. Shortly after, it started raining. What would later be called 'Black Rain.' This was a very different rain from what I knew. It was sticky, muddy drops that now fell through into the bombed-out house. It glued itself to a chest of drawers, to the exposed floors and walls. Now I know that it contained radioactive materials, but at the time, my mother was trying to wipe them away with a bucket and a rag."

Michiko's father settled the children down into a sheltered corner of the ground floor of the house, out of the rain, and talked with his wife for a few short minutes before heading out again, back to the family's original house close to Ground Zero. He needed to check on his nine siblings, who still lived close to where the bomb had detonated. Michiko would not see him again for another three days as he navigated the charred landscape searching for signs of them.

"While he was gone, that evening and the morning after, my relatives—grandfather, uncles and aunts and cousins—arrived at our house. Because we lived two miles away from Ground Zero, they thought it was safe and that they could rest there. All of them carried some injury. We didn't have any water, electricity, or anything at the time, but we had a well. Meanwhile my mother was trying to make bandages and towels by ripping old *yukata*, kimono, old sheets to wipe away everyone's blood and pus off their burned bodies. There was no sign of any official help from any medical team, the army, or local government. We were on our own."[13]

As her extended family reunited at her parents' wrecked house over the coming days, their mood reflected that of the wider city's survivors: there was bewilderment and shock as to what type of weapon the American bombers had dropped on Hiroshima to cause such catastrophic destruction and death, mixed with ever-increasing concern that the worst was not yet over.

"I was helping my mother treat everyone and I heard some noise from the front door. I went to open it, when I saw this figure that did not [seem] to have a human form. I became really scared and felt the urge to run and find my mother. That's when the figure called out my name: 'Micchan, Micchan.'

"With the voice, I realized it was my cousin, Onaichan ['Older Sister']. She had been working outside around five yards away from Ground Zero. Her face was now burned, with severe burns to her front, stomach area, and her back.

"As soon as I realized it was her, I invited her into the back room to look after her. But that summer was hot and so her wounds soon festered. I wiped away the pus and picked maggots that started to eat her wounds. As I remember, on the morning of the third day, I went to her bedside. I was going to pick out any maggots again, but I heard her utter 'water' in such a small voice. I went to the well in the garden to get some water. The inside of her mouth was burned, so she couldn't drink too much. I soaked a towel with water and held her in my arms in order to lift her head up, and I squeezed drops of water into her mouth.

"She couldn't swallow but only drool. She then took her last breath in my arms. I felt so extremely sad. Meanwhile some of my aunts and uncles were also dying at our house.

"We had nothing, no medical supplies. The doctors and nurses at a nearby Red Cross were all hurt. The entire Hiroshima city was like that. Doctors were treating patients even when they were injured themselves. There was no help from the government. I don't think the state was functioning. Individual residents like us who were treating the injured never received any support.

"My other cousin, ten years old at the time, was also staying at our house. When he had arrived, he seemed to have suffered only light injuries and luckily no burns. But he quickly developed severe diarrhea. At the beginning of September, he came out of the bathroom, one of several times that he had been throughout the day, and he came toward me where I was sitting facing the garden. He suddenly bled from his nose. At that moment this sight didn't shock me too much as I sometimes suffered the same ailment.

"Just as I was looking up at him thinking this, he began to cough, which gradually became more violent and shocking. Within minutes, he had keeled over and begun to vomit blood, in bigger and bigger amounts, until he was throwing up chunks. It was horrifying. He staggered around trying to maintain his balance but then collapsed and lay motionless on the mat. My mother ran to his motionless body, trying desperately to wake him up. But it became apparent he had died. It upset the whole family. I felt so scared for weeks, as I imagined that that is going to happen to me, too. I couldn't leave my mother's side for a long time afterward."

Michiko would discover much later that her original school had been destroyed. Of the four hundred students and eleven teachers of Honkowa School, all had perished.[14] Like tens of thousands of others that morning, there was nothing left of them to be recovered. Reliving this memory, which she herself admits she has buried for many years, brings forth further recollections that even my interpreter struggles to recount without becoming distressed:

"Two years later, I happened to be around that neighborhood—I can't remember why I was there. There was an older lady who walked toward me. I used to be called Micchan, but this lady grabbed my shoulders, shook them, asking, 'Aren't you Micchan?' It turned out she was the mother of my best friend. She said, 'My daughter hasn't come home! She hasn't come home! Why are you here!?'

"Tears were running down her face, and I shook off her hands and ran home. I don't remember how I got home. I asked myself if I had the right to be there—if I should even be alive. It was survivor's guilt."

As we continue to talk for almost three hours that morning, Michiko shares her family's story, as Japan became occupied by the victorious Allies before developing into a fledgling democracy by the start of the 1950s. The survivors of the atomic attacks on both Hiroshima and Nagasaki would struggle to rebuild their lives, forever tainted with the stigma of atomic disease. These hundreds of thousands of men, women. and children would be discriminated against as "Hibakusha" ("bomb-affected people"), suffering a lack of support from government as many succumbed to cancer-related illnesses, and those healthy enough to study and work shunned in higher education and the workplace. Even those who had legitimate reasons to travel to the United States to live with relatives and would later develop radiation-related illnesses had their pleas for medical assistance ignored.

"Even amid this type of prejudice, I met someone who wanted to marry me. I even declined him, but he insisted. His father had already died in the war. We decided to go meet his mother. I didn't know that there would be many of his aunts and uncles waiting to talk to me. They told me that they investigated me and my background, my family history because their son wanted to marry me. They said they found nothing wrong with that but found out that I was Hibakusha. 'We don't want any blood of the devil tainting our family.' The marriage was called off. I was rejected. We worked together, but that became too difficult for my boyfriend. He ended up leaving our workplace, too.

"I then made the decision to stay single for the remainder my life, and even though I had many men approach me, I declined their proposals. But eventually I met a man who knew I was also Hibakusha.

Though I turned him down at first, he said he just wanted to talk, and as time progressed, we became close and then decided to marry. There were many stories I heard of Hibakusha women who married without telling their spouses and ended up getting divorced when the spouses found out. Not only were we physically in pain, but Hibakusha lived with this mental trauma, too. My husband often had to relocate for his work, so I was constantly on my guard to not admit to anyone new that I was from Hiroshima.

"I now live in Chiba close to Tokyo Bay.[15] My mother died first. Although my father lived longer, he developed cancer on and off and went through several operations. When he died, his body had been devoured by two types of cancer. After many years of wondering whether I could have children, my husband and I did manage to have our daughter, who grew up healthy and cheerful. She almost never got sick. She went to school, graduated from university, and then landed a perfect job, as well as happily marrying. But in November 2010, she was diagnosed with cancer. We believed she was misdiagnosed. She went to several different doctors for treatment, some of whom asked if she had a Hibakusha in her family. I was truly shocked when she told me this. The second-generation Hibakusha does carry the DNA, the genes of Hibakusha, but the government does not recognize the need for any special, official support for them.

"In February 2011, she passed away, four months after the diagnosis."

Through the interpreter, I asked her how she has coped over the years without her daughter. She smiled and gestured to her side.

"She's still around here, hovering over me. I talk to her in the photo every day. Both my younger brothers died of multiple myelomas in late 2017. I have now lost my parents, my daughter, two of my brothers. Now it's my turn next."

I almost reach out to touch her hand. At the end of the table, like a referee overseeing a chess match, my interpreter simply stares at both of us, speechless. Silence settles on the room. Only the Tokyo rain drumming against the window disturbs the silence.

Introduction

THE GOOD WAR

The celebrations for America's "Navy Day" on October 27, 1945, were renamed "A Tribute to Victory," and a high-profile concert, live from the Los Angeles Memorial Coliseum,[1] would be broadcast by CBS Radio coast to coast. Across the US, most cities and towns were hosting their own tributes, marches, speeches, and stage shows to celebrate their military victory over Adolf Hitler's Germany and Emperor Hirohito's Imperial Japan. The country was coming together as one to almost close the chapter on the terrible conflict that had been won at great cost over four years since that "Day of Infamy"[2] on December 7, 1941, with the Japanese attack on Pearl Harbor. The biggest celebration was to be held close to Hollywood, and no expense was spared to create a show that would encapsulate this homage to the heroes of America and her allies.

The show would last for hours and be hosted by cinematic legend Edward G. Robinson,[3] supported by a cast of current stars, such as Henry Fonda, Judy Garland, Gregory Peck, Rita Hayworth, and Frank Sinatra. Over a hundred thousand people crammed into the stadium to watch awestruck as a huge cast of actors, complete with giant stage sets of ships, airplanes, tanks, and even parachutists recreated the key moments of America's role in the Second World War; from Pearl Harbor, the naval victory at Midway, the US Marine Corps's defense of Guadalcanal, the magnificence of D-Day, the heroics of the Battle of the Bulge, and of course the bloody victories achieved at Iwo Jima and Okinawa.

The crowd, many of whom were still dressed in service uniform, applauded, booed, and cheered as each pivotal moment was acted out with explosions, smoke, and Robinson's commentary. At one point, the concert's artistic director had outdone himself by constructing a fluorescent set of lines in the football field that burned furiously as flights of B-17 Flying Fortresses flew overhead to simulate incendiaries[4] dropping down onto enemy targets.[5] Many in the audience that night were themselves veterans not only of the European theater, but also of the Pacific war, still celebrating their good fortune in having escaped the trauma (and possibly death) of being part of the million-strong invasion of Japan slated for November 1945. The dropping of "the bomb" had instead brought about the enemy's speedy surrender.

To close the evening, as the Californian sun set and a cool sea breeze swept across the masses, eighty powerful searchlight beams encircling the stadium abruptly lit up the night sky. To those who witnessed it, it was reminiscent of the prewar Nazi rallies at Nuremberg. Robinson worked his audience masterfully as they scanned the night sky. What could they see? A searchlight suddenly picked out in the distance what seemed like a floating blimp. More beams found their target as it drew closer, the familiar drone of its four jet-propellered engines getting louder. A bomber was approaching. As Robinson declared to his audience, this was the US military's greatest weapon of the war, the B-29 bomber, the "Superfortress."

Tens of thousands of Californians fell silent as they strained to see the iconic bomber come in low above them, while millions of Americans across the country sat glued to their radios as if it was an actual raid they were listening to. With a deafening roar, three B-29s swept over the stadium at less than three hundred feet, so low the searchlight beams reflected off the plane's famous silver-plated fuselages, blinding those looking up at the monsters. A split second after the bombers disappeared into the night, a huge explosion wrenched the air, and the audience gasped as a giant mushroom cloud rose behind the stage where Robinson was standing.

"Ladies and gentlemen," he boomed, raising one hand in triumph toward the rising smoke, "I give you . . . Hiroshima!"

Even on the recorded broadcast, the roar of the Coliseum was mighty.

How does one explain this exultation of what was the first-ever atomic bomb—a weapon of mass destruction—being used on human beings for the first time? This narrative will lead you on a journey of the war, mostly in the Pacific and partly in Europe. Once the United States officially joined on December 8, 1941, it culminated forty-four months later in the fateful dropping of the atomic uranium bomb—Little Boy—on the Imperial Japanese city of Hiroshima on August 6, 1945, at 8:15 a.m., followed by a second attack on the port city of Nagasaki with a plutonium-made bomb called Fat Man on August 9 at 11:02 a.m.[6] The world would never be the same.

In the weeks and months after the ending of the war, the administration of Roosevelt's successor, President Harry S. Truman, would present this new weapon, the teams, technology that had built it, and the military who had trained to deliver it as a unique coming together of the power and ingenuity that only the United States could have achieved. The American public were drip-fed news of the top secret organization code-named the Manhattan Project, its military commander General Leslie Groves, and the multinational scientific team based at Los Alamos in the desert of New Mexico and directed by the brilliant physicist Professor J. Robert Oppenheimer. All would become household names as America led the way in what seemed a new, exciting postwar world, where democracy had prevailed over totalitarianism, and the Cold War with the Soviet Union was yet to develop.

Within a year of the Tribute to Victory celebrations, many Americans would be brought to tears as they read a thirty-thousand-word article in *The New Yorker* magazine, describing in graphic detail what the atomic bomb had inflicted upon its victims and the health

consequences for the survivors. The story was penned by the Pulitzer Prize–winning novelist and veteran war reporter John Hersey.
Titled simply "Hiroshima," it documented the personal stories of six
Japanese survivors after their city had been destroyed. The atomic
bomb had been celebrated as winning a vicious war against a fanatical
enemy, and that tyranny had been defeated in the race to invent such
a deadly weapon. Democracy had prevailed as America and her allies
had fought and won the "Good War." Hersey's reportage in *The New
Yorker* would forever question that mindset, not just in the United
States, but right across the Western world. *The New York Times* would
summarize the core message Hersey's sensational scoop had given
to the country: "The disasters at Hiroshima and Nagasaki were our
handiwork. They were defended then, and are defended now, by the
argument that they saved more lives than they took—more lives of
Japanese as well as more lives of Americans. The argument may be
sound, or it may be unsound. One may think it sound when he recalls
Tarawa, Iwo Jima, or Okinawa. One may think it unsound when he
reads Mr. Hersey."

He had changed the country's perceptions. A new, more dangerous era was dawning. This is the story of *The Hiroshima Men*.

As a historian, I have been always fascinated about the relation-
ships between emotion, memory, and facts. The Second World War
was undoubtedly the most brutal and bloody in modern history, a
true global conflict compared to its predecessor, the Great War of
1914–18, which had focused primarily on the European continent.
The losses from September 1, 1939, when Germany attacked Poland, until the ending of the war with the unconditional surrender
of Imperial Japan on August 15, 1945, are staggering. Over fifty to
fifty-six million people lost their lives directly as fighting spread
across the globe, with almost twenty million added because of fam-
ines and disease they brought in their wake. From this combined
total, it has been estimated that fifty-five million were civilians.[7] It
would be a war where the home could be and in many cases was "the
front line," and terms such as "appeasement," "mechanized warfare,"

"strategic airpower," "firebombing," "the Final Solution," and "genocide" would gain international recognition. "Total war" would now be added to the list.

President Roosevelt's administration, by breaking the Japanese diplomatic codes, knew an attack was coming. They simply didn't know where or when. The attack by aircraft of the Imperial Japanese Navy on the United States' Pacific Fleet at Pearl Harbor in Hawaii on December 7, 1941, would therefore come as a deadly surprise. Tension in the Pacific had been brewing for years over who was the dominant power in the region, the consequence of an economic-diplomatic confrontation over decades between Imperial Japan and the various Western colonial powers, Britain, France, Russia, the Netherlands, and the United States. At its heart: who could control East Asia and the Pacific, the abundance of natural resources it held such as rubber and petroleum, and of course the various populations within it who could be harnessed for economic growth. Much as we see with the rise of China today in the same part of the world, the United States had to contend with an economic adversary that had been growing in stature and now viewed itself as the primary power over its near neighbors and willing to use force to make it a reality.

Japan had been a feudal-based country, sealed off until the mid-nineteenth century, which was then opened to Western influence and trade at the point of naval cannons in the 1850s. Through bilateral agreements that heavily favored the colonial powers, Japan accepted Western influence, trade, and technology. By the turn of the 1940s it had rapidly transformed itself into a modern state, powered by a dynamic economy, a growing population of over seventy million, modern armed forces, and a political system wedded to the symbol of the imperial court being the highest power in the land. At the top of this pyramid, and the one source of stability for his country, was the slight, bespectacled figure of Emperor Hirohito. A divine monarch, whose key role in Japan's military advances was deftly overlooked and spun once the war was over and America needed him as a Cold War ally.

The first of the emperors had begun their reign in 660 BC. He and his successors were believed to be *arahitogami*, human and at the same time a god. Hirohito was no different, and emperor worship was central to the life of the Japanese people. As schoolboy, Hisashi Yamanka, recalled when Hirohito visited his city in the mid-1930s:

> Every school had to have a special little shrine, called a *honden*, with the photographs of the emperor and empress [that] had to be kept together with a copy of the Imperial Rescript. Every time we passed in front of this little shrine, we had to perform a deep bow. There are different degrees of bowing; from the lighter to the deeper, according to the occasion, but when it came to anything to do with the emperor, [or] his family, we had to lower our heads by forty-five degrees. When we looked in the direction of the photographs, we weren't supposed to look at them directly, we had to bow so deeply and so long that if we wanted to see the photographs themselves our only chance was to roll our eyes upwards very briefly.
>
> I remember when I was five years old, the emperor came and visited a military exercise in Hokkaido. A week before the emperor's visit the police went round every household ordering any invalid lying in an upstairs room to come down to the ground floor. They said no one should be on a higher level than the emperor.[8]

Race would play a significant part in the breakdown of relations between Japan and the foreign powers that had brought it into the modern age—especially her two primary competitors in Asia: Great Britain and the United States. Both powers held on to the vast colonial possessions they governed with policies rooted in notions of racial superiority. When the new heir in the Meiji line, the twenty-five-year-old Emperor Hirohito, came to the throne in 1926, Japan had already suffered the indignity of witnessing the US Congress pass the Immigration Act two years earlier. This statute detailed immigrant quotas that discriminated predominantly against "genetically inferior" races: Italians, Jews from Eastern Europe, and Japanese. This was after Japan had failed to get agreement at the newly created League of Nations on its proposed amendment for equal status among the victorious powers of the Great War. Then-president Woodrow Wilson had ensured its failure by voting against it.

For the Japanese, overpopulation was a key driver of the regime's colonial ambitions, supported by a racial doctrine of superiority. By the 1930s, the country contained seventy-three million people, a figure that made up approximately 5 percent of the world's population. Yet the Japanese existed on just 1 percent of the globe's landmass. The Japanese "Home Islands" consisted of Hokkaido, Honshu, Shikoku, and Kyushu,[9] with an added archipelago of over fourteen thousand islands and atolls, the primary island being Okinawa. Geographically, Japan was a land of mountains and forests, with little flat terrain to feed itself and house an industrial base that could compete on the world stage. For a country that had feared further Western encroachment, future economic growth ensured security. Government demographers calculated that to compete with the great powers of China, the Soviet Union, and the United States, Japan required a much larger workforce. The population needed to expand by another third, to at least one hundred million people. The Home Islands, plus colonies in Korea and Formosa, could not hope to accommodate such an increase. Hirohito's politicians and military looked covetously westward.[10]

The consequences of the Great Depression for Japan mirrored the path Germany took. The economies of both countries were devastated, and there was mass unemployment as foreign investment ground to a halt, high inflation, and an inexorable slide toward authoritarian military rule. By the early thirties, Japanese society witnessed political oppression and waves of high-profile assassinations in government, industry, and the media. Japan's military, with the emperor's knowledge, invaded Manchuria in northeast China in 1931, creating the puppet state of Manchukuo, with international censure (but no sanctions) resulting in Japanese diplomats walking out of the League of Nations in March 1933. Ultranationalists pushed for an ideology that ratified the emperor's right to rule as an absolute monarch and for an official policy for Japan to expand westward, even if it set in train hostilities with the colonial powers. The peoples Japan would conquer would be brought into the "East Asian Co-Prosperity Sphere"—an economic and military bloc that would shield members from Western colonization and manipulation. This was first articulated in 1940 by the Japanese prime minister, Fumimaro Konoe, and supported by Japanese intellectuals, likening it to the American Monroe Doctrine protecting US interests in South America from European intervention. For many of the Japanese-occupied states, it also meant enslavement.

By 1937, the United States and the European democracies, with colonial possessions, watched on as Japanese forces bludgeoned their way southwestward into China from their base in Manchuria, starting the Second Sino-Japanese War. In a prelude to Nazi Germany's race war against the Soviet Union in 1941, Imperial Japanese troops committed mass atrocities as they besieged the port of Shanghai and captured the temporary capital, Nanking. Hundreds of thousands of Chinese civilians were tortured, raped, and killed. The commander of the forces taking Nanking stated:

"The struggle between Japan and China was always a fight between brothers within the 'Asian Family'. . . . It has been my belief during all these days that we must regard this struggle as a method of making the Chinese undergo self-reflection."[11]

The war would drag on for several years as Chinese nationalist and communist forces combined in a tenuous pact to fight the Japanese, with the primary support of the United States. But as a result of an overly ambitious plan, Emperor Hirohito would see hundreds of thousands of his troops bogged down in China until the end of the Second World War.

The Japanese Imperial Army's shadow force (the "Kwantung Army," comprising some of the country's best units) had been spoiling for a fight on the western Mongolian border, which rubbed up against their Manchurian bases (renamed "Machukuo"). The goals of the Kwantung leadership were extreme, and to a degree at odds with their superiors in Tokyo, who were caught on the hop by their activities. Manufacturing an excuse to occupy Manchuria through the Nomonhan Incident in May 1939, by that August, what would prove to be the first combined-arms battle prior to the Second World War erupted. Soviet forces, led by General Georgy Zhukov, inflicted an embarrassing defeat on the Kwantung Army at the Battle of Halhgol.[12] Soviet estimates of Japanese casualties totalled sixty thousand killed or wounded. Whatever the cost, it ended Hirohito's ambitions of pushing westward from China. His military leadership now looked to Southeast Asia for obtaining the resources it needed to maintain its position of power.

On September 27, 1940, encouraged by Hitler's successes across Western Europe and Benito Mussolini's initial capture of territories in North Africa, Japan signed the Tripartite Pact with its authoritarian bedfellows in Berlin. Acknowledging each other's spheres of influence with promises of support in times of need, the geographical imposition of such a promise was seemingly ignored. But with such powerful European allies practicing their own racial and imperial agendas, the deal gave a sheen of respectability to the Japanese leadership on the international stage as relations with the United States worsened.

In late September 1940, to prevent further US-backed foreign aid reaching Chinese nationalist forces fighting her Imperial Army, Japan agreed to a deal with the Vichy French government that it would respect its sovereignty if Japanese troops, landing by sea, could both pass through and be stationed in French Indochina. Though the French had agreed, Japanese Army commanders on the ground proceeded to send in its forces by land, sparking firefights with French troops. After a few days of fighting, the matter was settled in a cease-fire. But the damage was done. The error prompted President Roosevelt's administration to later freeze Japanese assets on July 26, 1941, and eventually embargo all oil exports from the West to Japan on August 1. This move denied the Japanese war industry the essential supplies required to maintain its expansionist policy. Facing a stalemate in China, Japanese strategists, buoyed with an eighteen- to twenty-four-month supply of oil in reserve, gambled on a thrust south to capture Western oil, rubber, and mineral assets in Southeast Asia as Japan's best option. Mistakenly, they believed the Americans did not have the stomach for a protracted war and the British were preoccupied with Hitler's conquest of Europe. The plan of the military hard-liners was as daring as it was unrealistic; it was based on very little evidence or military intelligence reports. It would lead to war after December 7, 1941.

Warfare drives innovations in tactics and fighting, training one's forces, and crucially greater strides in science and technology. Of the main belligerents, the United States, led by President Roosevelt in his third term, was a sleeping superpower. Roosevelt had guided the country out of the Great Depression throughout the 1930s, reenergizing a wound-down industrial base and gearing it up for war, while remaining on the sidelines.[13] As David M. Kennedy in his seminal work *The American People in World War Two* concluded:

> Vast reservoirs of physical productive capacity lay unused, including factories, heavy construction equipment, machine-tool stocks, electrical generating plants, trucks, locomotives, and railcars. As much as fifty per cent [sic] capacity of automobile manufacturing plants stood idle. As the war crisis now snapped the drooping American economy to attention, all those dormant resources could be swiftly directed to martial purposes[.][14]

Roosevelt first pledged to be the "Arsenal of Democracy," but also to use the United States' manpower, industrial might, and wealth of science and technology to wage war like no empire before it. In short, American workers would put down tools for the consumer market and instead turn their energy toward outproducing all other countries in guns, tanks, ships, and planes. To achieve this, the United States had everything it needed from a continent teeming with minerals, oil, and gas. Unlike the fighting going on across Europe and the British Empire, North America remained shielded from its enemies by the barriers of the Pacific and Atlantic Oceans.[15]

He outlined his policy of Lend-Lease[16] to the American people in his "Fireside Chat" radio broadcast from the White House on March 15, 1941. The president detailed the current threats to "freedom" and "democracy" to his audience, and then how the Lend-Lease Act would allow America to deliver vital military matériel, as well as food supplies, to the Allies (at the time primarily Great Britain) in their hour of need. Nazi Germany now occupied the western half of continental Europe, leaving Great Britain and her commonwealth to fight on alone. At the policy level, the United States was poised to orchestrate a war of machines. Its vast industrial complex was now getting on a war footing. A prewar unemployment figure of three million was soon consigned to history. In a unique and rapid expansion, Roosevelt's administration traded armaments, vehicles, and war materials to its allies rather than expend the lives of its own people. America's allies could shoulder the burden of fighting, while American factories poured out the necessary implements of war to fight it. Striking the right balance with the American public was key if the country was to sign up to his policies to come. As David M. Kennedy summarizes: "The choices made [by Roosevelt's administration] in 1942 would deeply affect the course of the fighting, the shape of American society both during and after the war, and the fate of the wider post-war world."[17]

Lend-Lease would see the US workforce produce 60 percent of Allied munitions and 40 percent of all the world's arms. More than a quarter of all Britain's war supplies came from the United States. By war's end, the Americans provided as much as 30 percent of the Soviet Union's military needs,[18] as well as thirty-five thousand radio sets, 4.5 million tons of food, 1.5 million blankets, and fifteen million pairs of boots. After December 7, 1941, the Lend-Lease policy was never debated in Congress again. The signing of the later

Anglo-American Mutual Aid Agreement in February 1942 would cement deeper relations between the UK and the US and, as we shall see further in this story, would greatly support the United States' development of nuclear technology.[19]

Public support for the United States' participation in the war after Pearl Harbor was unanimous—with the American public assuming that the government knew best on military and foreign policy questions.[20] The country galvanized itself to fight major conflicts on both sides of the world, from the beaches of Normandy and France and the mountain passes of Italy to the jungles of Guadalcanal and the islands of the South Pacific. The war would activate the US government to harness the expertise of American industry and its workforce to achieve remarkable success. While human losses to the country were significant, with more than 290,000 killed in combat, the advances the United States made in science, technology, design, and supply inflicted far more damage to its enemies, particularly Imperial Japan. As John Dower outlines in *War Without Mercy*, "The human cost of the war for the Japanese themselves appears to be at least 2.5 million individuals—much smaller than the Chinese, and half the losses of Germany, but twenty-five times more than American combat deaths in the Pacific theatre, and eight or nine times greater than the total number of Americans killed in WWII."[21]

The campaign to defeat the Japanese Imperial Navy after Pearl Harbor began with victory at the Battle of Midway in June 1942. The United States, with its Western allies and those on the Chinese mainland, would then undertake a three-and-a-half-year war of attrition as it broke through Japan's outer perimeter that the early conquests had delivered, stretching from western Alaska to the Solomon Islands. A new "absolute zone of national defense" was established but would disintegrate in the wake of an American two-pronged assault from the South and Central Pacific, on land, sea, and in the air, stoked not just by patriotism, but by a thirst for revenge considering what was perceived as the Japaneses' treacherous attack on December 7, 1941. The fighting across the Pacific and East Asia would mirror to some degree the barbarity of the fighting on the Eastern Front, though it was far less ideologically driven and far more defined by race. Propaganda was ramped up as the war escalated in the Pacific and East Asia, spurring genocidal Japanese repression of occupied populations, brutal treatment of military prisoners, and a fanatical defense of its territory as the Allies fought to recapture lost territory and invade the Home Islands. The bloodletting would escalate a no-holds-barred attitude by the United States and the allies to defeating the Japanese. No weapon or method of fighting would be taken off the table if it brought unconditional surrender.

The US military had for many years drafted a strategy to achieve victory in the Pacific should a war with Japan come about—primarily led by the planners of the US Navy to develop "War Plan Orange." The concept was to achieve a decisive naval battle to destroy the Imperial Japanese Navy, to be followed by a naval blockade to bring the country to its knees. This plan had been drawn up as far back as the beginning of the twentieth century, after Japan's naval victory over the Russian tsar's fleet at Tsushima in May 1905. Over the ensuing decades, this plan had been incorporated into the United States Joint Chiefs strategy of fighting in multiple conflicts simultaneously: "Rainbow" plans.[22] The United States' actual strategy for fighting World War II would be distilled in "Rainbow 5": Countering the threat of a two-ocean war against multiple enemies, the United States would be allied with Britain and France to launch offensive operations by its forces in Europe, Africa, or both. Ideally, as the Roosevelt administration was aware, the United States did not want to fight such a dual-theater war, and given a choice, it would be going eastward to Asia. As the military historian Professor Tami Davis Biddle summarized:

"I think there was a strong sense that American isolationists were not isolationist towards the Pacific. They were rather gung ho about wanting to control the Pacific and the trade routes. Roosevelt didn't have to . . . make hard arguments about why it was important to have a large US Navy that could go into Asian waters. But I think it's important to say that no one in the US military was anxious to be in a two-front war, and we were really hoping to be able to just kind of push the probable future conflict with Japan down the road a bit."[23]

Within the framework of Rainbow 5 was a three-phase strategy to win a decisive war against Japan. Phase One envisaged the United States losing possessions to Japanese forces in the Pacific (which after the attack on Pearl Harbor would become a reality). Phase Two outlined the American counterattack by naval and army forces, which would sever and isolate Japanese lines of supply and communication. Finally, Phase Three would enforce a naval blockade of Japanese ports, the sinking of their mercantile fleet, and the bombardment of their coastal cities. This final phase made sense when measured against Japan's lack of natural resources and dependence on food imports for its burgeoning population. As one can see, this was always a US Navy–led strategy. American military planners would be forced to allow airpower into the equation after Pearl Harbor.

As early as 1940, to compound Japan's primary weakness of reliance on her seaborne trade routes to keep her going, the US military had pinpointed the country's infrastructural Achilles' heel. That September, Lieutenant Commander Henri Smith-Hutton, then the US naval attaché to Tokyo, reported back to his superiors that Japan's "firefighting facilities were woefully inadequate. Incendiary bombs sowed widely over an area of Japanese cities would result in the destruction of [a] major portion of the cities."[24]

It was a prophetic statement.

The war drove rapid innovation in aircraft design, technology, and the ordnance it could deliver upon the enemy. The culmination of such a policy (not just for the United States but for Great Britain, too) was the heavy bomber and the mass destruction it unleashed, whether through incendiary bombs or the atomic bomb. As *The Hiroshima Men* will detail, the prewar article of faith of how to defeat the enemy by targeting his industrial capacity to make war was ramped up, especially in Washington, DC. The result would be a speedier end to the fighting, but as Horatio Bond concludes in *Fire and the Air War*, the devastation that American bombers rained down on Japan was catastrophic:

"If one needs to be reminded that civilians were the real sufferers, he need only recall that the number of Japanese civilian casualties in the Japanese Homeland, inflicted entirely by your air force during a six-month period, was nearly twice the Japanese military casualties inflicted on our combined Army, Navy, Air Force, and Marines during a 45-month period."[25]

The American technology that produced a variety of four-engine, long-range bombers, and the deadly payloads of incendiary and high-explosive cannisters they would carry, reduced wide swaths of Japanese and German cities to rubble and ashes. As a microcosm of her industrial strength, more than two million American workers enlisted into the country's aircraft industry. Aircraft plants in Seattle, San Diego, Wichita, and Willow Run would turn out almost three hundred thousand airplanes between 1940 and 1945.[26] It would be the arrival into the war of the B-29 Superfortress that would fulfill the government and military's stated aim of forcing unconditional surrender on Japan.

Arguably the greatest weapon of the Second World War, the bomber pushed the frontiers of design, engineering, and technology in rapid time. As Jacob Vander Meulen summarizes in his excellent book *Building the B-29*, it was the vehicle from which the United States would deliver the knockout blow in indiscriminately firebombing the Japanese population in 1945.

"To take a 1945 military accountant's view of 'total war,' the B-29 program against Japan paid off brutally but handsomely. Taking the costs of bombing Japan with B-29s as a whole comparing then with the estimate of the total damage they caused produced the following: To drop one ton of bombs on Japan required 3.4 years of work by one American man or woman. To undo the damage one ton of bombs, a man and woman in Japan would have to work for 50 years."[27]

Yet despite this wholesale destruction, the Japanese leadership would finally submit only once an even more destructive force was unleashed, which would change the postwar world forever and which we are living with today.

Before these aircraft could unleash their firepower on the Japanese Home Islands, American forces and her allies would need to fight their way, step by bloody step, across the South and Central Pacific to get within striking distance. This would entail three and a half years of savage combat as the United States Navy, Marines, and Army[28] ground down the Japanese defensive perimeter while systematically destroying the Japanese merchant fleet, isolating the country from vital economic resources to continue the war and starving its population. The battles for Guadalcanal, New Guinea, Tarawa, the Marianas Islands, and Iwo Jima, culminating in the pivotal capture of Okinawa, inflicted devastating casualties on the enemy. Such was the level of Japanese fanaticism, the destruction inflicted by waves of kamikaze aircraft and mass suicides of the civilian population, that their dehumanization in the American and Allied press was reinforced. Media reports of their tactics had already hardened public opinion before the attack on Pearl Harbor. Once hostilities in the Pacific commenced, early reports of Japanese brutality against captured Allied forces and civilians in Singapore, Hong Kong, the Philippines, and Burma only served to weaponize Western bias. The stigma of taking civilian lives vanished during the Second World War, with all sides unconstrained in their targeting of them. For the United States, this unwritten policy would evolve into weapons of mass destruction being used for the first time to end the war in the Pacific.

The two atomic bombs—the uranium-made Little Boy and the plutonium Fat Man—dropped on Hiroshima and Nagasaki, respectively, brought a brutal conflict to a sudden end on August 15. President Truman's announcement caught most Americans by surprise when they believed the fighting would last considerably longer and entail significantly more losses. The Japanese empire's acceptance of unconditional surrender was a unique moment in history. Despite having close to two and a half million troops in readiness, a civilian population of millions conditioned to fight to the death, and thousands of kamikaze naval and air units prepared to inflict maximum casualties on the American invaders, they chose to surrender. It was the only time in modern history that a major industrial nation chose to do this without a single enemy soldier occupying its territory.

According to a November 30, 1945, *Fortune* survey, 17 percent of those Americans polled thought the bomb shortened the war by two to five months; 35.6 percent said from six months to a year; and 17.6 percent declared that without the bomb, the war would have lasted over a year.[29] The poll further indicated that 8.4 percent believed the bomb did not shorten the war at all, while 9.9 percent said it shortened the war by one month or less. But the initial feel-good effect the use of the bomb brought to an American public relieved the war was over would dissipate a year later thanks to John Hersey.

The atomic attack on Hiroshima marked the culmination of a new and terrifying way of humanity waging war within the prewar agreements drawn up in the Geneva Convention. In both the European and Pacific theaters, "total war" targeted civilian populations deemed as being on the front line. But whereas cities might be destroyed through traditional means of both artillery and aerial strikes, that could take days, weeks, and months of urban combat. The cities of Nanking in eastern China, Stalingrad in southern Russia, and Manila in the Philippines—all witnessed bloody fighting that drew in civilian populations and inflicted hundreds of thousands of casualties. Although in many cases these deaths would be called atrocities, one might argue they were achieved through traditional or acceptable methods—whether by bomb, shell, bullet, or bayonet.

For their respective populations, the harsh reprisals for Germany's surprise attack on the Soviet Union and Japan's on Pearl Harbor were justified. Hitler's armies inflicted almost twenty million civilian casualties as they overran and destroyed approximately seventy-eight thousand cities, towns, and villages. Their ideological war of extermination would be repaid in full by Joseph Stalin's Red Army as its armored forces battered their way into Central Europe, culminating in the mass rape of women as they captured Berlin. To an American audience, the Japanese were no better, if not worse. Across the Pacific and mainland China, Emperor Hirohito's forces had employed an almost medieval capacity for rape, murder, savagery, and destruction. Men, women, and children were indiscriminately killed by the countless millions driven by a racist Japanese ideology of supremacy.

The underlying message from Allied media was to portray the conflict as akin to a "holy war" against the "Jap."[30] As US naval and army units battled their way toward mainland Japan, racial undertones would become more explicit as the fighting intensified and enemy tactics became suicidally ferocious. Allied mass media portrayed their opponent as a bucktoothed savage, striking out of the shadows, showing little mercy to those it captured. Their demonization began on the front line, with reports of American troops taking trophies of enemy skulls, teeth, and bones, as well as mailing them back home to family and friends. Even President Roosevelt was given a trophy of a letter opener made from a Japanese soldier's arm.[31] Militarily, US forces realized that nothing was off the table in terms of waging and winning the war.[32]

The use of incendiary bombs and napalm during the Second World War sped up the rate of destruction and death, which I will argue paved the way, or morally prepared the United States and her allies, to push the envelope further in what was scientifically possible to quicken victory, no matter the cost in human life.[33] The apocalyptic destruction inflicted upon Hiroshima one sunny morning occurred in the blink of an eye, instantly killing over eighty thousand men, women, and children and leaving tens of thousands more to endure slow deaths from radiation poisoning. Consequently, every day since August 5, 1945, the repercussions and fears of what a nuclear global conflict might do to our world are still being examined and discussed.

The Hiroshima Men will reflect the personal experiences of key figures during the decade of 1936–46, as well as analyzing the experiences of diverse characters from science, politics, the military, and the media whose lives were inextricably linked by what happened before, during, and after the dropping of the world's first atomic bomb. All these men would be intimately involved with either the air war over Japan, the development of the world's first atomic weapon, its detonation over the Japanese city, or the subsequent postwar revelation of what its true cost to humanity might be. This story is based not only on archive research, but on access to unpublished family papers, the thoughts of a range of experts and writers, and some unique, heartrending eyewitness interviews recorded in the United States and Japan. It will navigate a journey across continents, secret government meetings, breakthroughs in engineering, design, science laboratories, and test sites amid a global war. All these paths would lead to Hiroshima.

This is that story.

Part I

THE RACE FOR URANIUM

Chapter One

FISSION

---

atom

/'atəm/

noun

1. the smallest particle of a chemical element that can exist.

<small>OXFORD DICTIONARY</small>

Fission, the basis for any atomic bomb, which had been actively sought after for almost fifty years, was finally discovered, by accident, at the Kaiser Wilhelm Institute for Chemistry in Berlin. Otto Hahn[1] and Fritz Strassman's research paper, published in December 1938, finally identified uranium-235 (U-235) as the key element that needed to be cultivated and enriched to create nuclear fission powerful enough to be used as a revolutionary energy source.

Uranium (the heaviest naturally occurring element in the periodic table) was so atomically fragile that if a neutron was fired at it, it would break up like a drop of water hitting the surface. More significantly, each uranium atom would break into two further neutrons, which in turn would strike more nuclei, thus creating a chain reaction in a process called "fission." This released a billion times more energy than a conventional chemical reaction. The result of their experiment proved that Albert Einstein's $E=mc^2$ equation was achievable. By breaking up the uranium nuclei, the loss of its mass from the splitting process would convert into kinetic energy, which could in turn be converted into heat. But it also, as a by-product, gave off more neutrons.

Hahn and Strassmann also concluded that the energy released when fission occurred in uranium caused several neutrons to "boil off," that is, break off into two main fragments as they flew apart. The German physicists wondered, given the right set of circumstances, could these secondary neutrons collide with yet more atoms and so release more neutrons? If they did, then the process would repeat ad nauseam, releasing more energy. Beginning with a single uranium nucleus, fission could not only produce significant amounts of energy but could also lead to a reaction creating ever-increasing energy, ultimately resulting in a chain reaction. Therefore, it was logical to assume that a controlled, self-sustaining reaction would generate heat, which, if allowed to go unchecked, would explode.

Hahn and Strassmann's findings were tested and reviewed by Hanh's former colleague Lise Meitner, a Jewish physicist who had fled Nazi Germany and was based in Sweden. Together with her nephew Otto Frisch, they confirmed what the German scientists had stumbled upon. The startling news spread rapidly throughout the scientific community. Their discovery had been years in the making. Many physicists around the world had researched the theory for years, among them James Chadwick, who had discovered the neutron at the Cavendish Laboratory at Cambridge University in February 1932, the Italian physicist Enrico Fermi, and the Hungarian Leo Szilard, who had conceived the theory of a chain reaction while crossing a London street in 1933. Many other scientists had come up with partial ideas and theories that explained segments of what Hahn and Strassmann had discovered.

Meitner and Frisch informed the great Danish physicist Niels Bohr, one of the world's great theoreticians, who since 1933 had helped scientists who were either Jewish or political opponents of the Nazis flee the country and set up in New York and elsewhere. Bohr confirmed the validity of the findings while sailing to New York City, arriving on January 16, 1939. Ten days later Bohr, accompanied by Enrico Fermi, whose own research five years previously had put him on the same track, traveled to Washington, DC, to present the news to an audience of European émigré scientists and members of the American scientific community. The news dominated the nuclear physics community, made more ominous as war loomed in Europe.

American scientists and university faculties worked closely with both Fermi and Bohr to build on the work Hahn and Strassmann had published. Bohr would focus on the theory of fission, while Fermi and Szilard, now working at Columbia University in New York, investigated with an American team the possibility of producing a nuclear chain reaction. By March 1940, American scientists had demonstrated conclusively that uranium-235 would fission with slow neutrons, not the more abundant uranium-238. The former was reactive, while the latter was docile. To make a modern-day analogy, it would be as if the Covid virus (neutron) struck and U-238 was the vaccinated host (i.e., no reaction), while the U-235 host would suffer a serious reaction that became more volatile if allowed to multiply. For a chain reaction to work using U-235, one would need a great deal of it. Bohr concluded so much effort would be required in terms of facilities required, a suitably trained workforce, huge amounts of natural uranium, and money to finance it all, building a bomb was simply not possible or worth the effort. The British chemist Sir Henry Tizard, the chairman of the Committee for the Scientific Survey of Air Warfare (CSSAW), analyzed the same scenario as Bohr and concluded to the British military that the chances of success were a hundred thousand to one.[2]

Despite the pessimism about success, the possibility of an atomic explosion still scared both European and American scientists alike, primarily because of Adolf Hitler. Europe looked to be plunging back into war within a matter of weeks. Germany was now threatening Poland, with Britain and France guaranteeing her borders. Émigré physicists living in the States, such as Fermi and Szilard, and his fellow Hungarian Jews, Eugene Wigner and Edward Teller, were adamant that the normal process of free-flowing communication within the science world now had to stop. They convinced most within the American and British scientific community to voluntarily withhold future publication of information that might aid a Nazi atomic bomb program. Not until late 1940, when European scientists had succeeded in enlisting government interest and support, did publication on nuclear research generally cease.

By then, two more European refugees, who had washed up on the shores of Great Britain, would shine a light on how to take a nuclear bomb off the mathematics blackboard and turn it into a reality.

Chapter Two

CONVINCING THE COMMANDER IN CHIEF

I am therefore addressing this urgent appeal to every
Government, which may be engaged in hostilities, publicly
to affirm its determination that its armed forces shall in no
event and under no circumstances undertake bombardment
from the air of civilian populations or unfortified cities. . . .[1]
PRESIDENT FRANKLIN D. ROOSEVELT[2]

October 11, 1939

What was keeping him?

Dr. Alexander Sachs had been pacing the same line along the carpet of the White House's State Dining Room for over an hour waiting to be called in to see the president since he had arrived at 7 a.m. The ex–investment banker had now worked in Franklin Roosevelt's National Recovery Administration for three years, met with him many times, and overseen key components of his boss's campaign to get the American economy back on track. Roosevelt, Sachs knew, respected and admired his capacity to handle big briefs, come up with answers, and get the job done. Yet here he was, pacing outside the Family Dining Room, working himself up into a state of panic, wishing yet not wanting to make a final plea to his president to listen to his concerns.

The fear that had kept him up all the previous night in his bed at the Carlton Hotel was still palpable. White House servants watched him warily, wondering what was causing this usually calm official to be acting so out of character. Oblivious to the onlookers, Sachs clasped his hands together again around the bulging manila envelope, staring up at the ceiling, almost speaking out loud as he rehearsed the lines he would say, slowly pacing up and down, up and down.

The previous meeting with the president the day before had not gone well. Sachs knew he had faltered in not arguing his case coherently and speedily enough. Roosevelt was known not to suffer fools, nor would he patiently sit through monotone seminars from his officials when there was work to be done and decisions to be made and a pile of paperwork stacked in his in tray to sign. But this issue needed to be fully aired and a decision made, Sachs knew, and he was thus determined to deliver a full report on a matter of national security—the threat to the country of a devastating new discovery that, if turned into a weapon, could theoretically destroy whole cities. This had been the message dictated to him by men far more aware of the danger than himself, one of whom was a world-renowned physicist who had brought news of worrying events in Germany.

The race to rearm had been well underway across Europe since the middle of the 1930s. As the decade now ended, Western Europe teetered on the brink as Hitler's forces stormed eastward into Poland on September 1, with Britain and France declaring war two days later. Hitler's allies in the Tripartite Pact, Italy and Japan, watched and waited, while the Soviet Union, cosignatory of the Ribbentrop-Molotov Pact, supplied Hitler's armored columns and took a chunk of eastern Poland in the bargain. The United States, still attached to isolationism, clung to its neutrality. Arguments raged in both the US Congress and Senate as to which side to show leniency to without being dragged into the cauldron. The news Alexander Sachs was about to deliver to his president, at the second time of asking, would ramp up the stakes even more.

The door swung open as a worried face familiar to Sachs stared intently back at him. Roosevelt's chief of staff, Harry Hopkins, was of similar age and build to Sachs, had the same receding hairline, and liked to dress in the same style of three-piece gray wool suits. The men were on familiar terms with each other, but there was no bonhomie that morning. Hopkins was still irked by Sachs's lackluster performance the day before. After much lobbying, he had carefully orchestrated his colleague's meeting with the president. Alas, Sachs's delivery had bordered on the comical as he stumbled through his words and looked like a man drowning in his brief until Roosevelt had simply lost patience and ended the meeting. Once Hopkins was alone with the president, Roosevelt admonished him for suggesting the meeting in the first place. As Hopkins's pallor whitened (his stomach cancer had been increasing in severity lately), Roosevelt eased off, mindful not to push him too hard. It was then that Sachs's head reappeared around the Oval Office door requesting to return the next morning and complete his presentation. He reminded both men that what he had to say was of national importance. Having vented his frustration, and with Hopkins remaining silent, Roosevelt nodded in acquiescence. Now the White House chief of staff ushered Sachs into the dining room, closed the door, and left him alone with the most powerful man in the world.

Roosevelt was sitting in his wheelchair by a dining table laid elaborately for one, ready to take breakfast. A steward stood beside him, a steaming silver jug in his white-gloved hands, ready to serve the president his morning coffee.

"What bright idea have you got now?" Roosevelt asked as he wafted his napkin across his lap. "How much time would you like to explain it today?"

It was sarcastic, but not brutal enough for Sachs to turn tail and walk out. He had waited many weeks to deliver this message.

"This won't take long, Mr. President."

Sachs moved toward the dining table, took the padded manila envelope from under his arm, and deftly placed it at the edge of the dining table, within easy reach of Roosevelt's grasp. The president picked it up and slowly read through the two-page letter and several pages of statistics and analysis that he knew had been signed off on by a man he knew to be a genius in his field—Albert Einstein.

The letter, though written months before, still commanded attention. Einstein and his fellow physicists, in two succinct pages, set out the danger the United States was now facing: their enemies, primarily the Nazis, had perfected the process of enriching uranium to create Uranium-235, an incredibly powerful source of energy that might soon enable them to create a superweapon—a bomb capable of immense destruction. The administration needed to take the threat seriously and step up to the challenge. The country had the people and technology to win this arms race, but it must act now. The president needed to set up a department to turn this theory into reality. There was still time.

Roosevelt didn't betray any emotion as he placed Einstein's letter aside, sipped a mouthful of coffee, and analyzed the accompanying report. The waiting Sachs now took this window of silence to deliver what he prayed would be the coup de grâce to galvanize the president into action.

"All I want to do is to tell you a story, Mr. President. During the Napoleonic Wars a young American inventor named Robert Fulton came to the French emperor and offered to build a fleet of steamships with the help of which Napoleon could, in spite of the uncertain weather, land his army in England. Ships without sails? This seemed to the great Corsican so impossible that he sent Fulton away. In the opinion of the English historian Lord Acton, this is an example of how England was saved by the shortsightedness of an adversary. Had Napoleon Bonaparte shown more imagination and humility at that time, the history of the nineteenth century would have taken a very different course."

Sachs waited for a response as Roosevelt stared back at him, lowering his gaze only to take his napkin from his lap to wipe his mouth. The younger man couldn't tell if he was deciding to dismiss him again or ask further questions. He willed the latter. Roosevelt put his hand into his jacket pocket, pulled out his fountain pen, and scribbled a note on his notepad, which he brusquely tore off and waved at his servant to take away. For an interminable few minutes, silence reigned between the pair, and then the servant returned to Roosevelt's side, placing a parcel on the table where his cup of coffee had been. He unwrapped it to reveal a dark bottle.

"Napoleonic brandy," the president exclaimed.

He poured out two glasses. Sachs took one from the servant. Roosevelt, remaining silent, toasted Sachs and drank his contents in one go. Sachs sipped his.

The wheelchair-bound leader studied the papers, now spread across the table before him. He gestured to the letter as he looked at Sachs:

"Alex, what you are after is to see that the Nazis don't blow us up?"

"Precisely, Mr. President," he replied. He sipped another mouthful of brandy in relief.

The president leaned to his left, looking over Sach's shoulder, toward the dining room door.

"Pa, come in here, please!"

Sachs turned to see the familiar and stocky figure of the president's military attaché, General Edwin "Pa" Watson, stride into the room past Sachs and come to attention beside Roosevelt's chair, a position he had taken up since Roosevelt had won the White House in 1933. The president smiled past Watson at the younger man, whose acute lack of sleep was now catching up with him, as he pointed at the papers in front of him.

"Pa, this requires action!"

Events over the coming months, not years, would make this one of Roosevelt's wisest prewar decisions. Six months after his meeting in the White House, two British-based, German-Jew émigrés, Rudolf Peierls and Otto Frisch, were about to cause their own reaction. The pair were just two of many refugee scientists who had been offered sanctuary and incorporated by the British government into the country's university system, under the leadership of Professor James Chadwick. Both men had been given work and accommodation by

Marcus Oliphant, an Australian teaching physics at Birmingham University, who had discussed electromagnetic separation with Ernest Lawrence at Berkeley and would become part of the British team that developed radar.

Peierls and Frisch examined the complications of producing a uranium bomb. They calculated that in theory, just a grapefruit-size sphere of pure uranium-235 could create the same strength of explosion as one thousand tons of TNT if developed into a bomb to deliver it. As German forces were driving a British expeditionary force out of Norway by March 1940,[3] their final paper was delivered to Oliphant. It would be known as the "Frisch-Peierls memorandum," and it would light a fire under the British physics establishment. Oliphant immediately discussed the paper with Henry Tizard, whereby it was decided to set up an offshoot group from his own Committee for the Scientific Survey of Air Warfare, to be called the MAUD Committee.[4] Within a year, the British would conclude that not only were Peierls and Frisch's [5] conclusions feasible, but with the requisite budget, they could be produced, for a great deal less than Niels Bohr had originally feared.

Chapter Three

THE WRITER FROM CHINA

Journalism allows its readers to witness history;
fiction gives readers an opportunity to live it.
JOHN HERSEY

Future Pulitzer Prize winner John Richard Hersey could understand and speak Chinese before he understood the English language. He would later state he could not recall much of the first ten years of his life being brought up by his missionary parents, Roscoe and Grace Hersey, in the port city of Tientsin (now Tianjin), in northern China. Like Shanghai to the south, this ancient city offered a direct trade route to the bigger markets of Beijing and had naturally been opened by the Great Powers. Decades before the Herseys arrived, the center of Tientsin had the air of a European city. Despite sporadic periods of fighting as the Qing dynasty struggled to maintain its rule, by the time the Great War raged in Europe, Tientsin was attracting both Protestant and Catholic missions. Hundreds of white European and American settlers worked alongside growing numbers of Chinese converts, attracted to a different faith but also to earning a regular wage that put food on the table. Roscoe Hersey had already traveled to Europe after the end of hostilities in 1918, supporting the tens of thousands of Chinese "coolies" who had been supplied by their government to assist the allies on the Western Front. He had volunteered for the YMCA (Young Men's Christian Association), which was the primary organization repatriating them back to the Far East.

Despite residing in an international community, like all Caucasians assimilating with their surroundings, Hersey and his brother must have been viewed with curiosity by the Chinese. He was caught between two worlds. Though he might speak their language, he was unfamiliar with Chinese customs and practices, attending the city's grammar school overseen by the British community, and then the American-run school. But his character would be influenced by what he encountered as he accompanied his parents on their missionary work in Tientsin. As the biographer of his life and career, Jeremy Treglown, summarizes in his book *Mr. Straight Arrow*, being out of the mainstream American attitudes and culture, Hersey would be influenced by the ordinary Chinese. "[T]he patience, the endurance, of these Chinese, their calmness as they talked, their acceptance of their hard circumstances, the many signs of their industry, frugality, and aspiration" were values that would stay with him as a writer.

In 1924, the family experienced a major change in their fortunes. Hersey's father fell ill with encephalitis, a potentially fatal inflammation of the brain.[1] Aged ten, he followed in their wake as his mother decided to relocate the family back to the United States, settling in Briarcliff Manor, in affluent Westchester County, a suburb of New York City, thirty miles to the south, and connected by a new railway line. During his teenage years, back in the bosom of white, Anglo-Saxon Protestant (WASP) New England, Hersey evolved into a typical all-American: tall, dark-haired, loving sports, and academically minded, though not a prodigy. He was able enough to win a scholarship to the prestigious boarding establishment of Hotchkiss Preparatory School.[2] Though separated from his family by eighty miles, the work ethic that would serve him well throughout his adult years as a writer drove him to supplement his good fortune at Hotchkiss by taking menial part-time jobs as a waiter and janitor. That work did not prevent him from excelling in his studies or other fields within the school, winning the accomplishment in his first year of being recognized as "the freshman who is most distinguished in scholarship, athletics and citizenship combined." He was popular, not prone to teenage exaggerations, and respected for his calmness and well-constructed arguments about most subjects. It would be at Hotchkiss, too, that Hersey would discover his love of and develop his appreciation for English literature. When he wasn't playing for the school football team, he would be practicing the violin or reading the new works of William Faulkner. It would be an easy decision to continue this life in higher education, and Yale University would have been natural for a Hotchkiss man in 1932. He would spend the next four years there in Trumbull College.

America was still in the weeds of the Great Depression, as Roosevelt's administration began the long road to tackle the severe economic decline and damage to the social fabric of the country. The priviledge of attending a prestigious center of learning was not lost on Hersey, and he embraced everything the university had to offer. He would fortuitously be provided with a secondhand typewriter—his first—by a member of the English department who twigged he had some talent. Outside the classroom, Hersey played tennis, went sailing, managed to be picked for the varsity football team—the Bulldogs—joined the secretive Skull and Bones Society, and crucially, now armed with his own typewriter, joined the board of the *Yale Daily News*.[3] Here he became part of team that produced articles and reports, some funny, others serious, as well as sports reports on the university's various teams. Though a small team and the bulk of its content lighthearted, it was a breeding ground for future novelists, correspondents, and journalists.[4] Hersey would establish himself as a team player within the office but still forge his own way, influenced by his background, bringing articles that fell back on his own family service in China. The timing was perfect. Japan's military had attacked Manchuria and was ravaging the Chinese province, without the international League of Nations raising a protest.

He was doing everything one needed to do to fit into the social groups who inhabited the college and collectively would join the East Coast elite. Balancing the missionary life he had been brought up in with the enjoyment he now got from mixing in such circles would be difficult and perhaps had a bigger influence in his later decision to become secular. He may not have mirrored his mother and father's missionary zeal, but he did have their love for travel. In 1936, with Nazi Germany brewing hostility in Europe, Hersey accepted a Mellon Scholarship to study eighteenth-century English literature at Clare College, Cambridge University. As he had done at Hotchkiss and at Yale, perhaps mindful of his invalid father back home, Hersey took on paid work to supplement his income. The English weather was worse, he thought, than New England, and despite having the company of various Yale contemporaries who were at Cambridge, he initially suffered homesickness the first few weeks of his stay, as he described in a letter to his parents that October: "This is the first time I have been homesick. I know I shouldn't be, but I can't seem to help it. Perhaps I shall get over it; it just seems so far and for so long."[5]

Gradually he warmed to the historic surroundings and marveled at what he deemed to be the quaintness of the people. He began to explore the rural countryside surrounding Cambridge, as he described to his mother in a letter two weeks later:

"At about three, starts the most enjoyable part of the day. High and I don old clothes, mount our bikes, and range out into the country villages 'round about here: lovely little spots, Coton Barton . . . wonderful names like Biggerswade, homely, thatched cottages which are the real thing, not clumsy fakes . . . farmers daughters on bicycles, the trees miles tall, clouds always scudding across deep, deep, blue . . . neat little pubs called The Lion and the Lamb, or the Broken Blind, or The White Horse. . . . Our rides seem the only real time of day."[6]

He was finally embracing life in England. He was making friendships, attending societies at college, and venturing to London, a hundred miles to the south, to enjoy parties and cultural events. All the while, he watched from afar the erosion of democracy in continental Europe as the Spanish Civil War raged, and he was shocked at the level of support for the Nazis in Britain.

His wandering bug also took him around the United Kingdom, with tours of the Lake District and an odyssey farther north to his mother's ancestral home in Dumfriesshire. He was experiencing a country that would be forever changed by the coming world war, and fascinated by the coming coronation of King Edward VIII in his spring term of 1937, describing to his parents how the capital was gearing up for the historic event: "All England buzzes with the coming coronation; Americans have begun to arrive in hordes; there are such crowds in London already, over a week before the event."[7]

Much as he wallowed in the pageantry, as the summer of 1937 approached, Hersey was in a quandary. The scholarship had not lived up to its billing. He was bored, feeling life was passing him by, and anxious to return to the United States to see family and friends. He informed his brother he had written to Henry Luce, owner and editor of *Time* magazine, in New York, requesting a summer internship. He hoped it would be an entry into full-time employment in the heart of where he wanted to be as a writer.

His happiness to be returning to New York that July was tempered by the news Luce had no room for him at *Time*; the magazine shied away from hiring interns. What was he to do? Through the Yale network, he discovered one of the country's greatest novelists, Sinclair Lewis, had lost his office gofer and needed a replacement. Hersey spent the following days applying to Lewis to fill the role, and to Cambridge University to terminate his scholarship. With his bridges burned and a ticket to return to the States, he needed the job.

The work with Lewis was both varied, as he expected, and colorful—Hersey encountering the many literary characters who drifted in and out of Lewis's household and getting to work close up with a once-great writer. Lewis encouraged Hersey's ambitions and quickly opened doors for him in New York. By that fall, Hersey was finally awarded an apprenticeship at *Time*, America's first weekly magazine and the place a budding writer with ambition could be exposed to some of New York's finest writers, columnists, editors, and publishers. Manhattan was indeed the place to be if you were an ambitious scholar, with a nose for a story and a skill of crafting great copy.

By the Roaring Twenties, as Hollywood on the West Coast became the mecca for the new film industry, so across on the East Coast, Manhattan grew into a powerhouse for literature and the arts. Some of America's most distinguished newspapers and magazines grew to prominence: *The Wall Street Journal, The Evening Post, The New York Times* bestriding Times Square, and weekly or monthly magazines such as *Fortune, Harper's, Vanity Fair, The New Yorker*, and of course *Time* and *Life* magazines. Occupying nearby neighborhoods close to and around midtown were publishing houses that would become world-renowned: Doubleday, Simon & Schuster, Charles Scribner's Sons, Random House, and Alfred A. Knopf. The development of critical analysis of published works, which could make or break an author, began with *The New York Herald Tribune*'s promoting its "Sunday Books" section.[8]

New York was a bright light attracting the country's finest minds and greatest writers of fiction, nonfiction, poetry, and prose, led by incredibly commercially minded, intelligent, and politically savvy characters, all fighting for space. Two such leaders would influence the career of John Hersey for the next decade: Henry Luce at *Time* and *Life* magazines and Harold Ross at *The New Yorker*. Both did not suffer fools, weak analysis for articles, or poorly written copy. They dominated their respective editorial teams and had differing political outlooks on the international scene, but each instinctively knew a good story and how to edit and publish it.

Henry Luce must have seen something in the twenty-five-year-old for him to take a chance on a novice. Like Hersey, though a generation before, Luce had been born in China to parents who were Presbyterian missionaries. He was a fellow alum of Hotchkiss Prep and Yale University, and had excelled at the *Yale Daily News*. Following university, Luce, along with longtime school friend Briton Hadden, had spotted a gap in the market to produce quality newsprint for the growing middle class across the United States. The young graduates left their full-time roles at *The Baltimore News* to set up their own magazine, *Time*, in 1923. Hadden took care of the financial aspects of locating funding, sponsorship, and advertisements that would fund the enterprise, while Luce excelled at staffing the magazine, overseeing its day-to-day running, and directing the content. He was revolutionary in how he wanted to present it, too. For the first time, Americans could navigate their magazine to easily find the sections they wished to read first, whether it be connected to domestic or foreign affairs, profiles on notable individuals, or culture, written by a wide variety of experts, novelists, and talented journalists. As Alan Brinkley, author of *The Publisher: Henry Luce and His American Century*, summarizes:

"Even in the earliest Twentieth century, most people lived in cities and towns that didn't have very much communication outside of their own communities. But starting, especially during World War One, but accelerating after the war, the idea of there being a national news source became very powerful. And *Time* was, in many ways, the first national news source for Americans, the first comprehensive treatment of the news that was available to people all over the United States. And, in fact, within a very short time, people in every state in the Union were getting subscriptions to *Time* magazine."[9]

The articles in *Time* had transformed how Americans saw their country and the world, while *Life*, an illustrated magazine created in 1936, helped them visualize it. He had ushered the magazine into the growing phenomenon that was radio as early as the mid-1920s. By 1931, through Luce's canny instinct to increase print circulation, *The March of Time* became one of the most popular radio programs in the country. The weekly thirty-minute program adapted stories from the printed magazine, both serious politics as well as culture, into ordinary Americans' homes. It helped Luce advance the Anglophile tastes he shared with Hersey. Luce had studied at Oxford in 1919 and seen the destruction the Great War had wrought on Western Europe. This had influenced his long-standing belief that the United States should take a primary role in world events. By the time Hersey appeared in the offices of *Time*, Luce had long monitored Europe's descent toward war, as well as the crisis building in Far East Asia and what it meant for war in the Pacific. The irony that *Time* had chosen Adolf Hitler as their "Man of the Year" the previous year in 1938 had been quietly put on the shelf.

Perhaps he looked at Hersey, saw something of himself, and decided he was the new breed of journalist who would move the magazine's breadth of international news toward the messaging it now needed to prepare the American public for war. By May 1939, with the Second Sino-Japanese War almost two years old, *Time* was one of the most read magazines in the country, and Luce had one of the largest journalistic staffs in New York. Despite others he could call on, he gave Hersey his first foreign posting. He would send him to China as the American correspondent at *Time*'s Chungking bureau. Hersey's brief was significant and high-profile for such a junior writer: travel throughout China and Japan, cover the ongoing conflict, send dispatches of the action from both sides, and interview key figures across the military and political spectrum, always with an eye on American interests and the potential that the United States might be drawn into a war with an aggressive opponent such as Japan. President Roosevelt's administration had galvanized Britain, France, and the Netherlands to begin the tightening of economic sanctions that could potentially cripple Japanese industry. Hitler had won concessions at Munich the year before, and now Japan was doing likewise in Asia. Luce needed to see a strong riposte, and he intended Hersey, now set up in Tokyo's Imperial Hotel,[10] to provide the stories to influence such a decision.

Hersey's timing was perfect, as the apprentice correspondent found himself meeting veteran foreign correspondents who provided excellent on-the-ground advice, such as Frank Hedges of the *Daily Telegraph*, "the second-best correspondent in Tokyo," and Hugh Byas of *The New York Times*,[11] whom Hersey rated "one of the most respected foreigners in Tokyo. He is a wonderfully genial Scot with a small moustache, a ruddy face, and a perpetual grin." The veteran Japanologist was at pains to highlight to Hersey that the polite, well-dressed, and well-behaved Japanese soldier he would spot on the streets of Tokyo was a million miles away from the soldier currently occupying swathes of mainland China: "overbearing, insulting, cruel. The behaviour of the soldiers in Nanking, which was really of an animal cruelty, was an extreme example. They slap Chinese and make them bow, and spit on them. There seems to be two levels of behaviour and thought in Japan, one civilised, the other imperial."

To try to counterbalance what he was being told by the likes of Byas, Hersey sought out interviews with ordinary Japanese to reveal to *Time* readers what lay beneath this bellicose attitude. One conversation in a Tokyo suburban office belonging to construction supervisor Bunichiro Sugimura was revealing: "We are tired of it [the war], We feel we have been dragged into something none of us wanted. No one dreamed that Manchuria and the petty incidents in North China would lead us as far in as we are. We all hope it will be over by the end of the year." Being a *Time* correspondent opened doors for Hersey to the Japanese government, too, who granted him an interview with the chief of the First Section of Japan's Foreign Office. Hersey came face-to-face with a youthful-looking, intelligence officer who praised the signing of the Anti-Comintern Pact, telling Hersey the colonial powers would now stay out of the conflict with China, "but when it does come, it is essential that Japan is guaranteed German assistance on the western border of Russia. . . . Joining the alliance . . . would finish the China incident in this way."

His decision to travel to northern China was perfect timing, as Japan's next moves provided the type of story Luce was after. Great Britain and Japan were increasingly at loggerheads from the latter's offensive in China. Though not in open hostilities, the British concession based in Hersey's old home of Tientsin was providing shelter and clandestine support for elements of the Chinese Republic's armed forces against the Japanese, in keeping with British foreign policy to prop up nationalist China in order to prevent further Japanese agression toward its own territories. It was a powder keg waiting to explode into open hostility, only requiring one major act of violence. In April 1939, it finally happened, with the assassination in Tientsin by Chinese operatives of a key financial ally to the Japanese.

It handed the Japanese the excuse they needed, and in June they blockaded Tientsin. Hersey would get himself to the city to provide Luce with on-the-ground reports.

His language skills and knowledge of the area proved hugely beneficial. His eye for the smaller, local detail, allied to the wider picture of a coming war, was an attractive mixture for the magazine proprietor. The eyewitness reports he cabled from the fighting around the port of Chunking were another example of the tone Luce was prepared to take against the Axis powers: "Some parts of the city are a dreadful shamble. There is no method to the Japanese bombing except to kill as many as possible. . . . This section was as bad a sight as Guernica and parts of Barcelona."[12] By July 1940, Luce had brought Hersey back to New York and promoted him to associate editor. He would specialize on the magazine's foreign news desk. With German tanks rolling across Poland a few weeks later, World War II had officially begun.[13]

The United States remained neutral as Great Britain and France prepared to meet the likely German onslaught in the spring of 1940. At *Time*, Luce drove his writers to look for stories that would promote the US position of supplying aid to Great Britain and to more strident sanctions against Japan. As he worked relentlessly to report on Asia, Hersey was by now dating socialite and wealthy heiress Frances Ann Cannon, so well-connected she had been presented at the court of King George VI and had dated the second son of the US ambassador to Great Britain, John F. Kennedy. Kennedy's father, Joseph, was a longtime friend of Henry Luce. Despite the disparity in their family backgrounds, the couple were in love and married within six months. JFK attended their wedding in late April. The ties of university, Connecticut, Manhattan, and ex-girlfriends who now existed between Hersey and Kennedy would combine to bring the scion of a Bostonian millionaire and the son of a missionary closer as both fretted about the state of Europe. They were right to do so.

By the late summer, across the Atlantic, Britain was losing its European allies one by one, until it now stood alone. Squadrons of the

Royal Air Force were contesting the very skies Hersey had gazed up to from his university quad at Cambridge three years earlier. By September, as the Battle of Britain went in the RAF's favor, the Luftwaffe turned to nighttime bombing of British cities—the Blitz had begun. Both men had little idea that war would bring them even closer, as Hersey's gift for a story would help promote the young Kennedy in wartime.

Hersey focused his talents as per the briefings of Luce as he sought to position *Time* and *Life* magazines behind the British effort, both in Europe, the Atlantic War now growing in intensity, and beyond to the Mediterranean, as the war escalated in North Africa and the Balkans. Luce was at the forefront of newspaper proprietors who lobbied Roosevelt's administration to counter the growing threat of Hitler, and to push Lend-Lease through the Senate by the spring of 1941.[14] In a *Life* editorial months before Pearl Harbor, Luce coined the immortal phrase that the world was inhabiting the "American Century." It was his vision of how the United States could use its enormous economic potential and influence to defend and spread the democratic values it held so dear, embodied in its own Constitution. But the world Luce argued that his country should build was abruptly stopped in its tracks on December 7.

For John Hersey, like so many American writers and photographers, the war would make their careers. It offered him extensive travel and the opportunity to bear witness to countless historic events in the Pacific and European theaters over the next four years and would would ultimately take him to Hiroshima. The Japanese city would make his name and forever be associated with arguably the greatest American invention that dominated the war against the Japanese, with a distinctive name—the "Superfortress."

Chapter Four

THE EMERGENCE OF AMERICAN AIRPOWER: THE B-29 PROGRAM

It seemed to me unavoidable that, in the long run,
Japan would be almost destroyed by air attack, so that,
merely on the basis of the B-29s alone, I was
convinced that Japan should sue for peace.
JAPANESE PREMIER KANTARO SUZUKI[1]

Of all the many weapons the United States would develop and use in the Second World War, the B-29 program was arguably the most decisive for victory. The plane's role was conceived from as early as the 1920s in the Air Corps Tactical Schools[2] of Virginia and Alabama and brought into reality in the dusty committee rooms of Washington, DC, before war had broken out in Europe in 1939. The men who studied and taught here would later form the elite command of what would become the Army Air Force in the Second World War. Their mantra would be the doctrine of strategic precision bombing. The B-29 bomber would be the ultimate tool of this theory. Driving it would be one man who had the foresight to understand what the long-range bomber could achieve and would lead the US Army Air Corps in World War II, Major General Henry "Hap" Arnold.

The concept of aerial bombing of an enemy, from safe at high altitude, that inflicted huge damage below, had galvanized a generation of American flyers who had come through the Great War intact. By the late 1930s, overall command of the country's air force had fallen to one of their number. Hap Arnold was a pre–Great War graduate of West Point, but a visionary of airpower. Arnold would be one of the first air force leaders who recognized the need for the military to nurture aircraft manufacturers for mass production should war come. He would lead a cadre of like-minded subordinates[3] such as Lieutenant General Ira Eaker,[4] General Haywood S. Hansell Jr.,[5] and Major General Carl A. Spaatz.[6] They were among many graduates of the school who believed America's next war would be won by airpower. Fleets of modern bombers, capable of flying unescorted behind front lines and even oceans, would deliver devastating, precision strikes from high altitude on the enemy's industry and means of waging war. The new strategy would minimize casualties in return for strategic victory.

The war in the Pacific against Japan would now test that theory. It was fought over thousands of square miles of ocean, dotted by small landmasses that would become battlefields as both sides sought strategic dominance. The United States Navy, led by Admiral Chester W. Nimitz, would work in tandem with its traditional rival, the US Army, led by General Douglas MacArthur, to achieve Japan's defeat. Their combined forces would seek to destroy the Imperial Navy, sink her carrier fleet, isolate her armies, and recapture New Guinea, the Philippines, and the many islands of the Central and South Pacific. Then they would blockade the Home Islands before invading Japan itself. Hap Arnold saw the Army Air Corps's role as equally pivotal. It would deliver the aerial destruction of Japan and break its people's will to fight once bases were established close enough to Japan. As we shall see, all three services would implement their respective policies as the war progressed. It would be Arnold's mission to protect the Army Air Corps's operational independence. The B-29 would be the plane that achieved this.

Though the Great Depression had curtailed any thoughts of an expensive development of their bomber program, by the mid-1930s the Roosevelt administration's New Deal had resuscitated the economy. Watching Europe march toward another continental war—

and ever mindful of the growing tension with the Japanese in the Pacific—convinced the military's representatives in Washington of the need for the country's armed forces to modernize. Airpower had to wait in line behind the traditional armed services. Both the Navy and Army lobbied hard for more jeeps, tanks, artillery, supply ships, carriers, and destroyers.[7]

Boeing's B-17 Flying Fortress first flew in 1936. A large metal single-winged plane with four powerful engines, heavily armed with a range of two thousand miles, it would go on to become the iconic American bomber of the European theater and the plane two of this narrative's central characters would fly with distinction: Paul Tibbetts Jr. and Curtis LeMay. The elections of November 1938 witnessed American voters returning many isolationist-minded congressmen to Washington and stymieing Roosevelt's domestic agenda.[8] Roosevelt had agreed to supply American-made fighter and bomber aircraft to both the French and British governments.[9] The domestic pressure on Roosevelt's administration only increased his fears as he watched by 1938 the deterioration in European politics that was pointing toward war. Hitler's demands for the Czech Sudetenland had already precipitated the crisis talks at Munich that September. The political fallout of Britain and France capitulating to his demands to avoid a continental war finally stirred the White House into action. But the president was walking a tightrope.

On the same day as the Munich Agreement was signed, disaster struck the Army Air Corps's command. Major General Oscar M. Westover, Hap Arnold's commander, died in a plane crash in California. Though heavily involved in discussions relating to the Air Corps's future strength and capability, Arnold was not guaranteed a promotion at the time. Various rumors of heavy drinking and questions about his intellect circled the corridors of the War Department. Thankfully, eight days later, he was officially appointed to the role.

In the same month, Roosevelt's administration finally woke up to the strength of Axis airpower. Hitler's rearmament of a lethal air force and motorized army had cowed both France and Britain into selling out the Czechs' sovereignty at the Munich Conference. It had also convinced the US president that airpower would dictate the coming war in Europe. As he confided to his Army Chief of Staff George Marshall, a powerful air force "was the only thing that Hitler understands." Marshall and Roosevelt's closest adviser, Harry Hopkins, would fall in line with his thinking.

Despite the constraints of the Neutrality Act, on October 14 the War Department was verbally put on notice to produce a plan to expand the Air Corps. The same day, now in full control of his brief, Arnold wrote to the country's leading aircraft manufacturers, asking for their opinions on adding detail to the plan. Over the next month, a series of meetings and upward revisions of what was required followed, influenced on the one hand by the Democratic Party's defeats in the US congressional elections and on the other by the terrible news of Nazi atrocities during Kristallnacht. A seeming reluctance by the American public to prepare for war needed to be balanced by the reality of preparing for one. The increase in Nazi anti-Semitism in Europe and Japanese troops' increased barbarism in China both helped turn the tide of public acceptance to rearm in FDR's favor.

The White House conference held on November 14[10] put in motion the increase of America's air strength, above all other aspects of rebuilding the country's military forces. Airpower was the key discussion that day. Roosevelt outlined the Axis Powers' current strength in depth: Germany had five to ten thousand planes, with the capacity to produce twelve thousand more each year. In view of this, he contended, the United States must be prepared to resist assault on the Western Hemisphere "from the North to the South Pole." The Army Air Corps must be built up rapidly, ideally to a strength of twenty thousand planes, with the country's aircraft industry expanded to supply a further twenty-four thousand aircraft each year.

The government would work with existing aircraft companies, as well as oversee the creation of new plants to fulfill such future quotas. The president wanted aircraft, but at this point the facilities, supplies, and personnel were numbers on a sheet. Like the Army,

Navy, and Coast Guard, the country's military arms would all have to be rebuilt from a low base. But it was the start. Outlining his reasons before Congress on January 4, 1939, the president explained that the world had grown so small "and weapons of attack so swift that no nation can be safe in its will to peace so long as any powerful nation refuses to settle its grievances at the council table. For if any government bristling with implements of war insists on policies of force, weapons of defence give the only safety."[11]

Events in the spring of 1939 finally silenced isolationists within Congress as the rump of Czechoslovakia was seized by Hitler, and Germany now looked ominously toward Poland. Such acts of aggression finally willed Congress to sign off on Roosevelt's preliminary budget of $2.5 billion for the US Army procurement plan. Hap Arnold gave the green light for a committee of officers and aviation experts, including American flying legend Charles Lindbergh, to draft a report, which they submitted by the end of June. One of its key recommendations was the need for the United States to develop its own long-range heavy bomber fleet. Continued fears of the strength of German airpower overwhelming France and Britain, and the superiority of Japanese planes flying in China, drove the debate in Washington. Of equal concern was the threat, however small, of German bombers attacking the American mainland. Much as the fear of Nazi scientists developing nuclear technology would influence Roosevelt to sign off on the Manhattan Project, so the Air Corps would be the beneficiary of an even bigger budget to create and mass-produce its new long-range bomber, which Arnold and his subordinates had believed could win any coming war. Before a full report for a super bomber was completed, Hitler invaded Poland on September 1. Two days later, Britain and France declared war on Germany, setting off another global conflict. Arnold's team now sped up the process of finalizing their feasibility study.

The operational demands for the plane might potentially be both offensive and defensive—able to fly thousands of miles in a single operation to deliver a devastating payload. The committee discussed its potential against both military and civilian targets. As Japanese and German tactics had shown, factories crucial to any enemy's war effort were now considered to be legitimate targets. The committee concluded a very large airplane was therefore required: Could it fly fast over five thousand miles at an altitude the enemy would struggle to defend against and carry tons of bombs? Working back from that decision enabled them to conceptualize a plane design that incorporated a large fuselage to store bombs and fuel tanks relevant to the operation required—whether long haul or over a short distance—and thus provide more room for more bombs.

By November 1939, the committee's report was delivered to Congress for sign-off to build a prototype. Studying the performance of German and British aircraft in combat in those early months of 1940, Arnold's team revised what they believed their own bomber would need, such as armored, leak-proof fuel tanks. Once a finalized statement of intent was drafted in April, Arnold invited the American aviation industry to pitch for the lucrative contracts. Or so he thought. Many aviation companies looked upon contracts to design and build new planes for the military as a poisoned chalice. The risk was loaded toward the manufacturer, and new technology could be dangerous and costly if rushed through. Government officials viewed advance payments as a risk. More worrisome was putting all their eggs in one (manufacturer's) basket. Value for money was paramount. Companies such as Boeing—from Seattle, Washington—employed a small workforce and needed regular cash flow. Committing to design and build a revolutionary aircraft that could run up to approximately $500,000[12] might ruin them. As one Boeing official put it: "There was no sound of coin in Uncle Sam's jeans; his pockets carried only marbles and chalk." Nevertheless, Roosevelt's administration lobbied Congress for the necessary funds. His new secretary of war, Henry L. Stimson, spoke to a congressional committee in August 1940 of the military's needs to catch up with its rivals:

"Air power today has decided the fate of nations. Germany with her powerful air armadas has vanquished one people after another.

On the ground, large armies have been mobilised to resist her, but each time it was the additional power in the air that decided the after of each individual nation. . . . [As a consequence] we are in the midst of a great crisis. The time factor is our principal obstacle."[13]

Four companies, all based on the West Coast of the United States, stepped forward to accept the challenge: Boeing which was set up in Seattle, Douglas Aircraft Company working out of Santa Monica, Lockheed Aircraft Corporation, based in Burbank, and Consolidated Aircraft Corporation operating out of San Diego. Douglas tried and failed to win the government contract with a preexisting concept, as did Consolidated. Across the Atlantic, as the Battle of Britain came to a head in early September, the Air Corps finally approved Boeing's design, titled Model 345,[14] in a contract worth $3.6 million.[15]

The company would supply two prototypes, to be renamed the "XB-29."[16] The number signified the twenty-ninth bomber design since the Martin B-1, built in 1918. As Boeing executives signed the contract, they were aware the XB-29 was still on the draftsman's table. Even so, they agreed that by April 1942 the prototype would be ready to test-fly. No one knew that by then the United States would have an urgent need for it. The main concern at Boeing was that their XB-29 would be built without the safety net of detailed engineering drawings and parts the workforce could fall back on should anything go wrong. The design, tooling of parts, and final stage of flight testing would all be conducted at the same time. This would lead to myriad production and design issues. America's entry into World War II was still six months away, but the rush was on to get the Superfortress into production.

Comprising a structure created from twenty-seven thousand pounds of aluminium sheeting, containing five thousand pounds of rubber, ten miles of wiring, over one thousand pounds of copper and brass, and nearly two miles of tubing, and with over sixty thousand separate parts, the XB-29 seemed like a giant jigsaw puzzle. The four-engine aircraft would weigh thirty-seven tons and have a smooth, circular fuselage measuring ninety-nine feet in length with a crawl tunnel large enough for an airman to navigate (thirty-four inches in diameter) connecting the cockpit to the bomb bay and tail gunner. The enormous wingspan of 141 feet would carry four air-cooled, supercharged engines, capable of producing 2,200 horse-power at takeoff. As we shall see, the design and manufacture of these engines would prove a running sore in the B-29 program throughout its infancy, and eventually into actual combat operations. It would almost undermine Arnold's whole program.

The XB-29 was twice the size of the B-17, faster, more heavily gunned, and with a fuel capacity to operate at twice the range. Just like the Flying Fortress, the XB-29 carried a crew of ten: a pilot, copilot, navigator, bombardier, engineer, radar operator, and four gunners manning positions in the front, middle, and the tail. Crucially, with relevance to the higher altitudes and lower temperatures the aircraft would be expected to operate in, the three cabin sections the crew occupied would be pressurized and heated. Ensuring these compartments were airtight would cause countless delays as the plane was manufactured, a problem repeated across the hundreds of techno-logical and engineering advances the XB-29 would contain. Boeing was building a plane it was still designing and hadn't yet tested. Once war erupted against Japan at the end of 1941, a construction process that normally took years was reduced to months.

The XB-29 enjoyed a wide variety of improvements on any long-range bomber that had gone before it, with armor-plated protection, advanced systems of radar, communications, navigational instru-ments, soundproofing, self-sealing fuel tanks to prevent fires, and a radical new computerized remote-control weapons system to defend the bomber. American planners had commissioned reports relating to the effectiveness of both German and British bombers' defensive guns and the protection given to their respective crews. Taking the good and bad points from both, their XB-29 prototype would be the answer to what they deduced was lacking in British and German heavy bombers operating in Europe.

The XB-29's enormous fuel tanks were constructed with a rubber lining to prevent catastrophic loss from punctures from enemy bullets or flak, and to protect the crews from fire breaking out, a common feature of aerial combat. Unlike the waste gunners of the B-17, handling heavy .50-cal. machine guns from an open waste hatch or in the ridiculously cramped belly turret, the XB-29 gunners would fire at the enemy through a remote-control system devised by the General Electric Company. Like the cabin, the turrets themselves, housing dual .50-cal machine guns and the 20 mm cannon in the tail section, would be pressurized. The aircraft's defensive firepower might give it an edge in combat. The new tricycle landing gear at the front of the XB-29 would keep the fuselage level, improving visibility and making it far easier for pilots to handle the plane on takeoff and landing.

Once all factors were considered, the initial weight increased to fifty-eight tons once one added the weight of the crew, the payload it would carry, and the fuel and equipment required. Within a month of the contract being signed, the Army Air Force had tabled an order for twelve more planes. Such was the urgency, the United States government and military were prepared to accept the risk of paying up front for a plane not even yet flying, nor its component parts given the all clear in testing. A month later, in November 1940, Boeing planners had completed only the construction of a wooden prototype! Though Roosevelt shied away from full mobilization in the summer of 1940, his government was now pouring money into military procurement. Over $8 billion was signed off on that year, followed by $26 billion in 1941. By the time Japan attacked Pearl Harbor, the expenditure exceeded the total spent on both the Army and Navy in the whole of the Great War.

The first test flight of the XB-29 took place on September 21, 1942, from Boeing's Seattle airfield base. At the helm was the country's foremost test pilot of multiple-engine, heavy aircraft, Edmund T. "Eddie" Allen. Hailing from Chicago, a Great War veteran now in his early forties, Allen was the golden boy of the American aviation industry, a gifted designer and builder of glider planes, as well as a pioneer of civilian and military test flying. By 1939, he had test-flown for Boeing, Douglas, and Sikorsky. As the new bomber program evolved, he was employed exclusively by Boeing to oversee testing of the B-17.

Allen was not just interested in test flying; he was at heart an engineer who pioneered new testing technology, such as the wind tunnel. This somewhat frail, soft-spoken pilot was at odds with the Hollywood vision of the 1940s. He was now at the sharp end of testing the US military's most expensive investment thus far. It would have deadly consequences. Before tests on the XB-29 began, at President Roosevelt's bidding, the Army Air Corps placed multiple contracts with Boeing for a total of 1,665 planes at a cost of over $750 million. This figure did not take into account the construction of the plants to build them.

To meet such a large order, government and Boeing planners worked alongside one another to create and build new manufacturing systems. To support their existing plant in Renton, Seattle, work began in October 1940 to build from scratch a new plant in Wichita, Kansas, at a cost of $13 million ($273 million today). Originally meant for turning out B-17s, it was decided to switch production exclusively in late 1941 to the XB-29 program. Two more companies would supply new plants to increase production: the Bell Aircraft Company (originally from Buffalo, New York), to be based in Marietta, Georgia, and the Martin Company, working out of Omaha, Nebraska. Why had the military chosen such disparate locations?

The choice was twofold: satisfying the military's needs for security and, secondly, aiding the government's drive to rejuvenate economically depressed areas of the United States. All four plants would be sited away from the Pacific and Atlantic coasts. The threat of a German attack from the Atlantic was perhaps remote, but an aerial attack from Japanese bombers was seen as a very real issue in 1942. Each facility's location enabled tighter security. New road and rail networks linked them to the thousands of subcontractors nationwide who would supply the tools and materials required. Placing these plants in rural areas would attract a workforce of hardworking patriots, not prone to strike action or falling for political propaganda from abroad. Over thirty-five thousand Americans would be employed to manufacture the planes, with 40 percent being women. African Americans were in general discouraged from working in the southern plants, and in the West, the large Japanese American communities on the Pacific coast had by now been forcibly interned for the war's duration.[17]

As ground was broken to build the giant facilities, new communities were also created. The Federal Housing Authority constructed thousands of homes for workers, the towns connected by new road systems and supported with shops, theaters, and schools. Wichita would become the program's star facility. It earned a reputation as an efficient production site. Its skilled workforce of fourteen thousand people was mainly drawn from an agricultural community experienced in handling machine tools and parts. Arguably paid more money than they had ever earned in their lives, they were motivated to produce the largest number of air-worthy B-29s across the program, with their surplus of spare parts shipped to other facilities. Bus services were created within a seventy-mile radius to bring the Wichita plant's workforce to and from their homes. The workers would pass through tight security, store their belongings in lockers, and punch in for their shift. Their breaks would be supplied by "floating cafeterias" providing them with everything they wanted to eat. Many workers had never eaten so well in their lives.

Roosevelt's commitment to supply the Allies with the Lend-Lease Act,[18] signed in March 1941, was by now in full swing once the US was committed to the war. Across the United States, millions of Americans were employed to deliver it. They would create and build ships to transport the food, matériel, and weapons of war to Great Britain and her Commonwealth, the Soviet Union, and the Republic of China. Even with these enormous priorities, the Roosevelt administration monitored the B-29 program carefully. In early 1942, the

War Production Board decided that Boeing would be the flagship manufacturer furnishing the other contractors. Apart from the workforce at the four facilities, hundreds of thousands of men and women were now under government contracts within the bomber program's budget to supply everything required to build the plane. By the time the XB-29 was on its inaugural test flight in September 1942, the cost to the US taxpayer stood at $1.5 billion.

Across all the plants, there were problems. Each one ate into Hap Arnold's schedule, from new, inexperienced workers getting to grips with construction and engineering techniques to the frustration of working with new technology. Many parts of the B-29 were untested. The initial method of production to meet such a tight schedule was failing, too. A manufacturing process intended to mirror the American car industry did not suit the method of constructing a complex and very large plane. The established method used in the automobile industry—a conveyor-belt-like process, with teams individually adding their respective piece to build it—was impracticable for the bomber. The many engineers, mechanics, welders, and electricians who were required might need extra time to problem-solve and complete their tasks before the plane could be moved on. Plus, the actual size of the thing limited speed and ease of production as it made its way through the plant.

Added to this were the many sporadic design changes as they came up, such as the rubber sealants for the crew cabin windows to enable pressurization, which took many adaptations before a solution was found. Perfecting the plane's computerized fire-control system; succeeding in the triangular, retractable forward landing gear; the correct speed of the pneumatic bomb-bay doors closing shut; the glass panes frosting over at high altitude; and crucially, the plane's massive engines overheating: they all caused delays. Sporadic shortages of materials and finding workers to complete each shift were issues, too, in some of the plants.

In response, innovative workflow analysis saw the creation of the "multiline system" of construction. It had workers operating in teams of six groups of lines, separately assembling the B-29's main pieces in "precompleted" form with all equipment installed. When each of the six main sections was complete, they would be hoisted up and brought to the huge final assembly bays by crane to be bolted and riveted together, connecting harnesses of electrical wiring and control systems, attaching props, and turning down the landing gear. They would then be inspected before being authorized to fly. That was the hope, anyway. By the end of 1943, as Hap Arnold signed off on the construction of air bases in China for the new squadrons, each B-29 now required twenty-five thousand man-hours to incorporate these modifications. For weeks thereafter, Arnold's gleaming silver bombers were parked idly on tarmacked runways from Seattle to Kansas, waiting their turn to be modified to become operational. It took more man-hours to modify a completed B-29 than it did to build one from scratch. Not only did Arnold have to figure out a way to increase speed of production, but he had lost his star test pilot earlier that year.

On February 18, 1943, Allen and his crew of eight were killed testing an XB-29—the cause of which would dog production of the program, as well as kill many frontline crews later in the war: the overheating and failure of the B-29 engines. Allen loved the bomber and had glowingly described it as "an excellent aircraft" in his initial flight in September 1942. On this fateful flight, taking off from the Boeing center in Seattle to test the company's second prototype, within eight minutes of takeoff, at five thousand feet, Allen's plane experienced a catastrophic engine fire. Two of his crew bailed out but died on landing. Allen and the remainder of his crew narrowly missed a skyscraper in downtown Seattle but crashed as they approached their home base. The plane plowed into a meatpacking plant, destroying it completely. All aboard—the cream of Boeing's technical team—were killed, as were twenty workers in the plant.

The ensuing investigation would be overseen by a certain senator from Missouri, Harry S. Truman, who would work alongside Arnold's designated leader of the B-29 program, Brigadier General

Kenneth B. Wolfe.[19] Wolfe would oversee not just the bomber's development, but the training and equipping of B-29 units and the bomber's first operational missions from Chinese bases. Truman's eventual report criticized the faulty design of the plane's engines (the R-3350 Cyclone built by Wright Aeronautical, based in Paterson, New Jersey) and the pressure the Army Air Force had placed on Boeing to speed up production. Engine issues would plague the B-29 all throughout the war.[20] The R-3550 Cyclone was an enormous, air-cooled duplex-piston engine, able to run at 2,000 horsepower when cruising at altitude, and 2,200 for actual takeoff. Like the B-29 design, it was revolutionary. Providing twice as much power as the B-17's engine, but crucially allowing for less drag due to the aircraft's design, it had the same air resistance. Such was the capability it gave to the aircraft, Arnold himself rated it as "the Number One requirement of the Army Air Forces."

Mirroring the technical problems arising from the whole plane, the R-3350 ran up thousands of issues and modifications that took time, money, and manpower to correct. Overheating was the major concern. The risk of fire within a heavily ladened bomber was deadly. The engine contained a major design fault in one of its component parts constructed with a magnesium lining. It was prone to ignite should the exhaust valves overheat. In flight, engines could easily burn through the wing spar and into the built-in fuel tanks. For Hap Arnold, it was an essential problem to be solved: without a durable engine, his bombers couldn't operate over long distances to attack Japan. Fixing the issue at the source was another. The groundbreaking concept and design of the R-3350 meant it needed highly skilled, experienced engineers and technicians to successfully put it together. Dozens of modifications made every week would mean new parts being redesigned and retooled. Hiring a workforce was one thing; training them on the job to deliver a working engine was another. This was one element that had to be perfect, since the crews flying into combat depended on it. There was no room for error.

Hap Arnold would find the manufacture of the R-3550 one of

his biggest challenges of the program. He berated the directors of Wright Aeronautical to employ a dedicated, motivated, and skilled workforce by ensuring they were well paid for their time and trained properly to do their jobs. Though he empathized with the problems arising from such a complex design, Arnold's forceful personality came to the fore within the corridors of power in Washington. He willingly took on the mantle of chief fixer to not only have Wright deliver what was required of them, but make the company an employer people would want to work for. Arnold would lobby the company to pull down the country's traditional gender and racial barriers in order to hire thousands of women and African Americans. Still, overheated engines caused a spate of fatal air crashes in the first nine months of the bomber's service in both China and the Pacific theaters.[21]

Unlike the paradise that was Wichita, Wright's base in Woodbridge, New Jersey, suffered from a shortage of skilled workers. Being near a metropolis offered better long-term jobs and rates of pay than other industries to an inexperienced workforce enduring long shifts for low pay. To assist the drive to produce enough engines, Chrysler would be pulled into the equation. The carmaker built the world's largest manufacturing plant in Chicago—complete with the world's largest parking lot. Through intense reviews, employing teams of engineers, and problem-solving on the factory floor, the issue was overcome, though not fully solved.

The mainstay of the program to deliver hundreds of B-29s ready for operations would be Wichita. Since the summer of 1940, when the plants had begun to be erected, the men, resources, and money pouring into the state to complete it had been a shot in the arm to the state's economy, lifting communities out of the poverty the Great Depression had left them with. The total floor area for the facility measured 2.8 million square feet, comprising the plants, warehousing, offices, runways, hardstands, barracks for military personnel, and the infrastructure to get the workforce to and from their homes. Wichita would employ the best skilled workers for the whole program, many of whom would be loaned out to other plants across the United States to iron out production problems. It was at Wichita that the "multiline" system was developed and perfected before it went nationwide.

It would be here, too, where Hap Arnold was driven to exasperation in production delays that were preventing Roosevelt's administration from honoring its pledge in 1944 to China that the B-29 would enhance its ability to defeat the Japanese. The B-29 aircrews Wolfe was assembling for combat in India and China had no actual airworthy planes to train in by the end of 1943. Militarily and politically, Arnold's expensive program was in danger of being delayed or even shelved if it could not deliver operational bombers the government had spent billions on. The "Battle of Kansas" would see him actively take control of the situation in early 1944, demanding that Boeing have the full complement ready by April 15, 1944. No matter if workers had to perfect engines, weld, solve electrical issues such as the new radar systems, or fit pressurized glass in the cockpit in a freezing Midwest winter, the planes would have their modifications completed and be ready to fly. They succeeded, and Wichita delivered the 175 Superfortresses General Wolfe's crews needed to take to India.

The B-29 was a miracle of design and technology, delivered by an economy and society flexible enough to adapt to new ways of manufacture and learn new skills, produced in record time. Over four thousand would be built by war's end. The bill to the American taxpayer would be more than the $2 billion cost of the Manhattan Project—$3.7 billion. As Jacob Vander Meulen concluded in *Building the B-29*: "The United States has built many bombers more complex and powerful than the B-29. But none were designed, developed, and mass-produced so quickly and with such urgency. None involved so much new planning and organisation in so short a time or posed so many challenges to the usual patterns of American social life."[22]

Building the B-29 had presented a giant jigsaw puzzle to American workers to figure out. The actual plane would now be part of an enormous operation in the Pacific theater. It would become the vehicle that the officers of the prewar "Bomber Mafia" had envisioned needing to implement their doctrine of precision aerial bombing. But that was three years hence in this story. At the same time Arnold had invited American aircraft manufacturers to design the plane, in Washington strategists and policymakers had been debating the merits of the United States developing a weapon of absolute destruction.

Chapter Five

COMMITTEES

I knew you couldn't get anything done in that damned town
unless you organised under the wing of the President.[1]
VANNEVAR BUSH

The theorization of atomic weaponry now began to gather momentum. In September 1940, as the Battle of Britain raged above the skies, the American and British scientific communities came together. A British delegation, authorized by Winston Churchill and led by Henry Tizard, chairman of the Aeronautical Research Committee, came to Washington bearing technological and scientific riches. In Tizard's team of military representatives were two radar experts, Edward Bowen and Professor John Cockcroft (from the MAUD committee). Both men had gathered a choice selection of plans, blueprints, circuit diagrams, and samples for their American hosts. They related to Britain's most sensitive plans for the jet engine, gyroscopic gun sight, and submarine detection. What the Americans were most keen to see, Cockcroft had brought them a prototype of— one of only a dozen that had been built thus far: the cavity magnetron, a revolution in radar technology. The crown jewels of British technology and science were placed in a traveling trunk and handed over to the Americans without anything expected in return. Churchill simply needed goodwill from Roosevelt's administration in his darkest hour.[2]

Tizard's team encountered Roosevelt's newly appointed adviser who would be instrumental in America's advance in science and weapons technology, and their atomic energy program: Vannevar Bush. Mindful of protecting American technology, engineering, and finance connected to this new weapons program, Bush would play a pivotal role in the relationship between Britain and the United States as he tried (many times unsuccessfully) to walk a tightrope between protecting American interests and retaining British support. The Tizard mission was an important step in cementing the Anglo-American alliance in the coming war. For now, Bush had what he wanted from the British. He had played a good game.

Known to his friends as "Van," the fifty-year-old president of the Carnegie Institute had been making a name for himself in Washington for the past year and a half. Six feet tall, debonair, dressed in neat pin-striped suits, puffing on his pipe, he stalked Capitol Hill with relentless energy. He was a sharp political operator, and though not a fan of Roosevelt's New Deal, he knew he had to gain his trust to get anywhere in government. Weaving from one group of scientists to administrators, he sensed their unease at the lack of progress in government to take the initiative and coalesce science with the military.

Bush had convinced Roosevelt to direct that the Uranium Committee be folded into the authority of the National Defense Research Committee (NDRC), as he began to establish a platform for American science to prepare for the coming war. He came armed with a formidable reputation to front the administration's program to steer science toward rearming the military. He was an electrical engineer by training, a former vice president of the Massachusetts Institute of Technology (MIT), president of the Carnegie Institute, and chairman of the National Advisory Committee for Aeronautics.

Bush could see that the United States was not yet fully prepared for war—if anything, its capability to conduct a multifront campaign in Asia and Europe was woeful. After discussions with fellow scientists and administrators, he evolved a plan for a committee, staffed with the finest science administrators the country had, that would organize science in military development. On June 12, 1940, as the

German blitzkrieg pushed France to defeat, Bush circumvented Congress and laid out his proposal directly before the president. His one-page plan, typed in four short paragraphs, mapped out what was required. The men were of similar mind, and Roosevelt gave it the green light. Three days later, Roosevelt formally appointed Bush chairman of an eight-person committee, with their work to be financed from his office's emergency fund.

The committee made room for two military representatives from the Army and Navy, but primarily was staffed with leading academics: Karl Taylor Compton, president of MIT; James B. Conant, the president of Harvard; Frank B. Jewett, president of the National Academy of Sciences and chairman of the board of directors of Bell Laboratories; and finally Richard C. Tolman, dean of Caltech. On June 27, an order was issued officially creating the NDRC. Bush was aware he was upsetting a well-established process for gaining funding for the development of military technology. The war in Europe had persuaded Roosevelt such laborious channels of administration had to be circumvented.

Bush's new role would have him expand the country's research base and recruit the personnel to achieve it, whether from academic or industry-related backgrounds. His new committee was to act as a rocket boost for the country's scientific resources, and crucially, it was not beholden to the military. The NDRC's reach now was enormous. It connected over two hundred thousand scientists around the country, as Bush was keen to state, from the lowest-paid lab technician to Albert Einstein himself. It had freedom to act as it pleased, devolving responsibility from government to his own office to kickstart scientific programs across the country. One of its first tasks was to bring in the Advisory Committee on Uranium to free up scientific progress into the issue of building an atomic bomb. Both Bush and Conant would now be the main driving force behind the US atomic program for the next two years.

Before it could begin its work, the Uranium Committee was redefined and retooled for the job. It was answerable to Bush, and he wanted it stocked with scientists, not with military figures, as his own NDRC would now maintain that link. The Uranium Committee was free to simply get on with the job at hand rather than be tangled up in military red tape. Security played a factor in no foreign-born scientists being eligible to join, and further articles on uranium being published or circulated were blocked without authorization.

In June 1941, Bush could recognize the committee's inherent weakness: it could support new research, but it did not have the authority, or budget control, to develop anything further. The NDRC was a great step forward, but a year's experience revealed certain imperfections. He lobbied the president's office once again for a department that had muscle, that could potentially take the best proposals from the drawing board and make them a reality. He created a new federal department—the Office of Scientific Research and Development (OSRD). Bush would now oversee a two-stage process. The NDRC (with the Uranium Committee), chaired by James Conant, would push through their recommendations on scientific proposals to the OSRD, overseen by Bush. His direct line would be to the Oval Office. He answered only to the president.

In July, the MAUD Report had been sent across by the British to the Uranium Committee's director, Lyman Briggs, a secretive man who unbelievably decided to store it in his office safe. It might have remained there but for the insistence of Marcus Oliphant, who undertook a perilous flight in a B-24 Liberator to fly to the United States, ostensibly to discuss radar but also to lobby for the report. Tizard wanted him to discover why there had been no reaction from the Americans to the findings in their feasibility study for the building of an atomic bomb, based, in part, on the theoretical work undertaken the previous year by Rudolf Peierls and Otto Frisch. The MAUD Report estimated that a critical mass weighing just twenty-two pounds was compact enough to be built into a casing, and with the correct firing mechanism could be stored in the bomb bay of a long-range bomber, such as a B-17 Flying Fortress. Twenty-two pounds of pure U-235 could potentially be made ready in less than two years. It would be enough to cause a colossal detonation that might destroy a town or a large harbor. Ultimately, it could affect the outcome of the war. Nazi Germany was clearly working on a similar line of inquiry, yet their paper was sitting in a safe, unread.

Oliphant set to work to ensure it received an audience. Within three weeks, he sat down with the Uranium Committee in New York and kicked up dirt. Samuel Allison, an experimental physicist, had recently joined the committee and recalled clearly the effect Oliphant had on the meeting: "He told us we must concentrate every effort on the bomb, and said we had no right to work on power plants or anything but the bomb. The bomb would cost 25 million dollars, he said, and Britain did not have the money or the manpower, so it was up to us."[3]

The Australian had the wind in his sales and flew across the country to have dinner with his friend Ernest Lawrence in Berkeley, where he handed him a copy of the memorandum. Lawrence passed it on to a friend of his at Berkeley, J. Robert Oppenheimer, to confirm the findings. His hard lobbying brought results. By the beginning of October, Vannevar Bush's right-hand man, James Conant, had read it and passed it to his office. By October 9 Bush was briefing President Roosevelt, who ordered him to open discussions with the British government, i.e., Winston Churchill.

The British leader would make a fatal mistake in underestimating the Americans' capacity to produce the bomb in record time and in sidelining his own scientists' endeavors.[4] By the time he replied, a full two months later, to Roosevelt's original offer to be a partner in the program, the chance had gone. Bush was determined that this would be an all-American affair, paid for by the American taxpayer. Allowing the British in had not been on his agenda: He would pick their brains, use their ideas and technology, and progress with his own plans.

Five months later, the world had been changed irrevocably by Japan's surprise attack on Pearl Harbor. Bush now ruled over the complete atomic energy program, with Conant taking control of the

Uranium Committee (now under the abbreviation of OSRD S-1 Section—Bush insisted the word *uranium* be deleted due to security considerations). Bush had a thorough review of the MAUD Report, with its findings verifying the British team's conclusions. They were still concerned, however, that Nazi Germany was pushing ahead its own feasibility studies. As the United States welcomed in 1942, if uranium was discussed, it was within the confines of what became known as the Top Policy Group—hosted by Roosevelt, with Bush, Conant, Vice President Wallace, Secretary of War Henry L. Stimson, and Army Chief of Staff George C. Marshall.

Once the US declared war against Japan, Churchill flew to Washington on December 22 to coordinate the Allied strategy as well as to discuss Lend-Lease and the Atlantic war, but curiously not the bomb. The two leaders were similar in backgrounds and upbringing, but whereas FDR was a tough, cunning politician, his aristocratic friend would ply the charm and, if that failed, shift to outraged bluster. They would enjoy an intimate political friendship. Once the British leader had departed, the president authorized Bush on January 19, 1942, to officially promote the program to development stage. It was going to be a solely American affair.

The government could pursue two pathways to create the bomb. A uranium bomb could be achieved if sufficient rare uranium-235 could be produced by one or more of the three isotope-separation methods under consideration: gaseous diffusion, centrifuge, and electromagnetic. A plutonium bomb might provide a quicker route, but it required plutonium to be produced in a uranium pile and then separated into usable quantities. To evaluate both pathways, Arthur Compton consolidated most plutonium research at the new Metallurgical Laboratory (Met Lab) at the University of Chicago. By May 1942, Bush and Stimson read Compton's review—there was as yet no leader in the race to build a bomb. It now recommended that the three isotope-separation methods and the pile project be pushed as fast as possible to full production planning.

The vast industrial engine of the American economy was starting to get into gear, millions of men were under arms and being trained in the bases now constructed by the US Army, and Roosevelt's Arsenal of Democracy was shipping supplies across the Atlantic to Britain and the Soviet Union. American naval forces had inflicted a morale-boosting defeat on the Imperial Japanese Navy at the Battle of the Coral Sea. Vannevar Bush sat in his Washington office and contented himself that he now had the limitless support of the American taxpayer to bring the atomic program to life. The issue was, how quickly could he do it?

Part II

WELCOME TO MANHATTAN

Chapter Six

"IF YOU DO THE JOB RIGHT, IT WILL WIN THE WAR!"

I don't want to stay in Washington!
COLONEL LESLIE R. GROVES, 1942[1]

"Groves is the biggest 'S.O.B.' I have ever worked for. He is [the] most demanding. He is [the] most critical. He is always a driver, never a praiser. He is abrasive and sarcastic. He disregards all normal organizational channels. He is extremely intelligent. He has the guts to make timely, difficult decisions. He is the most egotistical man I know. He knows he is right and so sticks by his decision. He abounds with energy and expects everyone to work as hard, or even harder, than he does . . . if I had to do my part of the atomic bomb project over again and had the privilege of picking my boss, I would pick General Groves."

This assessment by Colonel Kenneth D. Nichols eloquently summarized the kind of officer the US Army, and Vannevar Bush, knew the country's atomic program required to command it if it was ever to come to fruition. Forty-six-year-old Colonel Leslie R. Groves, of the Quartermaster's Corps within the US Army Corps of Engineers, was arguably one of the greatest project managers in the country, and he had worked wonders over the last thirty-six months. The Pentagon, the complex he had given the past two years of his life constructing, was now complete—the largest administrative installation in the United States as well as the world. It would become the epicenter of the country's mobilization efforts. The five-sided, five-story structure would house over forty thousand personnel, across an area of five million square feet, at an overall cost of $63 million (equating to $1.3 billion in today's money). As one of his trusted subordinates, Colonel Nichols had a front-row seat to Groves's fiery temper, but also his incisive, brilliant organizational ability. He had not only overseen the Pentagon's construction, but led the entire rebuilding of the military's infrastructure that would underpin President Roosevelt's rearmament program. Groves had directed the construction of airfields, ports, ordnance and chemical manufacturing plants, as well as accommodation and training facilities for millions of men.

He had succeeded in reinvigorating a program that had become tangled in the weeds of bureaucracy, delays, inefficiency, and poor management. Forming a team of talented officers, he had reshaped communications, improved adherence to schedules and budgets, and through their implementation, transformed morale and energy for the better. The opening of the Pentagon was the cherry on the cake. He had achieved almost the impossible, and more, as he stated in a postwar interview: "[W]ith most of the headaches of directing ten billion dollars' worth of military construction in the country behind me—for good, I hoped. I wanted out of Washington, and quickly."[2]

Now he wanted his reward. A transfer, possibly a promotion (during this period he had already risen from major to colonel), and with the United States fully engaged in the war against the Axis, a combat unit. He had entered middle age and knew this was his chance to serve with an engineer unit in theater—whether the Pacific, North Africa, or Europe. He expected his direct superior, Lieutenant General Brehon Somervell, commander of the Army Services Supply, an officer whom he had worked with intimately and who appreciated his experience to transfer to combat overseas. Groves believed his coveted posting overseas was in the pipeline once Somervell had rubber-stamped it. The military, and the war, had other plans. Groves had finished testifying in front of the Military

Affairs Committee, at the newly opened House of Representatives Building in Washington. As he stepped away from the meeting into the corridor, Somervell was waiting for him.

"To my great surprise," he later recalled, "he told me that I could not leave Washington. He went on to say: 'The Secretary of War has selected you for a very important assignment, and the President has approved the selection.'

"Where?" asked a stunned Groves.

"Washington," Somervell replied, deadpan.

Groves protested, "But I don't want to stay in Washington."

Somervell had the perfect riposte that arguably appealed to Groves's sense of duty. "If you do the job right, it will win the war."

Groves at last realized what they were talking about. "Oh, that thing."[3]

The "thing" Groves knew was the fledgling atomic program. The initial plans for sites, as well as allocation of men and equipment to build them, had passed by his desk. As he admitted, the confirmed cost thus far of $100 million was overly optimistic, though not a figure that daunted him. Over the past few years, he had overseen billions of taxpayer funds directed into the Army's restructuring program. It was not unusual for him to sign off bills for over $100 million in a single week! He had no choice. He had to take the position, realizing he would never command troops in combat. Groves had already discussed elements of the atomic bomb program with its then overseer, Lieutenant Colonel James C. Marshall, who had been put in place by Vannevar Bush in early June. Marshall had put in place new headquarters for the new engineer district—high up on the eighteenth floor of 270 Broadway in New York and named after its location: the Manhattan Engineer District. Colonel Nichols was at that point serving under Marshall, but as Marshall tried to come up to speed with the science behind the project, he was struggling to move forward with a fractured chain of command, waiting in line for scarce national resources, and frustrating scientists eager to get moving and establish facilities. Inertia bred impatience in the corridors of Washington, until two months into the job, Marshall was set aside and Groves was in the frame. Once he took up command, Nichols would become his point man.

Groves now met with the head of Army Services of Supply, Major General W. D. Styer, to be brought up to speed. The Army had been struggling to get the project underway successfully since being given the task that summer of laying the groundwork for the required facilities and materials. The top brass's estimates reflected their limited knowledge of what it would take to create sufficient supplies of the rare uranium-235, uranium-238, and plutonium-239. What was key was that the Army run the thing. Groves would later confess that Styer's conclusion that the bomb's research and development were complete and the initial tasks in his new in tray were nothing he hadn't done before were a tad overoptimistic. His role over the coming three years would not be as easy as building some plants and setting up the workforce to complete the job. What sugared the bitter pill of no combat posting and accepting a complex assignment was General Marshall's directive that Groves must be promoted forthwith to brigadier general—a reflection of his role in the coming task ahead. They knew they had the right man for the job.

His security vetting, overseen by J. Edgar Hoover at the FBI, highlighted Groves's passion for competitive tennis, an ability to solve complicated mathematical and engineering problems while eating, and comically, a love of candy, especially when stressed, which led to his half-joking fears of developing a middle-age spread. FBI files also highlighted that Groves, born in Albany, New York, in 1896, had been nicknamed "Greasy" at West Point, from where he graduated in 1918 as the Great War was coming to an end. The newly promoted brigadier general had few interests outside his work and thankfully enjoyed a stable, happy marriage. His record within the service was exemplary. He was highly experienced in working to schedule, leading multiple teams of personnel, and hardly ever exceeded budgets. General Marshal and Secretary Stimson assessed the many talents Groves could bring to the new role and balanced it against his well-known tendency not to suffer fools. He would be working alongside some of the country's top scientists, engineers, and technicians. It wasn't even an argument. Both men realized Somervell's recommendation of Groves gave them the best candidate to run the world's biggest-ever military project and deliver the bomb quickly. Groves would be given extraordinary powers—with command over all aspects of the nuclear program: construction, scientific research, the actual development program, while overseeing internal and external security and ultimately having a major role in the deployment and use of the bomb.

Groves would benefit from a direct line to the levers of power: Bush at the Office of Scientific Research and Development, Conant at the National Defense Research Committee, Secretary of War Stimson, and through him the ear of Roosevelt himself.[4] Outwardly, he was a mere brigadier general, but Groves now expected easy access to Joint Chief General George Marshall, a situation that bewildered many senior officers at first. Financially, and to get the project accelerated, he would be given the authority to sign off contracts up to a limit of $5 million.[5] The budget Groves was responsible for by the war's end would surpass the cost of running the entire American motor industry as he utilized the giants of the country's construction industry—Dupont, Tennessee Eastman, Chrysler, and Union Carbide—to build the program. Just as the country would offer the cream of its industry, design, and construction expertise to facilitate the creation of the infrastructure Groves required, so America's scientific community would now step forward to provide the teams to work in them.

Groves established his main headquarters in Washington on the fifth floor of the New War Department that he had helped build. From the outset, Groves was fanatically invested in the program, working fifteen hour days, seven days a week, with no letup. He gave up his beloved hobby of tennis to maximize his waking time on the job at hand. As a result, he put on weight. The stress of the job, as the

FBI had commented upon, had Groves sustain his energy levels with boxes of chocolates and jars of candy. His staff realized he had stashed away supplies in his office safe where he also stored the top secret paperwork for the Manhattan Project. He needed the energy as the construction of the key sites that had been chosen originally by Colonel Marshall began to take shape. Upon taking command, Groves immediately set about surveying what was planned to produce both uranium-235 and plutonium. Oak Ridge, Tennessee, which his predecessor Marshall had previously earmarked, would become the production base for uranium. Behind the scenes, Bush and Stimson created a more workable steering group—the Military Policy Committee, which would bring together the armed services to support him. Bush then ordered the overall command of the nuclear program to switch from the Office of Scientific Research and Development and be placed under the control of the Army. Groves now had to solve the debate of which fissionable material the program should get behind.

With his laser-like focus, Groves was fortunate to have someone like Vannevar Bush high up at the president's table. Bush, from his position running the OSRD, had already placed the right scientists in the best positions the previous December to deliver the kind of success the MAUD Report had concluded might be possible. Groves realized the time constraints meant mistakes might be made along the way, but a decision had to be made quickly. If they were going to use U-235 to make the bomb, what was the best process to create it quickly and in sufficient quantities?

Agreement had been reached that with the land at Oak Ridge now purchased, a full-scale production facility based upon Ernest Lawrence's pioneering isotope electromagnetic separation be created at his lab in Berkley. Meanwhile, Enrico Fermi and Leo Szilard were ensconced at the University of Chicago's Metallurgical Laboratory ("Chicago-Pile 1"), close to testing the world's first artificial nuclear reactor based on natural uranium. By December it would prove successful, offering the program limited supplies of enriched uranium. Working alongside them, the chemist Glenn T. Seaborg[6] studied the chemical process of extracting plutonium-239 from the mass of uranium. His success at the procedure that August produced a microscopic sample. He would eventually lead to full-scale production of plutonium at the Hanford Engineering Works in Washington State. To obtain the requisite materials, Groves dispatched Colonel Nichols to purchase 1,200 tons of high-grade uranium ore from Belgian firm Union Miniére, which had mines in both the Belgian Congo and the United States.

To bring these initiatives into mass production and construct the vast sites required, manufacture the machinery, supply the materials to kit them out, and hire a workforce that would reach over a hundred thousand by war's end, Groves needed the authority to get what he need when he needed it. When he assumed command, the project was not deemed the most vital aspect of the country's war effort. The highest rating in government for a share of resources and finance was AAA, rarely awarded to anything other than emergency requests. For essential weapons and equipment, AA-1 was the top rank, going down to the lowest, AA-4. Groves was enraged to discover his command was classed as AA-3. It would not suffice. Ignoring protocol, he warned the chairman of the War Production Board, Donald M. Nelson, that he would take his case to the president if the newly designated Manhattan Project, which Roosevelt himself had signed into being, was not granted AA-1 ranking. As with many fights he had inside the corridors of power in Washington and the Pentagon, Groves would get what he needed.

Groves had political and financial support, and the ear of the president, Stimson, Bush and the head of the Army. The scientific community was rallying to the project, the technology was evolving quickly in the right direction, and locations across the country for mass production were now selected and under speedy construction. And Groves now had the man he thought could lead the world's first atomic weapons program. As he was prone to do, Groves went against the recommendations and scientific prejudices of his senior advisers to offer the job of head of weapons technology for the Manhattan Project to the man without a Nobel prize, working in Berkeley, California: Professor J. Robert Oppenheimer.

Chapter Seven

THE MAN IN THE HAT

To me [the task at hand] is primarily the development in
time of war of a military weapon of some consequence.
J. ROBERT OPPENHEIMER

Groves required a brilliant theorist to pull together the various
threads of the program's research, inspire, and lead a team of different and, in some cases, temperamental characters. Many of
them were Nobel Prize winners. He had to maintain cordial relations with the country's main allies, the British, whose own atomic
program, Tube Alloys, seemed to be ahead of their own research.
Equally required was an appreciation of the practical obstacles he
had to overcome to build a weapon and do it quickly. Groves had
met with Oppenheimer in Chicago that October and invited him
to travel back with him and Colonels Marshall and Nichols to New
York aboard the *20th Century Limited*.[1] The Berkeley academic was
already invested in the program, having been brought in by Ernest
Lawrence to handle the bomb's design research. James Conant at
the NDRC had also wanted him to join the program. Groves had
picked up on this.

In his small, one-person compartment, the four men discussed
the program and the obstacles it presented in terms of access and
security. Groves felt he had the right man to lead the scientific team,
but Oppenheimer impressed him with his own ideas and solutions
to the many logistical issues it would bring. Groves had already met
many scientists, but Oppenheimer seemed to have a more worldly

view than any of them. Groves wanted him to construct and lead the secret research laboratory, the location yet to be established.

Born in Manhattan in 1904, Oppenheimer was from a privileged background. His father, a German Jewish immigrant, had carved out a hugely successful business empire in clothing, providing a lavish apartment on the Upper West Side. The family employed a live-in governess and maid. He was from an early age a loner, though he did love the outdoors. He mainly played alone and read poetry, and his parents encouraged his passion for collecting minerals. He attended the Ethical Culture School, which promoted ideals of liberalism, social justice, and how to support the poorer classes. To serve was at the core of the school's philosophy. Oppenheimer's subsequent life would be guided by what he learned there.

Harvard University, where he graduated in 1925, was his pathway to study chemistry, but he would discover and become obsessed with experimental physics. He moved on to Cambridge University to study alongside Ernest Rutherford and encountered for the first time the great Danish physicist Niels Bohr. He was deeply unhappy and felt alien to the work in the laboratory, where he was clumsy and slow. He confided to a friend, "I am having a pretty bad time. The lab work is a terrible bore, and I am so bad at it that it is impossible to feel that I am learning anything."[2]

He moved on to study for his PhD in physics at Gottingen University in 1926, where he would come under the influence of Max Born and met Werner Heisenberg, who would lead the German atomic program. It was the beginning of his path toward becoming a world-class theoretical physicist. He balanced his scientific work with exercising his religious and philosophical curiosity, studying the Hindu religion and teaching himself to read Sanskrit.

Europe had taken the lead in quantum physics (analyzing the behavior of nature at and below the level of atoms), but Oppenheimer relocated back to the States, just as the Great Depression was about to strike, to take up a position at University of California, Berkeley. For the next decade, Oppenheimer would be instrumental in developing Berkeley's school of theoretical physics into a world-renowned institution. As Algis Valiunas, a fellow at the Ethics and Public Policy Center, concludes in *The New Atlantis*,

"Oppenheimer's style of intelligence was perfectly suited to the seminar room: he possessed a mind quick as a striking cobra, capable of penetrating to the essentials of a new discovery while lesser men were fogged in by the details, recognizing straightaway the practical implications of abstruse theorizing, so thoroughly versed in the various relevant fields that concision and exactitude in explanation came naturally as breathing, and graced with a charm that captivated serious persons and drew the best out of them."[3]

The poverty and inequality of the Great Depression punctured the rarefied air of academia, as he listened to the complaints of many students who would graduate and struggle to find work. The poverty across the United States further fueled his social conscience, and he gravitated toward communism, which appealed to him, and many in his academic circle (including his younger brother Frank, who would join the Party), as a way to defeat the rise of fascism. Oppenheimer was aware that many German and Italian scientists were now fleeing their countries and washing up on the shores of America. He donated 3 percent of his university salary to support them. He would be drawn into left-wing politics further by marrying Katherine Puening Harrison,[4] who had been a Party member. As with a great many Americans from the cultural and scientific communities, this affiliation, or sympathy, would come to haunt him in later life.

With the company he kept and the need for complete secrecy for the atomic program, Groves was warned off selecting Oppenheimer by both the FBI and military intelligence. As he sat intently listening to the Berkeley professor articulately and coherently debate with him on the practicalities of running the program to a speedy, successful conclusion, Groves was intent on hiring him. The fear of the Nazis gaining the upper hand in nuclear technology allowed him the latitude of taking a calculated risk. For Oppenheimer, both fear of losing his job at Berkeley due to his past political dalliance and the chance to lead arguably the world's finest scientific team for the noble cause of defeating fascism were too good an opportunity to pass on. What he didn't know—how would he?—was that the FBI had opened up a file on him several months before he sat on the train with Groves heading toward Manhattan. He was on the Bureau's Custodial Detention Index. If there was a nationwide emergency, he was to be arrested.

He now joined Groves to scout where the research center could be set up. Oppenheimer's childhood relaxation had been the outdoors, the family vacationing in their holiday home amid the barren landscape and arid air of the high desert of northern New Mexico. A far cry from the hustle and bustle of city life on the Upper West Side of Manhattan, it was where both the young Oppenheimer boys learned to ride horses at the Los Alamos Ranch School for Boys, on the road to Santa Fe. The school had been built on flat tableland that made up part of the plateau of the Jemez Mountains, several thousand feet above sea level.

Pondering the issue of security for what was to be built, Oppenheimer knew how remote the laboratory had to be and that it had to provide a suitable, safe, test site. He remembered the ranch school where he had spent hours riding free through the hills and copses of deep green pine trees. He described to Groves just how secluded it was, with a vast expanse of remote territory surrounding it in every direction. They quickly flew down to New Mexico to ascertain its suitability. Groves and Nichols agreed it would be perfect. From a safety perspective, there would be no sizable civilian population nearby to be imperiled by the release of radioactivity. The hundreds of indigenous people who lived in the area would be relocated over the coming weeks. It would be code-named "Site Y."

By the early spring of 1943, once the government speedily made a compulsory land acquisition of the fifty-four-thousand-acre site, over fifteen hundred engineers and construction teams moved quickly to start building Site Y. It was a vast undertaking with Oppenheimer overseeing the setting up of laboratories, the continuous supply by fleets of military trucks of the specialized equipment, the building of housing, a canteen, movie theater, school, and church—situated on nameless streets. Groves was aware the occupants were no raw recruits to be trained and that the army could treat as it wished. The teams of scientists, some, like Oppenheimer, were bringing their families and needed to have some comforts of home in this wilderness if they were to successfully and rapidly, design, develop, and build the atomic bomb.

The heart of the camp, situated behind a guarded, high chain-link fence, was called the Main Technical Area, or as it was soon termed by the locals, the "Tech Area"—containing administrative buildings, the laboratories, warehouses with equipment, and various shops and auxiliary structures. Oppenheimer's main laboratory complex consisted of S, a technical warehouse; T, an office building to provide space for administration, the theoretical physics group, a library, a classified document vault, conference rooms, a photographic laboratory, and a drafting room; U, a general laboratory building; V, a shop building; W, X, Y, and Z, specialized laboratory buildings for the Van de Graaffs, cyclotron, cryogenic laboratory, and Cockcroft-Walton accelerator, respectively; J, an administration and physics laboratory used in connection with Building X; and M, Boiler House No. 1.[5]

Groves naturally named Oppenheimer as the director, announcing the title on February 25, 1943. Though Oppenheimer himself felt comfortable in military uniform,[6] Groves and Conant acquiesced to the protestations of some in his scientific team that they were not to be brought into the military. Los Alamos would be managed by the University of California, under contract from the War Department. Oppenheimer would learn on the job how to manage multiple teams of professionals, across a wide variety of scientific fields, in a confined, isolated area. It would be a baptism by fire. But he discovered quickly that he had the skill set to make it work.

Hundreds of scientists, technicians, their wives, and children now lived within the high-wire fences. Many of the technicians and lab assistants had been brought in via University of California, Berkeley, to whom Groves had entrusted filling the teams Oppenheimer required. Young scientists such as Richard Feynman and Klaus Fuchs (both remembered today for very different reasons) were recognized for their brilliance, recommended and given their opportunity by Oppenheimer. To serve and protect them were three hundred officers and men of the US Army military police and 160 civilian administrators.

Life at the camp was regimented and governed by the working hours, eight hours a day for six days a week, with longer shifts if specialists were committed to a longer project. Relaxation time was strictly controlled. In whatever direction one would walk toward the edges of the camp, residents would encounter the high barbed wire and armed guards. Correspondence with the outside was heavily monitored and, in some cases, censored. One scientist thought the place looked like a concentration camp, and to many of the wives expected to raise their families here, perhaps it was. Even travel outside the camp was restricted to certain distances. The house builders had not particularly outdone themselves on the materials either. Many were roughly constructed, with some families waiting weeks for toilets and running water to be installed. There were signs everywhere: RESTRICTED and MOST RESTRICTED.

Los Alamos was for the weapons program. To supply it with fissionable material, Groves now had Oakridge in Tennessee (opened in February 1943) producing the enriched uranium. Officially known as Clinton Engineering Works, it would grow rapidly to employ tens of thousands of workers, providing a bigger construction headache for the construction of a whole town and amenities as it became the fifth-largest urban area in Tennessee with a population of seventy-five thousand. The necessity for plutonium had Groves oversee the construction of the world's first reactors, housed within the Hanford Engineer Works, sited next to the Columbia River in the wilderness of northwest Washington State. Again, like Oak Ridge, a new community of over fifty thousand would be brought in to work at the vast, highly secretive complex. The geography and climate gave it a vibe to many inhabitants of gold mining a century before.

Both production sites cost millions of dollars to establish and run, with many workers having no idea what their link in the grand scheme was until after the war. Nor did the staff working at Berkeley, Chicago, and Columbia universities as they answered the call related to staffing issues or supplying equipment. Across the United States, dozens of engineering and industrial firms, plants and factories, motor shops, airfields, ports and supply depots were big or small links in a web overseen by Groves, set up within eighteen months and heading toward the common goal—for those involved at the top-secret level—of producing the bomb.

Meanwhile, the war went on. By 1943, as the Manhattan Project was fully underway, Allied forces prepared to invade mainland Europe for the first time in the war. John Hersey's war would now take him to the shores of North Africa and a remarkable escape.

Chapter Eight

"FIGHTING FOR APPLE PIE": JOHN HERSEY ON GUADALCANAL

My bedroom was the hollow empty sky,
and every once in a while, a 105mm shell would scream
in one window and out the other.

JOHN HERSEY[1]

Across the globe, by the spring of 1942, newspapers from London to Los Angeles, Auckland to Cairo, and New York to Cape Town brought bad headlines to their readers. In every theater of war, the Axis seemed to be on the move to victory. Adolf Hitler's forces had survived their winter storm on the Russian front, still held the strategic initiative, and were forging into southern Russia. In North Africa, Erwin Rommel's Afrika Korps were smashing the Allies once again, his panzers on the verge of capturing the vital port town of Tobruk with its thirty-three thousand Allied garrison with the intent of then driving on to Cairo. But it was the Pacific theater that the American public were most anxious about.

After their stunning successes at Pearl Harbor, the Japanese had run amok in the South and Central Pacific. The Dutch East Indies, Malaya, Singapore, Burma, Hong Kong, the Philippines, Wake Island, Guam, the Gilbert Islands, the Solomon Islands, and the strategically vital port of Rabaul, situated on the island of New Britain, all fell in quick succession. Though the United States had a foothold in the South Pacific, with bases in Samoa, Fiji, and New Hebrides, the battering of Pearl Harbor on Hawaii and the loss of the Philippines were grievous strategic defeats. They would start the fightback in 1942.

Eight months to the day that Japan had struck Pearl Harbor, the First Division, United States Marine Corps, experienced their baptism of war, as they began the country's fight to reclaim what they had lost. They would begin by assaulting the Solomon Islands. In a bloody campaign that would last six months, American naval, air, Marine, and Army units would seek to counter Japan's Second Operational Phase. By capturing Rabaul, the Japanese could launch their next offensive southward, using the large harbor and several nearby military airfields. It would, as American military planners knew, provide the perfect jumping-off point to threaten Australia itself. But they would overextend their reach.

By May 1942, American bases on Midway Atoll, the Aleutian Islands, New Guinea, and Fiji Samoa were now threatened. However, behind the jubilant scenes of their airmen and soldiers for the cameras, Japanese military and naval strategists were split on their next move. Mindful that the Pacific offensive was governed by the needs of the Imperial Japanese Navy, the Imperial Japanese Army argued it was at the limits of its operational effectiveness and would not countenance any further moves toward Australia. It had the manpower to support the capture and occupation only of smaller strategic point locations.

Within senior navy circles, debate raged as to their next move. Some strategists advocated slicing through Allied lines of supply and communication by securing the sea-lanes linking Australia to the United States. Admiral Isoroku Yamamoto, mindful the IJN had failed to achieve its objectives at Pearl Harbor, argued instead for a decisive strike to finish the job. Only with a victory at sea over what remained of the enemy's Pacific Fleet could Japan's strategic position be secured. With the admiral's threat to resign hanging over the discussions, a compromise was reached at headquarters. There would be multiple offensives by the Imperial Combined Fleet: striking into the South Pacific in May toward Port Moresby on New Guinea (Operation Mo),[2] taking the Aleutian Islands (Operation Al), and then capturing the American base and air base on Midway Atoll, to bring the US Pacific Fleet to battle and its destruction.

Upon America entering the war, the United States Navy, led by Admiral Ernest King (a member of the Joint Chiefs), mapped out a strategy to dominate the Central and South Pacific. President Roosevelt himself had promoted Admiral Nimitz, whose command style he favored, above other more senior qualified officers. Nimitz's first objectives from King mirrored Japanese intentions: protect and hold Hawaii the island base of Midway Atoll and secure the shipping lanes to Australia. Roosevelt's administration agreed with Winston Churchill that the US focus would be directed primarily toward a "Germany first" policy. This was the goal, but it did not reflect the inner workings of the Joint Chiefs, with Admiral King supported by Admiral William Leahy to ensure Nimitz's command received enough supplies throughout 1942, despite the intensification of the Atlantic War as American ships fought their way to British ports. For the summer of 1942, the policy was simple: Nimitz had to blunt Japan's momentum.

Their successes over the six months since Pearl Harbor encouraged the Japanese military leadership to believe they could expand upon their strategic objectives. They were unaware that American military analysts had broken their codes. Admiral Nimitz's headquarters was fed a stream of communications that detailed Japanese movements toward New Guinea. The first encounter, at the Coral Sea on May 4–8, would see history being made. Instead of battleships firing upon one another, airpower from each side's carrier fleets would be the deciding factor. Their primary job was to seek out and destroy one another's offensive capability—a new type of warfare that would swing the balance of power. In terms of carriers damaged or sunk, the Japanese came off second best at the Coral Sea, with one carrier sunk, one damaged, and the air group of the other destroyed, all for the loss of one US carrier. Such loss of ships and experienced naval pilots weakened one Japanese fleet, but Yamamoto had divided his strength as he steamed toward Midway, and the enemy knew where he was headed. American carrier-launched aircraft, together with land-based planes from Midway, held the balance of power for this encounter. United States Navy dive-bombers sank four Japanese carriers that Yamamoto could ill afford to lose. The spectacular American victory neutered Japan's plans for future offensive operations in the South and Central Pacific. King and Nimitz now looked to the South Pacific to take their own offensive action.

John Hersey had sought a commission in the US Navy, but by the early summer of 1942 he was aboard the aircraft carrier USS *Hornet*,[3] steaming toward the South Pacific as a uniformed war correspondent. He had gained popularity at home, and among the US military, with his first major work, *Men on Bataan*, published by Alfred A. Knopf in New York, based on extensive interviews with survivors. Despite describing the military reversal in the Philippines, his book unwittingly paid homage to the personality and military prowess of General Douglas MacArthur—despite the disaster he had left behind.[4] Though unintentional, Hersey's book would have favourable consequences once he was in Japan after the war was over and MacArthur was the de facto ruler of the country. *Men on Bataan* had sold well and had gained Hersey admirers.

Hersey's application to enlist was pending, and in the meantime he had a greater urge to cover the war at sea. The United States needed to get onto the front foot and gain a victory. Great battleships of the United States Navy's Pacific Fleet at Pearl Harbor lay in ruins, and MacArthur had been kicked out of the Philippines with his tail between his legs. Dan Longwell, the executive editor of *Life*, agreed to make Hersey a war correspondent. He would join the Allied expeditionary force to the Solomons, telling his readers, "The invasion of the Solomon Islands by U.S. forces must be followed up and maintained over a supply line more than five thousand miles long as the seagull flies. . . . There has never been a larger-scale expeditionary force operating so far from its mainland base."[5]

Many weeks after the victory at Midway, Hersey was enjoying his voyage to war aboard the USS *Hornet*, part of a carrier task force making its way toward the Solomons to protect vital shipping lanes. As he shielded his eyes against the noonday sun, he marveled at the composite task force of cruisers and destroyers that protected the *Hornet* and its fellow carrier, the USS *Wasp*. He spent days watching flights of reconnaissance aircraft dispatched for patrol and spent his evenings playing games of poker, gazing out at the black vastness of the ocean surrounding the *Hornet*, or laughing as new shipmates aboard his floating city baptized those new sailors crossing the Equator: "The whole affair was like a birthday party for twelve-year-old boys; it was as if, for one afternoon, those grown men on their way to the zone of death needed to pay a cleansing farewell visit to childhood."[6]

He was keen to get to where the Marines were fighting and re-layed his feelings of the Navy's ambitions for his *Time-Life* readers back home (though he was clearly no military strategist):

"We [at *Time-Life*] have been at considerable pains to point out that the campaigns of the war have all been battles of supply lines . . . our invasion of the Solomons, which we would not have undertaken if we had not intended to make it stick, is a perfect example of three kinds of battle, all relevant to supply: (1) It is intended to insure our lines to the southwest Pacific area and at the same time threaten the enemy's lines to the same area; (2) If successful, it gives us the perfect springboard; and (3) It is the greatest test yet of our own resource-fulness in supply.

"The Solomon Islands front, and to a lesser extent the Aleutians front—is an already operating, or perhaps you should call it third front, for the relief of the Russians . . . all we put into the Solomons and the Aleutians gives the Japanese something to think about be-sides Siberia—and I believe we are giving them quite a lot to think about."[7]

In their original offensive to occupy New Guinea that March, the Japanese had managed to capture the island of Tulagi in the southern Solomons island chain. Though unable to construct an airfield of suitable length for its planes, nearby Guadalcanal, a ninety-mile-long island of dense jungle, twenty miles to the south, was larger, with capability to construct land air bases. The Joint Chiefs created the South Pacific Area Command, with Vice Admiral Robert L. Ghormley[8] taking charge on June 19 to direct the offensive in the Solomons. Nimitz, based at Pearl Harbor, was designated as overall Allied commander in chief for Pacific forces. Many senior commanders in theater knew one another well, had studied at the naval academy together at Annapolis, and served with one another since the 1920s. These bonds of brotherhood would be tested as the campaign developed.

Admiral King and Army chief of staff George Marshall reached a deal on July 2 to move the command line so that the Solomons were placed in the South Pacific Area Command under Navy control. King ordered Nimitz to seize Tulagi and nearby islands on June 24, to lay the base for retaking New Britain and Rabaul. In early July, a US Navy reconnaissance flight had spotted Japanese construction workers building an airstrip on Guadalcanal. Thus, Guadalcanal was now added as a target of the impending invasion on July 5. On July 22, the First Marine Division departed New Zealand and headed for a rehearsal in Fiji.

At dawn on August 7, Operation Watchtower commenced, as American land forces went on the offensive for the first time in the war. The First Marine Division, commanded by Major General Alexander Vandegrift, supported by Rear Admiral Frank Jack Fletcher's Task Force 61, would assault Guadalcanal. Units of the Raiders from the Fifth Marines Regiment and paratroopers would tackle enemy positions on nearby islands. Vandegrift was an excellent choice to lead a "green" Marine division into its first action. He was a career officer and had seen action in various conflicts since the 1920s.

Ghormley, on the other hand, lacked combat experience, was beset by health issues, and was seen by many as an uninspiring choice. He would not step onto Guadalcanal throughout the campaign, but remain on his flagship, the USS *Argonne*, anchored in Nouméa, the capital of New Caledonia. His eyes and ears in the Solomons in charge of the Allied expeditionary force would be Vice Admiral Fletcher. Ghormley was skeptical of the tools he had at his disposal and of the plan itself. The First Marines were untested, there had been one failed attempt at a coordinated amphibious exercise in Fiji, and intelligence reports of where the enemy was in and around Guadalcanal were sketchy. Vandegrift had been frustrated in his attempt to persuade his senior commander of amphibious forces, Rear Admiral Richard Turner, that his men needed more time to prepare. They had been issued with supplies for sixty days instead of the agreed ninety. Marines listening to their officers joked their task was Operation Shoestring. The early weeks of the campaign would reflect Vandegrift's original concerns, as a lack of nighttime training at sea badly affected the Allies' performance in the first month of combat against a Japanese navy that was better prepared.

The Marines landing in the Solomons would be the first of up to sixty thousand, including US Army troops, who would contest ownership of Guadalcanal with over forty thousand Japanese soldiers. The fighting would last until the following February. It would be the longest campaign in the Pacific war, with the outcome tipping one way and then the other almost until the end six months later. But its consequences would be far-reaching. John Hersey's words would capture the American experience on Guadalcanal to those back home and make his name.

On D-Day, fortunately for Vandegrift's Marines, the Japanese defenders were caught by surprise, the first and second waves storming ashore without a single casualty, other than one embarrassed Marine who managed to cut his hand opening a coconut with a machete. Only on the neighboring smaller islands did the Raiders (a newly formed unit of Marines, schooled in irregular combat techniques) engage in firefights with local garrisons they had been sent to destroy. By day two, Vandegrift had landed two-thirds of his division and seized the Japanese airstrip, which they renamed "Henderson

Field"[9] and set up defensive positions around. It seemed as if there was no opposition on the island. That changed as darkness fell.

Under the noses of Australian and American naval ships defending the waters around the waters between Guadalcanal and Savo Island to the north, Japanese warships[10] adept at night fighting and armed with highly effective Type 93 torpedoes[11] infiltrated the defensive screen and struck the US task force. At what would later be christened "Iron Bottom Sound,"[12] Task Force 62 suffered the loss of four heavy cruisers, along with 1,077 sailors. News of the encounter was initially covered up so as not to influence American public opinion.

The loss of his cruisers and heavy air attacks from land-based Japanese bombers concerned Fletcher, forcing him into a decision that would forever cast a shadow over his performance. The order was given for the American carrier force to vacate the seas around Guadalcanal. Without air cover for his transports, which had landed only half of Vandegrift's supplies, Admiral Turner quickly followed suit with his transports. The watching Marines marooned on the island would now defend their positions against an enemy growing in strength. If they were to survive, Henderson Field needed to be made operational for incoming air relief. Vandegrift had less than ten days of ammunition landed so far from the transports. One relief: his Marines had discovered huge stores of rice that the Japanese had left behind, so they would not starve. They now grabbed whatever tools they could find and got to work to complete the airfield. One Marine erected a sign declaring, "Under new management!"

Guadalcanal, like many Pacific battlegrounds to come, made for arduous fighting conditions. Small areas of cleared, or cultivated, flat terrain housing naval or air bases, were surrounded by tall grass and coconut palm groves planted by Western settlers decades before. The island was scarred by a series of high ridges, dotted with caves and ravines, with the ground covered in impenetrable, tropical forest, split by small and large rivers, lacking any clear pathways, with rough tracks traversable by native guides who knew where the swamps lay.

As both sides would discover, military operations within the island's interior were extremely difficult and highly dangerous. Establishing a traditional defensive line was virtually impossible, the jungle limiting visibility and communication. The Marines opted throughout the campaign to conduct extensive patrols, establish contact with the enemy, work out his positions, and deduce where he would attempt to penetrate American lines. The campaign in the interior would become a series of intense skirmishes and firefights, while Henderson Field would witness savage fighting.

Major General Vandegrift studied the terrain and concluded the Japanese would not send reinforcements for counterattack across the whole island—the terrain would be too arduous to march across with provisions, artillery, and heavy weapons. The Japanese had one goal: they needed to capture Henderson Field as much as he needed to defend it. He calculated the points of attack: along the beaches to assault his fortified perimeter in the north, nearby rivers to the west, and up and over ridges south of the airfield. His issue would be having the airbase withstand naval bombardments, before his Marines fought off massed, frontal assaults. Pitted against growing enemy numbers, Vandegrift had to trust the veteran officers and NCOs who formed the spine of his battalions.[13] Cool heads, discipline, and the ability to make on-the-spot decisions to shore up penetrations would be the telling factor. Time and again, at places that would become infamous, such as Matanikau River and Bloody Ridge, repeated Japanese breakthroughs would be fought off in desperate hand-to-hand fighting and last-minute counterattacks. Rapid-fire support from Marine artillery and the few M3 light tanks Vandegrift had managed to get ashore would pay dividends and wreak havoc.[14]

By August 18, Henderson Field was operational. US Marine Corps Grumman F4F Wildcats and Douglas SBD Dauntless dive-bombers began to arrive on the base. They would defend Henderson Field, act as "eyes in the sky," and stop Japanese reinforcements arriving on the island by sea route. The Japanese Seventeenth Army commander, Lieutenant General Hyakutake Harukichi, expected to drive the

Marines off the island, just as the Imperial Navy had to their naval task force. Though limited in heavy equipment, his infantry were disciplined veterans and highly motivated. The fighting that erupted would see his men come up against the strength of the Marines' fire-power. The Marines would need it to stem the stream of reinforcements the Japanese navy was delivering from New Britain. Japanese destroyers and cruisers evaded the Allied navy to carry thousands of troops and supplies through the "The Slot"[15] onto Guadalcanal, in what would become known as the "Tokyo Express." Both sides had now determined that this isolated, insignificant island would be the key battleground of the South Pacific.

The first phase of massed, frontal bayonet assaults aimed at Henderson Field were mown down by US Marine machine gunners, supported by mortar and artillery barrages. On the night of August 21, a force of 917 veteran Japanese troops (the "Ichiki Detachment"[16]) was reduced to just twenty survivors against the Marines' positions on the western edge of the airfield, along Alligator Creek. The light of the morning revealed hundreds of Japanese corpses floating in the mouth of the river, or half-buried in the sandbar. It was their first major loss to an enemy they had confidently expected to melt away in panic. The Marines had suffered forty-four killed and seventy-one wounded. As the fighting progressed over the coming weeks, the resilience and tenacity of the Americans would not prevent Japanese commanders from ordering repeated attacks. The Marines cared for their dead and wounded, cleaned their weapons, smoked a cigarette, reinforced their dugouts, and waited for the next attack.

Sergeant William "Bill" Lansford hailed from East Los Angeles, where he lived above a garage with his single mother. In 1938, as a poor sixteen-year-old surviving the Depression, he had dropped out of school to work as a lumberjack to get physically fit, get out of the classroom, and earn some pay for his family. By October 1940, as war raged in Europe, he enlisted in the US Marine Corps, becoming a machine gunner in the Eighth Marines—the "Walking Eighth." By the time Pearl Harbor was attacked, Lansford's unit was training overseas in Iceland. The Marine Corps handed over its bases to the incoming US Army and were shipped back to their California bases via New York to prepare for combat in the Pacific.

With a thirst for adventure and to see action with a unit he could trust, Lansford had volunteered for a new unit within the Fifth Marine Regiment: a "behind the lines" force, trained in guerrilla warfare, with little attention paid to procedure, attire, or manners, and skilled in living off the land. They were conceived by a maverick military genius, Lieutenant Colonel Evans Carlson, who had honed his skills with Mao Tse Tung's communist forces in China fighting the Japanese in the mid-1930s. He returned to the United States a firm believer in the use of guerrilla tactics. It was a natural next step to want to evolve a unit within the Marine Corps. With the backing of President Roosevelt, whose own son James enlisted in his new outfit, Carlson selected, trained, and equipped two battalions by the time the First Marine Division were shipping out to Guadalcanal. They would become "Carlson's Raiders." Admiral Nimitz, himself a long-time admirer of Carlson, supported his formation's involvement in the upcoming operation. They needed every man they could muster. The First Battalion had trained as shock troops, skilled at taking out strategic targets, while the Second Battalion (the "Junior Raiders"), Lansford's unit, trained in straight-up guerrilla warfare. On D-Day of the Guadalcanal campaign, Carlson's men were given orders to seize and destroy smaller strategic garrisons on nearby Tulagi Island.

John Hersey had left the USS *Hornet* anchored in Nouméa and, together with the *Life* novelist writer and illustrator Thomas C. Lea,[17] begged a lift in a C-47 supply plane to Henderson Field by mid-September. By then the runway had been renovated by the Seabees, their trademark steel-meshed matting laid down on beds of crushed coral. Hersey studied the verdant green canopy and imagined what must be going on down below. He had read military reports while in New Caledonia of the type of fighting that was being carried out on the island, how the enemy's psychological warfare played on the exhausted minds of the young Marines, launching smoke grenades, shouting in English, "Gas attack!" and hurling insults toward American lines, hoping for a reaction to concentrate their fire. Wounded Marines in the hospital told of the Japanese committing atrocities against the local tribespeople and the Marines themselves, and Hersey thought about what he had experienced in China. Doctors aboard the *Hornet* had described to him the various diseases the fighting men would encounter: dysentery, dengue fever, malaria, and the soldiers' favorite, trench foot. The Marines were losing more men to disease than actual fighting. The monsoon rains had arrived, driving up the jungle's humidity. Still, he was relieved to be here, to discover the war for himself and relay what he could back to a readership desperate for good news about the battle's outcome, as well as news of their loved ones involved in the fighting.

"Home is what they talk about on Guadal. Women are almost never discussed; while white bread, still a luxury food, is dreamt about—the home-cooker kind. Within a few minutes, every conservation swings around to home."[18]

The Men on Bataan had been stories he had retold; now he was experiencing it himself.

The Japanese were still pouring troops onto the island, despite attempts by the American task force to stop them. They had driven off several naval assaults, including the night of October 11 at Cape Esperance, but they could not prevent the "Tokyo Express" unloading more men and supplies at the other end of Guadalcanal. The Seventh Marine Regiment and the first US Army units had now arrived, but Japanese naval bombardments continued to target Henderson Field as the American garrison frantically repaired the runway and unloaded what supplies were being flown in.

Admiral Nimitz finally lost patience with Ghormley's performance. Reports suggest he was concerned his old friend was nearing a mental breakdown under the weight of the campaign. He sought and received permission from Admiral King to relieve him of command on October 18 and replace him with Vice Admiral William "Bull" Halsey. As his nickname suggests, Halsey could be best described as a bulldog chewing a wasp. He was a fearless, profane, chain-smoking, and extremely aggressive naval commander. He worked arduous hours, sustained by copious cups of coffee, and expected his men to do likewise. After the attack on Pearl Harbor nine months before, he had been reported to have said that by the end of the war Japanese would be spoken only in hell. He had missed the victory at Midway and was anxious to get back into combat. Stepping on board the *Argonne* to relieve Ghormley, whom he had known well for years and considered a friend, was tough. The new job would be tougher. He confided to his chief of staff, "Jesus Christ and General Jackson, this is the hottest potato they have ever handed me!" He would oversee a seismic change in attitude for supporting the Marines on Guadalcanal.

Halsey immediately summoned Vandegrift to fly to Nouméa for a council of war. He would not be asking the Marine commander if he wanted to surrender. Instead, the major general departed hours later, satisfied the new man in charge would be as good as his word and support him with what he needed. Halsey would rapidly build a bond with the Marines fighting on Guadalcanal, installing confidence in his sailors who were suffering thousands of casualties around the waters of the Solomons.[19] He gave them all a single message: "Kill Japs, kill Japs, kill more Japs."

John Hersey was keen to interview the Marines who would do the killing. Ironically, his nose for a story almost killed him as soon as he arrived on the island. He seized the invitation to take the second seat aboard a sea-rescue biplane, heading with one other plane to the northern tip of the island to retrieve a downed flier being hidden by local islanders. In a relic from the Great War, Hersey marveled from the open cockpit as the wind and rain buffeted the bold aircraft, its enormous pontoon floats scarily close to the treetops a few feet below. Having found the young pilot and stored him in the second plane with local supplies from the friendly natives, they took off back to Henderson. Immediately Hersey's biplane ran into trouble. The undercarriage in the pontoon had failed to retract on takeoff, caught the water's surface, and flipped the biplane into a fatal somersault.

Hersey regained consciousness upside down, strapped into his seat as the wrecked plane sank deeper into the waters of the bay. He frantically unbuckled himself and kicked for the surface, almost blacking out with the effort. His instinct for the story never left him: "The first thing I saw, when my eyes cleared, was my small field notebook floating in front of me; I had sheathed it in a condom . . . [which] . . . I had bought on the [USS] *Hornet* for this very purpose— to keep notebooks dry."[20]

He retrieved the notebook, survived to tell the tale, and returned to Henderson lying flat in the floating pontoon of the plane, eating the fruit that the natives had stored around him. His next trip out would be far more dangerous as he joined a joint US Marine-Raider operation that would provide the title for his bestselling story "Into the Valley: The Marines at Guadalcanal."

What Hersey encountered with the Seventh Marine Regiment and Raider detachments would be later recorded as the "Third Battle of the Matanikau River." Armed with a sidearm pistol (which he later saw as a lucky talisman), he walked in line with ordinary Marines into the jungle on a "search and destroy" operation. He was honing his skill as a writer to encapsulate the feelings of the average American fighting man, not just on Guadalcanal but, he hoped, in any theater: the sheer boredom of waiting to move out, the constant delays of the march, the heat and humidity of the jungle, the whispered orders, and always in the back of his mind, the suppressed terror of giving one's position away or the crack from a Japanese sniper rifle the Marines knew was somewhere down in a valley amid the thick jungle screens. It was their job to flush this enemy out. His was recording, as he saw it, acts of ordinary heroism.

Hersey encountered Marine officers who would become household names in the Guadalcanal campaign, such as the Raiders' commander, Colonel Merritt Edson, and Lieutenant Colonel Lewis "Chesty" Puller of the First Battalion, whose inspirational leadership had already saved countless Marines' lives in the desperate firefights to protect Henderson Field. Before Hersey's voyage into the valley began, Edson spared him a few words on his Japanese opponent: "They're good, all right, but . . . I think we're better."[21]

The story was really about the men of Company H, led by a twentysomething young officer from Oriskany Falls, New York, Captain Alfred Rigaud. They were "a veteran unit. His boys were blooded. They had been in every battle so far . . . there was no unit which had been in such tough spots."[22] Hersey breathed life into the men of Company H, but the mission he would record was a typical tale of a solid military plan coming apart as soon as it contacted the enemy. "Into the Valley" would capture the nature of the fighting in the Pacific, by America's "Citizen Army" who were taking the fight to the "Superman" Japanese soldier. But at a cost.

Hersey did not try to con the reader; he didn't need to. His words described a Marine whom the American public could identify with, as just twelve months before, these young men were their sons, brothers, and husbands: "They were ex-grocery clerks, ex-highway laborers, ex-bank clerks, ex-schoolboys, boys with a clean record and maybe a little extra restlessness, but not killers. They had volunteered."[23]

But he was not afraid to highlight how they felt about the war, their leaders, and their enemy, no matter how offensive it would seem to postwar readers. As Hersey would later comment after the war, the American public and its armed forces seemed to hold their Axis enemies to different levels of hatred, as one Marine confided to Hersey as they rested on the jungle trail: "I wish we were fighting against Germans. They are human beings, like us. Fighting against them must be like an athletic performance—matching your skill against someone you know is good. . . . But the Japs are like animals. . . . They take to the jungle as if they have been bred there, and like some beasts you never see them until they are dead."[24]

He studied their young faces. Some were bored and gazed into nothing, a few sternly looked up into the canopy above for hidden Japanese snipers, while others wiped their necks and faces, their uniforms drenched in perspiration. Hersey could see Rigaud farther along the line with his radioman close by, waiting to get fresh orders to move along. He took the opportunity, leaning in toward three young riflemen next to him and asking, "Today here in this valley, what are you fighting for?"

"Their faces became pale. Their eyes wandered. They looked like men bothered by a memory. . . . 'Jesus, what I'd give for a piece of blueberry pie.'

"Another whispered: 'Personally, I prefer mince.'

"A third whispered: 'Make mine apple, with a few raisins in it and lots of cinnamon: you know Southern style.'"

His conclusion: these men were simply fighting to get home.

The fate of Company H in the valley would be repeated countless times throughout World War II and was a universal experience for both sides. Captain Rigaud's men would find themselves caught in a Japanese river ambush, almost cut off from retreat as their supporting flank rapidly withdrew, taking casualties from Japanese mortar, sniper, and machine-gun fire. "We hit the ground . . . like earthly insects with some great foot being set down in our midst. . . . All this hatred was pouring out of jungle too thick to see more than twenty or thirty feet."[25]

In what could have been a disaster, amid the cacophony of small arms, Rigaud methodically organized a fighting retreat back out of the valley floor, with Hersey following in his wake, the wounded and the dying taken with them as they retreated: "The walking wounded were magnificent. None of them complained about their own hurts but inquired politely of each other."

Eventually, the beleaguered company of Marines made it back, and their wounded were taken to the advanced dressing station along the lip of the valley. The dead were laid out on the grass, ready to transport back to Henderson Field. Hersey put aside his civilian role and became a stretcher bearer with the Navy medical corpsmen:

"Heaven, if it looks anything like the view that greeted us when we regained the top of the ridge, will be a welcome sight. I have never seen anything so beautiful."[26]

He could not figure out how many Marines had been killed in all the confusion of the retreat, but he marveled at how the men who had only hours before been in a firefight to save their lives now calmly settled down into the foxholes along the ridge overlooking the valley. As the sun set, Hersey joined them:

"My clothes were soaked and caked with mud, the Japs were much closer than they had been during the first, sleepless night, and artillery fire was just as frequent—but this time I dropped off within five minutes and slept dreamlessly all night long."[27]

By the time Hersey was on board a US Navy destroyer back to Nouméa, Bill Lansford's Raiders unit was in the midst of killing Japanese reinforcements they encountered marching in columns through the island's interior. Unlike Captain Rigaud's Company H, Lansford's unit was guided by the local native constabulary who had served the British Solomon Islands Protectorate.[28]

"We were six companies strong and fought for thirty days behind enemy lines throughout November 1942. I handled an air-cooled heavy machine gun. Our three-man squads had been reconfigured with M1s, B.A.R., Tommy Guns so we had tremendous firepower. We ambushed Japanese columns by attacking their rear from the flank out of the jungle. The press had made much of the Japanese being supreme jungle fighters, nobody could defeat them. We had local natives supporting us . . . they took us through the trails to attack the Japanese.

"We'd engage the Japanese many times in ambushes and retreat into the jungle. Our supplies, the thing we lived off, was in a sock. We would take one of our socks and fill it up to the head with rice. The other one would be filled with tea. And that was it. Occasionally the natives would supply bananas and papaya fruit. . . . Retreating through the jungle in the darkness, each man would hang onto the bayonet sheath of the man in front as they made their way along the trail. It was torrential rain as we made our way along through the mountains.

After thirty days of fighting, we were skeletons and exhausted after 150 miles of marching. We had killed over five hundred Japanese reinforcements and scattered the remainder. It would be called "The Long Patrol"—the most successful "behind the lines" USMC operation of World War Two. Most of the time we simply thought about food. But we had survived on this diet of rice, tea and raisins. We didn't leave our wounded but carried them down from the mountains to the beach and waited for the ships to pick us up and take us back to New Caledonia. When I got back to the hospital, they wanted to cut off my leg due to jungle rot. I refused. In the ward, I kept my pistol and a grenade under my pillow in case of any Japanese attacks behind our lines.[29]

As Marines battled inland, the decisive struggle for naval supremacy around the island's waters now began. On November 13, at the First Naval Battle of Guadalcanal, a Japanese supply convoy, carrying enough food and munitions for thirty thousand men, supported by battleships to bombard and knock out Henderson Field, was stopped by elements of Halsey's task force, but at a cost of 1,439 American sailors—a total that would exceed Marine losses for the whole campaign. But it did the job. Two nights later, one final enemy task force approached the island but was stopped. The failure of both operations would spell the Japanese's doom.

More American reinforcements poured in—Vandegrift's Marines finally giving way to the US Twenty-Fifth Infantry Division, commanded by Lieutenant General Alexander Patch, and the Second Marine Division. Of the eleven thousand sent in, the First Division had suffered 681 killed or missing in action and 1,278 wounded. The jungle had taken many more—over 8,500 Marines fell out of the line with malaria. They would return to Melbourne, Australia, to recuperate and refit for their next campaign in New Britain at the end of 1943.[30] On December 26, with the campaign in its fifth month, the Imperial General Headquarters finally succumbed to the inevitable. Maintaining the Tokyo Express cost too many warships and transports. It was an economic necessity to stop. Replacing them with ships closer to home would reduce supplies of raw materials coming to the Home Islands.

The Japanese had lost their test of will against the Americans. The evacuation of the Seventeenth Army, code-named KE, commenced on February 1, 1943. The Americans, still convinced of another Japanese counterattack, never realized what was happening until it was almost over. Twenty Imperial Japanese Navy destroyers fought off American air and PT boats to rescue almost five thousand emaciated troops. Two more destroyer runs ran the gauntlet until over ten thousand had been saved. It was, despite the strategic defeat, a remarkable achievement.

Despite their fanaticism, the Japanese had been blown away by American firepower. The Seventeenth Army had been crippled, with casualties of over twenty thousand men, at a cost of 1,769 US Marines and soldiers. Though the American media (including the US Marine Corps's own magazine *The Leatherneck*) would go into overdrive mocking the fighting ability of the "buck-toothed" "Yellow Monkeys," those new Marine recruits training for the Pacific battles to come would be wary of believing they could "Slap a Jap!"

Though a small island of only limited strategic value, psychologically the victory at Guadalcanal proved immense. It raised the morale of American and Allied forces in the Pacific, as well as the American public back home. What they had imagined as the "Superman" Japanese warrior had not just been defeated, but had been badly beaten. The timing was fortuitous for Hersey's article. His story from Guadalcanal came at the same time as the defeat of Hitler's Sixth Army at Stalingrad and of the Afrika Korps at El Alamein. On all fronts, including the South Pacific, the Axis powers had been beaten on land. Guadalcanal laid down a marker for the effective jungle performance of the US Marine Corps.

As US Marine and Army divisions completed the mop-up operations on Guadalcanal, *Into the Valley* was published by that February, receiving high praise from prestigious bodies such as the Council of Books in Wartime, as well as the ordinary serviceman in the street.[31] Hersey's life as a war correspondent took on more significance and earned him nationwide recognition. He was now valued by the military senior ranks. It opened the doors he would need to gain access to other theaters of operations. Eventually, it gave him access to occupied Japan, to research and write the article that would gain him worldwide recognition.

Recovering in Nouméa for two weeks with suspected broken ribs, possibly from the air crash weeks before, Hersey then returned to the United States to promote the book edition by Knopf. It was successful, selling twenty thousand copies, and he spoke at fundraising events in New York for a variety of war-related charity groups, spent time with his newly born second son, and sought clearance from the military to travel to the European theater. The Atlantic war was turning against the German U-boats' threat. The war in the air above Europe was starting to hit German industry, and the war on the Eastern Front would reach its climax at Kursk that summer. Hersey's application for officer training at Annapolis was turned down in December 1942. The fork in the road had been reached. He would not be picking up a rifle; his weapon of choice throughout the rest of the war would be the typewriter and pen. By June of the next year, Hersey was granted permission to board a troop ship heading to Morocco in the Eastern Mediterranean. The Allies, commanded by General Dwight D. Eisenhower, had finally driven the Afrika Korps out of North Africa and were now preparing to launch Operation Husky, the amphibious invasion of Sicily set for July 9, 1943. Here Hersey would really make his mark as a writer.

Part III

WORLDS COLLIDING (THE AIR WAR)

Chapter Nine

THE ROLE OF A LIFETIME

Get your bags packed, you are leaving right now!
GENERAL JIMMY DOOLITTLE, NORTH AFRICA, 1943

By February 1943, Germany had suffered calamitous defeat at Stalingrad, and Erwin Rommel was falling back in North Africa. Meanwhile, General Groves had in place the expertise to bring theories of nuclear weaponry off the drawing board, and he was constructing the facilities to produce a weapon of mass destruction and a revolutionary plane to deliver it. Now what he required was the right man to lead the mission. He would select a pilot who was born to fly and a natural leader of men. But his path to the Manhattan Project would read like a Hollywood film starring Erroll Flynn.

His passion for flight had all started sitting in the red cockpit of an old biplane as an excited twelve-year-old boy waited for takeoff from a grassy horse-racing track outside Miami in 1927. Paul Tibbetts Jr. clutched his giant bag of candy belonging to his confectionary-selling father and grinned ear to ear as the pilot, Doug Davis, known to locals for his barnstorming air shows, gunned the old aircraft's engine. Despite the fact it was January, it would never be as cold as where he had spent the first years of his life in Ohio, where the winters could be brutal for both farmer and livestock. His father's move to the warmer climate of Florida had suited his outdoor nature, though summer trips back to his uncle's farm in Ohio had taught him to look after cattle, hunt, and become a deadly shot. But here he now was, taking off into the blue, to drop his dad's candy on parachutes to the hundreds of eager children below, as part of a promotion. It would be the making of him, as he remembered in his memoir:

"No Arabian prince ever rode a magic carpet with a greater delight or sense of superiority to the rest of the human race. I could see the unfortunate earth-bound mortals crawling around like ants on the ground below. . . . Nothing else would satisfy me, once I was given an exhilarating sample of the life of an airman."[1]

Before such a life could begin, he first had to persuade his parents, Paul Sr. and Enola Gay. He worshipped his father, a veteran officer of the Great War, and loved his soft-spoken mother, a shy, Ohio farm girl. Both parents' expectations had been that Paul Jr. would take up a professional job, such as a doctor or dentist, and if that didn't work, then, as would transpire, the boy could follow in his father's footsteps and attend military school. Much to his consternation, Tibbets found himself bound for Missouri to attend the Blees Military Academy, where he would study for five years. Despite numerous pleas to be allowed home, he would find himself marooned there, knuckling down to graduate. What it left him with was an ability to assimilate, to be able to function within a group, and a code of conduct to live by and, as we shall see, to enforce. A classic battle raged between his hard-driven father and a seventeen-year-old seemingly off the leash of military discipline. Tibbets's time spent at the University of Florida was not a success. The family's hopes he might go on to study medicine fell by the wayside as the young man enjoyed life on campus a little too much. Only his father's contacts with the local police department managed to keep him from potentially acquiring a criminal record during one evening of drinking. Despite these setbacks, by 1933, he had rediscovered his love of flight since that day above the racecourse throwing out bundles of candy bars from a few thousand feet up. The Great Depression was still ravaging the country, but his heart was now set on becoming a flyer for the United States Army's newest creation—the Air Force.

He was accepted into the service to undergo the Army Air Corps pilot training program in 1937. He was twenty-two and bedazzled at the life ahead of him, getting to try out in an open-cockpit Consolidated PT-3, an aircraft similar to the one the legendary Charles Lindbergh had flown across the Atlantic—the *Spirit of St. Louis*. In these early years, he was flying aircraft with a high propensity to either stall in flight or succumb to structural or engine failure, leading to fatalities of both experienced airmen as well as rookies. It not only taught him to be cool under pressure and fly without fear, but also to accept the necessary losses that came with the occupation. He would graduate in February 1938 in front of his father—of 138 in his class, he would be one of fifty-eight to graduate. Paul Sr. extended his hand to his son, now a newly commissioned second lieutenant of the Army Air Corps, and said, "I feel a hell of a lot better about this thing. I can see why you like it and I think it's going to be great for you."

It would be.

His desire to fly and test himself against anything he could get into the cockpit of during these vital prewar years enabled Tibbets to hone his skills. Not for him were the thrill and speed of a fighter pilot. Instead, Tibbets chose to fly long-range aircraft, ideally bombers. It suited his skill set. By the time Japanese naval bombers were destroying the US Pacific Fleet at Pearl Harbor, the young pilot had logged over two thousand flying hours (including a stint as Brigadier General George S. Patton's personal pilot), and he had mastered the art of long-range flying. When the Japanese attack came, Captain Tibbets, as he now was, was serving as an engineer officer with the Twenty-Ninth Bombardment Group at MacDill Field, Florida. Now it was time to go war and put everything he had learned into practice. It was to be a baptism of his leadership skills as part of the newly constituted Ninety-Seventh Bombardment Group, of courage under fire that would scar him for life, where he served with men who would later fly with him over the city of Hiroshima and into history: bombardier Lieutenant Thomas Ferebee and navigator Captain Theodore Van Kirk. The three aviators would form a unique, almost brotherly, bond as they flew missions into Europe in some of the toughest conditions of the war.

The Ninety-Seventh Bombardment Group comprised four squadrons operating the Boeing Flying Fortress, or B-17. As discussed in chapter six, this remarkable four-engine aircraft was the workhorse of the Eighth Air Force. Tibbets would lead his squadron in Operation Bolero, as forty-nine B-17s were ferried with skeleton crews across the Atlantic from their jumping-off point in Bangor, Maine, to RAF Polebrook in Northamptonshire, via stopping-off points in Labrador, Greenland,[2] and Reykjavik, Iceland, with landfall after having crossed over three thousand miles of ocean at Prestwick, Scotland. As he recalled in his memoir, he marveled at the rawness of the men in his unit: "The B-17s that flew from New England to old England were piloted by boys in their late teens and early twenties and were guided by navigators of the same age. Most had never flown out of sight of land. In fact, a majority had never seen an ocean until recently."

Polebrook held diplomatic significance for the US government. It had received the first B-17s supplied through the Lend-Lease program and had launched the first raids across to Europe. In what was the very first transportation of an American air group across the Atlantic, Tibbets had flown thousands of miles to get to a war that was now separated only by the twenty-six miles of the English Channel. Now promoted to major, his early days were tough, primarily due to what was going on inside his own unit, and not what the enemy was up to. The majority of the group's commanders took to the cozy atmosphere of rural life in Northamptonshire, enjoying perhaps a little too much hospitality as well as letting discipline slip for what was expected of a frontline outfit. Tibbets was one of a few officers who tried to maintain active-duty standards, drilling the crews of the fifteen bombers under his command, relentlessly, in formation flying and navigation, often to the mirth of senior staff taking their leave of the station. It soon came to a head, with the Ninety-Seventh Group having its commander replaced and several officers reprimanded. Tibbets soon found himself promoted again to the new CO's executive officer, basically second in charge, to Colonel Frank Armstrong, a no-nonsense leader from the front. He would accompany Tibbets in the lead plane of the group's first combat mission on August 17, 1942, one that both British and American senior commanders looked upon as the Eighth's first test of bombing in daylight. They attacked the marshaling railway yards in Rouen, in northern France. The mission was a success, with no losses of planes or crews killed, though the novice crews had to learn their trade fast, as the author and aviator Robert Harder describes in *The Three Musketeers*:

"There was a great deal to learn about four- to five-mile-high bombing in a non-pressurized Flying Fortress. Wrapped in cumbersome flying suits, fur lined jackets and caps, and thick gloves and encumbered by an extremely irritating oxygen mask and dangling hoses, even the smallest of tasks could be performed only with great difficulty. Perhaps the most serious non hostile hazard at 25,000 feet was oxygen deprivation."[3]

Tibbets and his crew aboard the *Red Gremlin* earned their battle spurs a week later, on August 24, when their fifth mission had them bombing the port of Le Harve on the French coast. German fighters sneaked up on his group's rear as they headed for home. A breathtaking air battle ensued as the sky seemed filled with yellow-nosed Messerschmidt 109s, raking the flanks of several B-17s, whose disciplined flying ensured they remained within the relative safety of their box formation. Still, Tibbets, in the lead plane, almost came face-to-face with his own mortality, as an Me 109's 20mm cannon exploded in his cockpit, showering his right side with shrapnel and taking a part of his copilot's hand off. They somehow made it back to base. Too busy to think too much about what could have happened, Tibbets simply locked his fears away for another time. The missions were coming thick and fast as the Eighth Air Force began to suffer losses of men and aircraft. Tibbets would lead the first one-hundred-bomber raid on Europe, attacking fifty miles inland, against the French city of Lille, on October 9, 1942. The casualties were heavy, with over thirty aircraft lost to enemy action or aborting the mission with engine failure and returning to base.

The reputation Tibbets himself was earning as a remarkable, fearless pilot with a first-rate crew brought him to the attention of the commander of the Eighth Air Force, General Carl Spaatz, who had been ordered to supply his two most experienced pilots for top secret missions, transporting US Army top brass—General Mark W. Clark to Gibraltar, followed later by Lieutenant General Dwight D. Eisenhower. Both men were pivotal in the upcoming invasion by Allied forces of North Africa—Operation Torch, which would commence on November 8, 1942. It would be the first Anglo-American amphibious and air assault of World War II, and Axis forces were trapped in a classic pincer movement. Landings in Morocco, Algiers, and Tunisia were followed in the east by a general British advance from Egypt. It would force an Axis withdrawal from the continent and seal victory in North Africa as well as knock out Vichy French forces in the region.

The flying conditions were atrocious, but Tibbets and Van Kirk by this time worked effectively together, the latter's navigational skills on the return leg back to Britain averting a catastrophic error that would have had the B-17 unknowingly flying into the vastness of the Atlantic Ocean. Though it had been an arduous, stressful mission, for Tibbets, Ferebee, and Van Kirk it came with personal benefits. Sharing life-or-death experiences in the skies above Europe was one thing, but the officers had now spent many days in North Africa, sharing accommodation and eating together as they chauffeured General Clark and his staff back to his headquarters in Algiers, basing his unit of five B-17s on the captured air base of Maison Blanche, on the eastern end of the new front line of operations. They soon realized they were now in an actual war zone on the ground. Enemy air raids attacked their positions, Tibbets and his crews fast learning the need to scramble for the improvised air raid shelters as explosives rained down around them. His mini squadron would be flung into battle to stem a German counterattack as the winter rains developed and the bulk of USAAF reinforcements arrived, based farther back from the front lines close to Oran, south of the Atlas Mountains.

Among the many missions he would fly in what he himself described as the most difficult point in his wartime service, Tibbets became intimately familiar with the Algerian town of Bizerte. It would play a key part in the rest of his service in the war.

By the new year, Tibbets had been reassigned to the Twelfth Air Force, commanded by a force of nature, General Doolittle. He was off the front line and billeted in Algiers as the North African campaign gradually ground the Axis forces down, but at great cost. He was beginning to decompress from the weeks of combat missions and enjoying life in the Algerian capital as the Americans settled in as occupiers. But trouble followed him and would figuratively explode in his face, almost ending his career. All of it was connected to a clash of personalities and a German air base, ringed with extensive antiaircraft batteries, around the town of Bizerte.

As he stalked the corridors and planning rooms of the Twelfth Air Force, Tibbets was proud that at twenty-seven years old, he had earned the right to be seen as a combat veteran who had led dozens of missions across France and North Africa and survived. By rights, he should have been in his pomp. But events quickly spiraled, primarily due to an instinctive impulse not to back down and to tell it like it is. It had served him well so far as a lieutenant colonel who even General Spaatz believed was the best combat bomber pilot in the USAAF. It gave him a certain level of respect to air his views, but it did nothing to tame his temper or shield him from the internecine politics of senior command.

Colonel Lauris Norstad was the newly appointed chief of operations in Doolittle's staff. He was an officer on an even faster upward trajectory in the USAAF, a gifted strategist, well-connected in the Pentagon, and by the start of 1943, he was Tibbets's commanding officer. It was an instant personality clash. Norstad refused to sign off on Tibbets's battlefield promotion to full colonel and questioned his courage in a pivotal briefing for a low-level air raid on the German base at Bizerte, the same well-protected airstrip Tibbets had already successfully attacked weeks before at high altitude. Perhaps forgetting himself, or more accurately, refusing to agree to a plan he knew could cost the lives of his crews, he went head-to-head with Norstad in front of a room of gaping, wide-eyed junior officers. Clenching his fists, he stood up and challenged his CO:

"I'll tell you what I'm prepared to do, Colonel. I'll lead that raid myself at six thousand feet, if you will come along as my copilot?"

Norstad backed down, humiliated. The raid went ahead as Tibbets had planned at twenty thousand feet and was successful, without loss of aircraft or crews. But Norstad was a man to serve up revenge cold. Tibbets was called into General Doolittle's office a few days later. Norstad wanted to court-martial him for insubordination. Such were the colonel's contacts within the USAAF, even a war hero like Doolittle was powerless to prevent it. Tibbets was stunned. Doolittle soon snapped him back to reality. "Paul, I've just received a message from Hap Arnold. He wants an experienced bombardment pilot to come back to the States and help with the development of a big new bomber. I am naming you for the job. Get your bags packed, you are leaving right now!"[4]

It was imperative to get him away from Algiers and back to the United States as quickly as possible before Norstad could catch wind of the rescue and stir up trouble. Doolittle's personal staff car whisked him back to his quarters to pack a bag, before taking a C-47 transport to Liberia. From there he would fly across the South Atlantic to the United States, arriving in Miami in February 1943. He was not yet thirty years old and was a combat veteran, possibly suffering from post-traumatic stress disorder, haggard and underweight. But he was still in the USAAF. "I didn't realize until I arrived home how tightly my nerves had been wound by war. Every time I heard a siren on the street, I would jump. In the middle of the night I would wake up, listening for airplanes. I was home, but part of my subconscious was still at war."[5]

The many months of being away from family and home had begun to impact his home life, as it would do to many thousands of returning veterans from both Europe and the Pacific. But despite being back in America, trying to reconnect with his wife Lucy and his young son Paul III, the war would soon separate them again.

A week after Boeing's best test pilot Eddie Allen and a team of Boeing technicians died in the Seattle crash, Tibbets headed for Washington where he was offered the job of test pilot for the failing B-29 program. Brigadier General Eugene Eubank, USAAF director of bombardments, looked like a man who had been given the worst news in the world. The B-29 program was on its knees, its best pilot dead and the plane suffering a growing list of malfunctions, modifications, and delays. All the while its chief sponsor, Hap Arnold, was driving Eubank and other senior commanders insane with his daily requests and fiery outbursts. It was a technical, military, and, above all else, political issue. It had to succeed. Too much expense and too many man-hours had been sucked into it. Eubank promised Tibbets he would call for him when the plane was advanced enough that it was ready to fly and be tested. Five months later, Tibbets got the call. He was to proceed to the Wichita plant in Kansas.

Tibbets would spend the next year testing the plane and its myriad systems, improving where necessary and constantly taking it up into the air across the skies of Kansas and Nebraska. Above all, he would be central to the training of the first intake on crews for the new bomber, despite continued delays in modifications. By April 1944, Hap Arnold had his first 135 B-29s ready to dispatch to China, and Tibbets had helped ready the crews. On September 1, he was called to a meeting at Second USAAF headquarters in Colorado Springs to the office of its commanding officer, General Uzal G. Ent. It was a day that would change his life forever.

After initial handshakes with two uniformed officers—an Army colonel from intelligence called Lansdale, a naval captain, Deak Parsons, and finally a civilian sitting in the corner introduced as Professor Norman Ramsey—General Ent got down to business.

"Paul, you have been chosen to lead the operational phase of perhaps the most important project since hostilities began. If successful, its impact might be so great it could literally end the war. Let me very strongly emphasize at the outset this program is so very secret only a handful of senior leaders outside of the program even know of its existence. Your first directive is to keep it so. You must not in any way reveal what you are doing to anyone and that includes your wife, Lucy. Do you understand me, Paul?"[6]

Over the course of the morning, Tibbets was brought into the secret world of the Manhattan Project, the race to create enough atomic energy and matériel to drop a bomb on either Germany or Japan, or both. With a rudimentary high school understanding of physics, Tibbets comprehended the enormity of the undertaking. He waited for Ent to explain why he had brought him here. He was to form a brand-new outfit, a self-sufficient group, with its own airplanes, matériel, administration, maintenance, military police, housing, and mess halls. Everything. Ent leaned forward to emphasize his next point: "We can't afford security breaches of any sort, which means you cannot have any direct interaction with any other AAF unit . . . officially it will be the 509th Composite Group. And you'll be the boss of the entire operation."[7]

Tibbets was to take command of a newly trained B-29 squadron, the 393rd, flying fifteen B-29s, fresh off the Wichita plant conveyor belt, to the isolated USAAF air base in Wendover, Utah, where he would establish the 509th. As he studied the map, Tibbets concluded they had chosen the site well. As Colonel Lansdale and Captain Parsons listened in, General Ent outlined that the base was 120 miles away from Salt Lake City with hardly anything but desert and scrub in between, and therefore ideal from a security standpoint. It was also only five hundred air miles from the Salton Sea area in Southern California, which Ent told him would make an ideal bombing range. Colonel Lansdale took his time before interrupting to give him some good advice:

"Colonel, I want you to understand one thing. Security is first, last, and always. You will commit as little as possible to paper. You will tell only those who need to know what they must know to do their jobs properly. Understood?"

"Perfectly understood, Colonel," replied Tibbets.

General Ent closed the meeting. Tibbets had been given the command of his life—the world's first atomic strike force. Ent, Parsons, and Lansdale had ensured he knew that across all areas of the country connected to the operation, whether military, industrial, or the political corridors of power in Washington and the Pentagon, the needs of his command would enjoy top priority. Issuing the code name Silverplate would open any doors required, give him more power than he could ever have imagined. An ironic turn of events, he thought, considering what he had quickly left behind in Algiers. General's Ent's closing remarks soon brought him back down to earth:

"Colonel, if this is successful, you'll be a hero. But if it fails, you'll be the biggest scapegoat ever. You may even go to prison."

Undeterred, Tibbets took Ent's orders verbatim. If he was expected to achieve results with the best B-29 unit in the USAAF, then he needed people he trusted to train and lead them. Invoking Silverplate, he searched and found officers and men who had served with him in the European and North African combat theaters, with greater emphasis on bringing both Tom Ferebee and Theodore Van Kirk into his senior command group from their respective assignments since serving with Tibbets in North Africa the year before. He also made efforts to hire a variety of pilots and technicians who had worked with him on the B-29 testing and training program. Ever the all-seeing force behind the bomber program, Hap Arnold had made a point of calling him to reinforce Ent's promise made in Colorado:

"Colonel, if you get any trouble from anybody, you can call on me."

Chapter Ten

THE GOOD MAYOR

From now on, I will be living a true wartime life.
THE DIARY OF SENKICHI AWAYA, MAYOR OF HIROSHIMA[1]

He is a man lost to history. You may well find a few snippets of biographical information should you Google his name, but other than that, even visiting Japanese museums in the city of Hiroshima, you will be hard-pressed to discover his story. Yet he was a pivotal figure in the life of the city that would be forever linked to the dropping of the first atomic bomb. Senkichi Awaya's journey to be appointed mayor of Hiroshima in February 1943 mirrors both the rise and downfall of Imperial Japan in the decades after the Great War until its surrender on August 15, 1945.

Born in 1893 as his parents' second son, Senkichi Awaya was named after the town where his middle-class family resided at the time, Sendai. Japan by this point was over thirty years into accepting trade with the West following the Harris Treaty,[2] which was signed with the United States in 1858. Trade agreements with the Netherlands, Russia, Britain, and France soon followed, and like hundreds of towns and cities across the Home Islands, Sendai reflected the drive toward modernity.[3] Such trade agreements allowed Western firms access to establish themselves in the treaty ports of Nagasaki, Kobe, Niigata, Yokohama, and Edo, renamed Tokyo in 1868. Each international port developed its own specific enclave for foreign settlers known as "Gaijin" (Outsiders). Foreign companies eagerly arrived on the scene, such as the Hong Kong Shanghai Bank in 1866.

A transportation boom quickly ensued, led by an entrepreneur hired by one of the largest foreign investors, the business conglomerate Jardine Matheson. Thomas Blake Glover, a young Scot, who became one of Japan's most successful foreign businessmen, established a spectacular business empire in the early years of trade, from shipbuilding to green tea production to selling guns. Developing contacts at the court of Emperor Meiji, Glover would be at the forefront of rail construction across Japan, building the first railroad between Tokyo and Yokohama in 1872. Awaya's hometown of Sendai quickly evolved into a city when a new railway line connected it to the growing metropolis of Tokyo, bringing the town's inhabitants economic prosperity as well as cultural ties to the capital. Awaya's family would grow wealthy from the railways, too.

His father, Awaya Eisuke, was the first generation of the Japanese professional class to take advantage of the economic and social benefits that Western investment brought. He became a senior bureaucrat with one of the larger, foreign-owned railway companies whose lines were crisscrossing the country, linking Japan together and pushing her economy and society toward modernization. By the turn of the century, Japan was morphing from a semifeudal society into a mass-oriented, urban nation as new jobs brought them into the developing cities. Motorcars, trams, consumer goods such as fridges and electric fans, and the arrival of the first cinemas showing silent movies meant places such as Tokyo, Osaka, Niigata, and Hiroshima began to resemble their Western counterparts. This exciting modern age, however, eroded the delicate balance between town and country. Economic migration, as it had in the West, would bring poverty to rural communities and the spread of urban slums, disease, and harsh working conditions in heavy industry.

A snapshot of the Awayas at this time would show their prosperity. They were an ambitious middle-class family pursuing elite education, while exuding a healthy appreciation for Western culture. The Awayas can be seen in several photographs dressed in the kind of formal Sunday attire that Westerners might have worn attending an afternoon concert in Hyde Park, London, or strolling along the river Seine in Paris. But behind this image of familial contentment lay a slightly troubled household. His father was a stern disciplinarian and workaholic, often taken away on business across the country. He had also developed another Western trait, a taste for heavy drinking. Awaya never enjoyed the close bond with Eisuke that he shared with his mother. She would endow him with his devotion to public service, a love of family, and a deeply committed Christian faith. Though the family were patriotic and, like the rest of Japanese society, were devoted to the Meijii dynasty, they were not followers of the far-right nationalist cause that would sweep through Japan in the 1930s.

Despite the mild dysfunction at home, the family thrived as Japan threw off the shackles of Shogunate feudalism, embraced the country's path toward modernity, developed a universal education system and tolerance of Christianity, and became wealthy. Senkichi grew tall and wiry, sported a pencil-thin mustache, dressed in the Edwardian style, and excelled at his academic studies. Japan now raced toward the twentieth century, its industrial and economic transformation achieving in four decades what Western countries such as Germany had taken a century to do. It had also expanded and modernized its military, with its leaders displaying ambitions to become a local superpower.

Since concluding the Harris Treaty decades earlier, Japan had monitored the Great Powers and based its new constitution and social progress on what it deemed the strongest: the British Empire. It had signed the Anglo-Japanese Treaty, strengthening economic ties, including British industry helping it build up its naval forces. Japanese politicians and military leaders reviewed how efficient the British were in their land grabs across not only on the African continent, but closer to home in Asia. China by the turn of the nineteenth century was an example of what might happen should Japan not strengthen her defenses: riven by factionalism, warlords, and chronic corruption. Weakened by infighting, China was dominated by the Western powers, with the port city of Shanghai becoming a center

for international trade. Not for the benefit of the Chinese population, however; quite the contrary. Japanese politicians and military
concluded that security was guaranteed only through strength. A
strong economy was vital to modernize industry, develop powerful armed forces, and feed its growing population. Japan's historic
competitors, Korea and China, would in turn be cowed by Japanese
military prowess by the middle of the 1890s. Within a decade, the
first Great Power, Imperial Russia, was defeated on land by a mobile
and well-armed Imperial Japanese Army, while at sea its British-built
navy won a seismic victory at the Battle of Tsushima in May 1905.
The world woke up to the fact that Japan was now a serious international power, with ambitions to grow its influence in the Pacific and
East Asia. This was the new world for Senkichi Awaya as he grew
toward manhood.

Completing his studies at First Higher School paved the way for
Senkichi's admission to the Imperial University of Tokyo in 1916. A
prestigious center of learning since 1877, it was Japan's first Westernized university, created from several Westernized academic institutions. He graduated in 1919 and embarked on a lifelong career as
a civic administrator serving the Ministry of Home Affairs. He was
twenty-five years old and developing the skills required for a top-
level administrator who would play an integral part in the growing
empire, both home and abroad. Ironically, when one considers where
he would end his days, his first post was within agriculture, based in
Hiroshima Prefecture. Clearly when one looks at his early career, he
had been marked down as a safe pair of hands to handle important
roles in key cities throughout the Home Islands. Despite his Christian faith, he was resilient enough to display a loyalty to the civilian
legislature. This was at a time when the military was spreading its
influence throughout Japanese society, and a devotion to the emperor and his divine right to rule was expected. In the United States,
France, and Great Britain, whose administrative systems Japan had
copied, their people were "citizens." In Hirohito's Japan, Awaya, like
every other Japanese, was deemed a "subject."

The Japanese military, ascendant since the end of the Great War, became empowered by a deep-rooted resentment of the West when Japan was denied equality in the new international order. Sitting at the top table of the League of Nations, the covenant the Japanese delegation had put forward—the Racial Equality Proposal—was dismissed out of hand. The affront was then compounded by the United States, Great Britain, and France ensuring that Japan's spoils of Chinese territory were returned and her growing navy capped. Nationalistic fervor then fermented alongside the desire that Japan should forge its own "manifest destiny" in East Asia. Why, Japanese pamphlets asked, did Commonwealth countries such as Canada and Australia have such enormous landmasses to feed populations that were smaller than their own? Why did Great Britain, France, and the United States possess East Asian colonies with manpower that competed directly with Japan's own domestic workforce?

Many Japanese political leaders' careers either soared or were cut short by intrigue, betrayal, or assassination over the next two decades. Awaya would successfully ride this tumultuous wave while adhering to his principles and faith. He was a patriot but no zealot, who believed in Japan finding its natural place in East Asia; his personal writings tell us that. But his Christian faith, as well as a love of philosophy, prevented him going too far down the road of radical nationalism. He was a language expert, fluent in English and French, but especially in German, which he had continued to read every morning until the end of his studies. At university, he had made great efforts to practice his language skills, which would serve him well in his career. He tried to speak English as well as German in conversation when it was relevant. As Japan sleepwalked toward totalitarianism in the 1930s, such language skills and contacts with religious scholars and academics would provoke suspicion. But in the early stage of his career, his sharpened political antennae enabled him to navigate these waters and still retain the respect of those who worked for him, as well as impress those above him in the Ministry of Home Affairs.

Throughout the next two decades, as Japan endured economic woes amid a global depression, suffered a catastrophic earthquake in 1923 that leveled her capital, and her military lobbied for wars on the mainland, Awaya would climb the ladder, gaining management experience, dealing with staff, and overseeing larger budgets. He would travel the length and breadth of Japan's main islands of Kyushu in the south and Honshu and Hokkaido to the north, balancing work with marriage, his faith, and bringing up a large family.

He seemingly had a flare for judicial administration. At the age of just twenty-six, he was chosen above more experienced and older candidates to switch from his first job at the Agricultural Affairs Division to travel for the first time to Hiroshima and become the prefecture's superintendent of police and chief of security division. There he would meet and marry his wife, Sachiyo, two years later. Not only was he leading the police department, but he would oversee the next generation from the city's officer training school. Awaya would gain experience from this first role leading a police force, influencing many graduates who would go on to senior positions themselves by the time the country was at war with the United States.

Within a year, the couple had their first child, their eldest daughter, Motoko. Nine months later, Tokyo was struck by the great earthquake, which destroyed large parts of the city and surrounding towns and killed approximately 140,000 civilians. It traumatized the country, with structural damage estimated at $1 billion ($18 billion today), and stoked hard-line nationalism, leading to a deadly pogrom against ethnic Koreans (the Kanto Massacre[4]). In many districts the police conspired with the Japanese military to attack and murder political dissidents and journalists. Ironically, as the bodies were being cleaned from the streets, a sense of national renewal grew throughout both the capital—which would be rebuilt with Western aid and influence—and throughout Japan as a whole. This policy of rebuilding the country's sense of self would be led by the military as Japan embraced a road that led to the end of its constitution and subservience to a divine emperor.

In 1924, Awaya traveled yet again, this time heading north to Hokkaido to oversee urban planning. He had by now come under the influence of prewar Japan's biggest pacifist, Christian philosopher Uchimura Kanzō, an evangelist who had been one of the first scholars to benefit from the education policies influenced by the United States in the late nineteenth century.[5] Uchimura's teaching questioned the control of organized religion for one's own Christian beliefs. Awaya and his family became devotees, attending Bible study classes led by Uchimura on several occasions when they traveled to Tokyo, or he was giving lectures around Hokkaido prefecture. It would influence the young administrator for the rest of his life and career.

Family was at the heart of Awaya's life. Other than Bible studies, he gave little time to anything else. The next few years would prove tragic for them. By the winter of 1927, as the new emperor, Hirohito, spent his first year on the throne, the Awayas had welcomed two more children: a second daughter, Yasuko, and their first son, Yoshiyuki. It was a short-lived idyll. Within eighteen months, Yoshiyuki would succumb to illness and die. Grief-stricken, Awaya agreed to move the family farther south, close to the island of Kyushu, to accept the role as chief of police for a rural backwater at Kochi. His family sought solace in the countryside.

Primarily he would spend his time settling disputes of fishing rights between fishermen and the local government. Here his second son, Tsuyoshi, was born four months later after his family's arrival. Successfully settling a dispute that became national news elevated Awaya's profile. Within two years he was again selected over older, more experienced candidates to take up the position as head of the police department in the prefecture of Achi, close to Nagoya. And again, he was well liked as he handled his duties efficiently, even finding time to publish his thoughts on being a good policeman (*The Invisible Police*).

Events across the world, however, were to have a tumultuous effect on Japan, hastening its path toward totalitarianism, and Awaya was to come into conflict with the ultranationalists as they exerted their authority over the country's institutions.

The Great Depression had struck the United States. It had a domino effect on banks across the West, which collapsed or called in debts, ravaged the world economy, and plunged indebted countries like Germany into social chaos. Japanese nationalists blamed an attachment to Western values for the ills of their own society. Japan could not feed its population, which had been growing at a rate of a million people a year; much of Japan's staple food, rice, had to be imported. To pay for the rice, Japan exported silk. Prices collapsed, forcing Western countries to erect tariff barriers to protect their own industries. Japan's export trade sank to its lowest level, and millions went hungry. Protected to a degree through his office, Awaya witnessed the hunger in the countryside for himself as he toured the prefecture. His family suffered its own devastation when Tsuyoshi, his treasured second son, died. He collapsed suddenly while playing in the family garden with his five-year-old sister, Yasuko. Despite frantic care, he passed away a few weeks later. Such was Awaya's popularity and the outpouring of grief at such a sudden loss that hundreds of police and fellow Christians came from around the country to attend the funeral. Shows of public thanks and appreciation would be repeated throughout his career as Awaya traveled Japan from one key post to the next. He always left his mark.

By 1931, the military was now ascendant, with its eyes on China. Unable to reduce its surplus population by legitimate emigration, Japan turned to a drastic solution—the acquisition of living space on the Chinese mainland—Japan's manifest destiny. On September 18, an explosion destroyed Japanese-owned railway facilities near the Manchurian city of Mukden. Senior Japanese military commanders, operating independently on the Chinese mainland, used the event as an excuse to blame Chinese nationalists and to send their forces into Manchuria to protect Japanese possessions. Within six months, Manchuria, its resources central to Japan's East Asia dominance, would be fully occupied and renamed "Manchukuo." Japan was now on the path to being censured internationally, a move it used as an excuse to walk out of the League of Nations. The political fallout in Tokyo forced changes in the national and local government, as the regime sought to shape public opinion to embrace both nationalism and empire building and ultimately to move Japan to a constant war footing. Those seen as opposing the policy were removed from office. Though a junior official, this was Awaya's fate.

He relocated his family to Tokyo, to take up residence in a grand house that once belonged to his grandfather. Amid the splendor of this single-story mansion, which had many rooms, a spacious kitchen, and a regal courtyard, he would be reenergized. He studied languages again, reconnected with old friends from the Christian study groups he had belonged to as a young man, read the Bible with his wife, painted, and went for long walks. This was a happy time, made more so when his wife gave birth to another son, Shinobu, in May of 1932. Nothing pleased him more than to watch his family play in his grandfather's courtyard and spacious gardens. He enjoyed hearing their happy voices as they returned from nighttime adventures exploring the vast grounds with lit lanterns. Awaya would also take time to instill in his children the positive aspects of Western culture he had learned from his own parents when his father had worked for an American railroad company. But, like any Japanese patriarch, he expected adherence to the codes of conduct, manners, and obedience that governed Japanese society. Despite the family idyll inside the Awaya compound, major events were now happening within a few miles of their home.

The government's elderly prime minister, Inukai Tsuyoshi, had been murdered in his official residence by a cadre of junior naval officers. They had intended to kill his official guest, the Hollywood film star Charlie Chaplin (whom they missed, as he was attending a sumo wrestling match), hoping this would provoke hostilities with the United States. Though the death of Tsuyoshi was condemned and the coup d'état failed, the trial was used to platform the nationalist cause, which gained popularity across the country. The lenient

sentences handed out to the killers and the sympathetic press coverage emphasized to opposition groups that the military was the dominant force in Japan. The cabinet fell, and the party cabinet system
came to an end with the formation of a united cabinet headed by Vis-
count Saitō Makoto. Skilled administrators like Senkichi Awaya were
again needed to restore the public's faith in the system—whether
or not they agreed with it. He was appointed head of the police in
Osaka Prefecture the following month. Unfortunately for him, however, only a few months later he was drawn into a confrontation with
the Imperial Army.

A simple act of jaywalking by a young soldier turned into a contest of wills between the police force of Osaka and the Imperial Army,
whose officers wanted to use the incident to increase the dominance
of the Imperial Army at home. The army demanded an official apol-
ogy from the police.

Awaya, as director general of the Osaka Prefectural Police Department, stated his view: "If the army is His Majesty's army, then
the policemen are also His Majesty's policemen. There is no need to
apologize."

For months, Awaya would not back down, even though liberal-
minded politicians had been assassinated for less. Finally, five
months after the original incident, Awaya delivered an official apol-
ogy to the army's representatives. For his reward, he was moved to
the Agricultural Ministry in Oita Prefecture on Kyushu, far away
from Tokyo.

The family welcomed their fifth child, a daughter named
Chikako. Awaya had been diagnosed with diabetes in the early 1930s
but had managed to keep it under control through a strict diet. By
the time Japan was at war, he had almost lost a leg through cellulitis.
At the relatively young age of forty-eight, he took early retirement,
stepped back into private life, and hoped to be left alone. His eldest
daughter, Motoko, had married and moved to Kobe with her husband, also a senior civil servant.

But events would deem that Japan was in need of Awaya's stoicism and flare for command. In early 1943, with the tide of war turning against Japan in the Pacific, the minister of finance, Okinori Kaya (who also hailed from Hiroshima), offered Awaya the position of mayor of the city. Senior figures in the government and the military knew that there was a danger of the enemy assaulting the Home Islands. The Solomon Islands had fallen and the defence of New Guinea was underway. The strength of American forces on land, sea, and air was growing. Hiroshima continued to be a central military hub for supply and distribution. It was a key strategic city and needed a strong, calm hand to govern the city's administration. Despite his record of ill health, Awaya was the overwhelmingly popular candidate.

He accepted the role and relocated from the family home in Tokyo by July 1943, one year and four months after initially resigning from the ministry. Although he didn't know it, it would be his final civic duty to Japan.

Chapter Eleven
A LUCKY ESCAPE: JOHN HERSEY IN EUROPE

Wars fought without politics are wars lost.

JOHN HERSEY, 1944

As Tibbets took up the challenge of a lifetime in Utah, across the globe in the Mediterranean the Allies were now beginning what Churchill hoped would be the rupture of the Axis "soft underbelly" of Fortress Europe. The amphibious assault on Sicily—Operation Husky—on July 9, 1943, was overseen by General Dwight D. Eisenhower. The British prime minister had won over Roosevelt, from whom he needed men and supplies to undertake an operation he hoped would satisfy Joseph Stalin's demands for the Allies to open a second front in Europe. An assault on Hitler's Atlantic Wall was deemed too risky in the summer of 1943 following the disastrous Dieppe Raid the previous summer. Churchill's proposition to launch an offensive from Allied bases in North Africa was, for now, their only option to finally place troops onto the European continent since the fall of France in 1940.

Back from his first real taste of frontline reporting in the Solomons, John Hersey had returned to civilian life in Manhattan to take up his seat on the foreign desk for Henry Luce at *Time-Life*. His short memoir of his time in the South Pacific, *Into the Valley*, had been published in February 1943 and would prove to be a far stronger seller than his first book on MacArthur. His publisher, Alfred Knopf, congratulated him after Easter as sales peaked at twenty thousand copies. This perhaps compensated for the disappointment he had felt since Christmas, when official confirmation had arrived from the US Navy that they would not be offering him a commission. As Knopf called him to celebrate his bestseller, Hersey's life domestically and professionally was moving apace. He and his wife, Frances Ann, welcomed their second child, a boy—John Jr.—creating even more noise and fuss in the burgeoning family's apartment on the Upper West Side. Frances Ann would now be facing the rest of the year as thousands of other American mothers were. Her husband was shipping out to war.

Hersey and his *Time-Life* editor David Hulburd had agreed he should now go to Europe to cover the Allies' next move from North Africa. The Allied conference in Casablanca at the start of the year rubber-stamped Churchill's plan to invade Europe from the Mediterranean. "Husky" would be the largest amphibious and combined airborne operation in modern history: well over 150,000 Allied troops (British, American, and Canadian), supported by an armada of 2,590 vessels transporting them, plus thousands of vehicles and armor, that had sailed out of naval bases from Alexandria in Tunisia and the British naval fortress at Malta. The Allies had mounted a sophisticated deception operation to convince Adolf Hitler, via German military intelligence reports, that the landings would be aimed at Greece. The British operation of subterfuge worked, forcing Hitler to move valuable units in Italy to guard Greece. It enabled Allied troops to gain a toehold. Allied airpower was crucial in targeting and destroying enemy infrastructure, aircraft, and German and Italian columns prior to the invasion. Field Marshal Bernard Montgomery's Eighth Army landing in the southeast of the island would sweep up the coast to capture key ports, while Lieutenant General George Patton's Seventh Army would protect the flanks. But after quick, successful landings, both armies ran into heavy German resistance.

Hersey recounted for *Time-Life* the swift successes of Allied troops moving through Sicily and onto the Italian mainland, where the fighting became as intense as anything he had encountered. It was here Hersey almost lost his life when the C-47 transport plane he was in was shot down by enemy fighters and crash-landed in the Straits of Messina. History was almost repeating itself from his torrid adventures at Guadalcanal when his ancient biplane had clipped underwater coral and flipped over into the sea when rescuing a downed US Marine aviator. This time, amid the relentless resupply of an enormous amphibious invasion force below, the badly damaged C-47 transport attempted a crash landing on the sea. As soon as it hit the waves, it violently capsized and quickly began to sink. What must Hersey have been thinking as he scrambled to free himself, unbuckling his harness as water swept through the destroyed fuselage, the cries of his panicking fellow passengers ringing in his ears?

As at Guadalcanal, fortune again favored him. He managed to break free from his seat and, his lungs bursting for air, kicked for the surface as the wrecked plane descended into the blue depths. He had a habit of protecting his notebooks by placing them in rubber condoms that he then stored in the hip pockets of his US Army standard-issue trousers. Coming to the surface, waving his arms to survivors he could see in the distance, the thought suddenly gripped him—*the notebooks!* Kicking his legs frantically to maintain balance, he submerged his arms beneath the waves and felt his pockets beneath the water. Hersey immediately realized he couldn't feel their familiar shape. They were gone, perhaps lost in the wrecked plane now hundreds of feet below on the seabed. He recalled, "Then something bumped my head, and there they were floating in the water within easy reach. . . . I never could figure out how they got there. By rights they should have sunk straight off." Before the war was over, Hersey would have survived four air crashes: two in the Pacific theater and two in Europe.

The bitter fighting, in sweltering summer heat, would last several weeks before the remaining Axis forces were compelled to be evacuated to the Italian mainland by August 11. By then, Mussolini had been forced to abdicate his position on the Grand Council of Fascism. With Italian forces looking increasingly likely to surrender to the Allies, German forces commenced Operation AXIS, the seizure of all strategic points throughout Italy and Greece, and the forcible disarming of Italian forces where necessary. The Italian campaign would now be a relentless attritional struggle for many more months, as fourteen German divisions used the country's mountainous terrain to their advantage, turning it into a perfect natural defense that would stall the Allies' drive north, and inflict tens of thousands of casualties. Hersey would cover only the Sicily campaign and the first initial steps of the Allies into the toe of Italy.

Before he returned to New York, on July 19, he would take part in a 690-strong bombing raid over Rome as an observer in a B-26 Marauder, launched from air bases on Sicily. The air campaign against Rome was labeled a "hot potato" by Army Air Force chief Hap Arnold, concerned as to the reaction of the tens of thousands of Catholics serving in the US armed forces. Hersey's article was published in *Time* days later, in the magazine's "World" section, titled "The Mission of Ector Bolzoni." He would record the Allies' first-ever bombing raid on the Italian capital. But his article, perhaps mindful of the Catholic reaction, focused more on the human angle, through the thoughts of Italian American Lieutenant Bolzoni.

Bolzoni had enlisted from his home in Bristol, Connecticut, but as his surname suggests, he was of Italian origin. His older sister had visited Vatican City on a school trip in the 1930s and inspired him to visit, though the war had interrupted this plan. Wedged into the cockpit, both Hersey and Bolzoni pondered the nature of war, their place in it, and the pilot's feelings toward those civilians below he could argue were his fellow Italians.

"I wondered whether they looked up at us with fear and hatred, or whether there was secret happiness to see our bombs come down. Maybe they think they'll be free when we take over, or maybe they'll think it's just another bad thing. That depends on us, I guess. Some of my family is in Italy, and I know if I were down there with them, I would be glad to see bombs come down, even if they might hit me."

The raid would be deemed a success as Bolzoni's squadron struck the San Lorenzo Freight Yard, while others dropped their payloads onto the city's two airports.[1] *Time* gave it due recognition, and Luce lamented in an editorial that Hersey himself could not have told the American public of his adventure himself, and *Time* began publishing audio recordings from its correspondents soon after.

Hersey would be on the receiving end of a German air raid as he relaxed in Palermo two weeks later. Though Allied aircraft had begun to take control of the skies, a dawn sneak attack startled the local population, who ran to their shelters, some cursing the Americans. Along with a group of Allied journalists and officers, Hersey gazed up into the early morning light from his hotel lobby, watching as bombs fell on Allied shipping in Palermo harbor on August 3. A new, inexperienced US Army lieutenant sought reassurance from a veteran nearby:

"How long are these things supposed to last!?"

"There are no rules in this game, sir," came the sergeant's laconic reply.[2]

Hersey later described to *Time* readers how American fighters shot down four of the enemy planes in the raid.

The fighting in Sicily would inspire Hersey to produce arguably his finest work of fiction. One port that Patton's US Army engineers had converted into a major supply base was Licata, the first town the Allies had liberated on the continent of Europe and which was being hurriedly turned into a major supply operation as Montgomery's and Patton's armies fought their way through the rural countryside and back roads of the island. Licata offered a perfect strategic position to supply the push through Sicily. Hersey recorded and distilled it into a novel brimming with rich characters that offered a treatise on how a town and ancient community, with all the ebbs and flow of feuds, scandals, corruption, and criminality, reacts under the weight of military occupation. Hersey had originally written it as an article for *Life*, looking at how the town was handling its new masters through the prism of the Allied Military Government of Occupied Territories (AMGOT). Ever the reporter, Hersey was able to make himself almost invisible as daily life passed through the town, the headquarters of AMGOT, and the daily reports coming through of the fighting to the north. He left with the ingredients to fashion a story that he would complete in draft form back in New York in the autumn of 1943.

In place of the real Licata, Hersey created Adano. The plot for the story flowed around the title—*A Bell for Adano*—and followed the journey of an Italian American officer, Major Victor Joppolo, an administrator working for AMGOT. The eponymous bell of the town's church had been removed and melted down by Mussolini's fascists to make into rifles. Joppolo makes it his mission to bring the community together and accept the democratic values his army fights for by replacing the bell. Along the way, as the story progresses, he encounters characters Hersey himself discovered in Sicily, including a hard-nosed, disciplinarian US Army general who will ultimately clash with and punish Joppolo.

To many readers in 1944, when the book was published by Knopf, it was easy to recognize this heartless commander as General Patton himself. As far as Patton was concerned, it rubbed salt into his wounds, as Eisenhower had recently removed him from command after his altercation with American GIs suffering from Post-Traumatic Stress Disorder (PTSD).[3] *A Bell for Adano* was well received, selling over fifty thousand copies by Christmas 1944. It was dramatized for Broadway and for a Hollywood adaptation the following year. Hersey was only thirty years of age, with much more to come. A story from an old acquaintance would open one more pivotal door toward working for the magazine that would cement his future reputation.

Jack Kennedy was recuperating in Manhattan, a bitter, disillusioned man. The fun-loving millionaire's son from Boston had been blindsided by Hersey wooing and marrying his ex-girlfriend. To make matters worse, Hersey was also enjoying the kind of popularity Kennedy envied, and that he needed for the future postwar political career he had mapped out with his father. He himself was a combat veteran of the Solomons campaign in 1942, and he couldn't hide his bitterness at Hersey's good fortune, writing to his sister Kathleen that the author of *Into the Valley* was "sitting on top of the hill . . . a bestseller—my girl, two kids—big man on *Time*—while I'm the one that's down in the God damned valley."[4]

Kennedy had suffered an ordeal at sea when serving as a US Navy commander of a patrol torpedo (PT) boat. Though on the surface the job seemed exciting and significant, high-speed, heavily armed launchers taking on Japanese destroyers around the Solomons that ran the Tokyo Express, Kennedy's own boat (PT-109) met with disaster when attacking a Japanese convoy along with fifteen other PTs. His boat was rammed and sunk by an enemy destroyer, killing two of his thirteen-man crew. In shades of the adventurer Ernest Shackleton, the survivors swam three miles to nearby uninhabited Plum Pudding Island. Kennedy himself had dragged a severely burned crew member with a life jacket strap clenched between his teeth. Despite his own back injuries, he would galvanize his crew to hide from Japanese patrols and swim to a neighboring island offering more sustenance to survive for several more days until rescue arrived. He had been a strong swimmer and keen sailor before the war, but now he was in constant pain from a back injury that would plague him for the rest of his life. Yet here he was back home, one of tens of thousands of decorated war heroes, trying to recover.

When John and Frances Ann Hersey shared a drink with him in February 1944 at a Manhattan nightclub, Hersey's *A Bell for Adano* was racking up sales. During the evening of casual conversation, Hersey was taken by Kennedy's own account of the tragedy he had survived. The storyteller in him recognized it had all the elements required to repackage it to the American public in *Life*. Within a month, Hersey had interviewed Kennedy at length as well as the crew of PT-109. The trouble was, believing it was too negative a narrative, *Life* had turned it down. Undeterred and believing he had written something significant, Hersey turned to an editor he had encountered the night of the Kennedy drinks in Manhattan—William (Bill) Shawn of *The New Yorker*. He pitched to him the story, now titled "Survival." His theme of swimming against the tide of war to find rescue and redemption was a semi-fictionalized account of the rescue. Much to Hersey's approval, both Shawn and the magazine's owner, Harold Ross, would pour their own enthusiasm and experience into the piece, which was published in June as Allied troops sought to expand their foothold in Normandy, France. The story was a major success throughout the United States. It would push the young Kennedy into the national consciousness.[5]

But what now? *A Bell for Adano* was selling strongly, his stock was high at *Time-Life*, and despite having had "Survival" published by *The New Yorker*, he was still on good terms with Henry Luce. The war in the Pacific was far from decided. Though the Japanese Navy was not the powerhouse it had been during the Solomons campaign, it could still offer stiff resistance, as the US Pacific Fleet now pushed toward the Gilbert Islands chain, and Hersey's literary muse General MacArthur slogged through New Guinea toward the Philippines. His new assignment was at least going into a front where the Allies, this time Soviet, were smashing the Axis. Joseph Stalin's Red Army had recently launched their long-awaited offensive on the Eastern Front. Operation Bagration, begun on June 22, was chosen with dark humor by the Soviet dictator. It was the same date Hitler had launched his surprise attack on the Soviet Union with Operation Barbarossa. Three years later, and with western Russia destroyed, its cities leveled, and millions of his people dead, it was time for payback. A vast motorized Red Army was supported by tanks, trucks, and jeeps, courtesy of Uncle Sam. Hersey would now be commissioned by *Life* to find stories that highlighted to the American public where their tax-funded Lend-Lease supplies were going.

In the Pacific, the US Marines and army troops battled their way through the Gilbert and Marshall island chains. They gained valuable real estate to bring the US Army Air Force that little bit closer to the Japanese mainland. The harshest tests would come in early 1945.

Chapter Twelve
FIRE AND BRIMSTONE: IWO JIMA

Well, this will be easy. The Japanese will surrender
Iwo Jima without a fight.
ADMIRAL CHESTER W. NIMITZ

Iwo Jima, along with two smaller islands, Haha Jima and Chichi
Jima, made up the Bonin Islands. They had belonged to Japan since
1861, the local settlers naming them "Nanpo Shoto," meaning "Volcano Islands." There had been for decades a small economy on the
islands producing sugarcane and sulphur, but until the war it was
largely ignored. From the air, Iwo Jima resembled a pork chop, and
one that was overcooked. The island was literally smoking hot from
the sulphur beds below.

The small archipelago lay over three thousand miles from Pearl
Harbor, but much closer to the Home Islands. Admiral Chester Nim-
itz, Commander in Chief Pacific (CINCPAC), knew its significance.
Only several hundred miles from Japan's main island, Honshu, Iwo
Jima was vital for the next leg of his campaign to bring the war to
the enemy's backyard. He had taken the Gilbert Islands in 1943, the
Marshall Islands in early 1944, and the Marianas a few months later.
Operation Detachment would be one more nail hammered into the
enemy's defensive perimeter.

Nimitz had won the battle for military resources to assault the
tiny island. He argued to the Joint Chiefs of Staff that the next offensive General MacArthur planned for the capture of the island of Formosa, then to head into the Chinese mainland and eventually Japan,

would be too costly in men and matériel. His thrust through the islands of the Central Pacific to provide a base for growing American airpower was now in the ascendancy. While MacArthur's troops continued to battle their way through the Philippines to the capital, Manila, Nimitz assembled his commanders to plan the assault on Iwo Jima. Over the coming weeks the admiral would be in a constant battle to ensure both operational areas had the resources they required. But it was still a herculean effort. Nimitz continued to argue that the US Navy was still short of resources due to the European theater yet still had to cover millions of square miles in the Pacific.

Geographically the island's fate had been sealed years before by American military planners. Iwo Jima lay directly along the flight path of Hap Arnold's B-29 to the Japanese mainland. The Marianas chain was now one giant airfield for XXI Bomber Command, whose operational range now allowed them to strike the mainland. Though Nimitz had been keen to avoid battles for islands he considered strategically worthless when measured against the cost of men and matériel, taking Iwo Jima was very different. The small island was sovereign Japanese territory, forming an outpost of the Tokyo Prefecture. Psychologically, capturing it would be a hammer blow to Japanese morale—as pivotal as Commodore Matthew Perry's US naval flotilla sailing into the Bay of Tokyo in 1853 had been, which had opened Japan to Western trade at the point of a cannon.[1]

The tiny island measured roughly four miles in length, with a maximum width of two miles to its north, and less than half a mile in the south. In the center, on a plateau, were two operational air bases: Airfield Number One and Two. A third remained uncompleted nearby. Dominating the island on its southeastern tip was Mount Suribachi, a dormant volcano over five hundred feet high. Tactically it gave command of the whole island and the two-mile-long beach nearby. Though open to bombardment and machine-gun fire from both flanks, the long stretch of volcanic sand was the only logical landing site for the US Marines Fifth Amphibious Corps, which had been designated to take it. Consisting of the Third, Fourth, and Fifth

Marine Divisions, all told the operation consisted of one hundred thousand American personnel, supported by an armada of several hundred naval ships of the Fifth Fleet, commanded by Admiral Raymond Spruance.

American intelligence had badly underestimated the strength of the Japanese garrison—the 109th Infantry Division. What they believed to be a force of thirteen thousand men was in reality over twenty-one thousand strong, consisting of Imperial Army and Navy units. They were led by an ex–cavalry officer, Lieutenant General Kuribayashi Tadamichi, a veteran of thirty years' service who had been personally chosen by the Japanese prime minister, General Tojo, and had been given a personal audience with Emperor Hirohito. Despite the honor, he knew his appointment was a death sentence. As an experienced soldier descended from five generations of samurai, he wrote to his wife before taking command of the island, "Do not plan for my return."

Since the late summer of 1944, the Japanese garrison's air strength had been reduced by daily American air attacks from B-24s, B-25s, and B-29s, but their radar station was still intact. Its signals gave the mainland air defenses a two-hour early-warning signal of inbound American attacking bombers. Capturing the island's airfields would allow American sea rescue crews to operate closer to the target, as well as allow crippled B-29s to land on their return leg. The bases would also be home to squadrons of the new P-51 Mustang long-range fighter—an aircraft that far outperformed anything the enemy could throw up against it. Taking Iwo Jima all but ensured Japan would be defenseless against American air attacks.

Knowing this and taking lessons from how Japanese defenses had failed on Tarawa and other island strongholds, General Kuribayashi devised his strategy well. He knew he could not hold out, but his command, and the naval contingent alongside them, would inflict as many casualties as possible. Such bloodshed, he concluded, might blunt enemy morale before they considered striking out for the Japanese mainland. His primary concern was the poor quality of some units he had been bequeathed to hold the island. He had the veteran garrison unit, the 109th Division, but the remainder were a random mix of Imperial troops, sailors turned into infantry who lacked proper combat training, and airmen who thought themselves above such fighting. He had appealed to Tokyo, warning: "We cannot fight the Americans with them. Give me better trained troops and more guns, and I will hold Iwo!" His protestations were ignored.

He would not try to prevent a beach landing or waste his men's lives with futile banzai charges. Instead, he spent the nine months before the Americans arrived building an extensive honeycomb defensive system that created two defensive belts. Having to trust what he had at his disposal, the general could count on a few excellent combat leaders who would go on to prove their worth. The commander of the garrison's only armored formation, the Twenty-Sixth Tank Regiment, Lieutenant Colonel (Baron) Takeichi Nishi, would be one of the most effective and courageous Japanese officers during the battle. The son of a wealthy and ancient family, he spoke fluent English and was an ardent follower of the blood-oath code of *Bushido*. His tanks would be overwhelmed by Marine firepower. Once the crews lost their vehicles, they continued fighting as infantry. Nishi himself would die in the fighting.

As enemy fighter planes strafed anything that moved on the island in preparation for the invasion, Kuribayashi's men labored to build tunnels. Many were at least thirty feet below ground; his headquarters were placed seventy-five feet beneath the surface. Each tunnel was wide enough for a fully equipped soldier to move quickly to his next line of defense or come up behind the advancing enemy. To support the defense, supply channels, ammunition stores, and medical centers had all been meticulously carved out of the soft volcanic pumice rock and reinforced with wood, brick, and cement, to give excellent advantage to the defender. With electrical lighting, miles of communication lines, and ventilation shafts dug into the system, it was a formidable engineering feat. Aboveground, amid the island scrub and vegetation, Nishi sighted gun emplacements and mortar pits—all zeroed in on every inch of the three-thousand-yard-long beaches. The gun crews had trained for weeks and could recite their coordinates by heart if need be.

Kuribayashi knew that once the initial wave of Marines landed, meeting only light arms resistance, more waves would quickly follow. Then the attackers would realize the beach was enclosed by a fifteen-foot-high sand bank, which they would need to climb before tackling their objectives, his airfields. The Americans would be fish in a barrel for his well-hidden artillery to inflict maximum casualties. Should they get off the beachhead and push toward the interior, they would encounter his defensive belts containing hundreds of concealed concrete pillboxes, while his men would surprise them from tunnels to rake them with small-arms fire. The impetus would be on the Americans to capture the island, not sit behind defenses. He had spent months diligently training his inexperienced men in ambush tactics to kill infantry and destroy their tanks with bomb satchels on bamboo spears and grenades. Even caves had been excavated to create forts.

It was a deadly maze that Kuribayashi intended to draw the Marines into. Like the Soviet tactics at Stalingrad, his men would conduct a close, intimate battle that would deny the enemy air cover and bring them close enough to kill as many as possible. Aware of the enormity of what was to come and to stiffen his men's resolve, Kuribayashi declared:

"Each man should think of his defence position as his graveyard, fight until the last and inflict much damage to the enemy."[2]

A force of seventy thousand Marines, led by Major General Harry "Howlin' Mad" Schmidt, would be designated to assault and capture the island. The sixty-two-year-old three-star general had been given frontline command by President Roosevelt, who admired his battling qualities. "His Marines," as he called them, had fought and died through the islands of the Central Pacific, and though he accepted the risks, he was in constant war with the Navy for what he perceived as their interference in fighting a battle. Iwo Jima would be no different.

The Fourth and Fifth Marines would assault the beaches—designated from south to north: Green, Red 1, Red 2, Yellow 1, Yellow 2, Blue 1, and Blue 2. The beach could not take more than two divisions, otherwise the congestion would be detrimental to the overall offensive. Forty-two thousand Marines were still allocated to go in on day one. They would have the firepower of the US Fifth Fleet and Seventh Air Force behind them. By the time the American armada was steaming toward the island, Lieutenant Colonel Kaneji Nakane wrote to his wife before the invasion, reassuring her: "Everybody is in good shape, so you don't have to worry about me. . . . We have strong positions and God's soldiers and await the enemy with full hearts."[3]

A three-day naval and aerial bombardment commenced with mixed results before Schmidt sent in the assault of the southeast coast on February 19. The tremendous barrages unleashed created a lunar landscape, air reconnaissance photographs detailing as many as five thousand craters per square mile. Schmidt had requested at least ten days of bombardments to soften up the island fully, but operational requirements elsewhere left him with just seventy-two hours to do the job. As he feared, just three days of bombardments to soften up Kuribayashi's camouflaged defenses would prove completely ineffectual.

On their far-left flank, the Marines could see the brooding monster of Mount Suribachi, with dark clouds of volcanic dust swirling around from the countless naval artillery barrages striking it. A more deadly proposition was to the far right, an impregnable mound called the "Rock Quarry," its camouflaged guns enjoying a wide sweep of the whole beach. Even before the invasion, Fourth Division commander Major General Clifton Cates had raised his concerns: "You know if I knew the name of the man on the extreme right of the right-hand squad, of the right-hand company, of the right-hand battalion, I'd recommend him for a medal before we go in!"[4]

To men of the Fourth Marines like twenty-year-old Richard Jessor, serving with his headquarters company, First Battalion, Twenty-

Fifth Regiment, designated to assault Blue Beach, the journey to this small island had been an odyssey.[5]

"I was an intelligence scout with responsibilities for mapping and informing the commander where the enemy emplacements were. I was in charge of that kind of information and updating the maps as the lines changed, and we were successful in moving ahead.

"It was not a proximal concern throughout the training of whether one would survive the fighting to come. It became one as we got offshore. But there was sort of a low-level sense of apprehension, but more about the fact that we didn't know what war was like, or what was going to happen. We also weren't told where we were going when we boarded ships to leave Maui. We had been training, making mock invasions on some of the beaches of Maui. And so, we felt well-prepared."[6]

Initially unaware of which island they were assaulting or what kind of combat they would experience, Jessor and his buddies had perfected a method of communicating what news they could gather to send back home to loved ones.

"What a few of us had done was to get a map and see all of the islands in the Pacific and give them a woman's name. And then we sent that code to our family. And once we knew that we were headed for Iwo Jima, which was after we left Maui, we were able to write home, and I would say, 'I just heard from Aunt Mary . . . ' and then my mother knew that I was headed for Iwo Jima."

In the bunkers onshore overlooking the beaches about to be assaulted, eighteen-year-old naval radio operator Tsuruji Akikusa studied with growing alarm the size and power of the Fifth Fleet: "I was overwhelmed. How could they have so many ships? There were more than the entire [Imperial] Japanese Navy. It was then I realised we were going to lose the war."[7]

For Richard Jessor, reality struck him in the face as with his squad he watched the naval bombardment continue to pound the shoreline in the evening dusk. His division, veteran "old salts" and replacements like himself, had spent many weeks undergoing intense assault training on Maui.[8] Forced marches and combined arms training taking pillboxes under live fire had now brought him to this point. He looked on the many Marines in his battalion throwing from the heavy swell that had blighted naval actions over the previous two days.

"We knew, by then, that the mission was to take Iwo in four or five days, reboard the ships, and go to Japan. The night before the landing, we were called up on deck. The colonel just made this announcement:

"'Listen up, you guys. Tomorrow night, at this time, a lot of you are going to be dead. When you get shot, you fall forward. We need that extra six feet.'

"And he turned on his heel. That was his tribute to our impending invasion."

The bombardment pummeled the beaches, as well as the top of Mount Suribachi. Radioman Akikusa was badly wounded as his naval bunker was rocked by heavy artillery, three fingers on his right hand blown off. He managed to stagger back to a first-aid station for help and would be pulled back to another line of defense. There was no chance of being evacuated. He knew he would live or die on the island.

Despite the enormity of what he was witnessing from four thousand yards offshore, trying to suppress the fear of going into combat for the first time, Jessor took confidence from the power of the naval forces supporting the Marines and the words of comfort received from comrades:

"I was in the midst of experienced war veterans as a replacement who had no military experience. The guys I was with, we had trained together on Maui, and they gave me a sense that they were going to look out for me. They had my back, and I knew that I could count on them."

The battleships, cruisers, and destroyers continued to pound the island as a bright blue day developed, in ironic comparison to the previous week of appalling weather that had hampered American operations to soften up Japanese defenses. The Fourth Marines would be to the north of the Fifth Division, who were assaulting the beach-head closer to the base of Mount Suribachi.

"Dawn on February 19, the US Navy ships were still bombarding the island, and I think they were flyovers, dropping bombs. But we went over the side on these rope notes and dropped into the 'LVT Buffalo' [Landing Vehicle Track][9] that had pulled up right against the ship. When it was full, the tractor took off, and another one came up to the side of the ship. The tractor that I dropped into, like all the others, then went, and was just circling and waiting. We knew we were going to go in at some point, but the guys were vomiting off the side, and circling, and so on. We could see the artillery on the shore. The first wave and the second wave got in, and hit the beach, not under any fire whatsoever."

The bombardment continued as Marines of both divisions climbed over the side of their troopships, down the rope nets into their amtracs lying alongside. As their boats churned them toward the dark, crater-marked beach, the naval bombardment now rolled inland to suppress enemy activity. The waves were set to come in three hundred yards apart. It was 9 a.m. and all hell was about to be set loose. What they encountered, as General Kubayashi hoped, was the fifteen-foot-high terrace of coarse black volcanic ash. Men and machines sank into it as they tried advancing inland. Once the third wave had arrived, with bulldozers to excavate their way through the embankment, Kuribayashi gave the order for Japanese artillery to fire. The whole beachhead came under intense fire.

Richard Jessor, hunkering down in the fourth wave, now landed to a hot reception twenty minutes after the assault had begun:

"Our tractor hit the beach and got stuck in the soft, lava-black sand. The artillery shells were exploding all around it. We were getting enfilading fire, and it was incredible. We jumped out of the tractor, and ran around the front, and hit the beach. I looked over, and there was a Marine on his back, with frothy blood coming out of his mouth as he breathed. He died as I watched him. And that was the moment of my introduction to what war was about.

"It was terrifying, and what we did was what we were trained to do. And that is, after hitting the beach, and waiting for a lull in the shells exploding—you'd get up and run forward. Our mission was to reach the landing strip on the high ground of the interior."[10]

Jessor's five-man squad ran up the steep slope to get to higher ground, jumping into and out of bomb craters created by the Japanese bombardment. His squad continued toward Airfield Number One.

Coming ashore to tackle Airfield Number One, too, with the Twenty-Seventh Regiment of the Fifth Marines, was Sergeant Bill Lansford, a veteran of Guadalcanal two years before.

"I remember very clearly the battleships firing, 'Thump! Thump!' as they fired their fourteen-inch shells. It was a clear day and the island had smoke coming out of it, but [initially] it looked very peaceful. We entertained ourselves going in by watching the trajectory of the shells from the battleships going into the island. At one point I said, 'I hope the natives are friendly.' It was funny because a chaplain was in the boat with us as he later wrote in a paper that we were fearless, but we had been floating around in the water for an hour and were bored, we just wanted to get ashore. We thought the battle was over and the battleships were wasting their ammunition. Little did we know!

"All of a sudden, we reached the shore and the first thing I saw was two men carrying this guy and his head was all bloody—putting him in the boat where we were getting out. I began looking around and could see I was totally wrong—the artillery fire [from the Japanese] was coming in like crazy. Everybody was mixed up."

The concerns General Schmidt had voiced about the number of combat novices he had been obliged to fill within his corps's battered ranks now surfaced in action, as Lansford testified: "The enemy artillery was the worst I had ever seen. I started making my way up: ducking, sometimes hitting the deck, sometimes running. I got to the top of the third tier of sand, where it leveled off. I was just relieved to get out of that goddamned sand. There was a whole bunch of guys who had hit the deck. I saw some of the NCOs grabbing them to get them moving out of the artillery fire. I joined in, shouting 'Get moving!' They responded to that—they were trained to do that, but the poor kids didn't know what to do, they were brand new and had never been in combat."[11]

By the first day, despite Airfield Number One being captured, only a third of the objectives had been taken. But Mount Suribachi was now cut off from the bulk of the island's defenders to the north. Thirty thousand Marines had landed ashore, and of this total, five hundred had been killed and 1,775 wounded. The Marines dug in for the night as a cold front enveloped the area. New replacements like Richard Jessor, who had recently trained in Maui and were used to the tropical climate of the South Pacific, now shivered in their foxholes. The naval guns and Japanese counterbattery fire roared over the regiment's heads as the *whump, whump* of enemy mortars landed along their front lines all throughout the first night.

Sergeant Mike Mervosh of the Twenty-Third Marines had been a combat veteran since the start of the Pacific war, surviving the fighting on both Saipan and Tinian. He led a squad onto Yellow Beach in the second wave. Scanning the terrain with his combat field glasses, he realized with dread it was a defender's dream: "There was no place to hide and take cover, and no place to run."[12]

His unit assaulted what would become the infamous Rock Quarry on the right flank. His platoon rapidly suffered heavy casualties. He went in with a company of three hundred men. By the end of the battle, only thirty-one came off the island. As the fighting on and off the beach developed, all officers in his unit were killed or wounded. Mervosh became its temporary commander but was then wounded himself. Lying on the beach waiting for evacuation, he watched as Japanese artillery picked off LVTs scuttling back and forth from the naval armada. *If I am going to die*, he thought to himself, *it'll be here!* The medic gave him a shot of morphine and drew the letter *M* in blood on his forehead. Mervosh groggily sat up, wiped away the insignia of blood, grabbed his rifle, and staggered back to find his unit. "And man, that's when my adrenaline went up and the guys said I was even more combat crazy. . . . I threw more grenades than I fired my rifle. I had a sore arm."[13]

Richard Jessor's Twenty-Fifth Regiment had continued on to Airfield Number One. With its capture, by the fifth day after the Normandy landing (D+5) his entire division had wheeled right to strike north toward what they would painfully find out was the main belt of Japanese resistance. Major General Schmidt had ordered the capture of the isolated Japanese position atop Mount Suribachi, while the bulk of his corps pushed forward north along a broad front to capture the remaining airfields. As forward Marine units stumbled into intense firefights and endured powerful artillery bombardments or well-concealed deadly crossfires from multiple pillboxes and bunkers, Marine commanders realized they had reached the main Japanese defensive line. Enemy minefields and camouflaged antitank guns were starting to take their toll on American armor trying to provide the Marines with close fire support. The fighting over the coming two weeks would be intense, unrelenting, and extremely savage.

Jessor's unit's experience was typical of the fighting. The Twenty-Fifth Regiment encountered dozens of pillboxes, revealing themselves only when the Marines were in their kill zones. Each Japanese position fought to the end, with every defender killed or managing to pull back to the next redoubt. On many occasions it would take a few days to suppress and destroy a position before a fresh one was encountered a few hundred yards farther forward. The fighting was chaotic, as the fine weather of the first day's assault now turned to heavy rain. The hot volcanic ash quickly dissolved into warm clinging mud, prohibiting heavy vehicles offering close support and clogging the Marines' automatic weapons, negating their fire supremacy. Flamethrowers, grenades, and fixed bayonets in many instances became weapons of choice to attack enemy positions. Wielding a flamethrower was one of the most dangerous jobs within a Marine unit. Tackling larger bunkers or hilltop positions, the Marines would launch artillery barrages before sending in squad assaults, demolishing each position with incredible firepower—grenades, flamethrowers, and artillery support. The Japanese defenders would sometimes be wiped out but other times disappear without trace, only to pop up behind the lines to fire into their rear.

The casualties mounted, especially among frontline company and battalion commanders and platoon leaders. Privates, some of whom had experienced only a few days of combat, became squad leaders, corporals took charge of shattered platoons, and sergeants led threadbare companies. Schmidt committed his final reinforcements from Third Division to the battle. They had been watching from the boats offshore as the LSTs took their comrades onto Iwo. The calmness and comfort of their ship's quarters must have played on their minds as they heard the distant rumble of artillery and the smoke of mortar explosions while their sister divisions fought the Japanese. Now they were entering the fray.

The Fifth Division would advance on the left flank of the island, the Third Division would drive through the center, and the Fourth Division would come up along the right. Well-dug-in enemy positions became infamous: Hill 382, "Turkey Knob," the "Amphitheater," "Cushman's Pocket," and the "Meat Grinder." These took days and weeks to overcome. The Fourth Division would suffer 4,075 casualties in the two-week operation to capture the "Meat Grinder."

Richard Jessor, acting as his regimental commander's intelligence scout, witnessed daily firefights on the front line as he mapped out enemy positions. "All you experienced every day was people dying next to you, or around you, or behind you. It was, I think, the fourth day after the landing. My unit was pulled back from the frontline, and given a day of rest, and an opportunity to write one letter. I wrote to my parents, and said goodbye, and thanked them for everything they had done, and said, 'There's no chance I'll get off this island alive.'

"It was very clear to me, then, that it was just a matter of time before I got hit. There was a sense that this enemy was destroying us, and we couldn't see it. And this became a major frustration. We were angry that the Japanese wouldn't show up. And as a result, we would fire at them, whether with our rifles or the artillery would fire at where the fire towards us was coming from."[14]

On February 23, on the same day General MacArthur's forces captured Manila, the Marines finally scaled Mount Suribachi.[15] Frustratingly for Schmidt, the Japanese defenders used their hidden tunnel network to escape back to the main defensive line in the north. From their frontline position in the north, Richard Jessor's unit broke off their advance when they spotted the iconic flag flying in the distance: "I happened to look over my shoulder, and I saw the Stars and Stripes on Mount Suribachi. And I started screaming to the other guys near me, 'The flag is up! The flag is up!' After having written a goodbye letter to my parents—it was the first time I had a sense that maybe we can get through this, because now our rear was totally covered. The enemy was just on one side of us—and that was in front of us."

There would still be many days of fierce fighting to come. Taking Airfield Number Three on the northern end of the island and driving Kuribayashi's survivors back, breaking their lines into three separate pockets of resistance toward the northern coast of Iwo, had come at tremendous cost. General Schmidt's men had killed over twenty thousand Japanese, with only 216 taken prisoner. In return the Americans had lost over 5,800 killed, died of wounds, or missing in action.[16] Over seventeen thousand were wounded, including 826 officers. Japanese tactics had evolved as the tide of battle weighed against them. Their snipers enjoyed successes against advancing Marine flamethrower teams. Rumors spread of Marine units being ambushed by Japanese troops dressed in American uniforms; whether this was true, one cannot find reports. What certainly occurred was Marine medics and troops being killed when inspecting booby-trapped enemy corpses. To survive, some starving Japanese defenders would crawl out at night to scavenge food, water, and ammunition from nearby corpses and sometimes their wounded comrades. Some would be caught out in the open and killed by vigilant

Marine sentries or would simply crawl away to die. The island's vegetation they had last seen on February 19 was now a dystopian moonscape.

The Marines tried psychological methods to bring the fighting to a speedy conclusion, distributing leaflets containing messages from captured Japanese troops, like this one from Private Mamoda Hideo: "Comrades, I myself would have never believed that things could be this way if I hadn't seen it with my own eyes. At first, I was embarrassed to have been taken by the enemy but when I learned that several officers had the same experience I felt better. In our conversations we agreed that it is more honorable to live for the emperor and work for a greater Japan in the future, than merely to die like rats underground."[17]

The fanatical defenders simply scorned the attempt and continued the fight. But as the battle entered its fourth week, they were nearing the end of any meaningful, coordinated defense. Kuribayashi's men were short of food, ammunition, and water, but not lacking in fighting spirit. The general sent an assessment back to Tokyo headquarters: "The enemy's bombardments are very severe, so fierce that I cannot express or write it here. The troops are still fighting bravely and holding their positions thoroughly."

On the night of March 9, both warring armies trapped on the tiny island looked upward at the clear night sky. A low drone of engines was coming from the east of the vast ocean surrounding them. Sixty miles in length, it was the armada of Curtis LeMay's B-29s from the Twentieth Air Force striking out toward Tokyo to launch the great fire raid. LeMay with Admiral Nimitz would tell reporters at the next day's press conference that the loss of sixteen B-29s was worth the result: "We can take these losses but the Japanese sure as hell can't. With Iwo [Jima] in our hands, you can be damned certain this is only the beginning."[18]

The bulk of Nimitz's task force now left the Fifth Fleet off Iwo Jima to steam toward the next intended target—Okinawa. The battle raged on as thousands of US Army troops were taken ashore to be garrison units once the island was taken. More American ground-air support came in from carrier-based F-4U Corsairs, to drop bombs and deploy rockets to wheedle out enemy redoubts. The Japanese steadfastly remained underground, invisible to the Americans unless they appeared for close-quarter combat, or in last-ditch stands in the dozens of caves and ravines. Sergeant Mervosh's methods were brutally effective:

"I used a phosphorous grenade in a hole and four Japanese came running out coughing and smoking. One had a [samurai] saber over his head coming right at me. I shot him right in the face. I thought to get the other three [survivors] but that's when my rifle jammed on me.

"My BAR [Browning automatic rifle] man was a replacement. He started jumping up and down yelling: 'There are Japs!'

"I shouted back, 'Yeah, you son of a bitch, kill 'em!' And he mowed them down with his BAR. He saved my life. It wasn't half an hour later that I lost him. I didn't even get to know his name."[19]

Richard Jessor's unit was equally clinical: "Our tactics for taking a position were simple but effective. It was always rifles or grenades. If we identified a cave opening from which [enemy] fire was coming, we would provide cover for the flamethrower guy to get up to the opening of the cave, and fire his weapon into the caves, and incinerate where that fire was coming from.

"What we found incredulous was their lack of materials. An American grenade would have a steel ring as the pull ring. The Japanese used grenades that were armed by pulling a piece of string. Can you imagine using hand grenades with strings to pull? When we saw this kind of thing, we thought, 'Jesus, they must be in terrible shape, if they can't even manufacture a steel ring.'"

Most days the Marines were fortunate if they could move forward a hundred yards—what they titled, in a dead-pan manner, a "touchdown." Tanks with Zippo flamethrowers to support their advances were in constant use. By the end of the thirty-six-day battle, US tanks had expended over ten thousand gallons of fuel per day in support of the Marines. They had taken a dreadful pounding for their pains, with dozens of tanks destroyed by antitank fire, booby-trapped mines, and suicide charges with explosive satchels. One tank battalion lost three commanders in over a week of fighting.

Still the fighting raged in the tunnels and cave systems. Injured radioman Tsuruji Akikusa was by now desperately defending one such cave system, he and his comrades lacking food and water as they held off American assaults. Their end was inevitable as the Marines resorted to medieval methods to force them out of their natural fortress: "They pumped water into our cave. We were all filthy. The cave stank of excrement and dead bodies. So, some jumped into the water to wash. Then the water exploded. Gasoline had been mixed with the water. The cave became a sea of flame. People were burning; their skin was hanging and bleeding. It was like hell."[20]

The War Department in Washington declared Iwo Jima under American military control by March 14, but it was a PR exercise to limit US public concern for the mounting casualties. General Kuriyabashi, seemingly unaware of the news, carried on the fight with fifteen hundred men for another nine days. He made his final defense in the appropriately named "Death Valley," a seven-hundred-yard-long and three-hundred-yard-wide canyon, with dozens of gullies leading off from the main path. Kuribayashi's redoubt was concealed at the rear of the canyon. It was a killing ground for the Marines trying to reach it.

As Richard Jessor has described, the use of flamethrowers was a key weapon to subdue a defensive position, while demolition explosives could be made ready to drop into it. Bitter fighting, with tanks firing point blank into Japanese positions, drove them back until they were at the door of the island's commander. The end came on March 23. Kuribayashi's final message was cabled to the Japanese garrison on nearby Chichi Jima: "My officers and men are still fighting. The enemy front line is two hundred meters from us and they are attacking with flamethrowers and tanks. They have advised us to surrender by leaflets and loudspeakers, but we only laughed at this childish trick. All officers and men of Chichi Jima. Goodbye."[21]

Kuribayashi's body was never found by American troops. One rumor spread of his ritual suicide, another that he had led a banzai attack and been killed. Before he died, he had ordered staff to burn all his headquarters' paperwork, records, and regimental flags. He did not want the enemy celebrating cheap victories with Imperial Army insignia.

That evening, Radio Tokyo broadcast to the nation a speech by Premier Kuniaki Koiso announcing Iwo Jima's fall. To many listeners the bad news was a bolt from the blue. Koiso maintained the government's intent to fight on, despite the devastation being meted out from the waves of B-29 attacks on home soil: "There will be no unconditional surrender. So long as there is one Japanese living, we must fight to shatter the enemy's ambitions. We must not stop fighting until then."

If the premier wished to send a message to the United States of what the cost might be to invade the Home Islands, it worked. Of the twenty-one thousand Japanese defenders, nineteen thousand had perished, with just 1,083 taken prisoner. Many hundreds more would continue the fight and be killed by follow-up operations.[22] In return, Schmidt's Fifth Amphibious Corps had suffered 24,053 casualties, including 6,140 killed. The majority of them were between eighteen and twenty-one years of age. One corpsman in three who landed on the island was a casualty. Nineteen of the twenty-four battalion commanders were casualties.

Admiral Spruance's task force, parked off the island, suffered significant losses in dead and wounded from counterbattery fire from the shore, and kamikaze attacks claiming the carrier USS *Bismarck Sea*, with 218 men lost, on February 21. She would be the last US aircraft carrier to be lost in the Second World War. The reported losses were sobering news for a battle on such a small island, hundreds of miles from the Japanese mainland. It was the first time in the Pacific campaign that American casualties exceeded Japanese. It was the Stalingrad of the Pacific for the US Marine Corps.[23]

Considering the savagery of the encounters and the casualties his unit had endured, Richard Jessor experienced an epiphany during a particularly arduous assault, reminiscent of the trench fighting at Verdun. He would be one of a handful Marines to capture an enemy flag on the island: "One morning, I woke from where I was hiding, in a kind of foxhole, and there was a dead Japanese not far away—a soldier. It was quiet. I got up and went over to see if he had a flag under his shirt, because that's the souvenir that most of us, as Marines, were thinking were things to gather and take home. I went over to him, and bent over to pull up his shirt, and see if he had a flag tied around his waist. And as I bent over him, I saw that he had letters in his pocket. And I had letters in my pocket. And I had this sudden epiphany about: What are we doing here? We're both human beings, and I don't have anything against him. What is this about? Why are we fighting wars?"

Having survived days of intense combat, Jessor had finally come face-to-face with a live enemy. "I was asked to take that prisoner back to command center on the beach, where there were Japanese translators. There I am, twenty years old, with a live Japanese prisoner, and I'm pointing my rifle at him, and waving to get going. We had to get going through our rear lines and the artillery. The Japanese prisoner was very calm and quiet. He was very obedient. He looked back at me, over his shoulder, to be sure he was going in the right direction.

"A Marine from the side jumped up, and came running at us, shouting:

"'I'm going to kill that son of a bitch.'

"I pointed my rifle at his chest, and said, 'I have orders to shoot anybody who touches my prisoner.'

"And he stopped, and we had this confrontation. I just had my rifle pointed right at him, and he turned and went away. That happened one more time on the way down to the beach. When I got to the command tent, I sat him down and grabbed someone over, and said, 'He's yours.' And I got out of there. . . . I was twenty years old, and I'm not thinking that I make my own decisions."

It was D+36. Finally, what was left of Jessor's regiment had reached the northern coast of Iwo Jima. Upon news of the Japanese final redoubt being captured, Marine units began to march back to secured areas. Many exhausted Marines slept on the very beach their comrades had expended so much blood to capture. They lit oil drums as the sun went down, boiled up precious cups of fresh coffee, washed their dirty, battle-worn fatigues, and stared silently out to sea. Behind them the island had been reduced to a blackened wreck, littered with corpses, human excrement, and the detritus of battle. Some survivors took time to visit their dead comrades now lying in the three separate divisional cemeteries. Richard Jessor recalls:

"We marched back to the beach. We were coming off the high ground, and I could just see the entire expanse, and it was a sea of white crosses from one end to another. You saw in one image what the cost of the war had been, up until that point. My unit had taken a battering. I knew from personal experience that we had lost fifty percent to sixty percent of our strength."

Jessor's Fifth Division had arrived at the shores of Iwo Jima in twenty-two transports. They would sail away in eight: "We got down to the beach and boarded the LCIs that took us out to troopships, and went back to Maui, in Hawaii, and began training again for the big invasion of Japan itself."

Twenty-seven Marines and naval personnel would win the Congressional Medal of Honor for actions across the thirty-six days of combat on- and offshore of Iwo Jima—thirteen of them posthumously. Though recriminations would continue until well after the war about the failings in a preparatory bombardment before the Marines assaulted it, the capture of Iwo Jima and its conversion into a platform for the Seventh Fighter Command would be undeniably successful. Colonel Tibbets, still weeks away from transferring the 509th Composite Group across to the Marianas, would be grateful for the sacrifice the Marines had made on the island. During air combat missions from the Marianas over the last six months of the war, the Twentieth Air Force recorded that 2,251 B-29s landed on the runways created by the Seabees at Iwo Jima. The primary problems were mechanical issues or deteriorating flying conditions due to weather, or in some instances combat damage. They could now either make it to Iwo Jima's air base, only several hundred miles from the Japanese mainland, or at worst ditch in the sea, to be picked up by the US Navy's Catalina Flying Boats, now stationed just off the island.

The math suggests that over twenty-seven thousand US aircrews were saved by the sacrifice of the Marines, but it still raises questions about whether taking Iwo Jima was indeed worth a bloodbath. Nevertheless, the mistakes in assaulting the small island would be considered once Nimitz's task force anchored outside Japan's most coveted island territory. The battle for Okinawa would be many times more costly—for both sides. As the Marines packed up to head back to Maui to refit for the planned invasion of the Home Islands, a bullet-shredded Japanese security sign left on the landing beach had been taken by one corpsman as a trophy: "Trespassing, surveying, photographing, sketching, modeling, etc. upon or of these premises without previous official permission are prohibited by the Military Secrets Protection Law. Any offender in this regard will be punished with the full extent of the law."

The author with Michiko Kodama, assistant secretary general of the Nihon Hidankyo, Tokyo, November 2023.
© *Iain MacGregor*

Michiko Kodama standing next to her mother and infant brother, Hiroshima, 1940.
© *Michiko Kodama*

The simple memorial to Mayor Senkichi Awaya, along the banks of Motoyasu River, where his residence once stood several hundred yards away from the Atomic Bomb Dome.
© *Iain MacGregor*

Emperor Hirohito was a living god to the Japanese people, and one who rode the nationalist wave of his military's desire to forge an empire throughout East Asia. His part in the coming catastrophe in World War Two was not without blame.
PhotoQuest/Getty Images

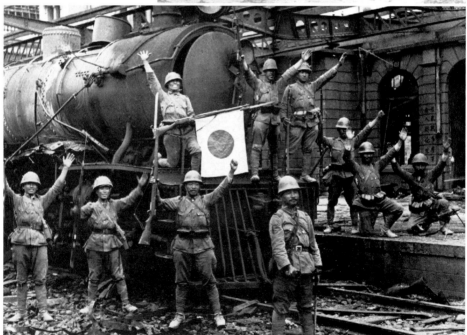

The Second Sino-Japanese War became a huge drain on Japanese economic resources, as well as diverting significant manpower to a conflict they realized they couldn't win.
Pictures from History/Universal Images via Getty Images

Prewar Hiroshima was built like the majority of Japanese towns and cities: one-and-two-story homes constructed from wood and paper, packed tightly together, with little shelter offered from air attacks.
© *The Hiroshima Peace Memorial Museum Archive*

Albert Einstein was driven out of Nazi Germany into the welcoming arms of first Great Britain and then the United States. He became an American citizen in October 1940.
Pictures from History/Universal Images via Getty Images

The surprise aerial attack on the United States Pacific Fleet by the Imperial Japanese Navy on December 7, 1941, was a stunning success. For the next six months, Japanese military forces were able to overrun vast portions of East Asia.
History/Universal Images via Getty Images

With the United States at war by the end of 1941, President Roosevelt's administration committed the bulk of its resources to winning the war against Nazi Germany in the European theater first. Here, he sits with the two men he hoped would have enough skill and drive to hold off and push back the Japanese threat, Fleet Admiral Chester W. Nimitz and General Douglas MacArthur. *Bettmann/Getty Images*

Major General Henry "Hap" Arnold would be the driving force behind the massive expansion of American air power during the war. He firmly believed the B-29 bomber program would deliver strategic victory, as well as place his command in prime position to dominate the country's future military decision-making. *Pictorial Press Ltd/Alamy Stock Photo*

The complexity of design and technology within the B-29 bomber was to many Americans, both civilian and military, almost like something from a Flash Gordon episode at the movies. That can be seen from the cockpit view of this B-29 "Wilde Hawg," based at the American Museum, RAF Duxford.
© *Iain MacGregor*

The vast amount of taxpayer's money that was allocated to the B-29 program was more than the cost of building the atomic bomb. Boeing's B-29 plant in Wichita was a vital cog in Hap Arnold's grand plan to quickly build a formidable fleet of bombers that would take the war to Japanese skies.
ART Collection/Alamy Stock Photo

Leader of the Office of Scientific Research and Development, hardheaded Vannevar Bush was President Roosevelt's trusted scientific adviser right from the start of the war who would eventually steer the United States to dominate the Allied nuclear program.
Everett Collection/Alamy Stock Photo

Sir James Chadwick had led the team that had first discovered the neutron, winning him the Nobel Prize in Physics in 1935. He was the choice by Churchill's government to lead Great Britain's delegation to the Manhattan Project.
Pictorial Press/Alamy Stock Photo

By the outbreak of war, the journalist John Hersey, like many young men, was keen to take up a commission in the United States Navy. He was talked down from such a move by his journalistic colleagues, who urged him to instead use his skills as a writer to report wherever American forces would be sent.
Granger Historical Picture Archive/Alamy Stock Photo

Perhaps as a way of excusing their disastrous early defeats, American and Allied propaganda initially eulogized the superhuman ability of the Japanese soldier. This would soon turn to vilification, bordering on outright racism, as the government sought to condition the country to support an all-out war in the Pacific.
Pictures from History/Getty Images

The battle between United States naval and marine forces and Imperial Japan on Guadalcanal in the Solomon Islands from late 1942 to the summer of 1943 ended in a pivotal victory for the Allies. Combined with the victory at Midway, it brought Japanese expansion in the southern Pacific to a juddering halt.
Historical/Getty Images

On April 20, 1943, General Leslie Groves of the US Army Corps of Engineers agreed for the University of California to operate the Manhattan Project's secret nuclear weapons laboratory. Robert J. Oppenheimer chose Los Alamos, a nondescript site in New Mexico.
John Dambik/Alamy Stock Photo

John Hersey covered the Allied landings on Sicily throughout the summer of 1943 and then the subsequent invasion of Italian mainland for *Time* magazine. He flew with the USAAF crew of a B-26 Marauder bomber in the first American raid on Rome.
Bettmann/Getty Images

The hundreds of scientists, technicians, and engineers that came to work at Los Alamos also brought their wives and children, requiring the need for better housing and facilities, such as shops, schools, libraries, theaters, and places of worship.
Bettmann/Getty Images

Chapter Thirteen

WELCOME TO "LEFT OVER"

Welcome to "Leftover Field"
Bob Hope[1]

Tibbets was no stranger to Wendover Field. Since its conception in the 1930s, the base and bombing and gunnery ranges close by had been getting larger and more complex since the beginning of the war with Japan. Close to the small community of one hundred–plus residents that bore its name, one didn't come here for anything else other than to learn to fly Air Corps fighter planes and bombers. Activated fully in April 1942, over a thousand aircrews who would fly the B-17 Flying Fortress and B-24 Liberator had earned their wings here.[2] After they had passed through by 1944, it was the turn of P-47 pilots of the Seventy-Second Fighter Wing to test their bomb-aiming skills on the nearby Bonneville Salt Flats. The rapid expansion of new housing and facilities had begun in late 1943, and by the time the 393rd arrived to take up residence, the air base measured 1.8 million acres.

When the officers and men of the 393rd Heavy Bombardment Squadron finally arrived at their windswept, barren new base in Wendover, they were greeted by high barbed-wire fencing, heavily armed military police, and a large white sign Tibbets had ordered erected at the entrance. Its black capital letters warned visitors:

WHAT YOU HEAR HERE
WHAT YOU SEE HERE

WHEN YOU LEAVE HERE
LET IT STAY HERE

Most men in the unit were perplexed at even being in Utah. They had expected to be sent oversees for combat in the Pacific. Here they were taking in their surroundings, reminiscent of Site Y at Los Alamos, freshly painted crew huts and larger hangars, some unapproachable, with signs warning: RESTRICTED AREA, or even more secretive: TECH AREA "C" MOST RESTRICTED. Many would never know the secret. Their commanding officer, Lieutenant Colonel Thomas Classen, a combat veteran, was now to run the day-to-day business of the base, but everyone knew it would be Colonel Tibbets who would be directing the new squadron.

Within a few days, there was yet another surprise, possibly to Tibbets, too. A party of thirty military officers under the command of Major William Uanna arrived at Wendover, sent by General Groves, to act as a further layer of security on behalf of the Manhattan Project supremo. Their role was to check and weed out any pilot, crewman, or ground staff of Tibbets's command who broke the rules Uanna set in place. Naturally, men of the 509th would refer to the agents as "the Creeps," with Uanna being "The Creep." Over the coming months, men of the 393rd and other squadrons that would make up the 509th Composite Group who fell afoul of this code would find themselves dispatched forthwith, either to another unit hundreds of miles away or to military jail. Many men fell for stings, as Uanna's agents had them voluntarily give classified information about their units, location, or simply who they were, whether getting drunk in the bars of Salt Lake City or farther afield when they were on their way home on leave. Secrecy for Uanna was everything. Discipline and adherence to training, Tibbets believed, were key.

The address he gave the 393rd typified the man:

"I've looked at you. You have looked at me. I'm not going to be stuck with all of you. But those of you whom remain are going to be stuck with me. You have been brought here to work on a very special mission which could end the war. Don't ask what your job is. That is a sure-fire way to be transferred out. Don't ask any questions from anybody not directly involved in what we will be doing. Do exactly what you are told, and you will get along fine. I know some of you are curious about all the security. Stop being so curious. This is part of the preparation of what is to come.

"Nobody will be allowed into a fenced-off area without a pass. Lose that pass and you face a court-martial. Never mention this base to anybody. That means your wives, girls, sisters, family.

"It's not going to be easy for any of us. But we will succeed by working together."

Catching them by surprise, he ended his speech by announcing a two-week furlough.[3] The work would soon begin. Other formations now arrived to support the 393rd, responsible for flying men and matériel in and out. The 390th Air Service Group acted as the basic support unit for the entire 509th. The 1027th Air Materiel Squadron provided quarters, rations, medical care, postal service, and other functions. The 320th Carrier Squadron and the 603rd Air Engineering Squadron worked exclusively on Tibbets's B-29s. They could even send bombers back to the plants for modifications if necessary.

Finally, and most secretive, was the First Ordnance Squadron. The self-contained unit was led by Captain William Parsons. From the look of them, Tibbets's men guessed, they were not military. They were technicians belonging to "Project Alberta," formed that March, consisting of fifty-one personnel recruited from the US Army, Navy, and civilians attached to the Manhattan Project. Under Parsons's supervision, his team would set up the facilities both at Wendover and in the Pacific once they were operational, to collect, store, and then assemble the components to build and arm the atomic bombs from Los Alamos. Their base at Wendover was behind TECH AREA "C" MOST RESTRICTED. Even though many of the civilian personnel kept to themselves, confusion about their identity extended even to Lucy Tibbets herself, who was by now looking after two children on the air base. Tibbets came home one day to find an eminent PhD physicist trying to fix the plumbing in the toilet. He hadn't wanted to reveal who he was to Lucy Tibbets, who had believed his repair man cover story.

Preparing a unit to successfully drop the bomb was one thing, but General Groves always knew that Tibbets and some of his key officers would need to be brought into the inner workings of the Manhattan Project to deal directly with Oppenheimer's teams at Site "Y"—Los Alamos. In September, Colonel Lansdale brought Tibbets and Lieutenant Jacob Beser, his radar specialist. J. Robert Oppenheimer himself conducted a personal tour of the facilities for the airmen. Tibbets felt he had been given "a better scientific education than all my years at school."

Oppenheimer wanted to understand the complexities and potential dangers Tibbets's crew would face once their mission had begun. Tibbets outlined the typical issues when on a bombing mission that he had seen himself over Europe with the Eighth Air Force two years before. The bomb payload, in this case, the one bomb, could jam in the new attachment mechanism that would be fitted into the B-29's bay. Without batting an eye, Tibbets stated matter-of-factly that a faulty mechanism could detonate the device on takeoff or in midflight. Oppenheimer was confident that such a risk could be eliminated if his team's design and construction were to the standard he expected.

Sitting back in his chair, Tibbets believed Oppenheimer was mulling over what he had just said. Instead, as if he had won an internal argument, he brought his chair back onto all four legs and stared at the group leader:

"Colonel, your biggest problem may be after the bomb has left your aircraft. The shock waves from the detonation could crush your plane. I am afraid that I can give you no guarantee that you will survive."

This would be the ongoing discussion between Tibbets, his senior crew whom he brought into the debate, and the many scientists he would encounter on his visits to Los Alamos over the coming weeks. Tibbets's first impression of an elite group of boffins he had nothing in common with was soon changed by men and women he respected and found common ground with to discuss a variety of subjects. More and more, Tibbets's time on the base was being limited by extended flights to Washington to update General Groves personally about the progress of the 509th, and time spent at Los Alamos to provide his opinion to Oppenheimer's team on how to solve a list of mechanical and performance issues with the bomb and its storage in the new B-29. The strain on his marriage, though evident, was shelved for resolving later. For now, Captain Parsons had a surprise in store for him.

Though he was wary of Uanna and his "Creeps," Tibbets had grown to like and respect Captain Parsons. He realized the influence the naval officer had within the hierarchy of the Manhattan Project once he saw how quickly serious issues that he brought to him were resolved. The biggest one was the plane itself. The original batch of B-29s his crews had been using were worn-out. The maintenance crews were overworked keeping them airworthy for the daily bombing practices at thirty thousand feet above the test bed of the Salton Sea. Much as Tibbets was driving the crews to excellence, a toll was being exacted on the aircraft. They needed replacing. Once Parsons knew of the problem in October, within days Tibbets was ordered to travel to the Glenn L. Martin bomber plant in Omaha, Nebraska, which was seen as one of the best producers of the B-29.

All fifteen new bombers would match the specifications Tibbets had said were necessary to take them into combat: Their armor plate and gun turrets were removed, except the two tail guns, saving several thousand pounds of built-in weight. Perhaps in answer to the fears Oppenheimer had expressed about detonation before dropping the bomb, new pneumatic bomb bay doors had been fitted, and a weaponeer station with atomic bomb monitoring instruments. Most importantly, the new bombers were to get the new fuel-injected Wright engine, with the revolutionary Curtis Electric reversible-pitch propellers. Both additions improved the Superfortress's performance, especially at high altitude, where they would be operating over Japan. It would be called the Silverplate series. Tibbets's own plane had been guaranteed by the plant foreman when he was showing him around. Pointing to model #86292, he had advised him, "Trust me, that's the one you want. It was built midweek, not on a Monday." What he meant was that the team assembling it would have been halfway into their weekly shift and therefore giving it their full attention.[4]

From April through to the end of May, the war won in Europe and news of the US Marines' victory at Iwo Jima in the Pacific, there had been a series of bad news, delays, and endless debates at Wendover. The men of the 509th were growing stale in the deserts of Utah. The relentless training schedule Tibbets had imposed upon them and still not having a date confirmed for active service overseas were now affecting their morale. Tibbets felt it, too. While they could let off steam in the bars of nearby Salt Lake City, he was in constant meetings with the boffins at Los Alamos, listening to their endless concerns about the bomb, the delays in testing, and new instructions on how his pilots should fly the bombing runs to drop the thing. Some of Oppenheimer's team were pessimistic about the chances of the gun mechanism even detonating the uranium device, and even if it did, about his crew's chances of survival.

Captain Parsons had already been dispatched by General Groves to find a suitable base for the 509th in the Marianas. Oppenheimer's team had informed Groves that the gun-type firing mechanism was ready for the uranium bomb, but a more sophisticated implosion mechanism was needed for the plutonium bomb, which would be tested in July. All being well, both bomb types would be ready for use the following month. Yet here he was, still kicking his heels in Utah, despite the intense training he had ordered his crews to undertake flying around the seas of Cuba. He knew the navigators needed experience flying over long stretches of open water if they intended to fly to Japan. In six weeks, that had been achieved, and the men were back at base. More and more scientists from Los Alamos were coming and going, with more requests and more problems to fix. He felt they were happiest trying to find problems with the device rather than having the confidence to test it.

Motivated by frustration and the fear his unit's logistical supplies would take weeks to get to Tinian, even if the planes could fly there in three days, Tibbets gambled. Without notifying anyone in the chain of command, he transmitted the code word Silverplate to Air Force Command in Washington, telling them the 509th was ready to go to war. Now his phone was ringing off the hook, and Tibbets knew who the caller would be. Groves ordered him immediately to the Pentagon.

"When I walked into his office, he kept me standing at attention while he gave me a thorough chewing-out, complete with profanity. He said my unilateral decision bordered on insubordination. Before he was through, I began to see myself as the oldest second lieutenant in the Air Corps, ferrying worn-out airplanes back from the war zones."[5]

The dressing-down suddenly halted.

"He gave me a big smile, and said: 'Goddammit, you've got us moving! Now they can't stop us!' He was tickled to death I had done it. Without my planes there was no way the scientists could keep tinkering with their toy."[6]

Tibbets got on a flight back to Wendover. The 509th was officially on their way to war.

Part IV

A WHIRLWIND IS COMING

Chapter Fourteen

A CHANGING OF THE GUARD

You've got to kill people and when you kill
enough of them, they stop fighting.
MAJOR GENERAL CURTIS LEMAY

The strategic bombing of the Home Islands by the United States Army Air Force was a uniquely ambitious plan. It would arguably become the most discussed and contested aerial campaign of World War II. The dropping of the atomic bombs would end the war, but was the changing of American air strategy against Japan worth it? It posed many issues for the American strategists. Geographically, from the Central Pacific theater, the Home Islands were protected by distance—at least seventeen hundred miles of ocean lay between any Allied air base and the Japanese mainland. From the Marianas Islands, it was approximately sixteen hundred miles to Hiroshima.

Since their resounding victory at Midway in June 1942 and the securing of the sea-lanes to Australia, the United States Navy had been retooled by the end of 1943 for the sole purpose of crossing this vast expanse to invade Japan. An enormous, self-sufficient fleet had been built, armed, and launched against the Japanese Empire. To increase the tempo of American naval operations, the single force would have alternative unit names to signify separate task forces. Therefore, the same actual fighting force had two commanders and planning teams, who would be rotated from active duty back to fleet headquarters with Nimitz. Task Force 38 would be commanded by Admiral Halsey and his team, then replaced by Admiral Raymond A.

Spruance and his own command structure, whereby it would become Task Force 58. The core of the fleet, whatever its call sign, was airpower; fourteen Essex-class carriers saw action during the war, plus the nine Independence-class light carriers, each capable of embarking over a hundred aircraft. The task force was protected by screens of battleships, cruisers, and destroyers and supplied by a naval conveyor belt that stretched thousands of miles back to the American West Coast.

For the Japanese, the following fifteen months had resulted in defeats at Guadalcanal, the Solomon Islands, and New Guinea, with the Imperial Navy suffering calamitous losses in ships, carriers, aircraft, and crucially, experienced pilots. On April 18, 1943, Admiral Yamamoto, the architect of Pearl Harbor and commander of the Combined Fleet, was killed when his plane was tracked by US military intelligence and shot down by fighters over Bougainville Island.[1] At the Imperial Court, the emperor expressed the fear that the momentum of the Pacific war had swung in the enemy's favor. Might they lose? Two key meetings brought this fear closer to home.

Between August 14 and 24, 1943, Roosevelt and Churchill and the combined chiefs of staff met in Quebec City, Canada, to formulate and agree on the next phase in the Allies' grand strategy against the Axis Powers. Within this framework of meetings, Hap Arnold showcased his "Air Plan for the Defeat of Japan." The aerial campaign would systematically destroy Japanese infrastructure. Arnold had envisaged four independent commands of B-29s, operating from China, the Marianas, the Philippines, and Shemya Island in the Aleutians. In the end, he designated two new combat commands: XX Bomber Command, sited in China, and XXI Bomber Command, based in the Marianas. As we shall see, his strategy to use them would evolve as the bombing campaign unfolded over the Home Islands and the fighting intensified in the Pacific.

Thousands of miles away from Quebec, on September 30, 1943, Hirohito's Imperial Command in Tokyo issued their own strategy to counter the Allies' progression in the Pacific: the "Absolute Zone of National Defense" policy. Japanese forces would coordinate their strategies to hold the line from Western New Guinea to the Marianas Islands in preparation for a decisive battle in the summer of 1944 that might force the enemy to accept a negotiated settlement. The Americans and the Allies had other ideas.

In a two-pronged advance, Admiral William Halsey's forces sprang from Guadalcanal and progressed up the Solomon chain as far as Bougainville. Within eight weeks, Allied forces had captured the bulk of New Britain Island—the Japanese garrison abandoned by its leaders to wither on the vine. Moving on from there, by mid-1944, the majority of New Guinea was occupied by US and Australian forces, forcing the Japanese to retreat farther westward to the Dutch East Indies. In October, studying a map of the region, it was clear the Imperial Command's strategy was now crumbling, made worse as General Douglas MacArthur's forces progressed through the Japanese-held Philippines. Though the fighting for the Philippines would be cataclysmic, the offensive was reinforced by the American victory at the Battle of Leyte Gulf. The losses inflicted by Halsey's ships and aircraft effectively neutralized the Japanese Imperial Navy as an effective sea and air threat.[2] Slowly, the net was closing in across the Pacific theater.

The first combat operations for the B-29 had begun on June 5, 1944, just before the US Marines stormed ashore on Saipan. India-based Superfortresses belonging to the USAAF General Hap Arnold's newly created Twentieth Air Force had their first experience of action. The mission statement of the Twentieth Air Force was destruction of Japan's industry and economy and to "undermine the morale of the Japanese people to the extent that their capacity for war is decisively weakened."[3]

The B-29s attacked Japanese facilities in and around the Makkasan Railway Depot, close to Bangkok. Unfortunately, the high-altitude precision strike proved a damp squib. The force of ninety-eight aircraft from the Fortieth Bomber Group took off from their bases in India, but cloud cover over the target had ruined any attempt at a precise strike. Their return journey was even worse, as five planes crashed landed back at base, and forty more made emergency landings at other airfields after running out of fuel. Luckily for the American crews, the Japanese defense had been nominal.

Japanese senior commanders had been forewarned of the B-29's existence. Early news reports in 1943 revealed the death of test pilot Eddie Allen and the crash of "a new Boeing bomber." Their intelligence services had managed to obtain valuable data and reports on this new long-range enemy bomber. Many details accurately outlined the B-29's composition: the plane had been built with mid-mounted wings, housed four engines, and weighed 120,000 pounds, capable of carrying a payload of twenty thousand pounds. Japanese spies had also reported the bomber's immense defensive armament of at least a dozen machine guns and the single 20mm cannon.

What created the biggest shock among Japanese aviation experts, however, was that the B-29 contained a pressurized cabin. They realized with some dread that their already weakened air defenses would face a plane capable of operating above thirty thousand feet. Their fighters, such as the nimble Ki-43 and the heavier Ki-44,[4] could not fly as high. The latter had been conceived before the war with no prior knowledge of the B-29, and thus operated below their level at twenty-seven thousand feet, though it had a faster rate of climb and dive than the Ki-43. From reports they received from their Axis partner, they understood the payloads the B-29 carried would inflict the kind of damage that the Royal Air Force had meted out on Germany for many months with their own heavy bomber fleet.

The Japanese got their first glimpse of the B-29 when aircraft landed in India in April 1944. Up to this point, Imperial Japanese Army Air Force (IJAAF) intelligence had failed to appreciate the enormity of the new enemy bomber for the air war to come. For the Japanese population, the lack of defensive preparations made by the IJAAF and Imperial Navy Air Force (IJNAF) to counter the B-29 would prove anemic at best and would soon turn desperate. In February 1944, the

JAAF issued a five-page pamphlet titled *Views on the Use of Crash Tactics in Aerial Protection of Vital Defence Areas—No.2.*

"We are now in a situation where we can demand nothing better than crash tactics which ensure the destruction of an enemy airplane at one fell swoop, thus striking terror into his heart and rendering his powerfully armed and well-equipped airplanes valueless by the sacrifice of one of our fighters."[5]

The American capture of the Marianas Islands would see a shift in the air strategy as the Army Air Force had attacked Japan from bases in India (Operation Matterhorn), but logistical concerns had driven Arnold to commit to operations solely from the Marianas. The B-29 needed paved runways of sufficient length, at least eight thousand feet, ideally more, to take off and land safely. With the capture of Saipan, Guam, and Tinian by the summer of 1944, engineers could now follow up to build them from scratch or replace existing Japanese runways. Across the next six months, air bases were built on all three islands: two on Saipan, four on Guam, and six on Tinian— all at least 8,500 feet in length. With these land-based aircraft carriers, the need for bases in China became negatable as supplying these islands was far easier from the United States and would pay huge dividends. The B-29 had been designed and built because of the loads in both fuel and bombs it could carry—twice as much as a B-17 with the same number of crew. With the bases built and the planes in place, the Marianas became the sole platform from which the B-29s would attack Japan. The issue would now be how to effectively use this deadly force. However much field commanders, such as General MacArthur and Lord Mountbatten, coveted the firepower the B-29s for their own specific areas of operations, the Twentieth was a strategic asset wholly belonging to Hap Arnold.

To him, this new weapon could not be corralled into spheres of influence; it was too important to the strategic war effort. The B-29's ability to strike far behind enemy lines, across thousands of miles, made such local tasks irrelevant. He had always envisaged that this new bombing force would bring about the very thing these commanders strove for on a local level: the defeat of Japan. Mindful of the effort and the billions of taxpayer dollars that had been spent on the program, Arnold lobbied aggressively in the corridors of Washington and the White House. He had battled to coalesce all B-29 units into the Twentieth Air Force, a single entity that he intended to command from Washington as he drove his subordinates relentlessly on the front line. That was the back story. It therefore made perfect sense he would insert his own commanders and micromanage their actions. Haywood Hansell was his choice to lead the premier XXI Bomber Command from the Marianas.

Hansell was the scion of a southern, aristocratic family, courteous to a fault, a lover of the classics, prone to singing when the moment took him, and a well-known raconteur with a raft of entertaining stories in the officers' club. He was a loyal staff officer, a true advocate of precision bombing as the future for the United States to win wars, and thought of as an excellent military strategist. Arnold valued his sharp mind, his belief in the tactics for the B-29, and had made him his chief of staff. The XXI Bomber Command had been activated in August 1944 and by October was set up on the Marianas, with Hansell flying in to take charge. Although he had served in Europe with the Eighth Air Force during the height of the air war over Germany, in Washington many questioned his ability to lead a successful campaign against Japan. It would play out like a Greek tragedy.

The precision attacks from high altitude on Japan failed from the beginning to hit their intended targets: the military production plants primarily based in the cities of Japan's coast, such as the Nakajima aircraft facility in Tokyo. If his fleets of B-29s could strike precisely from far above, safely out of range of antiaircraft fire and Japanese fighters, Hansell would shorten the war considerably. The issue was wind and weather. No American meteorologist had factored in the 125-mile-wide jet stream that sat above Japan, or the immense cloud coverage across the country that would allow only a few days a month of visibility to bomb from such a height.

In their debriefings back on the Marianas, pilots from the XXI would detail the vicious winds over the target, drastically increasing their speed if they flew with it or almost going backward if they flew into it. The former had them overshooting and their payloads landing many miles off target; the latter slowed them down and made them sitting ducks for enemy flak and fighters. Attempting to fly in the protection of a box formation was almost impossible, forcing pilots to fly in isolation and reducing the effectiveness of their payloads.

From below, and desperate to inflict damage on the enemy, the Japanese had formed special air-to-air ramming units called *Shinten Seiku Tai* ("Heaven-Shaking Air Superiority Units"). A unit contained four aircraft, each fighter shorn of its armor plating, gunsight, and radios, allowing them to fly quickly to gain height to engage the B-29s. These ramming units would become highly effective psychologically more than militarily. Mission after mission, from October to December 1944, Hansell repeated the same failure. And still, despite repeated requests for a change of tactics to fire raids, he would not contemplate shifting from his primary offensive tactic. Hansell remained committed to bombing from high altitude in daylight with high explosives—many operations still ending in failure and tempers fraying as Hansell questioned the ability of the wing commanders to come to grips with his way of aerial warfare. A remedy was required if XXI Bomber Command was to maintain its operational independence and be the service to deliver victory over the enemy.

Prone to impatience, and always the ruthless pragmatist, having watched from afar over the past few months, the air chief's decision, once made, was brutally swift. From his home in Florida as he recuperated from his fifth heart attack, Arnold cast aside ties of friendship and loyalty, to make one of the most significant decisions of the Pacific war. On January 6, 1945, his Chief of Staff, Lauris Norstad, flew to Guam to relieve Hansell of command. In his place Arnold elevated the more dynamic Curtis E. LeMay into the hot seat. He was a man who displayed the track record to deliver the necessary successes Arnold craved and the White House demanded.[6]

Arnold gave no thought to Hansell's embarrassment at being replaced by a man he had commanded in Europe. LeMay was the opposite in background and temperament. From a blue-collar upbringing in the Midwest, he had also progressed through the Army Air Corps ranks but without the patronage that class and birth provided. He was a tough-talking, decisive, cigar-chomping, somewhat brutal strategist, but a fearless pilot and successful frontline commander. Ironically, the day before Hansell was replaced, his final operation against the Kawasaki engine and airframe complex at Akashi was hit by B-29s on the morning of January 19. Out of a force of seventy-eight bombers, sixty-two hit the target, inflicting significant damage on the assembly plants, a vindication, perhaps, of his tactics. He was gracious enough to remain in Guam for two weeks while he briefed LeMay on the issues the crews faced over Japan, though photographs of the two men taken by the press did not hide the pained look on the fired commander's face. He would take command of a training wing in the southwestern United States until the end of the war.

A new, more robust air campaign would begin. As LeMay quipped to the media, his new command would now "stop swatting at flies and instead go after the manure pile!" LeMay's much publicized successes with the Eighth Air Force in Europe preceded him. The change of command hit the men of the XXI like a bolt of thunder:

"Big news of the day! Major General Curtis LeMay has arrived on Guam and the rumor is that he will soon relive General Hansell as Commander of the XXI Bomber Command. His reputation preceded him. The word is that he issues orders to hit a target, regardless of the cost. That is something we haven't been doing, even though the cost has been high. He is only thirty-eight years old, youngest major general in the whole Army, but he proved his mettle in Europe with the Eighth Air Force, and lately, with the 58th Wing in India."[7]

LeMay was acutely aware of the pressure of the job he had taken on, though he still publicly appeared confident that he could deliver and did not wilt under the incessant, daily communications from Arnold. The sole focus of the ailing head of the US Army Air Force

(Arnold would suffer four heart attacks during the war) was the success of the B-29s he had bestowed upon LeMay. Unlike his predecessor, this new commander of the Twentieth was not prepared to sacrifice his career for moral scruples. When one studies the casualty lists his new tactics would inflict upon the Home Islands over the coming few months, one could argue he was right up there with any commander, on any side, for mass civilian killings in World War II. LeMay had already made his peace with the use of incendiaries.

Bombing of civilians had occurred in the war in Europe already, but it would be the U.S. Army Air Corps, and specifically how their policy on aerial bombing would evolve over the coming years, that would determine a shift in American policy toward targeting not just their enemy's military, but their towns, cities, and civilians for destruction. President Roosevelt, in 1939, had appealed to the European powers now at war not to resort to the "mass barbarism" of indiscriminate aerial bombing. Adolf Hitler had ignored such demands as the Luftwaffe laid waste to the Dutch city of Rotterdam in May 1940 in prelude to the Germans invading and conquering France, and subsequently the Blitz on British cities. As the Royal Air Force's leader Arthur Harris saw it, his bombing campaign on German workers' housing was legitimate: "The cities themselves were the targets, they were to Germany what ganglia are to a living body. If enough of them were destroyed, the body would succumb."[8]

As America and her allies strove to push back Imperial Japanese forces from the Pacific theater, in terms of weapons of choice to achieve this, nothing was off the table for discussion. Among them was an incendiary, the M-69, featuring jellied gasoline, and was given its notorious name from its two chemical ingredients: naphthenate and palminate—napalm.

The M-69 was a plain steel pipe, 510 mm in length, 76 mm in diameter, and weighing six pounds. Thirty-eight of them would make up one cluster-type bomb, which would release its load at an approximate height of two thousand feet. The deadly devices would then separately fall to the earth, guided by a cotton streamer to ensure the fuse was pointing downward. Once it landed, within seconds the fuse would ignite, causing an explosive reaction, and ejecting the napalm stream up to a radius of one hundred feet, sticky, burning globules attaching themselves to the loft beams of a house, or the floor of a bedroom or kitchen.

The United States military embraced the new weapon without any qualms as to its morality. Napalm was first deployed by General Patton's troops on the battlefields of Sicily in August 1943. The following October, American planes were dropping napalm bombs on German factories. Two months later, US Marines were using it in flamethrowers, finding it essential to flush out Japanese defenders hidden in caves on the small New Guinea island of Pilelo. Within weeks of the reports of its successful performance, air crews were improvising designs and constructing homemade napalm bombs using gasoline tanks, as commanders realized the enormous potential of its firepower.

In January 1943, the US military had only one facility creating napalm, but by year's end there would be nine, the substance being shipped in hermetically sealed packages of various sizes, depending on whether they were being shipped overseas to units or sent onward to armaments factories to go into incendiary bombs. Production soared as the war progressed, from five-hundred-thousand pounds in 1943 to twelve million by war's end.[9]

The cost to enemy civilian populations, as we shall see, was biblical. The indiscriminate use of napalm and other incendiaries by the United States and her allies would, on the back of the propaganda campaign already in place toward Japan, arguably pave the way to an acceptance of embracing whatever weapons could be brought to bear to win the war. "No matter how you slice it, you're going to kill an awful lot of civilians. Thousands and thousands," ominously declared General Curtis LeMay.[10]

The previous November, while running XX Bomber Command in the Chinese theater, LeMay's units came under threat from the Japanese offensive Operation Ichi-Go.[11] Chiang Kai-shek's National

Revolutionary Army was driven back from the provinces of south-eastern China (Henan, Hunan, and Guangxi), and by December Commanding General Shunroku Hata's Imperial forces in French Indochina had captured some of LeMay's air bases. To stem their momentum, on December 13, LeMay ordered his available B-29s to bomb the captured city of Hankou (modern-day Wuhan) with the new M-69 incendiary. The attack was a success, leaving Hankou burning for three days as LeMay's crews dropped over five hundred tons of incendiaries. The operation left a positive impression on him about the effectiveness of this new ordnance and the ability of the B-29 to deliver it in significant numbers. Hata would be promoted to field marshal (*Gensui*) for the limited successes Ichi-Go had brought Japan. As LeMay's bombers dropped their incendiaries on Hankou, Hata was already on his way to take command of the Second Army at Hiroshima.

There were bigger issues at play for the new commander of XXI Bomber Command. In early February 1945, Soviet mech-anized forces were on the border of eastern Prussia, while British and American armies pushed into western and southern Germany. Everywhere in occupied Europe, Adolf Hitler's forces were in re-treat. The same month, President Roosevelt had met with Churchill and Stalin at Yalta in the Russian Crimea to debate both Germany's fate and future strategy against Japan. Mindful of public alarm at the heavy casualties from the fighting in the Pacific and the failing air campaign, Roosevelt debated with the Soviet leader his commit-ment to entering the war against Japan. Though Stalin promised to attack as soon as the European war was settled, beneath the bonho-mie, within Roosevelt's own administration, a war of strategy raged over how best to bring Japan to defeat. The US Army, with Chief of Staff George Marshall the main lobbyist, promoted a land invasion of the Home Islands, despite the carnage of taking Iwo Jima. Admiral Nimitz promoted the US Navy's continued blockade that was starv-ing Japan of food and the imports of oil and minerals to keep its war industry functioning. Meanwhile, Hap Arnold's bombers continued their fruitless campaign, with his political and military opponents arguing for a reason to break the bomber fleet up for various operational uses.

Sizing up his new command and unsure of the best policy to follow, LeMay persisted with his predecessor's tactics but spent time putting his crews through intense training as well as instilling more discipline in their commanders. His first operations repeated previous precision raids. The XXI crews once again flew at high altitudes and again experienced an aircraft difficult to control in the conditions. Multiple raids on the Nakajima plant from January through the beginning of March repeated the previous failures.[12] But there was a slight ray of light. An incendiary attack on the capital the month before on February 25, of lesser scale, had achieved some success.[13] Still wary of outright mass raids, LeMay again reverted to a high-altitude precision strike on March 4. It failed. His frustration at his lack of options broke into the open as he lambasted his crews: "This outfit has been getting a lot of publicity without having accomplished a hell of a lot in bombing results!"

Time was ticking as Major General William Norstad (the nemesis of Colonel Tibbets from his time spent in Algiers), sitting in Twentieth Air Force headquarters in Washington, pressed him on Arnold's behalf for results. As military historian Professor Tami Davis Biddle concludes:

"I have read the correspondence between LeMay and Hap Arnold between 1944 and 1945, and I've never seen anything like it. I've never seen a field commander placed under so much pressure by someone back in the Chateau, as it were. LeMay really understands he's been told to make this airplane justify itself. I think it was a mark of desperation, because the airplane was not able to perform under Haywood Hansell, the precision role that everyone hoped it would perform, and attack industry. This was just an expedient that LeMay came up with."[14]

Norstad was now the eyes and ears for the recuperating head of the Army Air Force and had played a significant role in Hansell's downfall. With the XX Bomber Command joining him in the Marianas in early March, LeMay knew he now commanded the most powerful bomber force of the war. Politically, the success of the Twentieth would energize Arnold's long-term objective to place his new bomber command into a postwar reorganization of the military. He envisaged an independent air force, but right now, the man who had overseen and relentlessly driven the B-29 program, at a cost of billions of dollars, needed results to prove its worth to Congress.

LeMay was savvy enough to understand the reality of his plight and buy into Norstad's embrace of the mass use of incendiaries to destroy Japan's ability to continue the fight. Deliver success or suffer Hansell's fate. At this point, sitting in his headquarters in Guam, slowly smoking his cigar, LeMay spent the evening mulling his next move. He recalled the conversation he'd had with Colonel Paul Tibbets at a barbecue held at the home of the commander of the B-29 flying school in Grand Island, Nebraska. Tibbets had walked LeMay through the attributes, good and bad, of the new bomber. It had left LeMay puzzled as how best to use it in the Pacific theater if he followed Tibbets's conclusion that it wasn't able to fly in formation at high altitude. Tibbets gave his usual forthright opinion: "I'd load the B-29s with firebombs for low altitude attacks of the kind the British employed against Germany. . . . All you need to do is area bomb these [Japanese] cities."

Finally, as dawn broke on March 6, he made the mental leap.[15]

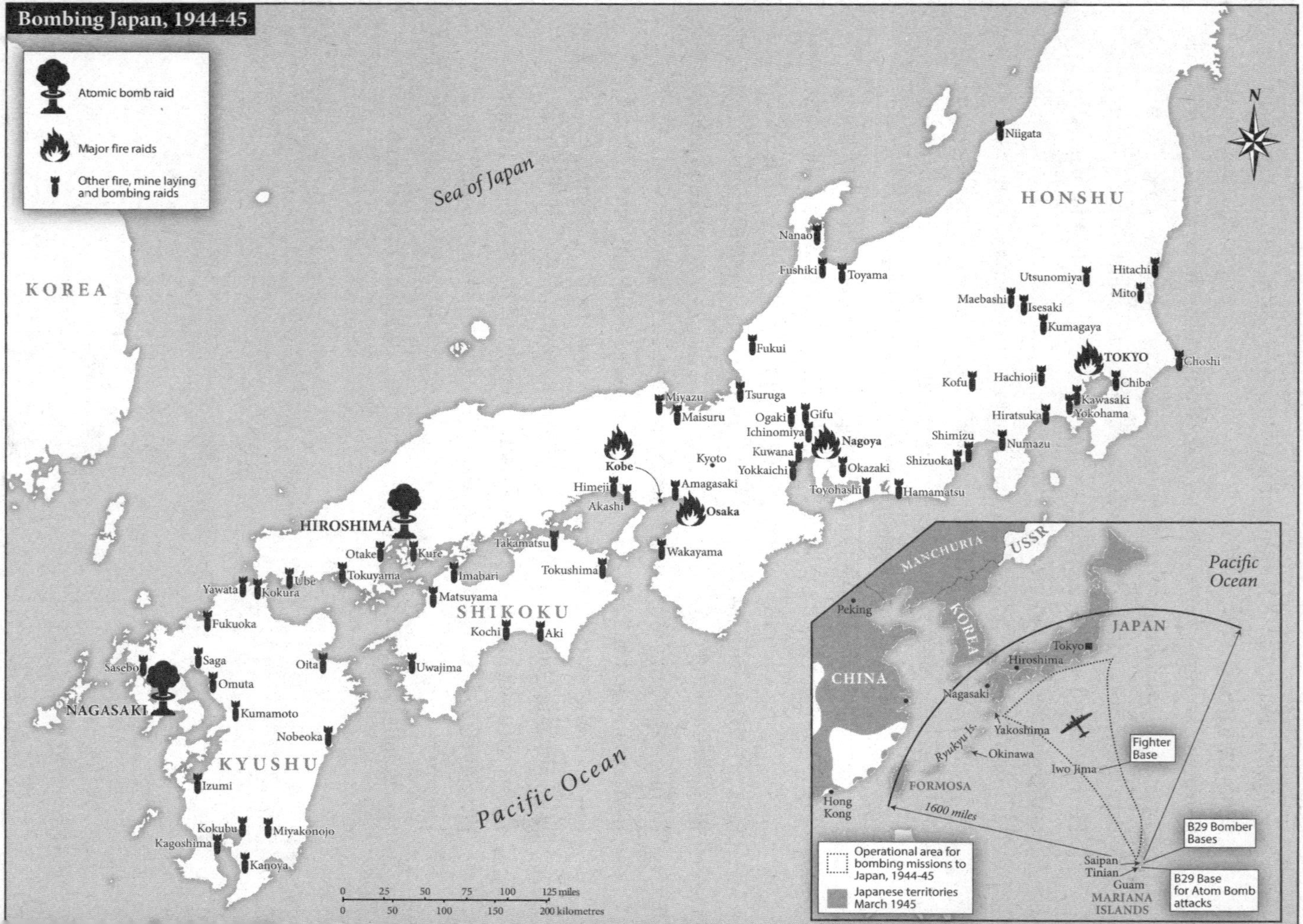

Bombing Japan, 1944-45
Atomic bomb raid
Major fire raids
Other fire, mine laying and bombing raids
Sea of Japan
KOREA
HONSHU
SHIKOKU
KYUSHU
Pacific Ocean
N
Niigata
Nanao
Fushiki
Toyama
Utsunomiya
Hitachi
Mito
Maebashi
Isesaki
Kumagaya
Fukui
TOKYO
Choshi
Kofu
Hachioji
Chiba
Kawasaki
Yokohama
Hiratsuka
Miyazu
Maisuru
Tsuruga
Ogaki
Gifu
Ichinomiya
Nagoya
Kuwana
Yokkaichi
Okazaki
Toyohashi
Hamamatsu
Shimizu
Shizuoka
Numazu
Kyoto
Kobe
Himeji
Akashi
Amagasaki
Osaka
Wakayama
HIROSHIMA
Otake
Kure
Tokuyama
Ube
Yawata
Kokura
Imabari
Matsuyama
Takamatsu
Tokushima
Kochi
Aki
Uwajima
Fukuoka
Saga
Sasebo
Omuta
Oita
NAGASAKI
Kumamoto
Nobeoka
Izumi
Kokubu
Miyakonojo
Kagoshima
Kanoya
0 25 50 75 100 125 miles
0 50 100 150 200 kilometres
MANCHURIA
USSR
Peking
KOREA
CHINA
JAPAN
Pacific Ocean
Tokyo
Hiroshima
Nagasaki
Yakoshima
Ryukyu Is.
Okinawa
Iwo Jima
Fighter Base
FORMOSA
Hong Kong
1600 miles
B29 Bomber Bases
Saipan
Tinian
Guam
MARIANA ISLANDS
B29 Base for Atom Bomb attacks
Operational area for bombing missions to Japan, 1944-45
Japanese territories March 1945

Chapter Fifteen

CROSSING THE RUBICON:
THE FIREBOMBING OF TOKYO

Properly kindled, Japanese cities will
burn like autumn leaves.[1]

TIME MAGAZINE

The straitjacket had been thrown away. The details for Operation Meetinghouse, Field Order No. 43, was issued on March 7 to the Twentieth Air Force. LeMay's plan was like the man himself: simple, brutal, but if successful, hugely effective. His crews would fly low and avoid the disruption caused by the jet stream. To afford some protection from Japanese air defenses, they would go in at night, give the enemy's radar stations little time to react, and be protected from Japanese interceptors. It was radical, but the leap of imagination, or the shelving of moral concern, finally had him order a full-scale incendiary attack on Tokyo. He concluded, as too few B-29s had been sent in before and they had flown too high, that the spread of bombs had not created a conflagration. He had ordered twelve B-29s to commit a test run at low level and bomb a small island off Saipan; it worked. This was followed up by more B-29 flights toward Tokyo for reconnaissance, at low-level altitudes, to identify enemy radar points that could be avoided for the coming operation.

With so many aircraft marked for the mission, the armada would take off on a timetable: squadrons from Guam, then Saipan, and finally Tinian, the wings assembling at different altitudes to avoid any midair collisions. They would be guided to the target by four specially fitted-out B-29s taking off twenty-five minutes prior to the armada to broadcast a homing signal. Twelve B-29s from each wing would serve as pathfinders ahead of the main assault, dropping the heavier M-47 gasoline gel bombs at one-hundred-foot intervals, to penetrate buildings' roofs and instantaneously start fires, marking the target. The streams would then follow with their cargos of napalm-filled M-69s set to detonate at two thousand feet and release the flame-packed bomblets to saturate the target zone.

The shoreline running along Tokyo Bay was home to hundreds of jetties, wharfs, and warehouses. The docks supported a supply chain that brought in 580 million tons of shipping per month. The downtown district, where the city's commercial center was, was also the country's banking hub. Japan's "shadow" factories, the thousands of workshops that maintained the war effort on a lower level, employing fifty people or less. Tokyo was the embodiment of this. Workers produced almost all Japan's radio equipment, three-quarters of its telephone parts, and under half of its motor vehicles.[2] Destroy them, LeMay knew, and you cripple the country's output. You also kill and displace the many tens of thousands of civilians living in and around them, in densely packed neighborhoods of housing constructed of perfect kindling materials—as the tests at Dugway Proving Ground in Utah the year before had highlighted.

Tokyo was rectangular shaped, roughly three miles east to west and four miles north to south, with the Sumida River running diagonally through it. In what would be designated "Zone I," many downtown neighborhoods LeMay's bombers would attack with firebombs were primarily residential, with a population density five times higher than most American cities. They were crisscrossed by tight alleyways, few bomb shelters, and inadequate firefighting centers. Approximately 1.1 million people lived in the target area of Zone I, 15 percent of the city's total population.

The plan was now outlined to the hundreds of aircrews sitting in briefing rooms in Guam, Saipan, and Tinian. Flight engineer Second

Lieutenant Chester Williams, of Combat Crew No. 25, 878th Squadron, 499th Bombardment Group, Seventy-Third Wing, noted in his diary afterward, "The briefing at eight o'clock this morning brought shocking, but not totally unexpected news. We will bomb Tokyo tonight. The target—a designated urban area in the north-eastern section of the city. The tactics to be used on this LeMay-ordered mission are so drastically different from the past raids that most of us sat in stunned in disbelief as the briefing progressed."[3]

These new tactics were music to the ears of Major General Norstad, who touched down in Guam the day before the operation. He was a political animal, a fan of incendiaries, and had fired Hansell to promote LeMay without compunction. He listened intently as his man briefed him on Operation Meetinghouse. Both men were aware of the hierarchy. It was unspoken, but LeMay knew if this operation went south, the consequences fell squarely on his shoulders. LeMay now outranked Norstad and didn't know or trust him. If Arnold approved of the operation, well, that kept him in his job, so he went through the motions of detailing the attack to Norstad.[4] The chief of staff listened and then alerted his public relations officer in Washington to prepare for "[w]hat may be an outstanding show."[5] He now had a commander who sang from the same hymn sheet.

The flights would come in between five and just over ten thousand feet and would not go in a tight box formation, as they did at high altitude, but rather as individuals at varying heights to confuse Japanese defenses. As one pilot of the 314th Wing later recalled, the planes had a plan to fly in "between 10,500 and maybe 11,500 feet. . . . We go over and we are separated only by a few minutes, only by five hundred feet. In other words, aircraft one will go at 11,000 feet. Aircraft two is at 11,500 feet, [and] two minutes behind, or three minutes behind. Aircraft three is at 10,500 feet. So that separates them both at altitude and gives them some distance. Airspeed is all the same. They all have to be at the same airspeed going across on their mission. To set it off, [there will be] at least three or five B-29's [going in] in at low altitude . . . [to] put their bombs on the strategic outer limits of the city and they go clockwise so the next aircraft that comes through at 11,000, he sees those fires already started by the spotting aircraft. All they do is then drop their bombs just short of those fires. They just keep adding, and adding, and adding until the whole city has been engulfed."[6]

Their antiaircraft shells were fused to explode at higher altitudes, thus buying time for the first few waves to hit the city while Japanese gunners recalibrated. Crucially, the enemy's early-warning radar would struggle to pick up the approaching fleet coming in so low. They would have the element of surprise. Intelligence reports convinced LeMay that enemy aircraft defenses were weak, still rebuilding from the air battles with American naval carrier forces the previous month. Still, the pressure was getting to LeMay, as he confided to an aide: "If we lose, we'll be tried as war criminals."

All measures had been taken to limit excess weight, and each plane's primary guns, bar the tail gunner, had been removed. Flying at low altitude would also save on fuel. All this made more room for more incendiaries—in this operation, LeMay's planes would be carrying twice their usual bombload. They would follow preplanned routes into the city, heading for the primary aiming point, a railway bridge spanning the Sumida River. The B-29s would fly lights out with the crews donning red goggles to protect their eyes from the expected glare of fires and searchlights. Walking out of the briefing for his Twenty-Ninth Bomb Group flying out of Guam, Captain Gordon B. Robertson Jr. recorded:

"We were dumbfounded and wondered if Bomber Command had gone crazy. The tactics to be used on this mission were a complete departure from the design objectives of the airplane and, to us, tantamount to a suicide strike."[7]

As the evening approached, crews from the three wings from Guam, Saipan, and Tinian began to arrive at their flight lines in trucks, drinking coffee and eating doughnuts distributed by the Red Cross vans parked nearby. Bomber pilots checked any issues with their planes with the ground crew before some of the crew embarked

and others assisted the ground staff with "pulling down" the enormous fifteen-foot props (it would take two men per prop) to clear out
any excess oil from the lower cylinders. A constant fear of engine fire
was foremost in their minds. Within minutes all four Wright engines
would be roaring, the noise deafening as each plane took its place in
the takeoff queue. The anticipation soon turned to controlled fear as
the giant plane, loaded this time with highly inflammable ordnance
as well as fuel, roared off into the darkness, slowly picking up speed
and using every inch of the 8,500-foot runway to finally leave the
ground. A green light flashed from the belly of the plane to tell the
next bomber to commence its takeoff.[8]

All 325 B-29s were airborne by 7:17 p.m. local time. Only once
they were free above the ocean did the crew begin to relax, set the
cabin pressure, and arm the payload of incendiaries.

LeMay had instructed that the best pilots, navigators, and bom-
bardiers be in the first wave to ensure the primary target within
Zone I—Asakusa district—was set alight for the following waves to
use as a homing beacon. Now, 279 bombers, led by Brigadier General Thomas S. Power, would attack Tokyo in echelon over the next
few hours. Conditions were good with sporadic cloud cover, and the
winds slightly below twenty miles per hour. They would pick up as
the night continued. Pilot Chester Williams, flying with the 499th
Bombardment Group of the Seventy-Third Wing could make out
the target glowing orange and red in the distance, "Our assigned
altitude was 7,000 feet and our take-off time positioned us in about
the middle of the strike force."[9]

Thirteen-year-old schoolgirl Toshiko Kameya had known Japan
only at war. She was born the year Japan invaded Manchuria in 1931,
and by the time of the Second Sino-Japanese war, her war work was
a key part of her schooling, she and her classmates making "comfort
bags" for Imperial troops fighting overseas.[10] By the fourth grade,
Japan had attacked Pearl Harbor. Within two years her sixteen-year-
old brother, the oldest of eight children, volunteered for military
service. Even though their parents had forbidden it, Toshiko assisted

with his paperwork. She had been sent out of Tokyo in 1943 to live with relatives in the countryside but had relocated to the capital by the summer of 1944. Despite attending National High School, the military authorities had constructed a munitions factory on the site, and along with hundreds of others, Toshiko spent hours polishing shell casings.

Her father, Kameji, was a manager for a nearby cement company, so the family's air raid shelter in their yard was relatively sturdy, though not bombproof. When Hansell's planes attacked from on high, like other families, Toshiko's ran for protection into the shelter they had built in their small yard.

Her mother, Asai, had taken a job working in a local miso factory—Suehiro Miso, which produced miso soup and rice—that overlooked the embankment by the Onagi River. With rationing becoming tighter, it made sense to work there as the whole family could get subsidized meals: "I would carry my youngest brother on my back and go to the diner to give him a baby-breakfast, and my mother's coworkers would say to me, 'Go ahead and eat a lot.' The leftovers were made into *onigiri* [rice balls] and brought back home. On Saturdays and Sundays, my mother worked there part-time, and on Saturday afternoons and Sundays, older kids like me would take care of the little ones."[11]

The family ate there frequently, to the point where all the children had put on weight. While Toshiko seemed healthy, she suffered from low blood pressure, making her sluggish and nauseous when she first woke up from her sleep. This ailment would save her life later that night.

"When the first wave of B-29s came across the city, I was awoken by my mother. The air raid seemed to be more intense than anything that we had suffered before, and she told me we should all go quickly to the area's designated shelter, her miso distribution store, which could shelter many hundreds of people. Because it was next to the Onagi River, it would offer protection if the heat became too great. We would be close to water."

The American pathfinders had done their job, dropping their

M-47 incendiaries to mark a flaming, giant X across Toshiko's southern district, which was why the family had awoken. By the time Chester Williams was over the target, the west side of the Sumida River was beginning to light up as the incendiaries struck. Soon, large fires could be seen around the city's central railway station. Fire teams were stretched as the multiple fires soon became uncontrollable and wind began to pick up. All Zone I was systematically being hit. As a pathfinder, whose payload had marked out the target for the oncoming squadrons of the 313th Wing, Lieutenant Leonard Carpi was one of the youngest pilots flying out of Tinian. He now watched the growing firestorm without any regret: "Our job was not to kill people, but to stop them from doing their job of supporting the war. Every time we turned [over a target] I thought of those people in the bottom of Pearl Harbor in the [USS] *Arizona*.[12] I thought of them every time."[13]

Within thirty minutes, fresh waves of B-29s arrived to drop their five-hundred-pound clusters of M-69 bombs. Across downtown Tokyo, people scrambled from their beds and took to their shelters or ran to join their fire associations. Toshiko, despite being hurriedly shaken awake, was not for moving:

"I told my mother I didn't care if I was going to die, so I would just stay in bed. No matter how much my mother tried to wake me up, it didn't help. So, she finally gave up and took my other siblings to her miso shop on Mitsume Street. As they were walking out the front door, my mother shouted above the noise, 'What's with the air raid sirens going off right now, and what is the military doing?' My mother was a rather outspoken person, so she left us saying such words. That was the last time I heard her voice."[14]

Pilot Chester Williams struggled to maintain his plane's altitude as the unrelenting heat from the fires created tremendously strong thermal air waves, which could cause a bomber to be bounced up by over two thousand feet in seconds: "As we closed on Tokyo, we looked upon the ghastly scene out before us. Giant searchlights scanned the sky trying to pick up the stream of Superfortresses enroute to their drop zone. It was then that we saw our first B-29 raiders since night-fall on the way up. To our right searchlights had picked up one of our planes and they locked on to it. Other lights immediately locked on and the B-29 glistened in the bright lights as if it were a ghost rider in the sky. We could see flak bursts around the plane, but it continued its path. Farther on, the fires had turned that section of the city into an inferno. Flames and debris were climbing several thousand feet and a dark cloud of smoke hurled upward to more than 20,000 feet.[15]

"Several times during the bomb run searchlights scanned across our nose and only the dark filtered glasses prevented the glare from blinding us. As the lights picked us up they would dart back trying to lock on. But evasive action . . . [meant] . . . they were never able to concentrate on us enough to give the anti-aircraft gunners below enough time to direct fire upon us.

"The whole area was lighted as if it were broad daylight when we entered the drop zone. The whole area changed to an eerie orange glow the closer we came to the inferno. I watched with amazement as the bombs from some of the planes struck the ground. On impact they resembled a lot of matches being struck, and within seconds the small flames integrated, becoming one big fire. . . . It was a great relief for us to exit the smoke, because the odor of burning flesh and debris was very nauseating."[16]

On the ground beneath them, Toshiko was awoken by her father, who had returned to the family home after making the rounds of his neighborhood association to issue the evacuation order to the community. He discovered his oldest daughter still in bed, despite the bedlam all around them:

"He shook me awake and shouted, 'Idiot, what are you doing, wake up! The whole area is on fire!' I scrambled to get dressed, and grabbing his hand, I rushed with him out of the house, and we ran towards the river. I could make out many figures in the shadows and smoke, all running along the streets. My father looked up and said, 'Is it raining?'

"I looked at the sky, and [despite the drone above] it was full of stars falling to earth—almost like fire flies. The starry sky was so beautiful in those days because of the light control system. I told him it wasn't raining."[17]

They continued on their way to find their family at the agreed meeting point in the miso factory close to Mitsume Street, which had been designated an evacuation shelter during air raids. It took them five minutes, but in that time the intensity of the lights falling to earth and the fires beginning to spread around grew. As they hurriedly walked along Mitsume Street, the sight that greeted them from the shelter was pandemonium. Hundreds of women, children, and the elderly were packed inside, with dozens waiting to get in, all trying to find shelter from the growing storm. Even though they were now by the river, the heat from the fires was incredible.

"The shelter was already packed. Many more than you would see if it was rush hour, and they wouldn't let us go inside. But we had left everything back at home on our futons soaked with water, so we had no luggage to bring in, so people made room for us, and we finally entered the doorway."

It was claustrophobic and getting hotter. And still more fiery lights dropped from the dark night sky, interspersed with the city's searchlights scanning the night sky for the "B-sans."[18]

Nineteen-year-old Second Lieutenant Donald W. Kearney was the navigator aboard the *Reamatroid*, belonging to the Sixth Bombardment Group, of the 313th Wing, flying out of Tinian. His wave had come in halfway through the operation. Inexperienced at flying so low amid the building flak and searchlights sweeping the orange sky, he recalled trying to quell his rising panic: "In this frightening situation, I had one real lucid thought; if we dropped the bombs right now and turned and fled, who would ever know the difference? With my map in front of me, I was the only one who really knew where we were—that the target was still several miles ahead."[19]

He looked out of the cabin widow, and even with his goggles on, a passing searchlight beam caught him square in the face. He instinctively ducked, as if scared of being identified: "All of my instincts said, 'Drop the bombs and get the hell out of here.' I wondered how many crews would take the easy way out and do just that. Never having been in such a mortally threatening situation before, I didn't know myself what I might do, so it was sort of a surprise to me when I rejected the temptation to drop the bombs short of the target. We were scared, but the bomb release went beautifully. We seemed to have exactly the right course, and we timed the drop precisely as prescribed."[20]

In the shelter, the situation was growing desperate as the fires spread and the wind they generated now took hold. Toshiko had been standing close to her father for thirty minutes. Neither of them had managed to see or hear anything from her mother and siblings. She held her father's hand tightly. After twenty to thirty minutes, there was a huge scream from the back of the building.

"I asked my father what happened, and he told me that the glass door at the back of the store had melted, and fire was now coming in. Then there was another huge scream from that direction, which caused people to panic. He shouted to me, 'If we stay here, we'll all die,' and he tried to go forward to open the door, but the fire wardens were blocking access to the door, saying, 'The front is on fire, too, and we'll all die if we go out there, so don't open it!'

"My father, however, argued with them and he forced it open and told everyone to get out."[21]

Dozens of people spilled out into the heat of the street. It was completely alien to the one Toshiko had walked down barely half an hour before. There were now flames spouting violently from every building in the vicinity, with great plumes of smoke bellowing into the air, with bright orange blobs, like volcanic lava, spread across the street. Along these streets she could see bodies lying motionless. From their sizes, they were both young and old. She was pushed to the ground as more people behind her started to escape from the shop. Many tripped over themselves as they stumbled out into the burning night, staggering in all directions. More and more of them headed across the road toward the river embankment. Some ran toward the nearby Otomibashi Bridge spanning the dark waters of the river below. It was winter and the water would be freezing cold, but with the firestorm building all around them, the waters would save them.

"As soon as I got out of the shelter, I was blown away by the strong wind, and the great swirl of flames in all directions—you couldn't remain standing up it was so strong. It resembled a sea of fire. My father got down on all fours and crawled right to the middle of the road. He shouted back that I should crawl toward him, which I did. My father thought we would be saved if we jumped into the river. The river was right in front of us, and there were many concrete buildings on the other side, such as the Takahashi Elementary School, a police station, and nearby it, a fire station. The tin sheets on the fire station's roof were ripped off in the strong gusts of wind and like wild kites flew in our direction. We couldn't reach the riverbank such was the intense heat and the size of the flames."[22]

Desperate to find safety as he and his daughter crouched in the middle of Mitsume Street, Toshiko's father picked up a fallen tin roof panel, scrambled over to her, and held it above their heads. "He tried to protect me from [the] flying debris and the flames, but my clothes still managed to catch fire. He patted my clothes with his hands trying to put out the burning cloth with his hands at first, but then he stopped doing anything, and I thought he was overcome with the heat.

"But he suddenly shouted, 'This way!' and pulled me along with him toward a military factory standing diagonally across the street which as yet wasn't ablaze. It was our only hope. He threw me over the wall onto a pile of rubbish which cushioned my landing. He then climbed over to join me. More tin sheets flew through the air and he managed to grab one and used it as protection as we sat there.[23]

"My father had been drafted to fight in Manchuria in 1918 when he was about twenty years old, and he received a lot of training. I think that must have helped him as he was able to make decisions in an emergency. So, there we were, the two of us, at the fence, with these flying tin sheets. I asked him, 'Dad, what if this fence falls down?'

"'Well, then, we will crawl to a lower place,' he replied calmly.

"A few minutes later we crawled farther along and into a culvert where there were piles of iron shavings. It was then that the fence was violently blown down by the wind with a mighty whack. My dad grunted in shock, but he was with me in a relatively low spot, so he didn't get hurt. Peering through the pile of scrap iron shavings I saw a B-29 bomber fly directly over our position."[24]

The fires would burn well into the next day. The cost to Le-May's bombing force was limited to single figures—only nine B-29s had been shot down by the Japanese air defenses, with forty-two damaged and four lost to mechanical issues. Enemy air opposition had been weak. Seventy-four Japanese fighters—primarily their Ki-44-II—of the Seventieth Hiko Sentai claimed two kills. The lack of ground-to-air coordination was compounded by the Japanese fighter pilots having limited, or no, night-fighting experience. Of the 287 fire stations based in the capital, a total of 100 were destroyed, along with 186 fire trucks. At least one hundred firemen died that night.

For LeMay's crews returning from their hot work above Tokyo, there was already a sense that their mission, despite their initial fears, had been a huge success. Tail gunners sitting a few miles up in their returning bombers could see the bright, orange glow of what they had accomplished. By the following afternoon, the last B-29 had touched down, and most crews had been debriefed over coffee and doughnuts. Many had simply gone to bed to rest. LeMay was relieved that his losses were lower than in any previous air raid. The initial reports of the debriefing crews spoke volumes. His strategy had worked. From his convalescence in Florida, Hap Arnold wired Guam immediately upon receiving the news, telling LeMay he was: "exceptionally well pleased" and that "this mission shows your crews have the guts for anything."[25]

The post-mission reconnaissance photographs would show the devastation: the flames had devoured almost sixteen square miles of the Japanese capital, destroyed some quarter of a million buildings and homes, and killed 85,000–120,000 men, women, and children (depending on which report you believed). Over a million people were now homeless—of which 25 percent were members of the industrial workforce. From a military perspective, twenty-two of twenty-nine aircraft-manufacturing targets had been wiped out and arguably thousands of small-scale "shadow" factories.

For Toshiko and her father, while B-29s were taking photographs from the safety of thirty thousand feet, the new day brought fresh horrors. Both she and her father had been overcome with smoke at various times, but they had survived the night. Now they crept out from under the tin roof that had saved them, staggered back out into the light and onto a street that was unrecognizable.

"I had to squint as I stumbled back toward the shelter. I stumbled over something, and when I tried my best to open my eyes, I found dead bodies—everywhere. The corpses were not completely black. They were all pink and all naked. Some of the bodies were still twitching. When I looked at the miso shop that we had escaped from, all the doors were melted down. Inside, some white bones were still bobbing and burning pink. No one had survived it."[26]

Her father stared in astonishment at the carnage, too. She took his hand and gripped it tightly, which seemed to snap him back to his senses. Speaking quietly to her, he told Toshiko her mother and siblings must have escaped and had survived the fire in a basement where they might have taken refuge somewhere. Or perhaps they made their way back to the family's own bomb shelter at home.

"My father first walked all the way to the shelter and came back saying that there was no one there—our home was badly damaged. I went to the Takabashi Fire Station, Takabashi Elementary School, Honkaga Elementary School, and other places where there were many people evacuating, but in the end, no one was there."[27]

Realizing there was no point staying near the family's destroyed house, they walked to her father's cement company offices, only to find that they, too, were burned to the ground. They then walked to the parent company, Asano Cement, in Kiyosubashi, and found that only the factory remained intact, though the roof was badly burned. Her father found some large jute bags that usually held cement but would do for that night as blankets. Without any food the whole day, Toshiko's stomach ached as she tried to settle down amid the debris of the factory. The stars shined through the shattered roof. *Will the bombers come again?* she thought. Exhaustion swept over her as she quickly fell asleep in her father's arms.

The next day, the pair continued their journey through the destroyed neighborhood. Her father had decided they would head west out of the downtown area toward Shinjuku, where his brother lived. He was sure they had not been hit by the raid and there would be food and shelter. To do so, they had to travel seven miles, taking them through the center of downtown Tokyo. Toshiko's sneakers had disintegrated from walking through hot ashes, and to protect her bare feet her father wrapped them in a jute bag before they could begin their journey. They searched for food and water as they walked. Her father told her they would try to get to the local subway line at Nihonbashi and then go to Shibuya, where there was a mainline train link to his brother's town.

"We walked to Nihonbashi. I thought that Tokyo had been wiped out. All the buildings were reduced to piles of rubble and ashes. Many were still smoking. The smell was terrible, beyond description. There had been a department store called Shiroki-ya on the corner by the subway, it was still burning from the third floor. We took the subway to Shibuya, and I was surprised to see that the town was still there, just as it had been. It was a surreal, refreshing change."

Back on the Marianas, LeMay had issued a press statement to the American public:

"I believe that all those under my command on these island bases have by their participation in this single operation shortened this war. . . . [T]hey are fighting for a quicker end to this war and will continue to fight for a quicker end to it with all the brains and strength they have."[28]

The strategists of XXI Bomber Command mapped out the new targets that would follow the same tactics as Tokyo. On March 11, 313 bombers carrying incendiaries flew toward the Home Islands. This time it would be Japan's third-largest city, Nagoya, also a center of Japan's aircraft industry. The light winds over the target were not as favorable for firebombing as they had been over the capital. The city's precaution of creating firebreaks and ensuring sufficient supplies of water for their emergency fire departments gave them a better chance of survival. For this attack, the B-29s were not exclusively carrying a payload of M-47 incendiaries. As a result, the forty-plus fires that erupted across Nagoya that night did not develop into the devastating conflagration that had destroyed downtown Tokyo.

The raid on Osaka the next night proved far more successful. Japan's second-largest city produced almost a quarter of the military's ammunition as well as being a key center of shipbuilding. LeMay sent in 301 bombers that bombed the city by radar instead of confirming a visual target. The results were far better, the raid succeeding in dropping a wide spread of incendiaries, which destroyed eight square miles of the city, and with it burned down Osaka's industrial cenrer and 130,000 buildings, all for the loss of two B-29s. The momentum was now with LeMay's strategy. Over the next few days, American bombers would strike the cities of Kobe and Nagoya once more.

Toshiko and her father stayed at her uncle's house until the night of March 14. Her father had made daily trips back to their destroyed neighborhood to look for her family, but as she was having balls of rice and milk for breakfast, he arrived through the door. His face was ashen.

"He told me, 'Today, they're going to bring out the dead bodies in the miso shop's basement, and I'm sorry, but you have to go too.' My father didn't want to take me with him because he thought it would shock me, but I knew what my mother and siblings were wearing. He didn't. So he had no choice but to take me with him."

She quickly got dressed, her uncle's family packed them food and drink to take with them, and they set off back to the city.

"When we got there, two or three military trucks of the military police [Kempeitai] were parked on Mitsume Street, close to the shop. The recovering team were pulling out more and more corpses from the wreckage and laying them down in long lines on the blackened pavement. A sergeant came over to my father and informed him that he would only allow us ten minutes to inspect the bodies. There weren't any complete corpses. The recovering parties brought out torsos and had left their hands, necks, and feet in the basement. The sergeant told my father there was simply no way to put them all together. It was such a cruel sight.

"At the time, the Kempeitai were feared by the population, but at the point, I admired the way they handled this terrible situation. Those trapped inside had used water to try to extinguish the flames, but it only created intense boiling steam. Everyone had either suffocated or been overcome with smoke. Ultimately, they had been boiled alive. The next day after the raid, no one could go in because it was too hot, so the Kempeitai finally took them out on the fourth day when we arrived."[29]

Toshiko's father now took her by the hand as together with her uncle they walked toward the lines of bodies. The police were wearing face masks, but they stopped their chatter and stood silently to one side of the road as the small group drew close to the long row of disfigured corpses. Toshiko slowly stepped along the line, pointing to specific bodies when she thought she recognized something familiar:

"They were all in a mess, but when I looked for them, my mother was [the only one] recognizable. She didn't have any hair, but the body was intact. My youngest brother was one and a half years old, but he was missing from the ankles and neck up, and you could only tell it was him by his kimono. My youngest sister, Fumiko, was five years old, and her upper torso remained covered in her kimono, too, so I could tell it was her. My ten-year-old sister, Chieko, I only recognized from the waist down. I had recognized the four corpses, and said [each time], 'Papa, here,' but I couldn't talk much. Each time, my father would then collect the body parts, little by little, with a fire hook that my uncle had brought, while the military policemen looked away. We went to the burnt ruins, lit a fire in a small pot, cremated them, and brought them back home."[30]

Many Japanese civilians who had survived the inferno like Toshiko, at some personal risk to themselves, now voiced their anger, despair, and frustration to the local authorities. When a detachment of Imperial Japanese troops was sent into one neighborhood to clear away the dead, they were confronted by an angry housewife who shouted: "You there, soldiers, how do you feel about all these people! Can you look at them!?"[31] The next day, Toshiko traveled to her aunt's house in the countryside, where she had lived in 1943 during the first year of evacuations. It was in her aunt's garden that her father conducted a simple funeral ceremony.

In less than two weeks, Curtis LeMay had succeeded to such a degree that he was forced to order a pause. He had run out of incendiaries to conduct more area bombing. But this period had provided valuable insight into how to tweak his plans. Critical density of incendiaries was essential to overwhelm firefighting units and destroy a target, the raid on Tokyo had shown. While the capital was spared further destruction, authorities began the cleanup. As Toshiko had experienced, survivors and neighborhood associations worked alongside the police and military relief units to clear the massive amounts of debris, restore transportation systems, and locate and dispose of the dead. By the end of the month, the survivors were able to obtain food and clothing from relief centers throughout the capital and receive some handouts from the government, though nothing could replace what they had lost. To prepare for further raids, firebreaks were created in bigger demolition programs, with those citizens affected told to leave the city as best they could. Every major city in Japan, including Hiroshima, took similar measures.

The evacuation program up until the fall of the Marianas in June 1944 had not been compulsory, merely encouraged. That summer, the government had published its *Outline for Encouraging the Evacuation of Schoolchildren*, the only compulsory evacuation measure enacted in the entire war. Now it went into overdrive. All nonessential workers were allowed to leave, with infants, schoolchildren, pregnant women, and those over sixty-five given priority. Free travel on the train system was provided, and the municipal authorities chose to waive the need for each citizen to obtain a certificate to change districts. Those who did take up this offer had to figure out their own place to stay once they reached their destination. The government was basically leaving their displaced citizens to fend for themselves. An emergency cabinet meeting the day after the fire raid issued the bleak official pronouncement that "every city must manage for itself."[32] Of the nearly three million without homes in the capital after March 10, 1945, two-thirds had found alternative accommodations by the end of April.

Despite their success, this did not mean the XXI Bomber Command was free to operate independently. American forces were preparing to assault and capture Okinawa. Though five hundred miles off the coast of Kyushu, it was a Japanese prefecture, and therefore considered inviolate. Their experience in taking the Marianas and Iwo Jima forced the US Navy, the Marines, Army, and Allied units to expect a baptism of fire. Hap Arnold and LeMay were tasked to support the operation by switching B-29s from attacks on the Home Islands' cities to tactical support to draw off Japanese aircraft in and around Okinawa. It would not be until mid-April that XXI Bomber Command's incendiary supply would be sufficient to restart the mass raids, with Tokyo successfully targeted once again.[33] Arnold held a press conference to laud XXI Bombardment Group's performance, telling reporters: "By the end of the summer, we are going to use every plane airplane we can effectively against Japan."[34]

Ominously, a columnist for the *Washington Star*, David Lawrence, noted: "It would not be surprising if it is in the Pacific war that air power demonstrates its real capacity for overall damage on the enemy."[35]

Throughout April, LeMay's forces now bombed military, industrial, and civilian targets in six major cities: Koriyama, Nagoya, Osaka, Kawasaki, Kobe, and Yokohama. The B-29, together with long-range fighter support, was free to fly almost unopposed across the Home Islands. Other service arms watched on from afar. One of General Douglas MacArthur's key aides, Brigadier General Bonner Fellers, concluded in June that the US air raids against Japan were "one of the most ruthless and barbaric killings of non-combatants in all history."[36]

And it was going to get far worse.

Chapter Sixteen

PREPARE FOR THE WORST

The enemy will return. That is the nature of war.

MAYOR SENKICHI AWAYA

Reports of the firebombing of Tokyo had not yet officially reached Hiroshima or any other city in the country. Up until that point, days later, the government censors had refused to issue detailed reports on the raid for the nation's media. Imperial Headquarters instead issued an understated news bulletin that was useless:

"Today, approximately 130 B-29s, with their main force, raided Tokyo from a little after midnight to 0240 and carried out blind bombing attacks on certain sections. . . . Various places within the city were set afire. . . . The war results thus far confirmed are as follows: 15 planes shot down [not true] and about 50 planes damaged [again, inaccurate]."

What Tokyo officials could not stop was the tragedy spreading by word of mouth as survivors traveled out of the capital to seek shelter elsewhere—many of whom now stepped off the few trains arriving at Hiroshima. Thus the news reached the city and was received with incredulity and fear. Mayor Awaya was informed of the disaster within minutes of refugees getting off the first train. Panic set in. Rushing to his office, he got on the telephone straightaway, hoping his government position would give him some luck in getting a message to his wife, Sachiyo.

After several hours of anxious waiting, he finally heard her faint voice down the line. She was unharmed. Instinctively, he asked her to now travel south to him, and perhaps they could bring the younger children to join him soon as possible in Hiroshima. Sachiyo Awaya hesitated. They had all survived the raid, she argued; the stories he must be hearing were exaggerated; and local officials were saying it was unlikely the enemy bombers would return, and if they did the city defenses would be ready this time. Aware that his line to Tokyo could be cut—official telephonists now had the authority to terminate any call which was not of a military nature—Awaya pressed her to agree to his suggestion: "The enemy will return. That is the nature of war. You and the children must come here. It is possible that we will all die in the battles to come. If that is to happen, I wish us to die together as one family."

Sachiyo relented. She promised to come down as soon as a train was available. Awaya asked their eldest son, fourteen-year-old Shinobu, whether he could travel, too. He agreed he would follow her down and continue his education at a school the mayor could arrange in Hiroshima.[1]

The level of destruction in Tokyo had been downplayed when he talked to military commanders in Hiroshima Castle. Despite their reassurances, Awaya put all civic offices, including the city police, on notice that dangerous times were approaching. In a general circular sent out on March 17, he detailed the preparations necessary for the speedy evacuation of the population if a heavy air attack came. If the Americans repeated a Tokyo-style raid on Hiroshima and no precautions were taken, would the city suffer the same fate as the tens of thousands who had died in the capital? As respectfully as he could, Awaya asked the military if there was a plan in place, or at least being discussed, for the protection of civilians.

"Based on the current information, there is a high possibility that our Hiroshima City would experience massive air raids. I predict it is just a matter of time. Thus, today I made an announcement to all citizens and told them to devote ourselves to national defense and protect with all our might the military-based city. However, if we lapse into a situation in which evacuation is inevitable, although I know it would be trouble for you and your citizens, I would highly appreciate it if you would help our citizens by accommodating them based on the Sufferers Evacuation Implementation Guidelines, which was decided by the decree. I would simply ask you for your generous sympathy and support."[2]

Two days later, with government-controlled radio now admitting the loss of Iwo Jima as a "strategic withdrawal," Hiroshima finally experienced its first visit from American planes, though fortunately it was not the dreaded B-29 bombers, or the "B-sans," as Japanese labeled them. At approximately 8 a.m., coming in low from the sea, four enemy carrier-based fighter-bombers had flown across the city. Only two bombs had been dropped: one falling into a tributary of the Ōta River, the other destroying a house and killing both occupants. It all happened so quickly that the American planes had successfully escaped back to the south before Japanese antiaircraft fire could engage them, or at least try to. Throughout the shops, factories, and tearooms of Hiroshima that day, and indeed into the following week, the brief aerial attack replaced the main topic of conversation and complaint—the official announcement that the people's daily rations were to be reduced yet again. Portions of rice would now be cut to three bowls a day for twenty days in the month. Ominously, there would be no other food available for the remaining days.

The American stranglehold on Japanese merchant shipping, from aerial minelaying and submarine attacks, but also the slow destruction of the country's production facilities and ability to transport it, were starting to bite. Hiroshima was mirroring the situation in many cities across the Home Islands. Failing rice harvests since 1942 were compounded by heavy government food controls, driving higher prices for most urban Japanese households to feed themselves. Only the wealthy and those lucky to be living in rural areas close to the sources of food production had a better chance of eating healthily. Bereft of the company of his wife and children, Awaya was suffering, too, but outwardly he continued to appear at peace, as he described in a letter to his daughter Yasuko on April 15:

Father is truly enjoying the feeling of being alone. He feels very close to God, and he feels as if he is together with everyone in Tokyo, transcending space and time. . . . It is cold if I sit too long, so now I sit in front of the round table in the center of the twelve-mat room and write this letter. . . .

The sweet food has completely ceased to exist. From now on, I will be living a true wartime life. I will try to simplify my hunger and make it a habit. It is said that a hungry stomach gives one more energy for mental and physical activities, and it also helps one's brain to think clearly. It seems that the more we eat out of habit, the less nutrition we need. Of course, it is good for your health, but it is not good for me in all circumstances.

Father is thinking only about the government office. He is thinking about the big job that will benefit Hiroshima. The important thing is to always keep your mind clear and be ready to face whatever comes your way. The secret is to think things through without preconceived notions or prejudice, to take matters into your own hands, and to naturally go where you need to go. It is not a good thing to draw a prejudiced conclusion from the start and try to force your way to it. It is the experience of fifty years of your father's life. It is not a loss. Keep it in your heart.

It's ten o'clock at night. I should go to bed soon, otherwise it will be bad for my health. Tomorrow morning will be another beautiful day, with the morning sun reflecting off the surface of the river. That's what I think about when I go to bed these days.[3]

Awaya and his departments could see how such food shortages and ineffectual, corrupt officials within local associations were now affecting food distribution throughout the city. This had been magnified especially since the Americans had begun their regular bombing raids in November 1944. Fatigue and illness were evident among the workforce. Teachers were reporting children falling asleep in lessons, or being too tired to complete their "spiritual training" classes.[4] Every day, Awaya couldn't help noticing the long lines for food in town, where prices rose daily, and reports of city dwellers walking or cycling into the local countryside to buy more food directly from farmers. It was technically breaking the law, but he knew it was a widespread practice throughout the country.

The mayor realized he could no longer turn a blind eye to the increasing military presence in and around the city as the southern half of the country built up its defenses. In April, in anticipation of invasion, the mayor's office was informed of the government's plans for reorganizing the military structure of the country. The creation of the First General Army would defend eastern Japan, with its headquarters in Tokyo. Western Japan would be governed by the Second General Army, based in Hiroshima. The chain of command from Hiroshima would incorporate the Fifteenth Area Army based in Osaka and the Sixteenth Area Army at Fukuoka. With the importance of Hiroshima's port facilities at nearby Ujina, the Imperial Army's Shipping Command would be based there with the authority of the Kure Naval District, an hour away to the south, which housed the biggest arsenal in western Japan. Overall, this new structure now based in and outside southwestern Japan, totaled more than three hundred thousand men and women.

Working in tandem with this new military system would be the "Chugoku Sokan-fu" (local government office), answerable to Tokyo. It would preside over five prefectures and be based in Hiroshima. Empowered with cast-iron rule over the civilian population, it would have no authority over the armed forces it worked alongside but could request deployment of troops by the army and navy when required. Mayor Awaya was informed that he would be reporting to Genshin Takano, the new governor of Hiroshima Prefecture, who would head the Chugoku regional administration council, too. Both men knew and respected each other's ability. Takano informed Awaya that a new commander of the Second General Army, with ultimate control of the region and authority over both men, would be announced shortly. In the meantime, they must continue to prepare the city and the prefecture's civil defenses.

Governor Takano dispatched orders for three hundred civil servants to be on duty at his prefectural office every night, to ensure his offices were secure should the city come under attack.[5] At Hiroshima City Office, sixty officers were to be on duty 24/7. Hiroshima would be divided into twenty-four sectors, with all city employees to be trained on evacuation procedures and then allocated to a specific sector for implementation and communicating to central headquarters. All eyes must focus on the battles to come, with the mayor's office telling the workforce, "with a spirit of sacrifice . . . discharge your duties and show yourself at your best in the decisive battle as governmental employees of the empire."[6]

Despite the official national mood of defiance, the enemy was dominating the skies over Japan. Waves of "B-sans" were remorselessly picking off city after city, and carrier-based fighter planes daily roamed the countryside at low level to strike fear into the population. Trains and road transport was being systematically shot up, and key power and water facilities destroyed. The Americans were laying thousands of mines to block shipping getting through to the Home Islands, too. Both civil leaders knew the tide of war was getting closer now that Iwo Jima had fallen, and the defenders of Okinawa, only 560 miles from the mainland, now prepared for their own defense. In meetings with senior police officials, concern about a future big air raid was continually raised. The number of troop and naval movements in and out of Hiroshima and Ujina meant the B-29s must strike soon. When would the war come to Hiroshima?

At a more local level, Awaya discussed privately with his personal assistant, Maruyama, his dread of the city's fate should it be firebombed. Over the past decade, mirroring the dire situation across the country, military and civilian authorities in Hiroshima had failed to construct many reinforced shelters capable of withstanding aerial attacks. Added to this was the lack of tools to fight a major fire.

The head of the city fire department had confirmed that the water pressure from the fire hydrants was too low to suppress multiple fires at once. Studying the city map, he drew a line with his finger, following the route of the fire lanes that had been created from the thousands of buildings that the authorities had ordered pulled down. On the one hand, he was confident that, with the many rivers cutting through the city, if fire did spread, the people could find refuge in the water itself, plus there was a ready-made source to fight the fires. What he feared most was that fire would take hold as it had in Tokyo. His fire chief had confided to him that though the lanes were far apart, they would ultimately be burned out. The fires could spread and conjoin.

Then it was only a matter of time.

Chapter Seventeen

MANHATTAN IN THE MARIANAS: THE ATOMIC WING COMES TO TINIAN

Into the air the secret rose,
Where they're going, nobody knows.
ANONYMOUS POEM, RELATING TO THE
509TH COMPOSITE GROUP[1]

By May 8, as the bulk of the 509th's men and supplies shipped out from a Seattle naval port heading toward the Central Pacific theater, news came that the war in Europe was won. President Harry S. Truman, fresh from spending his very first night in the White House, was ready to announce it to the American people and the millions of their countrymen fighting overseas. He sat behind the presidential desk in the Oval Office, flanked by his wife and daughter and surrounded by members of his cabinet and Senate and congressional leaders. The country's military representatives included Army Chief of Staff George Marshall and Head of the Chiefs of Staff Admiral William Leahy, who had enjoyed the position of Roosevelt's confidant. Truman read from a prepared script:

"I want to start by reading you a statement. This is a solemn but glorious hour. General Eisenhower informs me that the forces of Germany have surrendered to the United Nations. The flags of freedom fly all over Europe. It's celebrating my birthday, too—today, too."

"Happy birthday, Mr. President!" the audience in the Oval Office chorused.

Smiling, the new president gestured for quiet as he continued:

"Our rejoicing is sobered and subdued by a supreme conscious-ness of the terrible price we have paid to rid the world of Hitler and his evil band. Let us not forget, my fellow Americans, the sorrow and the heartache which today abide in the homes of so many of our neighbors.

"We are going to be in a position where we can turn the greatest war machine in the history of the world loose on the Japanese.

"Our victory is only half won. The West is free, but the East is still in bondage to the treacherous tyranny of the Japanese." And he called for their unconditional surrender.

Within twenty-four hours of VE Day, members of the new In-terim Committee, including Vannevar Bush of the NDRC, General Groves, and the president's personal representative James Byrnes,[2] sat down with Secretary of War Henry Stimson. The significance of the meeting became clear as Stimson declared: "Gentlemen, it is our responsibility to recommend action that may turn the course of civilization."

Across ninety minutes, the new committee discussed the bomb's completion at Los Alamos, the readiness of Tibbets's 509th Com-posite Group as they relocated to Tinian, the operational range of the B-29 to deliver the bomb, and the list of thirty-three potential targets in Japan that were still free from aerial raids that they would consider for attack. Groves for the first time highlighted Hiroshima as a primary target: "Hiroshima is the largest untouched target not on the 21st Bomber command priority list."[3]

The general outlined to Stimson and Byrnes that this city, situ-ated on the southern coast of Kyushu, was not just relevant militarily but had been deliberately spared from B-29 attacks by LeMay for an-other reason. It was a virgin target, Groves dryly concluded, and thus the damage of this new weapon could be gauged with more accuracy. Stimson called the meeting to a close and ordered regular briefings as testing for the bomb came closer at Los Alamos and Tibbets's unit was established on Tinian. At the committee's fourth meeting on

June 1, Groves brought in Oppenheimer and senior members of the Los Alamos team: the Nobel laureates Enrico Fermi, Arthur Compton, and Ernest Lawrence. The scientists briefed Stimson on the two types of bombs (uranium and plutonium). While the first was ready to go, the latter would be tested at Alamogordo in seven weeks.[4]

All eyes were now focused on defeating Japan in the Pacific. For the key military men in theater, despite the belief that they would receive everything they needed in men and supplies for the coming invasion of the Home Islands—(Operation Olympic)—Admiral Nimitz, LeMay's overall commander General Carl Spaatz, and General Douglas MacArthur, fresh from his bloody success in the Philippines, were all cognizant of the casualties that would follow. Tokyo would be badly firebombed again on May 24; this time LeMay's Twentieth Air Force sent in 550 B-29s flying at the higher altitude of ten thousand feet, but the result would be the same as the previous raid of March 10.

The Joint Chiefs, headed by Admiral William Leahy, had concluded that a ground invasion was necessary, with a tightening of the naval blockade and increased aerial attacks on the country's defenses and infrastructure. President Truman was buried in myriad briefings from Stimson and Byrnes as his administration formulated a policy on Soviet influence in Central Europe. The summit with Winston Churchill and Joseph Stalin would map out a postwar future with and calm Winston Churchill's fears of a communist takeover of Poland, Austria, the Balkans, and even Germany. While the meeting of the "Big Three" at Potsdam was agreed for mid-July, the Joint Chiefs pressed the new president as to the inevitability of American forces invading Japan to force unconditional surrender. The background of all this activity was the fighting to capture Okinawa and the horrendous casualties American forces were suffering on land and at sea.

As he flew his Douglas C-54 "Skymaster" across Saipan, gently descending south toward Tinian's North Field, Paul Tibbets was certain that his unit would deliver the weapon to make this fearful scenario academic, bring Japan to its knees, and possibly give the Allies the weapon it needed to rapidly solve any future war. He had been eager to scout out Tinian before the 509th's scheduled arrival. He had flown to the air base in mid-May to inspect the facilities and meet with the Twentieth's commander, Curtis LeMay, and Admiral Nimitz. "My first view of Tinian as I approached it from the air confirmed my preconceived notion of an island in the southern Pacific, a part of the world I was seeing for the first time. . . . I found [it] to be ideally suited to our purposes."[5]

The previous summer of 1944 had seen US forces make huge strides in their counteroffensive to penetrate the Japanese outer defensive line forces across the Pacific. The competition between General MacArthur's thrust into the southwest to regain the Philippines and Admiral Nimitz's island-hopping strategy through the Central Pacific had been decided in the latter's favor. And the lines of B-29s Tibbets now saw parked on multiple runways on Tinian were the reason. The key to Japan lay in the aerial campaign of the new long-range bomber. The Marianas island chain was crucial to this strategy, as its capture now placed Japan within reach of the B-29 and the new air bases could be easily supplied directly from the United States and from the sea as they returned from bombing the Home Islands.

As the Allies commenced their invasion of Europe on June 6, 1944, Campaign Granite II (the invasion of the Marian and Palau Islands) had commenced a six-month offensive in the Central Pacific. It would see Admiral Nimitz's Task Force 58 of the United States Navy decisively defeat the Imperial Japanese Navy Combined Fleet at the Battle of the Philippine Sea (June 19–20), and the destruction of their carrier air force in the "Great Marianas Turkey Shoot."[6] This decisive victory guaranteed the success of the United States Army and Marine units who were amphibiously assaulting Saipan, Guam, and Tinian. The whole campaign would be a taste of what was to come as American forces closed in on the Japanese Home Islands.

American forces on Saipan encountered ferocious, suicidal fighting from the Japanese defenders and witnessed the shocking sight of hundreds of Japanese civilians committing mass suicide rather than surrender. Those who hesitated were picked off by Japanese snipers. Many thousands more had died amid the fighting, caught up in crossfire, shelled by the US Navy, or bombed from the air. Practically the whole garrison of thirty thousand Japanese defenders had died in the fighting, with thousands more sailors and carrier pilots of the Imperial Navy killed at sea. American casualties numbered fourteen thousand wounded or killed, the costliest campaign up until that point of the Pacific war.[7] Robert Sherrod, a war correspondent for *Time*, summarized the lesson many American Marines took from the campaign: "What did all this self-destruction mean? . . . that the Japanese on Saipan believed their own propaganda which told them that Americans are beasts and would murder them all . . . ? Do the suicides of Saipan mean that the whole Japanese race will choose death before surrender?"[8]

Guam, the largest island in the Marianas chain, was assaulted on July 21 and would see a repeat of the fighting for Saipan. Of an original garrison twenty-two thousand strong, only 1,275 Japanese troops were taken alive. American losses were lower than on Saipan but still numbered approximately thirteen hundred killed and six thousand wounded.

Three miles to the south of Saipan, Tinian was smaller: twelve miles in length and six miles wide, primarily consisting of dense jungle, with cultivated land in the south. To the island's north and northwest lay urban areas, military installations, and the three of four active Japanese runways. A high five-hundred-foot plateau the locals named Mount Lasso dominated the views of the island. The nine-thousand-strong Japanese garrison on Tinian had, like the other major strongpoints in the Marianas, reinforced the island and had been determined to mount a last stand, despite the eighteen thousand civilians living alongside them. American strategists were keenly aware how big a thorn in their side Japanese naval and air units on the island might prove if they were not destroyed. From their air bases, Japanese aircraft could easily interdict American shipping, carrier aircraft, and merchant supply ships. American naval air attacks and bombardments had softened up the islands for six weeks. As nearby Saipan was overrun, American heavy artillery and air strikes then pounded the northern tip of Tinian relentlessly (approximately a shell a minute fell on the island) as two United States Marine divisions went ashore. The weeklong fighting through sugarcane fields and jungle was tough, Marine units methodically weeding out Japanese troops from caves and killing them in urban combat as they captured Tinian town and its naval base. Significantly, it would be the first time the Americans used aerial bombs containing napalm in the Pacific theater. Again, over five thousand Japanese were killed and just 252 prisoners taken, for the loss of one hundred American casualties. The predominantly Japanese civilian population, numbering over twelve thousand, was interned, but hundreds of enemy troops would remain at large, preferring to hide out in the jungle as American Seabee units arrived to build the biggest aircraft carrier in the world.

Tibbets banked the C-54 to get a better view of Tinian town. It was now the new naval base that would supply the island as it was converted for the Twentieth Air Force's use. He scanned the clear blue ocean around the island and the dozens of ships either coming in and out of the port or moored close by in the bay. The new air base always impressed him—it was a hive of activity. The island had now been leveled by teams of engineers and construction gangs. Over eight million cubic yards of coral fill had been mined from the nearby mountain to establish six main runways, taxiways, and hardstands. The coral was rolled smooth and constantly kept wet with seawater to ensure a smooth surface. The runways were supplemented by enormous support buildings and rows of huts and tents that acted as the living quarters required for the thousands of airmen, military police, and ancillary staff of the Twentieth Air Force. Tibbets couldn't help but see the rows of hospital huts and tents being erected now. A sure sign further island offensives were in the making.

The US Navy had taken control of the first operational airfield

(West Field) by November 1944, measuring 8,500 feet in length. Two further runways were added to West Field for the US Army Air Force by March 1945, with North Field operational soon after in May with four new runways. North Field would become the home of the 313th Bombardment Wing, their runways running east to west; the veteran Fifty-Eighth Wing, fresh from serving in airfields in China to bomb Japan, would fly from West Field.

The Seabees, with the support of hundreds of freed Korean laborers who had originally been brought to the Marianas by the Japanese, also landscaped and cleared foliage away from the air base. The asphalt roads were designed and laid out on the same grid as the streets of New York City, Broadway being the longest arterial road, stretching from North Field to Tinian town six miles away. Running parallel to it was Eighth Avenue, which linked West Field to the naval facilities built next to Tinian town. Crisscrossing to form a grid were smaller roads with names such as Park Row, Canal Street, Forty-Second Street, and Wall Street.

Many American personnel would be living in dozens of Quonset huts or tents. Twenty-nine feet wide by fifty feet long, lightweight, and constructed of prefabricated corrugated steel, with a semicircular cross section. Regulations on the base stipulated that each hut could accommodate twelve officers or twenty enlisted men. Senior commanders such as Tibbets would have the luxury, if it was such, of sharing his hut with three other officers of similar rank. Larger tents and prefabricated buildings served as mess halls, chapels, operational rooms, latrines, and medical centers. For recreation, the men could watch movies in an outdoor theater, play volleyball, pitch horseshoes, or travel into Tinian town—still showing all the signs of heavy fighting from the summer before. Being so close to the sea, swimming was an option, but the men had to don protective shoes and be mindful of the razor-sharp coral on the shallow ocean floor.

The whole airfield complex was fenced off, topped with barbed wire and multiple sentry posts guarded by armed military police units—the fear of Japanese troops roaming free in the jungle kept crews on their toes. Generally, these starving, raggedy men simply wanted to steal food from the base's canteens and kitchens. Periodically the men from the base, both aircrews and police, would go searching for them on hunting trips. From the air, the island's overall shape reminded Tibbets of the outline of South America. But now he brought the plane in to land on Manhattan. Whatever way he looked at it, it was now the largest airport ever constructed, which his unit was going to occupy, with the intention of launching the key operation on Japan that might end the war.

The 1,821 officers and men of the 509th would live in relative isolation near North Field, in a section reserved for them under the New York moniker of "Columbia University District." Captain Parsons's team of the First Ordnance of Project Alberta would operate out of a "base within a base" that had been set aside for him, complete with air-conditioned facilities to assemble the atomic bombs.

The First Ordnance area in the northwest corner of North Field was tucked out of the way of prying eyes, with a twenty-four-hour armed guard who inspected high-level passes required to gain entrance. The enclosure comprised several Quonset buildings and other facilities such as administration offices and a headquarters where all classified documents and orders, drawings, and correspondence were stored in safes. There was one large, windowless Quonset hut that stood aside from the others, where authorized personnel would open the crates carrying assembly parts for the bombs—Little Boy and Fat Man.[9] As Tibbets knew, this compound was arguably the most valuable asset on the whole island, as it held everything connected to the bomb sent from Los Alamos, Wendover, and other US Navy bases in the Pacific connected to it.

The 393rd Bomb Squadron consisted of fifteen Silverplate B-29s. They were numbered 1 through 15, with three flights (A, B, and C) containing five planes each. Their distinctive tail markings were a forward-pointing black arrow within a circle. The crews of the 509th would fly from the longest operational runways in the world. Much as this pleased them, they were still experienced enough to know that even that length of runway was dicey for a four-engine bomber to take off from, fully loaded with bombs and fuel for a twelve-hour round trip to Japan. There was a reason for a large, immaculately maintained military graveyard between the men's camp and the ocean. They had heard from veteran crews of the Twentieth that the casualty rates were high enough that the island's authorities kept fifteen freshly dug graves ready for use at the end of each operation.

Second Lieutenant Russell E. Gackenbach from Allentown, Pennsylvania, had enlisted in the Aviation Cadet Program at the beginning of 1943, completed his training as a navigator in February 1944, and now found himself stationed with Tibbets's unit as part of the 393rd Squadron. He would play a key role in the Hiroshima operation on August 6 and the attack on Nagasaki three days later. Once his squadron was established on the base, it was clear to him the 509th enjoyed their own special place compared to the other units of the Twentieth Air Force: "We moved into areas used by the Seabees. And first, we were in tents for about two weeks until they got things completely renovated for us to live in. Then we moved into the compound area guarded by fences. If somebody wanted to come to our outfit because we were known for our food, they couldn't get in unless they're verified by one of our guys. I had several friends come over, and I had to go down to the main gate, greet them, meet them, have a talk, but I never invited anyone back for lunch or dinner."[10]

This did not mean the 509th had complete freedom across the base, due to the secrecy of the mission and the secrecy around the technology: "We could leave the compound area, but there were certain places in the island we could not go to. Some were such that nobody except with the right patch on your sleeve could go there. There was a tech area where most of the scientists were. I couldn't go there. We couldn't go to the loading pits. That was all off-limits. Every man in the outfit had a badge: flying officers had a pink badge, enlisted men had a blue one, and then there were yellow passes, white passes, you name it, there was a pass for everything."[11]

A teletype operative in the 509th's Signal Office, Lieutenant

Patrick Grill, handled high-security communications going in and out of the 509th, situated in a hut guarded around the clock. Along with several other operatives, Grill coded and decoded all correspondence between Tibbets, Groves, Alamogordo, Los Alamos, and the Pentagon. The conditions at Wendover were luxurious compared to on Tinian.

"[It was] a cultural shock from that in Wendover. . . . Because of the uncomfortably hot, humid weather, almost overnight, most personnel had cut pants to shorts and nearly every day had to take a shower or two."

Conditions inside the Quonset huts were bearable with the men sleeping on camp beds and converting their spare blankets in the summer heat and humidity for extra pillows. As computer specialist for the 393rd Bomber Squadron Sergeant Ken Eide recalled, the men also had to contend with unexpected visitors:

"Rats infested our huts; food or candy could not be left out as they would eat it. The noise they made was loud and we would get up and chase them, using brooms or clubs, we would try to kill as many as we could."[12]

Time off duty for relaxation was limited for all men on the base: "A day in the ocean digging for shells was a welcome experience, but you had to avoid cutting your feet on the rocks. Sometimes we would drive into the wild jungle which was a dangerous thing to do as a number of [Japanese] were hiding and reports of gun shots made this very scary."[13]

Some, like Charles Perry, the group's catering officer, enjoyed what food was on offer: "In the 509th a PFC eats better than a five-star general." Lieutenant Grill arguably spoke for many enlisted men on the island: "The food, well, when hungry enough, you didn't mind waiting for the Australian Mutton, powdered milk, and dried eggs, because there was the Tinian Tavern where you could buy a beer. Most of us smoked and found solace in the nicotine habit even though they tasted musty and stale in the high humidity."[14]

Radar specialist Corporal Paul Metro gave credit to the cooks for trying to provide a taste of home to the thirty crews: "One time, they made a valiant effort to make ice cream, but it was a great milk-shake! . . . Anything cold was a great delight!"[15]

Tibbets maintained the 509th's training, especially on navigation at sea: "It was the same training we had been doing in the States, trying to maintain our familiarity with each other. Learning to operate together. Then we had to learn the surroundings. Navigating from the United States to Cuba is one thing. But when you go overseas, there's little islands [used for markers] that were very small and hard to find. There was this one [base]—Marcus Island, [with] only a mile-and-a-quarter runway. [Sometimes] you couldn't tell if you had found it, but I did three times. Of course, we had to rely on a lot of reckoning and on radar. And sometimes, the winds were very erratic. And they were changeable. It [was] easy to get lost."[16]

The arrival of the 509th among the veteran crews and service personnel of the Twentieth Air Force did not go unnoticed. As Tibbets maintained the readiness of the fifteen crews of the 393rd, their practice flights and live bombing runs with ten-thousand-pound bombs (called "Pumpkins") on Japanese-held islands close by were in stark contrast to the fate of the many B-29 squadrons actually bombing Japan. Despite requests from other wing commanders to know the 509th's actual intended mission, Tibbets batted all inquiries away, much to their annoyance. Even when he agreed some of his crews could attend lectures from flight officers discussing tactics and skills necessary to handle a B-29 over Japan, the 509th pilots would end up dispensing more knowledge than they received, such was their expertise. This only fueled further resentment. This was intensified at a higher level when General LeMay's director of matériel on the base, Colonel C. S. Irvine, demanded the 509th's maintenance depot and personnel be pulled into the Twentieth Air Force's pool, which was busy servicing a fleet of several hundred B-29s. Acutely aware of security, Tibbets refused, with the argument settled in his favor only once he had invoked the code name Silverplate to LeMay.

"To other outfits on Tinian, we were a bunch of pampered

dandies. While they were flying hazardous missions from which some did not return, our crews were making training flights with an occasional sortie into the enemy skies to drop a single bomb from high altitude."[17]

The 509th rapidly became a joke to the other units on the air base. Both the flight crews and ground personnel were constantly jeered at and made fun of, sometimes to the point of fistfights in Tinian town and on the designated beaches where they were allowed to relax. It was not uncommon for the men's sleep to be shattered in the dead of night by rocks being thrown onto their Quonset huts from passing jeeps. The unidentified miscreants sped off into the darkness to other parts of the base. A poem mocking them soon began to be circulated in the mess canteens, workshops, and bars, titled "Nobody Knows":

> Into the air the secret rose,
> Where they're going, nobody knows.
> Tomorrow they'll return again,
> But we'll never know where they've been.
> Don't ask us about results or such,
> Unless you want to get in Dutch.
> But take it from one who is sure of the score,
> The 509th is winning the war.
> When the other Groups are ready to go,
> We have a program of the whole damned show.
> And when Halsey's Fifth shells Nippon's shore,
> Why, shucks, we hear about it the day before.
> And MacArthur and Doolittle give out in advance,
> But with this new bunch we haven't a chance.
> We should have been home a month or more,
> For the 509th is winning the war.

Within a few weeks, thousands of copies of the poem were mimeographed and were read across hundreds of units of the Pacific command—from Hawaii to the Philippines. Even "Tokyo Rose," the Japanese propagandist, commented upon the arrival on Tinian of the "Black Arrow Squadron" of the 509th, warning of the hot reception they would face from Japanese fighter planes. No matter what criticism his command suffered from fellow airmen on Tinian, or threats that might be uttered by Tokyo Rose, Tibbets pushed the fifteen crews hard in their training. He pushed himself even farther, having to travel repeatedly back and forth to the United States for top-level briefings on target selection with Groves in the Pentagon or discussing issues with the devices Oppenheimer's team were completing at Los Alamos. He was proud of the speed with which a single trip might be completed—seventy-six hours being his record. Even for an energetic thirty-year-old colonel, it was exhausting.

Chapter Eighteen

ENDGAME: OKINAWA

Gunsei, Minshi
(The army survives, the people die.)

Since 1943, despite the Roosevelt administration's declared intention to fight a "Germany first" war, the successes in the Pacific had proven otherwise. The reality was reflected by how successful it had been for the United States Navy and Army in the Pacific to roll back the Japanese gains of 1942 until, by April 1, 1945, they were at the shores of sovereign Japanese territory, Okinawa. This had been achieved by the Pacific Fleet's Admiral Nimitz, supported by the Joint Chiefs head Admiral Leahy, being supplied with just enough for his command to get to this point. The Joint Chiefs, at the will of the president, allocated military resources across the globe. Admiral King had worked hard since 1942 to ensure Nimitz received a satisfactory share of the US Navy's force of carriers and warships. It was another story relating to logistical vessels ("liberty ships") that American industry was pumping out, and primarily allocated for the European theater, as was the bulk of aircraft. Nimitz managed to ensure an expanded Marine Corps was supported by a strong air wing. The United States Army was being allocated at a ratio of two-to-one in favor of the European theater. Nimitz, and to some degree General Douglas MacArthur when he lobbied hard enough,[1] needed ships, aircraft, men, and supplies to reconquer the Pacific.[2] At the same time, Hap Arnold's aerial bombing campaign and the submarine offensive against Japan's mercantile fleet were starting to limit its war industry. With Hitler dead and Germany defeated, American troops would soon be flooding back to the United States to be refitted for service in the Pacific. Nimitz was now receiving 90 percent of all American combatants.

Nimitz was at the head of a modern-day armada. Since the victory at Midway in June 1942, his navy had battered its way through the Japanese defensive perimeter as American industry supplied him with multiple large carrier battle groups. Like warring queen bees, the carrier groups were protected and supplied by a retinue of support vessels at sea and hundreds of fighters in the air, allowing them to roam at will across the vastness of the Central and Western Pacific. As we have seen already, the bloody victory in the Solomons and New Guinea in 1942–43 had been followed up by the brutal conquests of not only the Gilbert Islands, where the cost of capturing Tarawa toward the end of 1943 was particularly shocking, but then on to the Marshall and later the Marianas Islands, to allow the next step in the strategic campaign to bomb mainland Japan. Merely weeks after the Marines' success on Iwo Jima, Nimitz now parked his war machine off the final stepping stone toward the Home Islands.

The capture of Okinawa was vital to the US strategy in the Pacific for a variety of reasons.

From the perspective of the US Army's Air Force bombing campaign, neutralizing both Japan's early-warning radar systems and its air force on the island guaranteed greater success of the daily B-29 operations out of the Marianas. Several hundred miles to the southeast of Okinawa, their flight path was near the island. To defend Japanese airspace, both the Imperial Navy and Army ran independently of each other, with their own early-warning radar systems communicating to their respective air defense units. It was a system prone to break down, and thus far so uncoordinated that the major hurdle B-29 crews had to overcome was handling the atmospheric jet stream over the Home Islands to drop their payloads accurately. But the Allied occupation of Okinawa, like Iwo Jima, would offer operational naval bases for the planned invasion of the mainland, as well as bring the weight of American airpower within range of Japanese cities.

A nominal side effect was that it could act as a haven for American bomber crews. On the flights into Japan, the squadrons of B-29s coming in at lower altitudes before they gained height to their bombing altitude were less maneuverable, and therefore vulnerable to attack from Japanese fighters stationed on Okinawa and Kyushu. Capturing the island not only took away this obstruction but allowed the US military to convert and extend Japanese airstrips in the same fashion as Guam, Saipan, and Tinian. By August 1945, over 23 percent of American bomber and fighter crews who ditched in the sea between the Home Islands and Iwo Jima were saved by the superb air- and sea-rescue operation run by the US Navy.

Ultimately, Operation Iceberg, as it would be called, if successful, handed them the perfect base from which to invade Japan itself. The argument to take Okinawa instead of Admiral King's desire to move for Formosa had begun as far back as May of the previous year, before the capture of the Marianas. The US Navy had not opposed MacArthur's great strategy but ensured Okinawa would be on a list of future targets once the Philippines and Formosa campaigns were underway. What changed minds was the capture of the Marianas. One by one, the key decision-makers fell in line to endorse the new strategy. By October 1944, as Nimitz's carriers launched air raids against Okinawa, MacArthur's Sixth US Army, supported by the Seventh Fleet, had established himself in Leyte and would start their march up the archipelago toward Manila. The last great Imperial Japanese Navy task force was destroyed, along with over six hundred aircraft at the Battle of Leyte Gulf on October 23–26. By January 6, 1945, the US Tenth Army, commanded by General Simon B. Buckner, had submitted their operational plan for Iceberg.

Nimitz would provide practically every type of ship and submarine required for the campaign. The staging area for the fast-carrier force would be at the new naval base constructed by the Seabees at Ulithi Atoll, in the Caroline Islands, to the north of New Guinea.

Airstrips and Army and Marine bases to hold tens of thousands of men at a time were constructed on various islands, as well as docking piers, a seaplane base, and a spiderweb of pontoons to embark and disembark troops. A supply depot was built that could store the thousands of tons of fuel, ammunition, and spare parts for the invasion force. Over twenty thousand tons of supplies went through the base every month. Flying over Ulithi Atoll, twenty-year-old Marine pilot Sam Hynes, serving with the US Marine Torpedo Bombing Squadron 232, was dumbstruck at the sheer scale of Nimitz's fleet: "It was awesome. It was huge. The anchorage was miles across and it was covered with ships of all sizes. Carriers, battleships, destroyers, cruisers. I'd never seen so many ships. It was like seeing all the power in your corner. And there wasn't any power in the other corner."[3] Across Central and Western Pacific bases, American forces made ready to sail.

Okinawa, the fifth-largest island of Japan, lies over 350 nautical miles from the southern tip of Kyushu and had been an outlier of Imperial Japan for centuries. It is the largest island within the great sweeping curve of the Ryukyu island chain, spanning the East China Sea toward Formosa. As an isolated community, its history since the sixth century had been scarred by raiding parties from China, Korea, and Japan, but by 1853, it was occupied by American Navy commodore Matthew C. Perry as his "black ships" made their way to Japan, to open the country up from the end of his naval cannon. Admiral Nimitz viewed Okinawa in the same way his naval predecessor had; the island was "the very door of the Empire." Once Japan had embraced modernity, Okinawa was annexed formally in 1874, with Tokyo dispatching a governor to oversee it five years later. In 1920, it had been granted prefecture status, and two years into the Pacific war with the United States, it was officially absorbed into the mainland district of Kyushu.

The topography of the island mirrored Japan itself. It was a contrast in geography and climate. The south, where the capital Shuri was located, was a series of rolling hills and rich pastural land where the bulk of the island's 450,000-strong community resided.[4] They lived primarily in the hundreds of small towns, villages, and hamlets, and worked in farming and the fisheries dotted along the coast.[5] Actual roads to navigate the island were mainly single-track, made of crushed coral, which cut up fairly easily once American armor and heavy vehicles ran over it. When US Marines and Army units began their advance into the interior after April 1, 1945, they could not believe such a beautiful landscape, crisscrossed by well-manicured terraces, could be the site of a climactic battle. They failed to appreciate that this picture-perfect landscape was honeycombed with caves formed over hundreds of years by streams that ran down to the sea.

The island's prefecture capital and commercial hub was Naha, with a population of sixty thousand, many of Japanese origin, of whom hundreds served in the government civil service, healthcare, and police. Shuri was the historico-cultural capital of the island, although slightly smaller in size and population. Shuri was dominated by the ridge running through southern Okinawa. Overlooking the city was Shuri Castle, the military headquarters of the Imperial Army and historically the ancient throne of the original kings of Ryukyuan. Key to American strategists was the capture of the two primary airfields in the center of the island: Yontan and Kadena.

To the north, running off a rugged, mountainous spine approximately twenty miles in length, lay a series of ridges—some as high as fifteen hundred feet. At the northern tip, a small peninsula, covered in dense forests and brush, would prove to be one of the best natural defensive positions on the island and result in countless casualties toward the end of the campaign. As the battle raged over the coming weeks, hundreds of caves, gullies, and ravines would be viciously contested by fanatical Japanese soldiers and militia. Fenced in from the sea by high limestone cliffs, for many Okinawans, brainwashed to fear American brutality, they would be the platform from which hundreds would jump to their deaths rather than be taken prisoner.

The defense of the island was given to Lieutenant General

Mitsuru Ushijima—nicknamed the "Demon General," who left his position as commandant of the Military Academy in Tokyo to take up command of the Thirty-Second Army on August 8, 1944. While Ushijima was renowned and respected for his calm decision-making, his choice for chief of staff was certainly quite the opposite. Major General Isamu Cho reminds one of the heroes from Akira Kurosawa's epic postwar samurai film *Seven Samurai*. "Butcher" Cho was a throwback to the ancient warrior class, totally without fear but equally lacking any mercy toward the enemy—whether military or civilian. Though his military prowess was never in question, his politics were to the far right, having been involved in several coup attempts in the 1930s, as well as being at the forefront of the Imperial Army's many atrocities fighting in mainland China. He had played a pivotal role in the infamous "Rape of Nanjing" in 1937.[6] Now he would oversee the construction of the island's tunnel defenses, as well as ensuring all support was given to his troops, even at the cost of the Okinawans: "The Army's mission is to win, and it will not allow itself to be defeated by helping starving civilians." They would all soon find themselves in the eye of the storm once the fighting got underway.

The Thirty-Second Army had originally been 120,000 strong, but with reinforcements required for the fighting in the Philippines, it had fallen to seventy-seven thousand men—a combination of frontline combat units, augmented by various logistical, engineering, and signals troops. Korean laborers, as well as local civilian militia (*Boeitai*) and student volunteers ("Iron and Blood" Corps), bulked up the defensive force by a further twenty thousand. The Imperial Japanese Navy supplied 3,825 personnel who would man the island's fifteen coastal batteries—backed up by a six-thousand-strong civilian/combat force. They, too, counted on a civilian levee of Korean laborers and Okinawan conscripts press-ganged into service. The Thirty-Second Army could fall back on a wealth of artillery, mortar, antiaircraft, and automatic weapons due to an excess that had been previously meant for units fighting in the Philippines. The tightening of the American naval blockade on Japanese shipping had proved a boon for Ushijima's garrison. His men would also be able to defend their positions with copious amounts of satchel charges, grenades, mines, and bullets.

On Okinawa, the Japanese possessed artillery in greater quantity, size, and variety than had been available to them in any previous Pacific campaign. Using naval coastal batteries, they were able to concentrate a total of 287 guns and howitzers of 70mm or larger caliber for the defense of the island. Of this total, sixty-nine pieces could be classified as medium artillery, including fifty-two 150mm howitzers and twelve 150mm guns. The smaller pieces included 170 guns and howitzers of calibers of 70- and 75mm. In addition, seventy-two 75mm antiaircraft guns and fifty-four 20mm machine cannons were available for use in ground missions.

The principal mortar strength of the Thirty-Second Army was represented by ninety-six 81mm mortars of the two light mortar battalions. The Japanese also possessed, in greater numbers than had previously been encountered, the large 320mm mortars, commonly called "spigot mortars"; the First Artillery Mortar Regiment, reputed to be the only one of its kind in the Japanese Army, was armed with twenty-four. Standard equipment of the ground combat units of the army included about 1,100 50mm grenade dischargers ("knee mortars"). To counter American tank strength, the Japanese relied, among other things, on an unusually large number of antitank guns, especially the 47mm type. The independent antitank units had a total of fifty-two 47mm antitank guns, while twenty-seven 37mm antitank guns were distributed among the other units of the Army. The entire Japanese tank force, however, consisted of only fourteen medium and thirteen light tanks, the heaviest weapon of which was the 57mm gun mounted on the medium tanks.

Like the Imperial Army commanders who had held islands from the Gilberts to Iwo Jima over the past two years, Lieutenant General Mitsuru Ushijima and his immediate staff were under no illusions about what their duty demanded and what their fate would be. As the American historian David M. Kennedy summarized, "The Japanese on Okinawa knew their ultimate defeat was inevitable. Their goal was to buy time to prepare the defense of the home islands and to inflict the kind of damage that might even yet reduce the United States to sue for a compromise peace."[7]

The Japanese concept of the offensive spirit (*Bushido*) in warfare had seen incredible successes throughout the Second Sino-Japanese War, as well as the first year of conflict since Pearl Harbor. This doctrine had run its course by the time of heavy defeats in the Solomon Islands and then New Guinea in 1943, followed by similar defeats when attempts were made to defeat the US Marines assaulting the beaches of the Gilbert, Marshall, and Marianas island chains. In both cases of attacking first or fighting behind strong beach defenses, Japanese forces had been annihilated by extreme American air, naval, and land firepower. What could stop them? Imperial Japanese commanders fell back on their last throw of the dice—blood sacrifice. The fanatical defenses of both Peleliu and then Iwo Jima had come at a high cost in casualties for the US Marines, dented American public opinion, and worried political leaders in Washington. Though Imperial General Headquarters demanded Ushijima wage a "decisive battle" to make the enemy pay a high cost to capture the island and its airfields, the lieutenant general was influenced more by his mercurial chief of staff to dig instead.

Ushijima would order his defenders to press-gang the local population to assist in constructing lines of fortifications across the island anchored on dominating terrain. The complexity of the system in the south—the "Shuri Line"—would comprise thousands of bunkers, pillboxes, gun emplacements, and trenches. Fields of fire were coordinated to create deadly firetraps for the advancing American forces as they attempted to break through. Giving up the prized airfields was a price worth paying if they could draw the enemy into their killing fields, with less space to maneuver for their armored support and ground-attack aircraft that might hit their own side. By the new year, it was agreed, while the bloodletting erupted on the island, Japanese "special attack units" would smash the American fleet anchored offshore. Thousands of aircraft and pilots would be made ready for their one-way mission to assault the Fifth Fleet over the coming weeks.

Assaulting the island would be 170,000 Marines and US Army soldiers, supported by a logistical train that needed 120,000 personnel, under the supervision of the US Navy, which would land them via Admiral Turner's (of Guadalcanal fame) amphibious force. Neighboring islands housing small garrisons or simply strategically important to the success of the main event were to be taken prior to L-Day ("Love Day"). Leading them would be an untested American commander: Lieutenant General Simon Bolivar Buckner Jr. The son of a former Confederate general, he had never led troops in battle but had the support of Army chief of staff General George Marshall, who moved him from garrisoning the North Pacific to command the Tenth Army at the sharp end of the war. Buckner would walk a tightrope of winning one of the arduous campaigns of the Pacific War while keeping a lid on tensions between the US Army and Navy. Unlike his peers in Europe, such as General Patton, Buckner was not prone to make decisive, strategic decisions or be aggressive or innovative in his planning. This he would leave to his subordinates.

Before Iceberg commenced, American submarines and aircraft sought out and destroyed dozens of Japanese cargo ships, isolating the island's garrison from relief and supply. The Thirty-Second Army would fight and die with what it had on the island. On March 25, on the western side of Okinawa, the Fifth Fleet's Gunfire and Covering Force unleashed hell along the length of the island to disguise their intended landing zone. The combined firepower of battleships, cruisers, destroyers, and dozens of gunboats opened up a 24/7 bombardment for the next week that fired over ninety thousand rounds.[8] The US Navy carrier force flew over three thousand missions, and B-29 bombers coming from the Marianas several hundred miles away devastated the island's infrastructure, wrecking airfields, supply dumps, military barracks, as well as civic headquarters and warehouses. The capital, Naha, was reduced to rubble, the beaches cratered, but the island's defenses remained intact and hidden. The Allies were simply bombarding locations where the enemy wasn't.

Okinawans scrambled to hide in whatever shelter they could find, and those who had prepared shelters were often driven out by local Imperial Japanese troops seeking protection themselves, many stealing the civilians' meager food supplies. Overhead, American aircraft dropped millions of leaflets urging them not to resist the invasion and to surrender at the earliest possible moment. Ironically, the Americans asked that Okinawan civilians seek shelter. On nearby islands, the first wave of civilian deaths by organized suicide would play out tragically as terrified old men, women, and children who had been conditioned by the regime's propaganda that they would be tortured at best, and raped and murdered at worst, took their lives, egged on by local Japanese troops.

Kinjo Shigeaki, a young sixteen-year-old living on Tokashiki Island, part of the Kerama island chain west of Okinawa, heard from the authorities that Americans were landing on March 26, days before the main event. He, along with his village, were ordered on a rapid nighttime march in the pouring rain, to the north of the island to the military garrison at Nishiyama. By the morning, over eight hundred people had been gathered into the base, where the headman, an ex-soldier, ordered them to cry out *Banzai!* What followed would be repeated throughout the islands over the coming weeks as Okinawans chose death before capture. Shigeaki recalled:

"Soldiers distributed grenades among us, we were told that after you pull out the pin, you had to wait three seconds before the grenade exploded. There weren't enough grenades to go around because there were so many of us. . . . The grenades were detonated, but there were few of them, so most people survived the blasts. Then people began to use clubs or scythes on each other—various things were used. It was the father's role to kill his own family, but my father had already died. . . . My older brother and I didn't discuss how we would do it, but we both knew we had been ordered to kill ourselves and our family.

"I don't remember exactly how we killed our mother, maybe we tried to use rope at first, but in the end, we hit her over the head with stones. I was crying as I did it and she was crying too. My younger sister would have been about to become a fourth grader in elementary school and my little brother would have been about to start first grade. I don't remember exactly how we killed our little brother and sister, but it wasn't difficult because they were so small—I think we used a kind of spear. There was wailing and screaming on all sides as people were killing and being killed. If there were knives, knives were used."[9]

Distraught, both Shigeaki and his elder brother prepared to kill themselves, but their bloody rampage was halted by a teenage boy who urged them to follow him instead to die attacking the American forces coming onto the island. They all hid in the mountains over the next few weeks as the Allies bombed the islands relentlessly, destroying empty villages. They avoided American patrols and lived off their discarded rations and any shellfish they could find on the beaches. Eventually they were captured and would survive the campaign. They were the lucky ones.[10]

L-Day was approaching—ironically, in Western tradition, April Fool's Day. Marines aboard their transport ships, waiting to disembark the next morning onto a hot beach, were shocked to hear Tokyo Rose's broadcast welcoming them to Okinawa and promising their "hot reception." They had been briefed that this operation would most likely be the fiercest battle yet and to expect eight of ten of each squad to be dead or wounded by the end of the first day.

As the troops of the US Army's Seventh and Ninety-Sixth Divisions, along with the US Marines' First and Sixth Divisions, came ashore in waves that Sunday, their grim expectation of carnage turned to stunned relief as they stepped onto a quiet beach, disturbed only by dozens of craters created from days of naval bombardment. Unlike the casualties the Marines had suffered on the first day tackling

Iwo Jima and Peleliu, there was no enemy here to fight. Or so it appeared. The celebrated war correspondent Ernie Pyle, a veteran of recording the fighting in Europe, concluded: "[T]he carnage that is almost inevitable on an invasion was wonderfully and beautifully not there. . . . Like a man in the movies who looks away and then suddenly looks back unbelieving, I realized there were no bodies anywhere—and no wounded."[11]

By day's end, four divisions comprising a total of over seventy thousand men had been safely landed onshore, and the primary objectives of the island's airfields at Yontan and Kadena were in American hands for the loss of only twenty-eight dead, twenty-seven missing, and 104 wounded. Both airfields would be converted and operational for American air units within forty-eight hours.

Despite American ground forces developing the beachhead to a depth of five thousand yards, still no enemy counterattack occurred. The only Japanese response was on the mainland, where news of the invasion was announced to the public on April 3, a national holiday, "Emperor Jimmu Day," celebrating 2,500 years since Japan's founding. Perhaps nationalist fervor for the date magnified what was seen as a disaster. It brought down the government of Prime Minister Kuniaki Koiso. Emperor Hirohito finally instructed the inner circle of his new government, led by Baron Kantaro Suzuki, that they should prepare for an honorable end to the conflict.

On April 2, the day after landing, advancing in fine weather, US forces reached the eastern coast, splitting the island in two. The Tenth Army would turn south toward Shuri, while the First and Sixth Marine divisions would advance northward. All units were now secure in positions military planners had estimated they would not occupy until two weeks of fighting had been endured with significant casualties. Marching in columns through the lush farmland of the southern half of the island, veteran Marines and soldiers who had fought in the dense jungles of the South Pacific could not believe such a tranquil landscape would be turned into a major battlefield. Still, there was no sign of the main Japanese force. Captured local

Okinawans revealed to intelligence officers they were indeed present on Okinawa and in the area to the south that had been heavily fortified, even though American reconnaissance planes could not detect them in their underground bunkers and tunnels. On L-Day+3, US Army forces moved south to engage what they could find, while the two Marine divisions moved north. As the bright weather turned to rain, a typhoon developed offshore, and the island's roads and bridges became impassable without renovation from engineer units, so the fighting finally erupted on April 6.

On land, General Buckner's Tenth Army would begin their long slog to penetrate the vast fortifications that covered the last six miles of the island's southern end. The Thirty-Second Army's headquarters lay behind the heavily defended Shuri Line, circling the destroyed capital, Naha. Buckner took a sledgehammer to such a daunting nut. Assaulting one ridge after another, his army would implement the less-than-subtle frontal-assault tactics of "blowtorch and corkscrew." As discussed in a previous chapter, the Allies' willingness to use Louis Fieser's invention of napalm was a game changer in close-quarter combat against the Axis powers, but even more so in the Pacific. M4 Sherman tanks were now modified to use it as a jet stream, belly tanks were fitted to US Navy aircraft containing gallons to drop on enemy positions, and of course US Marine and Army teams were trained to carry napalm flamethrowers into action. In Europe, the Germans might call upon their own heavy artillery, tanks, and air cover to destroy these new units before they could strike, but the Japanese defenders on Tinian and Leyte had no such support. At Iwo Jima months before, and now on Okinawa, Japanese artillery and mortar support would play a significant part in inflicting casualties upon the Americans.[12]

"Blowtorch" referred to Sherman M4 tanks flooding Japanese positions in their fortifications with burning oil. The results were terrifying for the defenders. "The tank moved up to shoot streams of napalm into the cave. . . . Japanese soldiers who ran from the furnace were squirted with napalm—which, however, failed to ignite. One of the tankers saw to that with a tracer bullet, turning a fleeing man into a torch—which prompted a throaty cheer from the platoon. . . . [W]e cheered that incredibly horrible sight, the burning of another human. Whatever the justification, we'd become savages, too."[13]

Assaulting each position forced the advancing Americans to show themselves to Japanese observation positions, before tackling minefields, booby traps, hidden machine-gun nests, as well as trying to survive intense Japanese artillery fire.[14] Large formations of troops contesting such a small, constricted space proved fatal for many on both sides, as the rain swept down across the island, turning the battlefields to mud, reminiscent of Verdun. Swarms of fleas covered the dead and dying. But Ushijima's men were dying at an atrocious rate—almost six-to-one compared to the enemy, especially when up against American armor or air support. Still, the daily casualty reports stirred up interservice rivalries between Marine and Army senior commanders on the front line and dented American public support back home. Buckner refused to contemplate a plan by the Marines to launch an amphibious assault on the southern coast and thus envelop the Shuri Line, and instead chose the methodical and costly process of slogging forward incrementally. Some have argued he was mindful of not repeating the mistakes that the US Army had made at the Anzio landings in Italy the previous year, where an initial success had almost resulted in disaster once the Germans had counterattacked with reinforcements. It is hard to see where Japanese reinforcements would have come from, but Buckner continued the bitterest of paths to victory.

The Japanese plan to wear down the Americans with fanatical defense ran parallel with a two-pronged assault at sea: one a symbolic act of fanatical stupidity, the other hugely effective. Operation Ten-Go was initiated by the Imperial Japanese Navy's Combined Fleet, and a mix of cruisers and destroyers were led toward Okinawa by Japan's greatest battleship, the *Yamato*, to engage the US armada in what was a suicide mission. The plan was for the giant battleship to disrupt the American fleet before running aground on the island, to give fire support to the defenders and for the bulk of its crew to disembark and fight on land. The flotilla, however, without air cover, was spotted and destroyed by US carrier-based aircraft 210 miles to the north of Okinawa, with the loss of over four thousand Japanese seamen. It was the last major naval engagement of the Pacific war.

Beginning on April 6, the Japanese Navy's "special attack unit" launched *kamikaze* ("divine wind")[15] suicide air attacks on the Fifth Fleet and the British Royal Navy's Task Force 57 (British Pacific Fleet).[16] Slower than their American counterparts, the British carrier fleet enjoyed armored decking that could withstand a kamikaze strike. The first special attack units had been officially sanctioned and developed toward the end of the previous year, though the concept of suicide tactics (or "body-crashing," *taiatari*) had been discussed as early as June–July 1944, once Saipan was lost and senior Japanese commanders acknowledged how the tide had turned against them in the air war. Their aircraft, such as the Mitsubishi A6M Zero, once the best pound-for-pound warplane in the Pacific, was now up against US Navy aircraft such as the F6F Hellcat and the F4U Corsair. The Zero would be the plane of choice to send young, inexperienced pilots on one-way missions to attack the Allied fleet.

Operation Ten-Go would see the Allied fleet fight off repeated suicide attacks from the air over the course of the campaign. Commanded by Vice Admiral Matome Ugaki of the Fifth Air Fleet and launched from bases on the southern tip of Kyushu, over 4,500 Japanese Army and Navy aircraft would be launched in predominantly conventional attacks over the next weeks. Though the initial assaults were small-scale and easily beaten off, by April 6 Ugaki sent in massed flights, justifying their usefulness to the war effort: "We were losing the war and pilots were constantly being killed in combat. We felt that a man might just as well sacrifice his life deliberately as lose it in an air battle."[17]

The first operation of over seven hundred aircraft, 355 which were kamikazes, sank six ships and damaged twenty-one more. US Navy carriers could not put up enough fighters to contend with them, and the men aboard the destroyer monitoring the radar screen could not swiftly tell friend from foe. The cost to the fleet, both physical and psychological, was immense. During the air campaign, over fifteen hundred Japanese pilots dived to their deaths, destroying twenty-seven of Admiral Spruance's ships and damaging 164.[18] They inflicted more damage on the US Pacific Fleet than in any naval engagement since the Guadalcanal campaign, or in the Philippines, where kamikaze units had been first deployed. The human losses they inflicted were staggering, too: 3,048 killed and 6,035 wounded. The intensity of the attacks caused some US Navy men to crack as they strove to defend their ships against planes coming straight at them. The service would suffer the highest casualty rate of the entire war in this two-month period.

On April 13, news broke of the sudden death of President Roosevelt. He had been driven to exhaustion by the arduous trip to Yalta to hold the Big Three conference with Churchill and Stalin in the Crimea, where the strategy to finish off Nazi Germany before then turning to defeat Japan was agreed upon. Increasingly debilitated by his failing heart, he had been recuperating in Warm Springs, Georgia, when he suffered a brain hemorrhage. The American public, ignorant of how ill he was, lapsed into grief and deep shock. Many Marines and soldiers fighting in the mud and blood of Okinawa for tactical positions within the greatest battle of the Pacific war—Sugar Loaf Hill, Awacha Gulch, and of course, Shuri Castle—had a hard time recalling the record of the man from Missouri who was replacing him: their new commander in chief, Harry S. Truman.

On land, the fighting to break the Shuri continued as Buckner's forces launched repeated frontal assaults. A request by the commander of the Seventy-Seventh Infantry Division to attack the southern coast to outflank Ushijima's defenders was refused. Admiral Nimitz, shocked by the news his fleet was losing a "ship and a half" a day to kamikaze attacks, flew to Okinawa to urge Buckner to take the amphibious option. He was also ignored. Stubbornly, Buckner continued his war of attrition, his three divisions wearing down and breaking through the concentric lines of defenses through brute force, explosives, napalm, and hand-to-hand fighting.

By April 20, the US Marines had succeeded in occupying the north of the island, but, like Saipan in 1944, they had witnessed shocking sights. Hundreds of Okinawans, the elderly, women, and children who had hidden in the mountainous areas, had died, many from malaria or starvation, but also caught in the fighting or killed by Japanese troops retreating across the island. Marines once again witnessed mass suicides by locals conditioned to fear them, jumping off the high cliffs into the sea or murdered by their own side for trying to surrender. Buckner could now bring all his force to bear in the south. Perhaps this move broke Japanese discipline, with Ushijima finally being convinced by his senior commanders to launch his own assault in the American rear to encircle and destroy them. It was a disaster, in which he lost more than several thousand men to American firepower. Though several more weeks of fighting remained, this would be seen as the decisive action of the Okinawan campaign.

From May 11, the Marines were given the task of breaking the Shuri Line, the fiercest and longest stretch of fighting taking place on Sugar Loaf Hill. Ushijima had chosen Sugar Loaf Hill precisely because it offered the best opportunity to kill as many of the enemy as possible. Consisting of coral and volcanic rock, rising to a height of one hundred feet, and three hundred feet long, it was flanked by high ground on both sides, creating a perfect arena of crossfire. Marines advancing up its slopes would be cut down by murderous machine-gun fire, as well as supporting artillery barrages. The fighting and shelling, combined with torrential rains that began to fall on May 21, created a hellscape reminiscent of the Western Front in France. Bodies and body parts of the fallen were strewn everywhere, blown up repeatedly by barrages. Retrieving the wounded was nearly impossible. Men fell out in large numbers with battle fatigue. Such was the accurate concentration of fire from Japanese positions that rumors persisted the defenders must have received training from German gunners.

On May 17, a Marine battalion from the Sixth Division battled up one hill on Sugar Loaf's flank, enabling American artillery to suppress Japanese counterfire. Within forty-eight hours, diversionary attacks lured Ushijima to miscalculate his allocation of defenders, thus opening up his rear positions for an assault on Sugar Loaf Hill by Marines with armored support. It finally cracked open the Japanese defenses. On May 27, 1945, Japanese units retreated from their underground headquarters in Shuri to caves on the Kiyamu Peninsula. Approximately thirty thousand Japanese troops now occupied the peninsula, and over sixty thousand were dead. Buckner's forces had captured fewer than five hundred alive. It was now a matter of a few weeks until the official end of the fighting.

In Washington, President Truman was having to find his feet quickly. Supported by Roosevelt's trusted chief of staff, Admiral Leahy, his secretary of war Henry Stimson, and his close friend Secretary of State James Byrnes, the man from Missouri was gaining a positive reputation for making swift decisions on establishing a satisfactory end to hostilities in Europe and winning the war in the Pacific. Victory in Europe came on May 8. Soviet and American forces had met on the Elbe, and Germany was under occupation. Debate would build between the hawks and doves about how best to deal with Joseph Stalin, given Allied fears of a communist takeover throughout Eastern and Central Europe and potentially any move toward Japan. In Europe, the Allied occupation of Berlin was set to begin on June 5.

At the beginning of the month, with Japan's main Axis partner defeated and mindful of the fighting on Okinawa, the White House issued Truman's message to the Japanese people of what was in store for them should they resist further:

We are now engaged in the process of deploying millions of our armed forces against Japan in a mass movement of troops and supplies and weapons over 14,000 miles—a military feat unequaled in history. The Japanese have more than four million troops under arms—a force larger than the Germans were able to put against us on the Western Front. . . . We have not yet come up against the main strength of the Japanese military force. . . . Substantial portions of Japan's key industrial centers have been leveled to the ground in a series of record incendiary raids. What has happened to Tokyo will happen to every Japanese city whose industries feed the Japanese war machine. I urge Japanese civilians to leave these cities if they wish to save their lives.[19]

Amid the endgame for Okinawa, the two opposing commanders would not live for that day of surrender. Amid the continued sporadic fighting in the south, on June 18 Lieutenant General Buckner took the opportunity, yet again, to visit the front line, conspicuous in his three-star general's uniform and insignia, as well as the pendant flying from his chauffeured jeep. Despite warnings from nearby units who feared being targeted with such a high-ranking officer standing nearby, Buckner repeatedly stood out in the open as he scanned Japanese positions. The Japanese obliged, firing an artillery round in his direction, striking the volcanic rock and mortally wounding him. Buckner died a few hours later. He would be one of only four lieutenant generals to die in combat in World War Two.

Finding their position impossible to defend, on June 19 Lieutenant General Ushijima ordered his headquarters staff to disperse and for the surviving army to conduct guerrilla attacks. Two days later, together with his chief of staff, Isamu Cho, he committed ritual suicide, while several of his senior staff shot themselves. All organized resistance was now at an end. American forces carried on suppressing pockets of resistance until July 2, 1945.[20] The eighty-two-day campaign had been costly for both sides. Such was the level of destruction that accurate figures of civilian losses are elusive, but historians agree that at least one hundred thousand Okinawans, a quarter of the island's population, were killed. Ushijima's army was decimated by the fighting. Estimated losses were over seventy to a hundred thousand men killed. The Tenth Army would take over ten thousand prisoners. At sea, the kamikaze campaign had claimed the lives of over nineteen hundred pilots, together with an overall loss of several thousand aircraft.

The Tenth Army had suffered 7,603 killed, 36,613 wounded, with over twenty-six thousand men dropping out of the line with battle fatigue.[21] The US Navy's losses were frightening. Thirty-two Allied ships and craft had been sunk and a staggering 368 had been damaged, with 4,907 men killed in action and 4,824 wounded. It would be the US Navy's greatest losses in any operational theater. The ferocity of the Japanese defense, the brutality of their treatment of the civilian population, the suicide of so many Okinawans, and the determination of the massed kamikaze attacks shocked not only American military commanders in the field and strategists at Nimitz's headquarters, but also the War Department and President Truman's administration in Washington. The figures spoke for themselves: for each day of the campaign, over three thousand people had died. How would this figure play out once the United States and the Allies commenced Operation Olympic—the invasion of Kyushu, set to begin in a matter of months.

For Truman, the next weeks would be a whirlwind as he led his nation toward the ultimate prize—the defeat of Japan—and the biggest decision of his life.

Chapter Nineteen

THE CITY OF WATER

The Japanese have rites and customs so different
from those other nations that it looks as if they studied of a
set purpose to be unlike any other race on earth.
JESUIT PADRE ALESSANDRO VALIGNANO, 1599[1]

Situated in the southwestern part of Honshu Island, at the outbreak
of war with the United States in 1941 Hiroshima was the seventh-
largest city in the country. It served as the principal administrative
heart of that part of the country and was also the headquarters of
the Second Army, a key position of defense for the nation by 1945,
in terms of supply depots and shipping routes to the outer empire.
Serving this requirement meant that the prewar population of the
city was a little over 340,000 people.

From the beginning of Japanese imperial rule, Hiroshima Prefecture was divided between two provinces, Bingo and Aki. Long
before Hiroshima was founded as a city, the Aki region was known
for its religious significance. Possibly dating from as early as the late
sixth century, the famous Itsukushima Shrine (Shinto) was located
in Aki province on a small island (Miyajima, Shrine Island), a short
distance west of where Hiroshima would later evolve. Over time, this
shrine to the sacred island became an important pilgrimage site.[2]

The city of Hiroshima itself was founded as a castle town on
Hiroshima Bay in the late sixteenth century, a period when most
of Japan's medium- and large-size cities were founded, nearly all of
them as castle towns constructed throughout Japan by competing

warlords. The city was founded just above sea level, on a broad, fan-shaped delta of the Ota River, with seven tributaries pouring out to Hiroshima Bay, logically dividing the city into six separate islands, on flat terrain, interrupted only by a single, one-and-a-half-mile-long, kidney-shaped hill that rose to 221 feet and dominated the vicinity.

The early history of the city is thus closely linked to the broader—and relatively long—history of urbanization in Japan. Urbanization began in this period of civil warfare and later witnessed, under different circumstances, successive waves of expansion in later centuries, particularly in the decades after the Meiji Restoration, then in the 1910s and 1920s.

The founder of Hiroshima was the powerful warlord Môri Terumoto, who was closely aligned by the late 1580s with Toyotomi Hideyoshi, the lord who was rapidly bringing the warring clans of sixteenth-century Japan under his dominion. In 1589, Terumoto set about building a grand castle headquarters for his clan on the shores of Hiroshima Bay, a location blessed by strategic and commercial advantages. This building project followed a pattern being repeated all over the country as warlords, either in open battle with one another or newly victorious, built immense fortifications and lavish headquarters. The derivation of the name of Hiroshima Castle is that the fortification was constructed on the largest of the low, flat islands of the time (*hiro* meaning wide and *shima* meaning island). From this location, the Môri clan controlled a large part of the commerce in the western portion of the Seto Inland Sea.

Hiroshima soon became more than just a castle fortification as it evolved into a bustling castle town with artisans, merchants, and workers of all stripes who lived cheek by jowl with samurai warriors serving the clan chieftain. Eventually the Sanyô highway, which connected the expanding city to points east and west, was redirected so that the road went directly through the burgeoning commercial center. The city would become by far the largest in the area of the main island of Japan and grow into a significant center in Japan itself over the course of the next three centuries.

As the largest city located on the inland sea shipping route, the city had a thriving economy, with a steady flow of shipping in and out of the ports, which began to expand over the decades. Numerous local products from surrounding areas (such as cotton grown in the coastal regions; hemp jute, paper, bamboo wares, and vegetables from the Ota River basin; and seaweed, oysters, and other marine products from Hiroshima Bay) were all brought into the area near Hiroshima Castle, where they were consolidated and shipped off to Kyoto and Osaka.[3] Hiroshima by this period had constructed a highly developed bridge system, linking the six islands across the many tributaries.

By the nineteenth century, following the Meiji revolution, the new government set about reshaping the city's administration and economic-political base. In 1871, despite local unrest and protest, the new national government in Tokyo remodeled Hiroshima and the neighboring Fukuyama into Hiroshima Prefecture (*ken*), a new category of administrative unit whose top executive official would be an appointed governor. Under this modern system of local and municipal administration, the national government in Tokyo officially designated Hiroshima as an incorporated city. It had roughly eighty-three thousand residents. One of thirty-one cities recognized under the new system, Hiroshima now resided within a more modern, centralized state that finally broke away from the centuries of feudal rule that had originally given birth to it.

As Japan began a race to modernization to thwart the danger of Western colonialization toward the end of the nineteenth century, Hiroshima began to grow in importance as a city of heavy industrial manufacturing and export trade. As the city grew, so did the its capitalist class of merchants and industrialists. It was geographically in the right place at the right time, at the crossroads of the industrial centers of Kyushu, the Inland Sea, and industrial cities farther east that gave it an integral position within Japan's emerging industrial strength and global position.

Once the port of Ujina had been constructed at the end of the

1880s, Hiroshima's long-term economic future was secure. It was now a critical modern transportation hub for civilians and military alike. By the mid-1890s, the Sanyô Railroad was extended to the city, providing a link to Kobe and Shimonoseki in the east, and a new branch line from Ujina connected the port to the main Sanyô Railroad station in the heart of the city. Entrepreneurs also constructed the sorts of light-industrial plants that formed the basis of much of Japanese early industrialization during the modern period, especially cotton mills. Located near the coal-producing regions of northern Kyushu and able to receive shipments of coal from overseas suppliers, the iron and steel industries also flourished in Hiroshima.[4] By the wartime 1940s, Mitsubishi Heavy Industries constructed a major naval shipbuilding factory on the port waterfront of the city.

The evolution of Hiroshima encapsulated not only the country's advance toward modernity but also its embrace of imperialism. Through the latter half of the nineteenth and early twentieth century, the country's military (both navy and army) would play a crucial role in the city's life. As Professor Scott O'Bryan summarized in his paper "Hiroshima: History, City, Event":

"Hiroshima was a city where hundreds of thousands of civilians made their lives. Shops, small businesses, factories, banks, schools, hospitals, and government offices lined its streets. It was, however, also a military city. So common was the image of military personnel in the daily life of the city that it was dubbed by residents a 'soldier's city.' Military personnel could regularly be seen at the Chûgoku Regional Army and Fifth Army Division headquarters complex at Hiroshima castle, at their barracks and on drill grounds, and marching to and from transport ships and train stations as they entered the city or shipped out during the successive wars of the modern period by which Japanese extended their imperial reach."[5]

As Japan set out on its rapid Westernization, it became known as a garrison city by the late 1880s. The Imperial Army's Fifth Division (of six total) was headquartered at the old castle in the heart of the city. The Japanese Imperial Naval Academy was then also relocated from Tokyo to the large island of Etajima in Hiroshima Bay. Etajima remained the officer-training facility for the navy until the end of World War II.[6]

As a staging post, Hiroshima played a vital role in the country's military campaigns abroad, beginning with the First Sino-Japanese war of 1894–95. Once the naval port of Ujina had been completed, the city acted as an assembly area for troops from all over the rest of the country shipping out to the war zones in China, and then the war with Russia in 1904–05. By the end of these successful campaigns, Hiroshima would be seen as a pivotal communications, transportation, and supply hub for the military. This would only gain in significance with the coming of the Pacific war in 1941.

In addition, one consequence of the conflict in China was returning troops bringing with them not only the garlands of victory, but also infections and transmissible diseases picked up on the campaign. Therefore, military commanders ordered the construction of a quarantine facility on the harbor island of Ninojima. As Japan's empire building increased after December 7, 1941, the facility increased in size to accommodate more troops.[7]

For a remarkable moment, Hiroshima's place in the history of imperial wars even included the transformation of the city into the virtual imperial capital of the nation. During the First Sino-Japanese War, leaders moved the Meiji emperor's imperial command headquarters from Tokyo to Hiroshima to be at the center of the military logistics of this most important city in the war effort. During much of the war, the emperor thus resided in Hiroshima. Even the national parliament pulled up stakes and moved to Hiroshima, convening for a time during the war in a building hastily constructed for the purpose.

The fighting in Manchuria and the Chinese mainland in the 1930s, and subsequent rapid expansion throughout East Asia and the South Pacific after their surprise attack on the US Navy at Pearl Harbor in late 1941, placed Hiroshima on the front line of Japanese military life. The military authorities had been purchasing increasing amounts of city land for development for a decade. Hiroshima was now a clear military target for aerial bombing, but also lay in the path of any possible invasion of the southern islands of Kyushu. The city was pivotal in the country's strategic defense. As the war against the United States and her allies took an increasing turn for the worse, Japan's defensive perimeter was supported by supplies coming from the city.

In the South Pacific, by the beginning of April 1945, American naval forces had now fought their way to the shores of Okinawa. It would be the final island battle before the much-anticipated attack on the actual mainland. The headquarters for the Second General Army, which had the job of defending the entire western part of Japan, was therefore relocated from Okinawa back to Hiroshima, northeast of the central military complex at the castle.

By 1945, the city boundary measured just over twenty-six square miles (50 percent of which had been developed for residential living), which now bordered the low hills surrounding the city on three sides. Of the total amount of developed land, half was heavily built up, and the remaining 50 percent occupied by poor-quality residential, storage, and transportation areas. Between these were lower developed patches of land, containing a mixture of wooded forests and gardens, man-made water courses, and vegetable farms developed by residents.

Heavy industry was logically sited at the outskirts of the city, with easier access to transportation hubs on land, sea, and to the new airport, while Hiroshima's commercial district was located alongside the Regional Army Headquarters in the center of the city, which together dominated the greater portion of town. The densely built-up area in the heart of the city that had evolved over decades now contained over 190,000 of the city's total population of 320,000.

Residents' dwellings were primarily constructed of wood, a mixture of one and two stories. The roof coverings were mostly hardburnt black tile.[8] There were no masonry division walls, and large groups of dwellings clustered together. The construction, coupled with outdated firefighting equipment and poorly trained personnel, risked serious fires breaking out even in peacetime.[9] As had been analyzed by the United States Chemical Weapons Service, many Japanese wood-framed residential and industrial buildings were of poor construction by American standards. As the CWS technicians had pinpointed at Dugway Proving Ground, their points of weakness were throughout the supporting beams in the roofs and ceilings. Though building standards had been tightened prewar because of the Tokyo earthquake in 1923, industrial buildings had an array of their own weak points, too—primarily the mixed quality of the materials. As we shall see in later chapters, this would play a crucial role in what emergency services were functioning in the aftermath of the atomic attack.

It was now three years since the outbreak of the war, Italy was almost knocked out, and Germany was on the retreat in France and Eastern Europe. Senkichi Awaya could see that in East Asia, American and Allied forces were ever nearer the Home Islands. He sensed the mortal danger Japan faced could become a reality without a change in her fortunes. Like any government official or military officer, such defeatist thoughts he kept to himself. Though the Japanese public were shielded by government propaganda, it was obvious from his own government and police contacts in Tokyo, as well as private discussions with his son-in-law, Hiroshi Sakama, who now managed the labor department in Kobe, that the future looked grim. Too many "ash boxes" were coming home now to hide the scale of the Imperial Army's losses. The one outlet he had to express such fears daily was with his assistant, Kazumasa Maruyama, a fellow Christian he trusted completely. Both men read the Bible together and found time to share whispered conversations.

The firebombing of Tokyo and other cities had forced his hand. Although it dismayed him, he authorized the demolition of sections of the city, damage not seen since the infamous floods of 1653. It would leave thousands homeless, many of whom he now encountered every day queuing outside the mayoral department seeking compensation and advice on where to go and how to get there. What remained of the prefecture's railway system, much like the national network, was now monopolized by the Army as it transported thousands of men and supplies south for the expected American invasion. Seeing so many people—the elderly, women, and children sleeping on the streets, housed in tents, many left to scratch out survival begging for help and food—left Awaya distraught.

But there was nothing he could do. The order had come down from the central government's Department of the Interior, the same department that had appointed him as mayor two summers ago. He had the military and the secret police to contend with, too, he knew. The one relief of the demolitions came from Field Marshal Hata's military headquarters. The bridges would not be pulled down. Even Hata could agree that would be impractical for his soldiers' mobility. Once the time came to defend Hiroshima or fight the Americans in urban combat, his men and the Hiroshima militia needed to be able to navigate the city quickly.

In the late summer of 1944, the Christian church in Hiroshima where Awaya regularly worshipped closed. Despite Japan signing the Tripartite Pact in 1940, such Christian orders run by Germans and Italian priests were viewed suspiciously by the military regime, in keeping with their xenophobic policies since the 1930s. Awaya now chose to worship at home, singing to himself the hymns missionaries had introduced to Japan. But he had a reputation for honesty, his office was open to ordinary citizens to voice their complaints, and he seemed to care. As a result, he was one of the most popular mayors the city had ever known. Such popularity afforded him a degree of protection from Army interference. Awaya wasn't foolish enough to believe he was untouchable. He knew the military ruled the city and that attempts had been made to subvert his staff, but they were in the main loyal to him.

City after city across Japan had suffered a similar fate to Tokyo's on March 10. Reports came through every other day of yet more places attacked, suffering heavy civilian casualties. The port city of

Kobe, two hundred miles north of Hiroshima in Hyogo Prefecture, in particular had suffered great damage on March 17 when a force of 331 B-29s destroyed several square miles of the city, killing almost 9,000 people and displacing 650,000. Both civic and military authorities in Hiroshima looked on from a distance and made what preparations they could. But still, by the early summer of 1945, no enemy bombers had attacked the city or the naval dockyard in any great numbers. Awaya was initially confident about the likelihood of Hiroshima not being targeted by the American bombers. His wife and eldest son had listened to his fears about what could happen to Tokyo. Mrs. Awaya had arrived from the capital by train on April 28. Her journey had been severely delayed due to several impromptu stops as carrier-based enemy fighters had been spotted flying above looking for targets.

She would scout out the city for their third son, fourteen-year-old Shinobu, to join them, where he could continue his studies. Their remaining second daughter, Yasuko, would remain in the capital, where she worked in a munitions factory. Her older sister, Motoko, was now a mother and, for now, living out of harm's way on the outskirts of Kobe. Her husband had been hospitalized with a stomach complaint. The mayor had dispatched his assistant Maruyama to welcome his wife off the packed Tokyo train. As he guided the exhausted mother and son through the throng to a waiting car, Maruyama urged her to be confident in the decision to move:

And here you will be safe. Hiroshima is not a large city. They will bomb other places first. By the time it is our turn to be attacked the war will be over.[10]

She was taken to Senkichi's mayoral residence in the government district of Kako-michi, nestled in relative peace and quiet on the island between the Ota and Motoyadu Rivers. After the trauma of Tokyo, she slowly relaxed. It was now the weekend, with time to settle in with her husband and perhaps contemplate prayer and sing hymns. The new accommodation was a world away from the war she had left behind a few days earlier. Already she was keen that their Shinobu should follow her here as soon as possible. Maruyama, however, had spoken too soon. Two days later, as the city bustled with the start of the workweek, Hiroshima suffered its first attack from a B-29 bomber. Fortunately, it was not a major air raid, but a lone plane, perhaps lost or suffering some form of damage, that flew across the city and caused pandemonium.

It appeared out of the blue at over twenty thousand feet, coming in from the north undetected until it was too late, and it dropped its payload into the heart of the city before antiaircraft batteries could engage. Twenty-four buildings were caught in the blasts, with the Nomura Life Insurance Building taking the brunt. Ten people had been killed and thirty more injured. Perhaps mindful of how badly the defense of Okinawa was going, the military authorities in the city ordered an immediate news blackout.

As Awaya and his officers took stock of the damage and casualties, the reality that a storm was coming could not be ignored. If they believed the various reports from the government, the prefecture governor's office, and the headquarters of the Second General Army, Hiroshima would be firmly in the path of the enemy's invasion plans.

Chapter Twenty

NATIONAL SUICIDE

Within four months we shall in all probability have
completed the most terrible weapon ever known in human
history, one bomb of which could destroy a whole city.
TOP SECRET MEMO[1]

At the foot of Mount Futaba, a twenty-minute walk from the center
of the city, ensconced in a well-dug bunker, and surrounded by a
copse of pine trees, sat Field Marshal Shunroku Hata's headquarters.
It was an apt choice. The mountain sat at the *kimon* ("demon gate"),
to the northwest of his military compound at Hiroshima Castle. Historically, this was the direction from which misfortune was thought
to come, and Hiroshima's feudal rulers had taken the threat seriously.
To stop such evil in its tracks, they had commissioned the building of
a string of temples and shrines along the foot of the mountain. Hata
was wise enough to know superstition and tradition wouldn't keep an
American bomber, or the US Marines, from attacking the city. Each
morning, he was fully prepared to meet the enemy head-on.

Hata was one of the most successful and respected commanders in Japan, so he knew how badly the war was going. Though he
supported the government propaganda that a "divine wind" (*shimpu*)
might arrive to rescue Japan, he was realistic enough to understand
the task ahead. He was confident, with the reinforcements arriving
daily to bolster Kyushu's defense, that he *might* be able to stifle the
enemy's invasion plans.

The field marshal's life had prepared him for this moment. The sixty-five-year-old commander was a respected military hero, with strong ties to the highest reaches of Japanese society. He had fought valiantly and been wounded during the Russo-Japanese War in 1904–05 and had attended the Paris Peace Conference. In the war with China in the 1930s, he had led the offensive against Chinese forces around Nanking, and though his army had committed horrendous atrocities against the local population, his reputation had not been tarnished. As war came to Europe in 1939, Hata was Japan's minister of war and had also served as Emperor Hirohito's chief aide-de-camp. But it would be China that again drew him back to fighting command.

In 1941, as he campaigned like a feudal lord of old leading his samurai retinue, he had ruled over much of central China with more than a half-million troops. While proclaiming that his policy was to "defeat Chiang but love his people," Hata would again be accused of turning a blind eye to the repeated atrocities committed by his troops, both against the civilian population and American fliers who had the misfortune of falling into the hands of his soldiers. He had overseen the semi-victorious Ichi-Go offensive the previous year, which pushed into southeastern China to destroy Chiang Kai-shek's Nationalist forces and capture the US air bases from which Curtis LeMay's B-29s attacked Japanese shipping and mainland targets. Having reached a bloody stalemate, Hata again emerged with his reputation seemingly intact, Hirohito decorating him with the First-Class Order of the Golden Kite.

Returning to the Home Islands in June 1944, he was made a field marshal and by the year's end was appointed inspector general of military training, a pivotal position within the Imperial Army. With the country being firebombed from the air, the fall of Iwo Jima, and American forces looking likely to take Okinawa, the invasion of Japan's southern island Kyushu seemed imminent. Hata was seen by both the military and political elite as the best person to install discipline and raise the morale of the ragtag forces he would have under his command. He would gather many of his former trusted subordinates from earlier campaigns to comprise his personal staff.

Japanese military strategists at Imperial General Headquarters had been debating for many months where the Americans would launch their invasion of the Home Islands. Would it be targeted toward Kyushu in the south or would they drive directly on Honshu to take Tokyo lying on the Kanto Plain?[2] Since the early spring, the War Ministry and the military had been busy mobilizing the country's remaining forces. Forty-two divisions and eighteen independent brigades would be assembled, totaling over 1.5 million troops, to defend Japan to the bitter end.

Imperial Army commanders had received detailed instructions on April 8 to conduct homeland defense preparations. Code-named Katsu-Go, the nationwide plan would try to destroy any American fleet intending to invade the country while still at sea. Like Iwo Jima before and the ongoing battle on Okinawa, the defenders' sole aim was to inflict heavy casualties that would stop the Americans from establishing a bridgehead on the mainland. Such a price in blood would sap their willingness to continue the fight. Imperial Japanese Army and Navy formations would coordinate strikes on land and at sea to achieve this aim. The First General Army would protect and defend the main island of Honshu and the capital Tokyo. The Second General Army, under Hata's command, would assume the pivotal role of resisting any American assault on Kyushu. Hata's Second General Army senior staff were convinced that Kyushu would be the enemy's objective. By establishing a bridgehead, the Americans could repeat what they had done on other captured islands: construct bases for their air and naval forces to then pound the defenders farther north as US Army and Marines fought their way toward the capital. If that happened, the battle for the nation was lost. Hata was aware that government officials had given his command a higher priority than ones on Honshu.

Remarkably, the Japanese had guessed accurately where and how the enemy would strike—code-named Operation Downfall. Since March, debate continued within Truman's administration and the Pentagon whether to invade the Home Islands. There were arguments for and against, measured with how many American and Japanese casualties might result, magnified by the actual losses suffered at Okinawa and the recapture of the Philippines by General MacArthur. The president refereed the arguments for and against between, among others, Army Chief General Marshall and the president's chief of staff, Admiral Leahy. The former pushed for Downfall, while the latter blanched at the expected human cost. The president, with no other military alternative, had approved the start of preparations. General MacArthur and Admiral Nimitz would now formulate their plans.

Downfall would be a two-phased offensive: The amphibious landing and capture of the southern island (Operation Olympic) would see the American invasion fleet launch MacArthur's Sixth Army (comprising nine US Army and three Marine Corps divisions) along three bays of western Kyushu. They would establish a bridgehead, push through the limited number of mountain passes that encircled the coastline, and drive northward. Once southern Kyushu was cleared, engineers would build airfields, and Kagoshima Bay would serve as a major naval base and port for preparing for the second phase should Japan not surrender: Operation Coronet.

Coronet envisaged an initial assault by the First and Eighth Armies, composed of nine infantry and three Marine Corps divisions. After the initial amphibious landings, a force of three infantry, one Marine division, and two Army divisions would come ashore at two sites on the eastern coast of central Honshu. Allied military forces would drive to envelop Tokyo and Yokohama and the remainder of the Kanto Plain. MacArthur's planners believed up to twenty-five divisions would be needed to seize all the objectives. Despite concerns about terrain and the winter weather in Japan, Olympic was to launch by November 1, 1945.

Upon arriving to take command of the Second General Army, Field Marshal Hata was acutely aware that the coastal defenses needed reinforcement. Hiroshima and the whole prefecture's civilian population would have to shoulder the burden if his plans were to be successful. For a man who commanded respect from his subordinates, the relationship with the city's mayor was one he would need to handle differently.

Hata intended to make the Americans pay dearly for every inch of Japanese soil. The price in blood the defenders of Okinawa were making the Americans pay would be nothing compared to what he intended. Kyushu would be converted into one enormous killing zone for the enemy. From the Goto Islands in the north to the Osumi Peninsula to the south, Hata's military administrators would oversee a system of interlocking defenses—much in the way that German forces had done throughout Normandy in France. A series of layered, heavily fortified defensive lines would stretch back from the coast, line by line. They would be coordinated via a complex communications network, controlled via Hiroshima to Hata's headquarters at the base of Mount Fuma. Hiroshima itself would be guarded by forty thousand Imperial troops, primarily around the castle complex.

Aware of the overwhelming strength of American forces, Hata was convinced that only fanatical resistance could blunt their momentum and, if they were lucky, bring the United States to the negotiating table. His staff officers were overseeing an army of four hundred thousand, though of various fighting quality. He had been pleased when given the news that one of the key architects of the Imperial Navy's victory at Pearl Harbor, General Minoru Genda, had been sent to Kyushu to command a fighter group, though he would not oversee the expected hundreds of kamikaze units now stationed throughout Kyushu and ready to inflict even greater casualties on the US Navy. Suicide strikes would not just come from the air. Thousands of Japanese marines were currently putting the finishing touches on seaborne kamikaze units. Hundreds of small boats outfitted with motors were being packed with high-explosive charges. Camouflaged in hard-to-find inlets and coves around Hiroshima Bay, these boats and their sole occupants would ram US Navy landing craft.

But fanaticism was not exclusive to the Japanese military. Hata expected every Japanese citizen to sacrifice him- or herself once the enemy had landed and urban fighting began. Young and old, healthy or infirm—it was to be a nationwide fight to the death, from throwing bamboo spears at advancing American troops to children throwing the three million petrol bombs or planting booby traps that were currently being created in hundreds of small workshops. Though many Japanese publicly went along with such plans, many privately knew it was folly. One government official overhearing an evacuated civilian complained: "As the war progressed, even some soldiers were unable to get their guns and other war equipment. We, too, drilled for the approaching battle for the homeland with bamboo spears. How can a man fight a mechanized army with bamboo spears? We were deceived by the army leaders who constantly told the people that Japan will emerge victorious in the end."[3]

For military men like Hata, it was more than symbolism. This sacrifice, however futile, might still bring some sort of strategic victory. Nevertheless, it was beyond his imagination that Hiroshima itself would become the target for a superweapon.

With the city's civilian and judicial departments reorganizing to work alongside the Imperial Army, Awaya had urgent concerns only Hata could address. The mayor read more bulletins of American firebombing attacks that seemed to be happening almost daily. Large parts of Tokyo were a smoking ruin, the Imperial Palace had been struck and lightly damaged, and one by one, cities throughout the Home Islands were being reduced to rubble and ashes. And now, he knew, Okinawa had been lost to the enemy—at great cost to the local population. The field marshal needed to address the civilian authorities' concerns about the city's children, food supplies, and air raid protection.

Awaya delicately questioned the plans for the evacuation of the city's population. He had informed Hata's headquarters that of the prewar total of 320,000, only sixty thousand had thus far relocated. What would now be the fate of the thousands of young teenagers who currently worked in the many small-arms factories and workshops dotted throughout the city? Hiroshima was no different from the rest of Japan: it housed a widespread cottage industry that created and supplied arms, munitions, clothing, and other supplies to the military. Awaya voiced concern about their education, knowing it was a low priority for the military. Daily memos from his council officers described teachers forced to travel from one factory to the next to provide basic lessons. Many were forced to conduct impromptu lessons on the factory floor due to time constraints on delivery quotas as local firms managed twenty-four-hour shifts.

Just as concerning was the military's new law of corralling thousands of older schoolchildren to work alongside soldiers and construction gangs to assist with the forced demolition of whole streets in the city to create firebreaks.[4] The mayor's office was handling complaints from thousands of Hiroshima residents whose buildings were being torn down by order of the military authorities. The previous November, 291,809 square feet had been cleared at 133 different locations around the city. By the time Field Marshal Hata took up his command, over three thousand more buildings had followed suit, with hundreds of others earmarked to be pulled down by the teams of special district guards and volunteer citizen corps.

Many were now forced to live in the streets, move in with relatives, or leave the city. On the one hand, this final option alleviated Mayor Awaya's fears to relocate the population out of harm's way, but the homeless were now clogging up the city's transport network as more troops came into the prefecture. It was stress and paperwork the mayor's departments could do without as they tried to solve the city's most urgent issue—a lack of food.

Since the spring, civilian authorities had worried about dwindling food supplies in the government warehouses as well as stores, shops, and school kitchens. The American blockade of the country had strangled imports of basic foodstuffs. Japan's prewar merchant fleet had measured almost 6.5 million tons, but by the beginning of 1945, it had fallen sharply to 2.5 million. American submarines had sunk over 1,100 merchant ships, and US carrier fleets now dominated the waters around the Home Islands.

Apart from American firebombing raids, enemy bombers had been targeting supply lines and rice production areas. What reserve food stocks Awaya's officials had were being drained by the increasing number of troops arriving in the region. This could be seen on the streets of the city. Prewar shops in Hiroshima had totaled over two thousand before 1941, but now there were fewer than 150 open for business, offering few essentials and fewer stocks of the much-prized cooking oil.

Hiroshima mirrored every other major city and town in the country, with hundreds of "victory gardens" sprouting in all manner of places, for locals to grow what they could to survive. Corruption within local government, the occupying military, and the black market all took their share of what little there was. The city was slowly starving, with no expectation it would get better anytime soon. Morale was ebbing.

A month before the field marshal's headquarters became fully operational, Awaya had decided to travel to Tokyo. His wife's vivid descriptions of the firebombing had left him frantic about what to do with his remaining children who had now been evacuated from the capital. He worried about all four of his children. Their eldest daughter, Motoko, living with her husband and two-year-old daughter Ayako in Kobe, was now enduring B-29 air raids; his second-oldest daughter, Yasuko, had now been mobilized to serve in Nigata on the west coast of Honshu, and he longed to see his youngest daughter, Chikaku (nine years old), and his two sons, Shinobu (fourteen years old) and Tadashi (twelve years old), all of whom had now been evacuated to the relatively safety of central Japan. Like hundreds of thousands of other Japanese children, Awaya's youngest offspring had been moved away from the cities and towns when the bombing increased. The hope was they would be safe in the countryside.

Awaya would also take advantage of the trip to meet trusted friends at his local Bible society and also colleagues in the government and police. They might add detail to his growing concerns about supplies to Hiroshima and what the military's plan was for the coming year. Yasuko was permitted to meet him in the capital, and Shinobu was leaving the place of his evacuation to travel to meet them, too. He hoped they could make a decision about their continued education as well as what to do with the now-empty family residence.

Taking the train the four hundred miles north to Tokyo was a stop-start affair. Enemy aircraft activity caused delays, or his train was sidelined by troop trains heading south. He looked out his window to study what he was passing by, catching the eye every now and again of a young man's face, usually serious looking, the odd one in animated conversation with friends he couldn't see farther inside the carriage. Many of them seemed no older than Shinobu, and he was barely fourteen. When his train was sitting idly in a queue, it was stopped at security checkpoints, overseen by the Kempeitai, where travelers had to hand over their papers. Despite his position as mayor, he was still checked and formally questioned before being politely waved on his way. He noticed how intimidated his fellow passengers were by the intrusion.

Since the unconditional surrender of Germany on May 8, the Kempeitai were rounding up anyone they believed to be a subversive or citizens overheard complaining about the conduct of the war. The authorities were aware that many Japanese were tuning in to American broadcast radio to get a true picture of the war's progress.[5] Operating from their base in Hiroshima Castle, the several-hundred-strong security force had full powers of arrest over every civilian and soldier in the city. Over four hundred prominent public figures had been taken in by the summer, including a high-court judge and a former ambassador. If anything, the closer his train got to Tokyo, the tighter the internal security seemed to be.

After he saw the smoking ruins of cities en route to the capital, Awaya's concerns turned to dread once he caught sight of Tokyo in the twilight. The center of the city in Chiyoda Ward was a charred ruin. Though the train station was functioning and still in relatively good shape, as he walked through the lines of tents and crowds of people, the mayor didn't recognize his old surroundings. Many landmark streets had simply disappeared. The incendiaries had gutted the southern wing of the Imperial Hotel, Tokyo's iconic place to stay, designed by the renowned American architect Frank Lloyd Wright in 1923. He could only tell which direction to head toward home by the piles of rubble denoting where a road had been.

As he progressed farther to the north and past the Imperial Palace, the buildings that had survived were covered in government slogans: *Forget Self! All Out for Your Country!* In some places, the slogans were covered in hundreds of scraps of paper. As he stopped to study them, he recognized them as burial notes. There were also desperate messages looking for loved ones, telling them where the writer had gone and how to find them. It was both traumatic and depressing.

It was getting dark, and the blackout transformed the city into a surreal, alien world where he would recognize a neighborhood, only to then take another turn into a smoking wasteland. Several times he had to retrace his steps to take the correct route to his neighborhood. As he walked on, so his anger grew. The military in Hiroshima had hidden the true scale of the destruction from him. Their accusations of scaremongering leveled against the refugees who had flooded into Hiroshima were lies. What these terrified survivors had said was true.

His black mood lifted only once he caught sight of Yasuko. He gave thanks to God that she and the other children had been spared so far, as had the family's house in the northwest of the city. He handed over what little food he had managed to bring with him from Hiroshima and over dinner discussed with the children how they should now look after it when he returned to Hiroshima and what to do in the event of further air raids. He felt sure more would come. The next day, he visited his government contacts to give an update on events in the city and his ongoing relationship with the military, and he caught up on gossip about the war in general. That evening, he attended a Bible study group.

Early the next morning, accompanied by Yasuko, Awaya traveled back into the center of Tokyo to take the train south to Hiroshima. He felt a great weight on his shoulders, and they spoke very little as the taxi trundled along the six miles to Shibuya Station. He hated leaving the children alone when he knew the city was still a major target. Around the station were all the sights of destruction, with the sides of buildings scorched black from the firebombing. Yasuko walked arm in arm with him to the platform, through the crowds of soldiers boarding the two dozen carriages and their loved ones standing back to see them off. The street hawkers had fewer things to sell than in Hiroshima, he thought. As he placed his suitcase up into the doorway of his compartment, he turned to embrace his daughter. He gripped her arms and spoke above the station noise into her ear:

"We are both living on the edge of life and death, and we must think that this is the last time we will be parted."

He tightened his grip and repeated: "We must think that this is the last time we will be parted!"

He stepped back. She tried to smile as she wiped away her tears.

He wanted to leave her with some hope. He leaned forward again and kissed her tenderly on the cheek. She embraced him again before he ripped himself away to step up to board the train. Two old women eyed him as he took his seat opposite them. They seemed very much alike, perhaps elderly sisters. Both were dressed in dark blue kimonos, their silver hair trussed up in buns. One carried a book, while her companion clutched her small wicker case to her stomach. He wondered if it had food inside. He bowed and formally greeted them as he took his seat in the six-berth cabin. It would be close to midnight by the time the train got into Hiroshima, if they were lucky.

Finally arriving home, Awaya provided his wife with details of the trip and news on their children. He had arranged for Shinobu to travel down in June to be with them, while Yasuko would stay to manage the house. He saved describing the full extent of the destruction he had seen all around him in Tokyo. There was little need to worry her further; he had enough anxiety for both of them. After their meal, he went to his study to read passages from the Bible.

Back at his city office the next day, Awaya discovered Genshin Takano would be the new governor of Hiroshima Prefecture after Isei Otsuka left to become the head of Chugoku Sokan-fu. As the person in charge of civil air defense and having experienced the bombing of Osaka, Takano had a sense of the danger of the delay in preliminary measures against air raids.

"Currently, this city has relatively few air raids, but I am ready for possible massive air raids in the near future. As this is a small city with many rivers, most of the buildings are built of wood. In the event of a fire, we would have a difficult situation. I am alarmed and worried."

Although there was no way for the mayor to know that air raids on Hiroshima had been forbidden because the city was the future target of atomic bombing, Takano expressed worry in a letter written on July 20 about the lack of air raids and hastened the process of organizing an evacuation: "Amid the situation where many medium- and small-sized cities were destroyed, our Hiroshima City has had only minor damage. I feel rather uneasy about it. I am unsure if preparations for evacuation can be completed before a possible at- tack, but I have implemented them on a large scale."

Still, the firebombing continued throughout the coastal cities, as Osaka and Kobe once again took a pounding, the naval ports being crippled. Along with the rest of the city, Field Marshal Hata would catch sight of American carrier-based P-38 fighter-bombers swooping across the bay, having strafed targets inland. Since his arrival in Hiro- shima, the commander would rise at 6 a.m. in the house he'd had built closer to his headquarters. After a bath, he would dress in his kimono to have breakfast with his wife, then dress in his military uniform, con- duct prayers, and tend to his vegetable garden. By 8 a.m. he was ready to travel the short distance to his offices. Unlike most of his staff of- ficers, who rode in on horseback, Hata took a chauffeured limousine.

As the field marshal discussed reports of nearby air raids and lone B-29s flying at high altitudes, at City Hall Awaya studied the new lists of demolished streets and met with a fresh line of homeless residents. He studied the long line of concerned, tired citizens, who he worried now faced a future of slow starvation. He thanked the lord that his eldest son, Shinobu, was safe at his residence with his wife. He then took an extended lunch to do something that had been on his mind since he returned from Tokyo. He wrote to Yasuko. She needed to hear his confidence about the future: "Let us do our best and live like Japanese. There is no doubt that we will win. But I may collapse before then, and we will meet in heaven."[6]

They were prophetic words.

Chapter Twenty-One

THE DETONATION DEBATE

---

*The various waterways give ideal conditions. They allow
for no chance of mistaking the city. Hiroshima can be
approached from any direction for a perfect bombing run.*
COLONEL PAUL TIBBETS JR.[1]

It was July 1945, and MacArthur's and Nimitz's staffs were well underway laying the foundations for Operation Olympic. Yet there was still disharmony about when it should be given the go-ahead. The United States was in a state of semi-celebration. The war in Europe had been won, American troops in that theater were starting to return home, and even their supreme commander, General Dwight D. Eisenhower, had returned to a ticker-tape hero's welcome in New York. But still, the casualties continued every day in the Pacific, and the heartbreaking letters from parents who had lost young sons arrived at the door of the White House. Truman was a soldier's soldier, a veteran of the Great War, and a man who felt the responsibility of command deeply.

The previous month, on June 18, he had overseen a frank discussion of opinions in the Oval Office. Presenting the plan for the invasion of Japan, the Joint Chiefs sat alongside Henry Stimson, Secretary of the Navy James Forrestal, Assistant Secretary of War John McCloy, and General Ira Eaker, representing Hap Arnold, still recuperating from his recent heart attack. Though most attendees supported Olympic and the acceptance of Soviet forces' involvement in the Pacific, one dissenting voice held sway due to his position:

Truman's chief of staff, Admiral Leahy. The old sailor and wily politician who had previously been President Roosevelt's right-hand man now took issue with General Marshall and Admiral King over predicted casualties should Olympic go ahead.

Whereas the chiefs of the Army and Navy sided with research that reflected American losses suffered in MacArthur's Philippines campaign—one for every five Japanese killed—Leahy argued for realism. He cited the brutal statistics from the fighting in Okinawa, which ran much higher, at 35 percent. If this rate was repeated on the Japanese mainland, then what could they expect from sending in over 750,000 soldiers, sailors, and Marines? Despite his protestations, Leahy was outnumbered as Stimson, Forrestal, and Eaker joined to support the other Joint Chiefs and argued for Olympic.

Still Leahy persisted, looking for an option, however remote. The meeting's minutes recorded the moment: "Admiral Leahy said that he could not agree with those who said to him that unless we obtain the unconditional surrender of the Japanese that we will have lost the war. He feared no menace from Japan in the foreseeable future, even if we were unsuccessful in forcing unconditional surrender. What he did fear was that our insistence on unconditional surrender would result only in making the Japanese desperate and thereby increase our casualty lists. He did not think this was at all necessary."[2]

The elephant in the room that dogged American decision-making was the lack of accurate data on enemy numbers and their fighting ability. United States Army intelligence intercepts could provide information on Japanese troop movements, but no actual hard evidence as to their strategic intentions. Olympic was therefore based on a series of theories about how the enemy could defend against the invasion. It was not based on reality.

Since May, American analysts had continually changed their figures, and always upward. Two days before the meeting in Truman's office, a new estimate of three hundred thousand casualties had been stated. By August 2, this figure was drastically revised to 534,000, with the added fear that the Japanese were mobilizing civilians to replace Imperial Japanese Army logistical personnel, who could then be mustered for combat duty. Further decrypted Japanese coded messages, supported by Allied aerial reconnaissance photography, now reported a fleet of 3,335 combat and 3,530 obsolete training aircraft to be used for kamikaze attacks that required limited fuel and only basic piloting skills for such one-way missions. This figure was revised upward by Admiral Nimitz's intelligence staff, to 10,290 aircraft.

The fear of kamikaze attacks only depressed American military planners further. Studies of Okinawa had shown that a kamikaze had a 32 percent chance of hitting a US Navy ship—a success rate almost 1,000 percent greater than conventional aircraft attacks by bombing. Moreover, MacArthur's Olympic planners did not know how the Japanese military intended to defend the country, generalizing only that "troop movements and dispositions clearly emphasise preparation for all-out defense of the home islands," and that Tokyo considered invasion "certain, if not imminent." Another fear was that Japan would use "chemical or new kinds of weapons."

Admiral Leahy was still attempting to argue the case for accepting what lay in store for such a large-scale military offensive. He brought up the topic of the government's demands for unconditional surrender. How, he argued, might that influence Japanese determination to defend their emperor? He threw in another argument to the discussion. Could there be an argument to keep Hirohito in place? Truman quickly shut the topic down, saying they must respect public opinion, the losses the United States had and still was incurring, and the fact that the country had been attacked without warning at Pearl Harbor. It was now that Stimson's assistant secretary of war, John McCloy, voiced his idea about "the bomb." Leahy frowned at the introduction of the subject. He had always argued with Roosevelt against the Manhattan Project, not just on moral grounds but in the belief it would not work and was a waste of time, resources, and money. Aware of Leahy's opinion, McCloy ignored him anyway and asked the question: Should the American government warn the

Japanese of its impending use? Perhaps to spare his chief of staff's further ire, having lost the argument on Olympic, President Truman declared he would postpone that discussion until the "device" had been successfully tested.

Truman had been miserable all summer long. Casualty reports continued to come from all parts of the Pacific theater, approximately seven thousand dead a week. Though he had signed off on Olympic, it left him depressed and fearful it could turn out to be a giant Okinawa, which would itself then be dwarfed in comparison to the eventual assault on Honshu. Alone in the White House, his family still residing in Missouri, the new president agonized over his decision in his diary entry at night: "I have to decide Japanese strategy—shall we invade Japan proper, or shall we bomb and blockade? This is my hardest decision to date. But I'll make it when I have all the facts."

Despite his concerns about the cost in young American lives for the final act in the Pacific campaign, Truman failed to mention in his diary that the work done by General Groves, Oppenheimer, and his team in the New Mexico desert was about to come to fruition. How could he? It was top secret. But the tectonic plates of the war were shifting into final gear.

Four days after the Olympic meeting in the Oval Office, in Tokyo, Emperor Hirohito finally ordered his inner cabinet to initiate peace discussions via the Soviets. Forty-eight hours later, his former prime minister Koki Hirota met with the Soviet ambassador in Tokyo, Jacob Malik, to request a stronger agreement to replace their neutrality pact. Malik was no fool and had been warned by Moscow that the Japanese could lobby to keep Stalin away from the Pacific— he waited two days in an effort to show he considered it a serious discussion, before rebuffing it. For Stalin, bigger rewards than peace with Japan were to be had elsewhere. Truman had agreed to meet with him and his old adversary Winston Churchill in Potsdam, Germany. As his office made plans for the trip to Europe, battalions of Seabee engineers and construction workers were busy turning the wreckage of Okinawa into a purpose-built aircraft carrier and naval facility with one goal in mind—the invasion of Japan.

Truman was lonely, away from his family and venturing across the Atlantic for the first time since he was an artillery officer in the Great War. He was naturally apprehensive about how he would perform against the political titans Churchill and Stalin at the Potsdam Conference. The British prime minister was about to find out whether he would survive the coming general election. Truman had bigger issues on his mind, dealing with the world's greatest political survivor, Joseph Stalin. The president was an enthusiastic cardplayer, but this was for higher stakes: the postwar settlement in Europe, with Red Army tanks parked on the river Elbe, splitting Germany in two; and of course, how to bring the war with Japan to a speedy close. In his corner he would have two of Roosevelt's men, Secretary of War Henry Stimson and Truman's chief of staff, Admiral Leahy. His new secretary of state, James Byrnes, was as green as the president when it came to international diplomacy. The Grand Alliance was coming to its natural conclusion, with the once-fervent suitors now growing tired and wary of one another. He confided to his wife in a note just before departing on the USS *Augusta*, "I sure dread this trip worse than anything I've had to face."[3] He hoped for imminent news from New Mexico that would strengthen his hand.

Until he had confirmation that the Gadget worked, his future plans were in the air. Oppenheimer's team, setting up the vast metal tower at the test site at Alamogordo Bombing Range some two hundred miles to the south of Los Alamos, still had little idea whether it would work and, if so, how powerful the explosion would be. With the supply of plutonium successfully operational form the Hanford site, both Groves and his weapons director knew they had to test it. The locals had fortuitously nicknamed the area where the site was set up "Jornada del Muerto," or "Journey of Death." It was an apt name. For the past several weeks, preparations had been made. Three observation bunkers had been built. Each bunker, sited ten thousand yards north, west, and south of the test tower, titled Ground Zero, would attempt to measure key aspects of the reaction, the size of the fireball, and radioactivity.

On July 15, the site was struck by a thunderstorm. The Gadget was in place, suspended one hundred feet within a specially constructed metal tower, ready for firing. In the command bunker, Oppenheimer waited anxiously with Groves for the go-ahead. Waiting with Groves and his assistant brigadier general, Thomas Farrell, at base camp were the main players from Washington who had gotten the Gadget this far: Vannevar Bush and James Conant. The top scientists from Los Alamos were elsewhere within the bunkers—Enrico Fermi, Edward Teller, and Ernest Lawrence. Groves had dictated three separate letters once the Gadget had detonated, the third to be opened only if they were all killed.

At precisely 5:30 a.m., the Gadget detonated. The New Mexico desert was lit up as if it was midday. The tower instantly vaporized, the asphalt base was turned into green sand, and an orange-and-red fireball grew in intensity, evolving into a mushroom shape as it ascended ten thousand feet into the brightly illuminated heavens. Grove shook hands with both Bush and Conant, and when Oppenheimer appeared after the test, the general warmly congratulated him, saying, "I'm proud of you." The military man in Farrell led him to succinctly summarize his conclusion as he shook his superior officer's hand: "The war's over." The test would later be measured as giving off the energy equivalent of twenty thousand tons of TNT.

The United States finally had the bomb. Groves sent his coded report to Henry Stimson, who read it aloud to the president. Within twenty-four hours, both men were informed that a uranium bomb would be ready for use at "the first favorable opportunity in August." He may have been excited when Stimson and Bush had first informed him of the Manhattan Project's existence, but now, with the Trinity test successful, his private papers from Potsdam reveal a different side, a sudden wariness in the ex-artilleryman of how such an extraordinary weapon should be used:

We have discovered the most terrible bomb in the history of the world. It may be the fore prophesised in the Euphrates Valley Era, after Noah and his fabulous Ark. . . . An experiment in the New Mexico desert was startling—to put it mildly. Thirteen pounds of the explosive caused the complete disintegration of a steel tower 60 feet high, created a crater 6 feet deep and 1200 feet in diameter, knocked over a steel tower 1/2 mile away and knocked men down 10,000 yards away. The explosion was visible for more than 200 miles and audible for miles or more.

The weapon is to be used against Japan between now and August 10th. I have told Sec. of War Mr. Stimson to use it so that military objectives and soldiers and sailors are the target and not women and children. Even if the Japs are savages, ruthless, merciless and fanatic, we as the leader of the world for the common welfare cannot drop this terrible bomb on the old Capitol or the new.[4]

Potsdam showcased the poker face of Joseph Stalin at its stoniest. Truman discussed with Winston Churchill how the news to the Soviet leader should be delivered. Their conversations took on an almost funereal atmosphere as news came through of Churchill's defeat at the polls. Great Britain had a new leader, Clement Attlee, who would fly out to Potsdam two weeks after Trinity.

Potsdam was marred by bitter recriminations among the three leaders about the postwar status of Poland, and indeed the rest of Soviet-occupied Eastern Europe. Despite this, with regard to Japan, the president followed his predecessor's gamble of desiring Russian entry into the East Asian theater. If it could bring about a rapid victory over the fanatical Japanese and save American lives, Truman would accept it. The daily news from Okinawa was bad. It was proving to be a bloodbath. The Potsdam Declaration was issued to Japan on July 26: Britain, the United States, and the Allies wanted nothing short of unconditional surrender. Despite the continued discussions of Russian troops coming in to support the final push on Japan, Stalin was not formally given the green light, nor had he been consulted on the declaration. He was furious. In any event, Japan officially responded to the declaration two days later. It was negative.

Amid the high-stakes debate, the day before the declaration was issued General Spaatz, now leading the Strategic Air Forces for the coming invasion of Japan, discussed Groves's written order to use the atomic strike weapon with a select group of senior officers in the office of his new chief of staff, Curtis LeMay, on Guam. Operation Centerboard had chosen Hiroshima as the top target for a strike. After discussing with Tibbets the mission's specifics, Spaatz then briefed the most senior Army commander in the Pacific theater, Douglas MacArthur, who replied, "This will completely change all our ideas of warfare."

On August 1, Truman was back on board the USS *Augusta*, with Byrnes secretly briefing members of the press he trusted about the Trinity test. News came through of yet further air raids from LeMay's B-29s: over sixty Japanese cities had been pounded to rubble or reduced to ashes. The president would be making his way home across the Atlantic, now free of any German U-boat threat.

Part V

FALLOUT

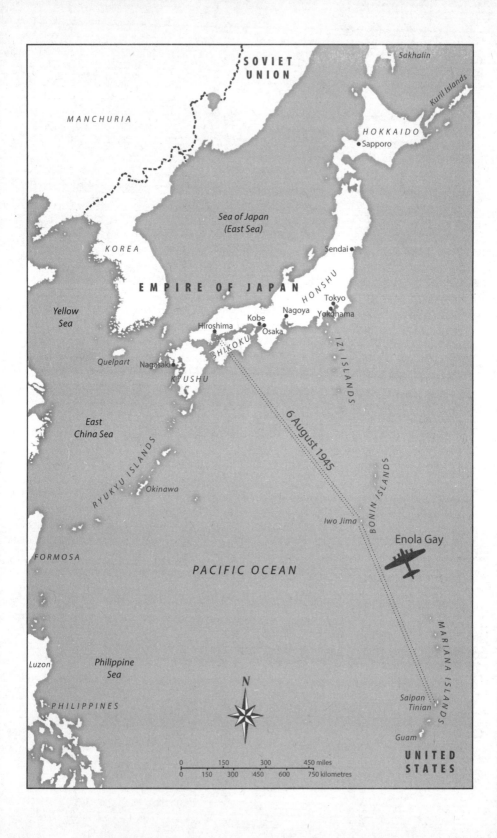

Chapter Twenty-Two

SPECIAL BOMBING MISSION NO. 13

Right after we dropped the bomb,
I felt much the same as I do now except that
I hadn't drunk as much coffee that morning.
COMMANDER PAUL TIBBETS JR. [1]

General Curtis LeMay had now been with the 509th for a few days, having landed on Tinian on August 3. There was a reason the commander was making a personal, somewhat unusual visit to the island airstrip. He was carrying sealed orders for Tibbets: "Special Bombing Mission No. 13." Within it, and what he would discuss with the strike leader, was the authorized date for the attack on Japan with the weapon. The date agreed was August 6, and LeMay discussed with Tibbets the targets that had been assigned:

Primary—Hiroshima urban industrial area
Secondary—Kokura arsenal and city
Tertiary—Nagasaki urban area.

The order confirmed that no friendly aircraft, "other than those listed herein, will be within a fifty-mile area of any of the targets for this strike during the period of four hours prior to and six subsequent to strike time."

Thirty-two copies were distributed to commands in Guam, Iwo Jima, and Tinian. Tibbets locked his copy in the office safe and then departed with LeMay to inspect Little Boy, nestling on its cradle in the Tech Area. The most important commanders on the base were barred from entry by one vigilant MP who demanded LeMay first hand over his cigars and matches. Earlier that morning, the senior military men and scientists on Tinian had agreed that Tibbets's weaponeer for the mission, Captain William S. "Deak" Parsons, would arm the device in flight.[2] Parsons had made a convincing case that to have the bomb armed before actual takeoff risked destroying the whole island should the *Enola Gay* suffer a malfunction and crash—as so many other B-29s had over the past months. The fear of catastrophic engine failure haunted all of them. Parsons would crawl to the bomb bay early in the flight to insert one of the uranium plugs and the explosive charge into the bomb to fully arm it.

In the baking midday heat, Tibbets had decided to go and judge the finished livery he had instructed the crews to paint on the newly christened *Enola Gay*. He admired his mother's name in a bold black font beneath the pilot's side of the cockpit. The imposing bomber, along with the other six that would accompany him on the mission, had their distinctive 509th arrow inside a circle insignia removed and replaced with a simple large black *R*. Tibbets worried that any deviation might lead an inquisitive Japanese interceptor to attack them. He now oversaw the plane being towed to the loading pit. He studied the weapon as it was slowly and carefully hoisted into the bomb bay of the *Enola Gay* by the technical staff. Wiping the sweat from his forehead with his handkerchief, Tibbets could make out a variety of scrawled messages; one declared, *To Emperor Hirohito, from the Boys of the* Indianapolis. He recognized the tribute to the old battleship that had delivered parts of the bomb to Tinian.[3] He took in the familiar dimensions of the plumb-shaped, gunmetal-gray ordnance: nine hundred pounds, twelve feet long, a diameter of twenty-eight inches, and sharp tailfins protruding. Tibbets later recalled in his memoir: "Looking at the huge bomb with its blunt nose and four tail fins, I wondered why we were calling it 'Little Boy.' It was not little by any standard. It was a monster compared with any bomb that I had ever dropped."[4]

Later that evening, Tibbets called the crews together for a briefing. Theodore Van Kirk recalled: "We knew this was going to be a very important thing because they had guys with Tommy Guns out situated around the briefing hut. Who's going to go on the mission, what the course is going to be, what the bomb heading is going to be and all that kind of stuff. Then they tell us to go and get some sleep and they'll call us at 10 p.m. for the final briefing, the final breakfast and then we'll go down to the airplane. How are they supposed to tell you you're going out to drop the first atomic bomb and then go and get some sleep is absolutely beyond me. I know Tibbets didn't sleep, and I know Ferebee didn't sleep, and I know I didn't sleep, because we were [all] still in the same poker game, and I don't even remember who won!"[5]

The crews had been informed that there would be two deviations from the procedures they had practiced. Tibbets had decided to change the *Enola Gay*'s call sign from "Victor" to "Dimples." Just as he feared an air attack from enemy interceptors, so he fretted that they might also pick up his call sign via radio traffic. Secondly, now that Parsons had won his argument to arm the bomb in flight, Tibbets announced they would remain at an altitude of five thousand feet for the first leg of the flight. Parsons needed as much stability in flight as possible to do the job safely. He assured the crews precautions had been taken with the US Navy for a thorough safety net of vessels and submarines situated at points along the route below, to retrieve them should the *Enola Gay* or any other plane on the mission ditch in the sea.

At 11 p.m., the three crews were brought together one final time for Tibbets to address them: "Tonight is the night we have all been waiting for. Our long months of training are to be put to the test. We will soon know if we have been successful or failed. Upon our efforts tonight it is possible that history will be made. We are going on a mission to drop a bomb different from any you have ever seen or heard about. This bomb contains a destructive force equivalent to twenty thousand tons of TNT."[6]

Van Kirk remembered their final orders. "We were given instructions that when we dropped the bomb . . . we have to do it visually, otherwise take it out and drop it into the ocean. Do not bring it back with you. That's all there was to it."[7]

As if to confirm the scientific nature of the mission, what resembled welder's goggles, but fitted with Polaroid lenses, were then distributed to all of them. Professor Ramsey from the Manhattan Project reassured them that they were to prevent blindness from a bomb flash that was intended to be brighter than the sun. An hour later, they all made their way to the mess hall to eat a breakfast of eggs, sausage, rolled oats, pineapple fritters, apple butter, and plenty of coffee. While his men ate, Tibbets quietly, without them noticing, tucked away a packet of cyanide pills into his breast pocket. The roar of engines in the distance told them the three weather planes—*Straight Flush*, *Jabbitt III*, and *Full House*—had successfully taken off. They would fly an hour ahead of the strike force to report back weather conditions for a visual bomb-drop over the principal targets.

At 1:45 a.m., they finished their last cup of coffee, and Van Kirk found himself in Tibbets's jeep as they drove down to the flight line. "We got down to the airplane and that was our first surprise. Lights beamed all over the plane and people were interviewing the crew, taking photographs and movies. We hadn't expected this. All the [senior] command of the Manhattan Project [were present] to record the moment for historical purposes. The *Enola Gay* was heavily ladened (over 15,000 pounds more than usual): the bomb, plus gasoline stored in the rear bomb bay to balance out the aircraft." Takeoff was scheduled for 2:45 a.m. In the dark, humid night, watched by a crowd of at least a hundred officers and men, as well as reporter Bill Laurence, Tibbets watched his crew board the plane. His copilot, Captain Robert Lewis, his best friends, bombardier Major Ferebee and navigator Captain Van Kirk, radarman Lieutenant Jacob Beser, weaponeer Navy Captain Parsons, assistant weaponeer Lieutenant Morris Jeppson, radar operator Sergeant Joseph Stilborik, tail gunner Staff Sergeant George Caron, assistant flight engineer Sergeant

Robert Shumard, radio operator PFC Richard Nelson, and flight engineer Technical Sergeant Wayne Duzenbury now boarded the *Enola Gay* to write their names in history. Van Kirk recalled with a smile how his friend ensured no one was mistaken about who was running this mission, even if this wasn't his usual plane to fly: "Tibbets scolded Lewis: 'Keep your damned hands off [the controls]. I'm flying the aircraft!'"[8]

Tibbets focused on the 8,500 feet of coral runway ahead, checked in with his crew to confirm all was ready, wiped the sweat from his palms as he gripped the stick, and gunned the mighty Wright Cyclone engines. All his training, all the sacrifices, and all the secrecy came down to ensuring he got the *Enola Gay* off safely and didn't join the blackened wrecks of B-29s he could make out in the artificial light lying close by.

"Dimples Eight Two to North Tinian Tower. Ready for takeoff on Runway Able."

Less than a second later came the reply: "Dimples Eight Two. Dimples Eight Two. Cleared for takeoff."

Special Bombing Mission was now a go!

As he lifted the *Enola Gay* into the night sky, three more B-29s roared behind him, making ready to follow suit. The *Great Artiste*, commanded and piloted by Major Charles Sweeney and Lieutenant Charles Albury, would carry the observation equipment, *No. 91* (later renamed *Necessary Evil*), flown by Captain George Marquardt, was kitted out to photograph the detonation, and *Big Stink*, piloted by Lieutenant Charles McKnight, would act as standby until they reached Iwo Jima, where it would land.

Aboard the *Necessary Evil* in his navigator's seat was Lieutenant Russell Gackenbach, plotting the course where the three strike planes would coordinate their flight paths once weather conditions over the target sites had been confirmed. He recalled: "At Iwo Jima, we met each other, formed up in the V-formation and flew up to the IP. At the IP, *Enola Gay* and the *Great Artiste* flew in toward the city of Hiroshima."[9]

Long after Tibbets had launched the *Enola Gay* from the Tinian runway, right across all wards of Hiroshima city, teams of air defense officers and fire wardens had been in action following the false air raid warning. The "B-sans" had bombed Ube City in Yamaguchi Prefecture, ninety miles to the southwest of Hiroshima, which had brought the city's fire defenses to high alert. Mayor Awaya had risen from his bed to take reports from his head of fire department, before he, his wife Sachiyo, and his eldest son Shinobu tried to settle down again by 3 a.m. Luckily it had not woken their young granddaughter, Ayako. Across the city, many citizens followed the mayor's example and returned to their homes in the early morning sunrise, while a few remained at their posts and continued to work their shift.[10]

Tibbets's B-29 crews knew it was going to be a long flight: six hours and fifteen minutes out and six hours and ten minutes back. With little to worry about as the *Enola Gay* cruised along at five thousand feet, still some miles to the south of Iwo Jima, his own crew relaxed as best they could. Or at least most of them did. For Theordore Van Kirk, the strain began almost immediately as he studied his charts. "I was the only guy working the whole time! If you had seen my log, I'm recording our instrument readings and location every fifteen to twenty minutes. The way navigators screwed up was that they didn't keep up with the airplane. I didn't want to just keep up with it, I wanted to keep ahead of it."

As they approached Iwo Jima, Parsons and Jeppson announced to Tibbets it was time to arm Little Boy. He nodded his consent and looked down at Iwo Jima, easily spotting the distinctive shape of Mount Suribachi. He immediately thought about the thousands of US Marines who had died taking the island before they had finally managed to plant the flag at the summit. The two weaponeers disappeared to crawl back to the bomb bay. Though he had spent hours practicing the routine of taking out the green plugs to insert the red plugs to make the bomb live, the US Navy captain sweated as he did it for real. Checking that the colors were correct, he patted the steel plum and gestured to Jeppson that they should return to the cockpit. Van Kirk looked up from his charts as the officers reappeared from the bomb bay: "Parsons sat next to me monitoring the console," he recalled. "I asked him, 'What happens if any of the green lights come on?'

"He replied: 'We're in a helluva lot of trouble!'"

Parsons leaned next to Tibbets's seat and informed him the bomb was now good to go. Tibbets seemed more relaxed than he'd ever seen him. Indeed, he was. The mission was for now going according to plan. He pulled back the controls, and the *Enola Gay* steadily climbed to her operational height of thirty thousand feet. The weather was perfect for a bombing run. He could see the coastline of Japan from a hundred miles away. By the time they were just seventy-five miles away, he could clearly see Hiroshima itself. Van Kirk continued:

"We wanted to bomb on a heading of 270 degrees as Ferebee wanted to hit the target. Escaping fast with a tailwind wasn't an option. Accuracy was. It didn't make any difference [anyway] as the winds from the south were very light. We sat on the bomb run for a long time. I shouted to Tom, 'If we had sat on a bomb run this long in Europe, we wouldn't be here.'"[11]

Everyone in the cabin was now laser focused, and chatter throughout the plane had stopped. Their training kicked in as they prepared to release Little Boy. Tibbets broke the silence to remind his crew to put on their goggles. They would lower the Polaroid dark lenses once the bomb was on its way. Studying his own charts aboard *Necessary Evil* as it flew behind Tibbets, Russell Gackenbach watched his own crew don their goggles as his plane made a 360-degree turn lasting six minutes, plus fifteen seconds. "When we came out of that turn, we were headed directly for Hiroshima."[12]

To the north, two miles from Aioi Bridge, eight-year-old Howard Kakita was excited he might enjoy a day off school if his grandparents allowed. Perhaps he and his brother might even catch sight of a plane flying overhead. They had forgotten their lives back in California, where the boys had been born before the war. Howard's extended family had several relatives who had made the decision in the 1920s to build their future in the United States. His parents had made the fateful decision to send their two young sons to their parents in Hiroshima just before the attack on Pearl Harbor as an extended holiday. Now, four years into the Pacific war, they lived in a Midwest internment camp as "enemy aliens" while Howard and his brother had grown up fully Japanese.

Like thousands across the city, the alarms that had warned of an impending air raid had caused Kakita's family to seek shelter in their purpose-built shelter his grandfather had decided to construct in the courtyard. "During that night, there had been an air raid siren, and my grandmother woke us up to take shelter. Once the all clear had been given, we came back out of the shelter and went to bed. It was a Monday morning with beautiful weather. Our grandmother got us up at around seven o'clock in the morning to go to school. On the way to school, we saw a bunch of children coming back toward our direction and saying that school was cancelled because there's still some enemy aircraft in the neighborhood. So, we came home and changed into our play clothes."[13]

Sumiko Ogata's family home had been pulled down by the firebreak squads, forcing them to relocate closer to the river in the city center. Her new home was only several hundred yards from Little Boy's designated target. Her father had been called up to fight in China in August 1941 and had not been home since. Sumiko's mother had departed the day before to visit her oldest brother, who had been evacuated, leaving her sister in charge of the house, Sumiko, and her two younger brothers (five and three years old). She had been given the day off from school due to feeling unwell and from lack of sleep from the air raid sirens that had gone off earlier that night.

Thirteen-year-old Setuko Thurlow had been assigned with other classmates as part of the Student Mobilization Program to Field Marshal Hata's military headquarters. Her primary function every day was to decode messages in a two-story old wooden school now called the Bureau. She worked on the second floor, surrounded by dozens of others, all listening to radios, their pencils and paper at the ready to take down any enemy communications they might pick up. A lot was American music, or civilian chatter, but sometimes they would detect radio tests made by incoming B-29s. These would be passed on urgently to the air defense headquarters. The morning had started like most others, her team listening intently to a morning pep talk from the Army major in charge of her section. She noticed many of her young friends stifling yawns. She, too, felt incredibly tired, having had been deprived of sleep by the B-San, and was now dreading the long day ahead as the morning's heat increased.

Seventeen-year-old Mitsuko Koshimizu had rushed to her class at Jogakuin College of Economics. Her daily commute on the train from her family's home at Iwakuni, twenty-five miles to the southwest of the city, had been frustratingly delayed. She wasn't to know that the enemy plane flying over that had set off the alarms in the city was the B-29 weather plane scouting for the *Enola Gay*. The summer heat had been oppressive, and Mitsuko had decided to wear her pale purple short-sleeved uniform instead of the heavier black long-sleeved version. Despite the lighter clothes, she had sweated running to college to register, before heading to chapel while most of her friends stayed in class. She took her place at the back and settled down to pray. She then headed to the first class of the morning with her friends.

Fusako Nobe had left for school from his family home in Teppo-cho in Naka Ward, to the east of Hiroshima Castle. Like everyone else, he was relieved the air raid warning had been lifted. Although he was still a college student, he had been working at the factory as a mobilization workforce student. On August 1, he had been given permission to start school again and had begun studying hard. The morning service had just finished, and, along with dozens of other students, he exited the assembly hall to start his day. He recognized the tune the piano played in the background as the students chatted and walked into the morning sunshine.

Having completed her second year at high school, Junko Yoshinari was now part of the mobilization student workforce, working at the Ujina Railroad Station some miles outside Hiroshima to the southeast. As the war worsened, her office had become unsafe due to enemy bombing raids, and her administrative department had been relocated in the city, transferring to one of the school buildings at Hiroshima Jogakuin, east of where Little Boy was heading. With the morning heat already intense, she had decided not to walk and instead take a streetcar to her job. Arriving, she greeted some work-mates as she went to the relevant desk to sign in for work.

Far up in the clear blue sky, Tom Ferebee was crouched in the nose of the *Enola Gay*, studying the city below through the bomb-sight as he worked to correct the plane's drift. Talking with Van Kirk, as they had on countless missions, they conferred notes and then agreed that at their speed of 330 miles per hour, Ferebee should ad-just the bombsight by eight degrees to allow for the *Enola Gay's* drift. They were now ten miles away from the target and had engaged the autopilot, which now guided by the bombsight was leading them to the aiming point. Suddenly, Ferebee announced he had sight of the familiar T-shaped Aioi Bridge. He was certain; they had studied it dozens of times back at base. At that signal, Ferebee was in charge. Tibbets let go of the controls. It was now a matter of seconds.

Behind them, in the *Necessary Evil*, the team of observers posi-tioned themselves, ready for the detonation. Russell Gackenbach rec-ognized the signal they were all waiting for: "We were in the bomb run, and the radio went dead. That was done on purpose. When that radio went dead, it told us 'Bomb-bay doors are open, bomb is gone.' At that point, the scientists aboard our plane pushed a button on a stopwatch. So many seconds later, he pushed a button on the camera, which is mounted on our bomb site. And then they proceeded to take the film."[14]

Theordore Van Kirk suddenly felt the *Enola Gay* surge upward as their nine-hundred-pound bomb left the bomb bay. "Immediately Paul switched off the autopilot and started to go into the turn to get away from it—160 degrees to the right. Steep as you can make it. Pushed the throttles all forward, put the nose down to get enough

The fighting on the volcanic island of Iwo Jima showcased the brutal simplicity of Japanese defensive tactics at inflicting maximum casualties on the US Marine Corps in their island-hopping campaign toward the Home Islands. A suicidal defense ensured the Americans would pay a heavy price, and would influence public opinion in the United States.
Photo by Warrant Officer Obie Newcomb/Archive Photos/Getty Images

US Marine Corpsman Richard Jessor would survive the five weeks of vicious fighting to capture Iwo Jima. He would go on to build a successful postwar academic career.
© Professor Richard Jessor

The capture by American forces of the Mariana Islands in 1944 would prove cataclysmic for Japan. "Hap" Arnold set up his B-29 fleets on giant, purpose-built airstrips, such as this one on Tinian. From here, American bombers could take the war across all Japanese cities.
Photo Quest/Getty Images

The invention of the M-47 incendiary bomb was a major turning point in aerial warfare in the Pacific. Its cargo of flammable mixtures or white phosphorous would prove lethal to Japanese housing, resulting in hundreds of thousands of casualties in the final year of the conflict. Over 175 square miles of Japanese cities would be turned to ashes.
© *Iain MacGregor*

Operation Meetinghouse, conducted by the USAAF and commanded by General Curtis LeMay against Tokyo, finally proved the effectiveness of the B-29 as a terror weapon. The low-level raid on March 9–10, 1945, decimated large sections of the city and killed well over a hundred thousand civilians.
Photo by Prisma Bildagentur/Universal Images via Getty Images

A child's artwork of the Great Tokyo Fire Raid, March 9–10, 1945.
© *The Centre of the Tokyo Raids and Fire Damage*

The brutal Japanese defense of Okinawa against overwhelming enemy air and naval forces, inflicted so many American casualties that it hardened attitudes across President Truman's administration of what had to be done to defeat Japan.
Interim Archives/Getty Images

Robert Oppenheimer's Manhattan Project team, together with the US Army, conducted the world's first nuclear bomb test on July 16, 1945, codenamed Trinity. The implosion-designed plutonium bomb successfully detonated, with a strength of 25 kilotons of TNT.
Everett Collection/Alamy Stock Photo

The "Big Three" of Churchill, Truman, and Stalin met at the Potsdam Conference in July 1945. News from General Groves as to the success of Trinity convinced President Truman he had a trump card to negotiate with Joseph Stalin. However, spies within the Manhattan Project had already given the Soviet leader information on American progress toward a nuclear weapon.
Pictorial Press/Alamy Stock Photo

Special Mission Number 13. The *Enola Gay*, piloted by Colonel Paul Tibbets Jr., flew into history on August 6, 1945, after successfully dropping Little Boy over Hiroshima.
Photo12/Universal Images via Getty Images

Little Boy missed its intended target, the Aioi Bridge by several hundred feet, but still successfully detonated, wiping out a radius of 4.7 square miles.
Science History Images/ Alamy Stock Photo

The jubilant crew of the *Enola Gay* pose for the cameras after their successful flight.
Like many of the fellow airmen on the island, they believed Japan could not withstand
the power of this new weapon and the war would quickly be over.
Keystone/Hulton Archive/Getty Images

Survivors of the world's first atomic bomb attack stagger out of the city, seeking shelter in
the surrounding mountains. Tens of thousands would perish from their injuries
and the unknown effects of radiation poisoning.
© *The Hiroshima Peace Memorial Museum Archive*

"All the News That's Fit to Print"

The New York Times.

LATE CITY EDITION

Copyright, 1945, by The New York Times Company.

VOL. XCIV...No. 31,972.   NEW YORK, TUESDAY, AUGUST 7, 1945.   THREE CENTS NEW YORK CITY

FIRST ATOMIC BOMB DROPPED ON JAPAN; MISSILE IS EQUAL TO 20,000 TONS OF TNT; TRUMAN WARNS FOE OF A 'RAIN OF RUIN'

HIRAM W. JOHNSON, REPUBLICAN DEAN IN THE SENATE, DIES

Isolationist Helped Prevent U. S. Entry Into League—Opposed World Charter

CALIFORNIA EX-GOVERNOR

Ran for Vice President With Theodore Roosevelt in '12 —In Washington Since '17

Jet Plane Explosion Kills Major Bong, Top U. S. Ace

Flier Who Downed 40 Japanese Craft, Sent Home to Be 'Safe,' Was Flying New 'Shooting Star' as a Test Pilot

ROCKET SITE IS SEEN

125 B-29's Hit Japan's Toyokawa Naval Arsenal in Demolition Strike

KYUSHU CITY RAZED

Kenney's Planes Blast Tarumizu in Record Blow From Okinawa

REPORT BY BRITAIN

'By God's Mercy' We Beat Nazis to Bomb, Churchill Says

ROOSEVELT AID CITED

Raiders Wrecked Norse Laboratory in Race for Key to Victory

Steel Tower 'Vaporized' In Trial of Mighty Bomb

Scientists Awe-Struck as Blinding Flash Lighted New Mexico Desert and Great Cloud Bore 40,000 Feet Into Sky

NEW AGE USHERED

Day of Atomic Energy Hailed by President, Revealing Weapon

HIROSHIMA IS TARGET

'Impenetrable' Cloud of Dust Hides City After Single Bomb Strikes

MORRIS IS ACCUSED OF TAKING A WALK

Company—McGoldrick Sees Only Tammany

CHINESE WIN MORE OF INVASION COAST

Smash Into Port 121 Miles Southwest of Canton—Big Area Open for Landing

ATOM BOMBS MADE IN 3 HIDDEN 'CITIES'

Secrecy on Weapon So Great That Not Even Workers Knew of Their Product

TRAINS CANCELED IN STRICKEN AREA

Traffic Around Hiroshima Disrupted—Japanese Still Sift Havoc by Split Atoms

News of the bombing of Hiroshima was quickly seized upon by the Allied press, as well as reports of secret cities hidden throughout the United States that had constructed this new wonder weapon. *Granger Historical Picture Archive/Alamy Stock Photo*

Five days after the original surrender document was signed by the Japanese delegation aboard the USS *Missouri* in Tokyo Bay on September 2, 1945, President Truman displays it to the American media in the White House. *Fox Photos/Stringer/ Getty Images*

The powerful searchlights surrounding the Tribute to Victory concert in Los Angeles, on October 27, 1945, was akin to the spectacular showpieces in Nuremberg under the Nazis.
Associated Press/Alamy Stock Photo

Harold Ross, the influential editor of *The New Yorker*. He was determined that John Hersey's article would receive maximum support, which resulted in both his assistant editor William Shawn and himself becoming heavily involved.
Bachrach/Getty Images

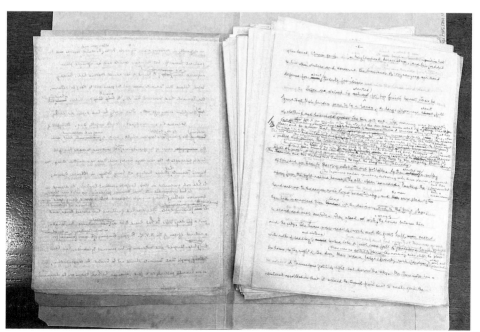

The original first draft of John Hersey's Hiroshima article, complete with annotations from Harold Ross, stored in the Hersey Archives in the Beinecke Library, Yale University.
© *Iain MacGregor*

The family of Senkichi Awaya. Having already lost two sons to infection and disease before the outbreak of war with the United States, his remaining wife and five children would suffer like many Japanese families.
© *Family of Motoko Sakama*

An original copy of *The New Yorker* magazine containing John Hersey's story.
© *Iain MacGregor*

The Atomic Bomb Dome, now part of the Hiroshima Peace Memorial Park, was the only building left standing in the vicinity where Little Boy exploded on August 6, 1945.
© *Iain MacGregor*

speed to get away in the forty-three seconds at which the bomb would reach its altitude where it would explode."[15]

Little Boy hurtled toward earth, heading for the Aioi Bridge. At five miles down, the bomb's fin radar system activated the detonator. At 8:15 a.m., some forty-three seconds after Ferebee had dropped it from the *Enola Gay*'s bomb bay, the weapon exploded at 1,890ft above the ground. Tibbets and his crew were by then approximately six miles away, having turned away as instructed by Oppenheimer. Ferebee's aim, however, had been off, missing the bridge by approximately eight hundred feet. The atomic bomb detonated instead above the Shima Surgical Hospital. It didn't matter for the men, women, and children of Hiroshima within the blast radius; the effect would be the same.

Van Kirk recalled, "Everyone in the airplane didn't have a watch, they were counting, '1001, 1002, 1003, etc.' I think we had concluded it was a dud, as it seemed to be a long forty-three seconds. Then suddenly, there was a bright flash in the air and very shortly after, the first shockwave hit the *Enola Gay*. The sound was worse than the shockwave. It sounded like a piece of sheet metal snapping. Somebody onboard [mistakenly] called out 'flak!' but George Caron in the tail gunner's position confirmed it was a shockwave, and another one was about to strike, though less intensity than the first.

"It was then that Bob Lewis [exclaimed] second statement in the log [probably once he got on the ground at Tinian—'My God, what have we done?'—it was a better quote]. What he actually said in the aircraft was: 'Look at that son of a bitch go!'"[16]

Aboard the *Necessary Evil*, Russell Gackenbach felt the sonic boom. "The echo just bounced off the nose of our plane because of streamlining. The other two planes were heading away from the blast, so their tails felt the blast. As a result, [the *Enola Gay*] were rocking for a little while until their tail gunner says, 'Here comes another sonic bomb.'"[17]

"We looked now at what had happened," recounted Van Kirk. "The first thing you saw was that there was a large white cloud over the target, well above our altitude of 45,000 feet already and rising. At the base of the cloud, the entire city was covered in a thick blanket of smoke, dust and anything that was kicked up by the blast. It was obvious we weren't going to make any visualization down there. We did not circle the city. We flew a southeast quadrant of Hiroshima and then flew home."[18]

Observing from the *Enola Gay* at twenty-nine thousand feet, as Tibbets steered the plane away from the blast, Flight Sergeant George Caron looked at what they had "achieved." The planned coded message was now transmitted:

82 V 670. Able, Line 1, Line 2, Line 6, Line 9.
Clear cut. Successful in all respects. Visible effects greater than Alamogordo. Conditions normal in airplane following delivery. Proceeding to base.

The shock waves that struck the plane had spooked the crew until Caron reassured them it wasn't enemy flak. All of them had declined to don their metal protective vests. Tibbets, Ferebee, and Van Kirk were very familiar with them from their countless bombing runs in Europe, where they had contended with strong antiaircraft fire. Right now, on a gloriously sunny morning over Hiroshima, there were no Japanese interceptors to be seen at the altitude they were flying. Nor would there be. Tibbets and Lewis relaxed a little in their seats as the *Enola Gay* quickly headed back out to sea. The main subject of conversation as they flew back home was the end of the war with Japan. How could they withstand such a weapon? They could not visualize the destruction they had left in their wake.

Aboard the *Necessary Evil*, Russell Gackenbach felt the atmosphere in the cockpit was unusual: "Normally, as you dropped your bombs, you're heading home, you're happy. You're okay. You're cracking jokes in a hilarious mood. This mission, we did not have that. It was quiet, subdued, awesome. We didn't realize what it was, and by the time we got the fifteen miles from where the bomb had been released to where it exploded, the cloud was already higher than we were. We could see the cloud a hundred miles away. Especially the tail gunner."[19]

For Tibbets, the sight before him as he had circled the *Enola Gay* to get a good view of the target before they departed to the southwest would remain with him for the rest of his life: "The giant purple mushroom, which [Caron] had described, had already risen to a height of 45,000 feet. Three miles above our own altitude and was still boiling upward like something terribly alive. It was a frightening sight, and even though we were several miles away, it gave the appearance of something that was about to engulf us. . . . If Dante had been with us in the plane, he would have been terrified!"[20]

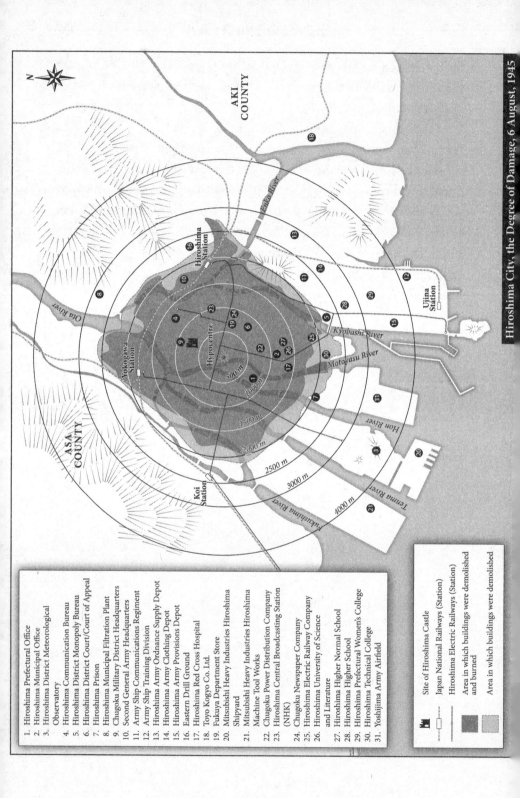

Hiroshima City, the Degree of Damage, 6 August, 1945

1. Hiroshima Prefectural Office
2. Hiroshima Municipal Office
3. Hiroshima District Meteorological Observatory
4. Hiroshima Communication Bureau
5. Hiroshima District Monopoly Bureau
6. Hiroshima District Court/Court of Appeal
7. Hiroshima Prison
8. Hiroshima Municipal Filtration Plant
9. Chugoku Military District Headquarters
10. Second General Army Headquarters
11. Army Ship Communications Regiment
12. Army Ship Training Division
13. Hiroshima Army Ordnance Supply Depot
14. Hiroshima Army Clothing Depot
15. Hiroshima Army Provisions Depot
16. Eastern Drill Ground
17. Hiroshima Red Cross Hospital
18. Toyo Kogyo Co. Ltd.
19. Fukuya Department Store
20. Mitsubishi Heavy Industries Hiroshima Shipyard
21. Mitsubishi Heavy Industries Hiroshima Machine Tool Works
22. Chugoku Power Distribution Company
23. Hiroshima Central Broadcasting Station (NHK)
24. Chugoku Newspaper Company
25. Hiroshima Electric Railway Company
26. Hiroshima University of Science and Literature
27. Hiroshima Higher Normal School
28. Hiroshima Higher School
29. Hiroshima Prefectural Women's College
30. Hiroshima Technical College
31. Yoshijima Army Airfield

🏯   Site of Hiroshima Castle

Japan National Railways (Station)

Hiroshima Electric Railways (Station)

Area in which buildings were demolished and burned

Area in which buildings were demolished

Chapter Twenty-Three

THE SHIMMERING LEAVES

The whole city of Hiroshima was destroyed
instantly by a single bomb.
DISPATCH FROM SECOND GENERAL ARMY HEADQUARTERS,
HIROSHIMA, AUGUST 7, 1945[1]

At 8:15 a.m., Mayor Awaya had been in the dining room as he had breakfast with Shinobu and Ayako. His wife had walked across the courtyard to the rear of the residence to retrieve some fruit from the store next to the shrine they prayed at daily. As Awaya urged his granddaughter to eat her food, a blinding flash of brilliant light filled the room, and then the fireball struck the city. Situated just over a half mile from Ground Zero, the front of his residence was swept away in a cauldron of violence and heat.

Mrs. Awaya had lost consciousness immediately. When she came to, she found herself in the dark under the collapsed residence. She desperately crawled out from under the wreckage of the house, the effort exhausting her as she lay in the residence compound. Incredulity and shock rapidly turned to panic. What had happened to Senkichi, Shinobu, and Ayako? They were nowhere in sight. Although bleeding from wounds to her head and arms, she hadn't seemed to have suffered any major trauma. She shouted for her husband. Nothing. The sky was gone. The brilliant light had now suddenly turned to a dark gray, and the hot wind was unbearable. She had to find help. She managed to stand, staggered out of the destroyed residence, and slowly headed toward the nearby bridge. In the distance, her eyes must be deceiving her. The city seemed to have disappeared and been replaced by a great wall of flames. She knew she needed to find any officer from the mayor's office or fire wardens.

But she would find no one. Governor Takano's prefecture office based at Kokomachi, close to her family residence, had been obliterated. The majority of his seven hundred staff who had been there at the time were dead or dying under the collapsed building. The mayor's office based at City Hall was a half mile from the detonation of Little Boy. Originally constructed of wood in 1878, it had not been fireproofed for air raids, and instead firebreaks had been created by pulling down all the buildings surrounding the complex. The heat from the bomb blast had engulfed the buildings, incinerating many of the office workers who had spent the night there.

Howard Kakita and his brother had excitedly climbed on top of their grandparents' bathhouse to get a better view of enemy planes. "We climbed on top of the roof of the bathhouse, where my grandmother would dry her laundry. It had a flat roof that you could stand on and was good to get a bird's-eye view. We stood there, our necks craning to scan the sky, and we detected a distant vapor trail. It was the B-29 and was clearly coming closer in our direction. Our grandmother was washing dishes in the kitchen, which looked out onto the courtyard, and spotted us. She marched out and gruffly ordered Kenny and I to come down off the roof immediately. We begrudgingly came down, and I went back into the bathhouse, and Kenny disappeared into the main building and that's when the bomb exploded.[2]

"Now, most of the people in the neighborhood will say that they saw a huge, blinding flash—an orange color, followed by a huge boom. But I didn't see the flash, and I didn't hear anything."

Howard was knocked out instantaneously. When he regained consciousness, what was left of his grandparents' prestigious residence was on fire. The bathroom had collapsed on top of him, but fortunately, although suffering a mild concussion, he was not seriously injured and he quickly dug himself out. He found his brother nearby, who had also escaped serious injury, suffering only a burn to his forehead. He had gone back inside the house and was walking down a side room when the building collapsed.

"My grandmother, however, had returned back into the kitchen to finish washing her dishes. She was standing in front of the window looking out to the yard when the explosion occurred. She was engulfed in dozens of shards of glass as the windows shattered from the blast, many of which struck and embedded in her body. She was bleeding badly, though no arteries had been severed. She was buried under the rubble of the house, where the kitchen had been. My grandfather was safe and upon arriving at the scene, he managed to find several neighbors who helped him dig her out.

"Once Grandfather extricated her, she was able to stand and walk, though her clothes were covered in blood, and she was in a lot of pain. As she rested on the ground, I could take in the view around me. What remained of our once-grand house was now destroyed or on fire. My grandfather and his neighbors tried to douse the flames, not realizing it wasn't just our house but the whole city."

Howard's grandfather ordered his wife to take the young boys and escape out of the city toward the mountains. She took their hands, and they headed west on the road adjacent to the river Ota. It would act as a topographical guide to get to the mountain roads. The banks of the river were lined with bodies of the dead, the dying, and others struggling to get out of the water. As Howard watched them, he could see they were covered in raw, bloody burns, some from head to feet, stripped naked by the blast. They had jumped into the river to cool their burns. Bodies of the drowned floated face down.

"As we walked, we started to encounter dozens, then hundreds of survivors, all from the direction of the inner city, who were now making their way in the same direction to escape. Hordes of them were walking like semi-naked zombies, oblivious it seemed to the horrendous wounds and burns on their bodies. The worst cases I witnessed, their skin was literally hanging off their bodies. Many of them had little or no hair, it had been burnt off, so I couldn't tell whether they were male or female. Some survivors were painfully dragging themselves along with broken limbs. One lady was clutching her stomach, trying to keep her intestines from falling out. I walked along in shock as I looked upon these nightmare scenes. It was pure survival. We passed by countless dying people who had collapsed all along the road. Many of them reached out and pleaded for water. I could see some adults who were in good shape, dismissing their pleading, and telling others, 'Don't give them water, because they will die anyway.'"

Sumiko Ogata had suffered a similar fate as Howard Kakita: her world fell on top of her. "The moment I came out of the bathroom that morning, there was a sudden roar. I was suddenly trapped under the house, and I fainted. I only regained consciousness upon hearing my aunt's voice as she frantically looked for me from somewhere above. I answered in desperation."

Her aunt rapidly tore away at the roof tiles one by one as Sumiko began to fight her way through the debris trapping her. By the time she had been freed and was standing on the wreck of the house, she was surrounded by fire. Sumiko's aunt now dug out her brothers from under the rubble. After half an hour of digging, when everyone was accounted for, the dazed family fled, Sumiko carrying her youngest brother on her back while her aunt carried the other. Spotting the Western Telephone Company building, they focused on it as a spot to make for amid the destruction and fire. "We weaved through hundreds of survivors crawling out from under their destroyed homes, groaning and unable to move from their injuries. We dashed like mad and came to Hirose Bridge. The rail track was already on fire, and the bridge was about to collapse. We kept walking due west to try and escape the city. The river was full of people who had jumped in to escape the heat. I'm not sure how many hours we had been walking. I ran out of strength and sat down when we came by the next river. I reached to my back and noticed my brother was still clinging on with all his strength. I was overwhelmed with joy and hugged him tightly. Tears flowed from my eyes. Then I started vomiting and experienced uncontrollable diarrhea and was unable to leave the river.

"Suddenly the sky was covered in clouds and black rain showered us. As I got soaked, I watched bewildered as my brother and others were dyed black. Then, snapping out of my daze, I looked at myself and realized that the bottoms of my bare feet were tingling in pain from burns. My clothes were tattered like everyone else wearing rags. Red and swollen dead bodies lay about. We moved toward the railroad and climbed up to the tracks and saw the city completely engulfed in flames."[3]

At Field Marshal Hata's headquarters close to Mount Futaba, the wooden two-story bureau had taken the brunt of the blast. The field marshal had escaped any injury, but his wife had been severely burned. Setuko Thurlow noticed a bluish-white flash like a magnesium flare outside the window, then a sensation of floating through the air. "As I regained consciousness in the total darkness and silence, I realized that I was pinned in the ruins of the collapsed building. Gradually I began to hear my classmates' faint cries for help. Then, suddenly, a man's voice said, 'Don't give up! I'm trying to free you! Keep moving! See the light coming through that opening. Crawl toward it and try to get out!'"

She managed to scramble out to freedom as a nearby soldier ordered the few surviving girls from the building to get out and seek shelter in the nearby hills. Dozens had been left buried alive or dead. Coughing violently and wiping her eyes to see clearly, she got her bearings, but did not recognize where she stood: "Although it was morning, it resembled twilight probably because of the dust and dirt sucked skyward. People at a distance saw the mushroom cloud and heard a thunderous roar. But I did not see the cloud because I was in the middle of it. I did not hear the roar, just the deathly silence broken by the groans of the injured."

With the survivors from her building, Setuko joined the streams of semi-naked and charcoal-looking people who were shuffling up from the city center to escape into the nearby hills. She was shocked to see so many naked and with horrendous injuries: blackened, swollen faces, severe burns, some with their eyeballs gone, staggering forward with their hands placed on the shoulder of the person in front. Their groans and whimpers of pain were pitiful to hear. Within a mile, the procession came to the foot of a hill where a military training ground had been. Approximately the size of two football fields, every inch of its ground was now covered with the dead and dying. There were no medical units to be seen, nor was there water to give relief to those suffering from burns.

Along with others, Setuko went to a nearby stream to clean up and provide water to the sick: "We tore off parts of our clothes, soaked them with water and hurried back to hold them to the mouths of the dying, who desperately sucked the moisture. We kept busy at this task all day. When darkness fell, we sat on the hillside, numbed by the massive scale of death and suffering we had witnessed, watching the entire city burn all night. In the background were the low rhythmic whispers from the swollen lips of the ghostly figures, still begging for water."[4]

At Jogakuin College of Economics, Mitsuko Tanaka had completed her prayers and was making her way to her first lesson of the day, when a red-blue flash passed by as quick as lightning, startling the students. A split second later, in an almost out-of-body experience, she found herself lying under a beam of the collapsed building. "I heard someone urgently crying for help. I wondered for a moment whether we had suffered a direct hit by a bomber. My friend, who had been full of life just seconds earlier, was lying dead under a beam nearby. I was now covered in her blood."

Feeling around her face, neck, and legs, she ascertained that she had only suffered cuts to her head and elbows. She struggled fiercely to gain some space to wriggle from under the beam that had crushed her friend. After what seemed like hours frantically wriggling through the dark and dust, Metsuko finally made it out to the roof. As she squinted in the light, the sight before her eyes chilled her. "The assembly hall and classrooms were all flattened, with fires sprouting out of the rubble in various places. My friends, who [had] stayed in the classroom, were all crushed between desks under the school building and couldn't escape the fire. It was a living hell."

She investigated muffled sounds and cries coming from the ruins, as more survivors began to appear out of the ruined building and ran for safety. Mitsuko recognized one cry for help instantly: it was her classmate. She staggered over the rubble and investigated the collapsed, smoking classroom. Her heart sank. Her friend was trapped under several desks, pinning her legs tightly to the floor. She spotted Mitsuko coming toward her: "Please help me! Cut my leg off to save me!"

She desperately squirmed against the weight on top of her as she implored her friend to help her. Her own strength vanishing as the adrenaline rush passed, Mitsuko begged her forgiveness, but she couldn't free her. It seemed impossible that she could get out of the trap as she froze in despair. A male teacher suddenly arrived and ordered Mitsuko to escape the burning wreckage while he tried to pull her friend out. She staggered out of the college, still taking in the scale of destruction all around her. A body lay in her path as she came to the entrance, and she recognized the trembling woman from the teaching staff, but she was covered head to foot in blood. Mitsuko knelt to comfort her and asked if she could walk. In a daze, she mumbled that she would try. Ignoring her yelps of pain, she pulled her arm around her neck and coaxed her up to stand. The survivors stumbled into the main road. Hundreds of ghostlike figures were limping, crawling, or being carried in the direction of the Sentei Garden, close to where Hiroshima Castle had stood.

By the time they arrived, the garden was teeming with a mass of survivors. They looked like the living dead resting in a blackened, charred landscape that Mitsuko didn't recognize at all. She found a place for them to sit, and the teacher collapsed, exhausted. Within minutes, Mitsuko made the decision to keep moving; she needed to get away from the devastation and attempt to get home. She set off into the city. "There were injured people, burned people, and people unable to move. Everywhere I looked, it was people, people, people in hell. People dead with their heads stuck in the fire cisterns; babies clinging to dead mothers; people trapped in a burning streetcar.

Walking over dead bodies, I finally made it to the riverside where the fire couldn't reach. Nearby was a unit of engineering officers, and there were many soldiers lying on their sides. Their hair remained only where the metal helmet protected them. The rest of their bodies were completely burned black, and had it not been for the mark of their helmets you couldn't even tell if they were men or women. They were still alive and breathing faintly."

She wandered along the river heading west toward home. The riverbank was packed with the dead and dying, and bloated corpses and animals floated in the polluted water. Passing by dozens of survivors lying by the bank, those who could still speak gave her their names and addresses in the hope Mitsuko might contact their families. "I cannot forget their desperation to communicate with their loved ones they were about to leave behind. I saw many soldiers who had gone mad fall over as they yelled 'Mother, Mother!' 'Banzai to the Emperor!' We could feel the heat across the river when the old pine tree at a shrine caught fire. . . . I saw someone running away holding a large squash. Another was walking with a cow in tow, headed into the city. As I came toward an army camp, the campsite and nearby street were filled with injured soldiers sprawled around, their bodies burned black. I passed by, stepping over bodies as I apologized to each of them. A woman walked by with manure barrels balanced from a bar over her shoulders. She was carrying a dead child in each barrel. There is just no end to the madness I saw."

Eventually, as she continued her journey west, Mitsuko came upon a crowd of injured people waiting in line. It was a first-aid station. After a few hours of waiting, her light wounds were treated, and she then continued her trek home for another four to five hours. Despite the heat of the day, she dared not drink the water from the river for fear of the dozens of dead floating in it. "We crossed the river on a boat and arrived at the Kenjo High School for women, where I was told to seek refuge. They fed us some cucumbers grown in their garden. I remember the juicy sweetness of the cucumber quenching my thirst. I savoured the delicious vegetable."[5]

Fusako Nobe had been humming along to the faint piano music echoing from the main hall as she walked toward her classroom, when she saw people meandering about in a blue light that resembled a gas flame. Then everything went black. "When I came to, I was trapped under the building. I looked around and saw people covered in blood. Some were calling for their mother. I didn't know what had happened and for a while I stayed there, in astonishment. My classmates were calling out words of encouragement toward each other. Then I noticed sunlight shining through a hole about the size of my body. I gathered all my strength to crawl out and found myself standing on top of the roof that had fallen flat on the ground. I stepped over fences and clung to telephone poles and finally came to the road. I heard a voice say, 'Escape, hurry,' so I quickly walked to Sentei Garden [Shukkeien]. We were all walking in bewilderment.

"I heard [another] cry, 'Somebody please help! My child is trapped under the house!' but we walked by them in silence.

"'The fire is approaching, hurry up,' somebody [else] yelled.

"Pushed by the wave of people, I arrived at the riverbank of the Ota River in Hakushima-cho. The row of houses along the river had caught fire and the flames were coming closer. Masses of injured people were being brought to the area. The riverbank was filled with people whose skin was dangling from their hands. People's backs were split open, revealing what looked like the inside of a pomegranate. A soldier ordered me to help him take care of the injured. The people's faces were swelling, and they cried, 'It's hot, so hot.' Some dove into the river and floated away. I was bleeding from the back of my ear and my neck was becoming stiff. Thankfully I was with my best friend, who kept encouraging me."

She spent the night on the riverbank. "The city was engulfed in red flames and looked like a giant campfire, except in this fire I could see silhouettes of people burning. The next day, not knowing whether any of my family members survived, I headed for my home with my best friend. When I arrived, I saw my house had burned to the ground. I found a concrete surface and used a broken piece of roof shingle to write, *Fusako is well.*

"Nobody was around, not even the cat. I found ashy remains of a mother and child on the side of the street. Another mother in a fire cistern clutched her child close to her body. Their skin was pink like a boiled octopus. Not having a place to stay, I went to the house of my friend's relatives, in the countryside. We walked for about six miles. We passed by a grade school full of injured people. I could hear them say, 'Water please' from behind the burned masks of their swollen faces. It was like hell on earth."[6]

At her temporary workplace at Hiroshima Jogakuin, Junko Yoshinari was making her way to register for the day's shift. "I went straight to the attendance roster, which was lying open on a desk, by the windows on the south side of the room. Just as I was about to stamp the roster, there was a sharp hissing sound, and a flash of light ran across the windows. The windows of a small building sandwiched by the gym and art room flashed brightly. I was startled but continued to press down on my stamp. Then I walked two or three steps toward the entrance, wondering what the light was. That's when I lost consciousness.

"I have no recollection of the sound of the bomb or how I became trapped under the building. I'm not sure how many minutes had passed. I heard a small voice, 'Help, help . . . ' as if I were in a dream, which grew louder as I came to my senses. I was surrounded in darkness and couldn't tell what was going on. Slimy liquid poured out of my head onto my face, and slowly I gathered that I was bleeding, lying face down under the fallen building. In the midst of voices calling for help, I heard Ms. Fujita [say], 'Help, I can't breathe. Please get this off my neck. . . .' But help never came. I heard Ms. Fujita say, 'Goodbye, everyone.' And then I noticed I could no longer hear the voice belonging to my senior, who had been saying, 'If I escape, I'm going to help all of you get out.'

"I felt the need to urgently do something. In the darkness, I called out to Ms. Nakaoka, whose voice seemed to be closest to me.

She answered immediately, so I asked her 'Is there a place to get out somewhere?' 'I'll take a look,' she said, and shortly later, 'We can get out here!' I wiggled my body toward the direction that she indicated, and soon I saw some light. I scooted over farther, but there was a mass of wires that had spilled out from above the ceiling, blocking my way. I closed my eyes and passed under them. That was the most nerve-recking experience the whole of that day."

Junko crawled her way into the light and to what she thought was safety, with no idea of the true extent of what had just occurred. "When I finally stood on top of the collapsed school building and looked at the schoolyard, I was astounded. The yard was eerily quiet without a single soul. I could tell that all the school buildings had collapsed. . . . A ghostly atmosphere hung in the air."

Her body trembling in shock, she staggered through the rubble trying to gather her thoughts as the various voices crying for help gradually all died away. She was urged by a staff worker who suddenly appeared from the nearby kindergarten to leave the ruined building quickly in case of further attacks. Looking around, she realized that many buildings that had surrounded the school were either wrecks or on fire. Together with the coworker, plus another manager they encountered who was bleeding profusely, she scrambled down a wall and jumped down to the street. Like many thousands of citizens, her primary thought was to escape the city and head to the mountains to seek safety.

"In the street there were many refugees walking in a line. They seemed to be covered in dust, and I wondered if they had all escaped from under collapsed buildings and homes. The line moved silently toward Hakushima, bending toward the right after crossing Tokiwa Bridge. We wanted to go toward the farm in Ushita, so we turned left after crossing the bridge. When we passed by the Nigitsu Shrine, a large tree on the temple grounds was on fire. The leaves on the branches that were outstretched to the street were burning furiously, and I was worried that a branch might break and fall on us. We ran past it in a hurry. We walked along the river and turned right onto a small street that led toward the Jogakuin farm, until we realized the houses along this street were also on fire. We gave up going to the farm and walked instead toward Ushita-waseda, in order to get into the mountains."

The first report that Hiroshima had been destroyed was sent by fourteen-year-old Yoshie Oka, a communications officer at the Chugoku Military District Headquarters half a mile away from the epicenter. Part of the student volunteer force working alongside the military, Oka served in the communications division monitoring air defenses situated below the surface in a concrete bunker—which saved her life. The initial explosion rocked the underground bunker, and despite the protection it offered she was knocked off her feet and for a moment lost consciousness. When she recovered after a few seconds, she called Fukuyama headquarters on a special hotline. At first her call was not believed by the officer at Fukuyama, so Oka went out above ground into what was now a wasteland of burned destruction and, amid the clouds of debris, spotted a soldier staggering toward her, covered in burns. As she tried to comfort him, he murmured the enemy must have used a new type of bomb. Once Oka was down below in the safety of the bunkers, she repeated his words to Fukuyama.

"Hiroshima has been attacked by a new type of bomb. The city is in a state of near-total destruction."

The core of Hiroshima's municipal government office had been destroyed, as had 90 percent of buildings within the city center. Of the thousand employees fit for work the day before the *Enola Gay* attacked, just eighty reported for duty the next day. The scale of the task at hand was beyond comprehension. Mayor Awaya was presumed dead. The few civil servants alive and able to walk now attempted to deal with supplying emergency medical treatment for the tens of thousands of people badly injured and the dying. Throughout the next forty-eight hours, huge columns of survivors and those injured but able to move slowly made their way out of the city to seek shelter in the surrounding mountains.

The city's emergency medical services had been decimated. Fourteen of the sixteen major hospitals in and around Hiroshima no longer stood. Of medical personnel, 270 of 298 hospital doctors were dead, along with 1,654 of 1,780 registered nurses. The central telephone exchange was in ruins and all its employees dead. The tram car system was no longer tenable as the tracks running through the center of town had melted. Streetcars caught in the blast were charred husks. The main train station was a wreck, too, and Hiroshima Harbor was in ruins. To tackle the thousands of fires now out of control in and around the city, only sixteen firefighting equipment pieces of the hundreds that had been available seconds before now actually worked. Reminiscent of the catastrophic fire raids on Tokyo, most firemen had been killed and the main pumping stations were wrecked. The military complex based within Hiroshima Castle ceased to function as the castle complex was destroyed, with several thousand people dead or dying, including the two dozen American POWs who had been tending the gardens that morning—their shadows burned into the ground where they had stood. Of the estimated 320,000 human beings present within the city boundaries that morning, approximately eighty thousand were dead.

At Field Marshal Hata's Second General Army Headquarters, the injured commander had moved his command post to an underground bunker. With what remained of his military personnel, he worked tirelessly to restore some order and communicate to the outside world for aid.[7] But Hiroshima's communications were down; telegraph and phone lines destroyed throughout the city, severing any contact with survivors. The train line running from Hiroshima was now inoperable due to the damage to the main rail hub, with all scheduled trains coming from the south and north diverted elsewhere. A calamity had struck Hiroshima, but very few people outside military and government officials in Tokyo knew the extent of it. By that evening, Domei, the state-run news service, issued bulletins to calm the rumors:

A few B-29s hit Hiroshima city at 8:20 a.m. August 6 and fled after dropping incendiaries and bombs. The extent of the damage is now under survey.

Earlier that afternoon, at 2:58 p.m., Tibbets and the crew of the *Enola Gay* had finally returned to their air base on Tinian, soon followed by *Necessary Evil* and *The Great Artiste*. Their mission had covered 2,960 miles, taken twelve hours and thirteen minutes, and used over six thousand gallons of fuel.[8] Without the weight of the fuel and the payload of Little Boy, Tibbets and Lewis relaxed as the giant bomber serenely came in to land thousands of pounds lighter. An even bigger crowd awaited them than had seen them off the night before. Two hundred officers and men crowded on the apron, ready to greet her. Several thousand more lined the taxiways. As soon as Tibbets managed to park the plane and disembark onto dry land, General Carl Spaatz quickly marched up to shake his hand for the cameras and pin the Distinguished Service Cross on his chest. Once the festivities and photographs were over, all crews drove for the debriefing.

Theodore Van Kirk remembered: "When we got back to Tinian there were more admirals and generals than I'd ever seen in my life. Curtis LeMay said to Paul [Tibbets]:

"Do you have any more of those damned things?"

Paul answered: "Yes, sir, we have one more at Wendover."

LeMay replied: "Get it over here!"

Jimmy Doolittle made a comment: "If you drop it on Tokyo, who you going to make peace with?"[9]

At 11:45 a.m., as the USS *Augusta* plowed through the dark waters of the North Atlantic, President Harry Truman was sitting down for breakfast in the aft mess hall with Secretary of State James Byrnes, his chief of staff Admiral William Leahy, and the ship's captain, James K. Foskett. It was now sixteen hours since Ferebee had released Little Boy over Hiroshima when the news arrived of its success:

"Hiroshima" bombed visually with only one tenth cover at 052315A. There was no fighter opposition and flak. Parsons reports 15 minutes after drop as follows: results clear cut and successful in all respects. Visible effects greater than in any test. Conditions normal in airplane following delivery.[10]

Truman launched himself from his seat, startling everyone sitting close to him, and pumped the young messenger's hand. He exclaimed to Foskett: "Captain, this is the greatest thing in history." James Byrnes seemed unfazed at the fuss, while Leahy would retire quickly back to his quarters.[11]

While the buzz among the ship's crew drowned out any private conversation, another cable arrived, this time from Henry Stimson:

To the President
From the Secretary of War

Big bomb dropped on Hiroshima August 5 at 7:15 p.m. Washington time. First reports indicate complete success which was even more conspicuous than earlier test.

Clutching both communiqués in his hand, he exultantly turned to Secretary of State Byrnes and shouted over the noisy canteen hubbub: "It's time for us to get on home!" Turning to the dozens of men now looking at him, he picked up his fork and struck it against his glass to quiet the excited room of crewmen to bring them to attention. The officers and men hushed. Truman read the news of the atomic bombing of Hiroshima. The room exploded in ecstatic cheering, applause, and backslapping. As the day progressed, the news spread throughout the crew of the USS *Augusta*, with the mood throughout the ship palpably changing. The years of fighting since Pearl Harbor had exacted a heavy mental toll. Suddenly, their fear for the future, and of surviving the war with Japan, was potentially over.

Chapter Twenty-Four

A DISHONORABLE DEFEAT

There was no change in the way we felt:
we all felt the horror of being defeated and the inexpressible
horror of being the citizens of a defeated country.
What will happen now? I wondered.[1]
TANAKA JINGO, FARMER, KYUSHU

Hard-liners within the Japanese leadership, despite governing from
the burnt-out ruins in Tokyo, continued to believe the country and
the emperor could survive. As Curtis LeMay ordered further raids
on cities in Hokkaido, Japanese civilians based in the south were
bombarded by his leaflets, millions of which were dropped from
B-29s, warning of fresh attacks like those that had destroyed Hiroshima. Emperor Hirohito's government was at a crisis point. Hawks
in the military still desired to continue the fight and inflict Okinawa
levels of casualties on any American invasion, even with the imminent threat of further aerial annihilation. The peace group, headed
by Prime Minister Suzuki, continued to chase a forlorn hope of a
diplomatic solution through the Soviet ambassador to Tokyo. A negotiated settlement that kept intact the sovereignty of the emperor
was paramount for all. On August 8, that hope was extinguished for
good.

Targeting further acquisitions in the east as part of the postwar
settlement, Stalin ordered the invasion of Japanese-occupied Manchuria in northeastern China. Truman had already authorized the
use of further atomic weapons on July 25. The Target Committee

concluded from weather reports they had three more days to deploy the plutonium bomb before a storm front moved in that could cover southern Japan for almost a week. The target was to be the military industrial complex of Kokura, situated at the northern tip of Kyushu, over 120 miles south of Hiroshima.

If weather prevented an attack, the secondary target was to be Nagasaki, a further 125 miles southwest of Kokura and one of the largest ports in southern Japan. Unlike Hiroshima, Nagasaki had not been taken off LeMay's target list for heavy raids.[2] The population had increased through imported Korean forced labor as well as a strengthening of Japanese troops for the expected invasion. Over 240,000 people now resided in the old city, primarily constructed from wood and paper, with the vast majority of its workforce employed in shipyards, steel plants, and armament works.

As he had expected, Tibbets's 509th Group were again given the mission. This time, it would be *Bockscar*, commanded by Major Charles W. Sweeney with, among other supporting aircraft, Tibbets in the *Enola Gay*. Unlike the first mission, the attack to drop the plutonium bomb, Fat Man, was beset by incremental weather and operational confusion. At 3:47 a.m. on August 9, Sweeney took off for Kokura Arsenal, but by the time he had avoided a storm-ladened weather front, the target was covered in cloud. The option for Nagasaki was taken with the crew aware the bomb could not be brought back, and a technical fault robbed Sweeney of valuable spare fuel. He had to drop the bomb quickly even to make it back to the base on Okinawa. Like Kokura, Nagasaki was wreathed in cloud and ringed by heavy antiaircraft batteries that homed in on Sweeney's aircraft as he was forced to make repeated passes over the port trying to get visual recognition of the target. At 11:02 a.m., having decided to drop the bomb by radar, his bombardier, Captain Kermit Beahan, spotted a feature of the city and let Fat Man go. The detonation would be 40 percent greater than Little Boy and kill approximately forty thousand people, including hundreds of American POWs.[3]

Between August 12 and 14, the Inner Cabinet, protected in the imperial bunker, once again debated the next steps, if indeed there were any to follow. While Hirohito's cabinet argued, Chief of Staff General Marshall conducted discussions at the US War Department for gathering several more atomic bombs by October to be used in tactical support of the coming ground invasion—despite continued ignorance of the dangers of gamma radiation on American forces once such weapons were deployed against the enemy. Intercepted radio signals from Japanese military units convinced American commanders that continued bombing was necessary. To maintain the pressure on the Japanese government, both carrier-based aircraft as well as B-29s from the Marianas flew multiple, devastating raids across the Home Islands. B-29s again dropped leaflets with the US response to the original Japanese reply of conditional surrender. This act caused consternation within the Inner Cabinet, fearful that the Japanese public and junior members of the military would finally rise in revolt against a continued struggle that was going to be lost. On the American side, Groves was asked by Stimson to ship further materials to construct a third atomic bomb on Tinian, while Hap Arnold sent over his last vast air armada, over a thousand B-29s and other bombers dropping over twelve million pounds of high-explosive ordnance to destroy the cities of Kumagaya and Isezaki.[4]

At 10:20 a.m., the emperor met with Prime Minister Suzuki to inform him of acceptance of the American ultimatum: unconditional surrender. Hirohito then met with his key military leaders, including Field Marshal Hata, who had flown up from Hiroshima that morning. It would be his opinion the emperor sought out. With tears in his eyes, the old warrior, the man the emperor had trusted to fight off the American invasion, admitted he could not hope to prevent it. It was over. Hirohito would direct his Inner Cabinet forty minutes later to accept the Potsdam Declaration in full:

"In order that the people may know of my decision, I request you to prepare at once an imperial rescript so that I may broadcast to the nation. Finally, I call upon each and every one of you to exert himself to the utmost so that we may meet the trying days which lie ahead."[5]

A radio broadcast informed Japan of an "important announcement at noon tomorrow." The country was still gearing itself up for the imminent invasion. An End-of-Days mentality dominated citizens' minds as they prepared themselves for the upcoming "final battle" the regime had prepared them for against the American invaders. At noon, on August 15, millions of Japanese heard their emperor's voice for the very first time announcing he would accept the Potsdam terms, though he was careful not to utter the word *surrender*. Plots and coups to stop the broadcast and to continue the struggle were all defeated by August 23.

And still the Soviets advanced in Manchuria against stiff Japanese opposition as they prepared to assault the northern Home Island of Hokkaido. It would take the diplomatic intervention of Truman's government for the Soviet advance to stop, sending Stalin General MacArthur's General Order Number One, which detailed the future American occupation of Japan. It would take a further rebuke on August 18 before Stalin got the tone of Truman's mettle and made the sensible decision not to invade the Japanese Home Islands.

The day after the emperor's radio announcement of surrender, Motoko's freight train from Osaka finally pulled into the shattered remains of Hiroshima Station. The journey had been delayed and stressful. She worried about her husband, still lying sick in bed with typhoid fever back home, but he had insisted she travel. Both had been shocked at the news, realizing their young daughter, Ayako, was almost certainly dead. But she wanted to see for herself. As she had slept in the crowded carriage, her provisions of food and medicines she had spent valuable time buying in Osaka were stolen. The care she hoped to bring to her seriously ill mother went with it. Now she was pulling into a city she did not recognize. As the midday sun glared down, Motoko stepped down off the train and took in the alien landscape.

She could not believe her eyes. The city of her birth, which she had been proud to say her father governed and was her mother's hometown, too, was now gone. Up until last year, this was where she, her husband, and her family had lived until he had been ordered to relocate to Kobe. The destruction was total in all directions. As she shielded her eyes from the sun, dozens of people drifted past her through the rubble of what had once been a busy thoroughfare. It was surreal. She could not get any bearing on where she was. Everything had gone. What would normally be a bustling disembarkation was now dominated by an eerie atmosphere of silence in her wagon as the freight train emptied. She walked along the concourse, or what was left of it, her thoughts broken by the low murmurings of her fellow travelers as they themselves took in the horrific landscape.

As far as the eye could see, looking down toward the coast, there was nothing left standing other than a few isolated, ruined concrete buildings. Everything else of memory had been erased, save for the faint outlines of where the main thoroughfares had been. The normal landmarks that would indicate a neighborhood, civic building, police headquarters, or the many tea shops set along the riverbanks—gone. *This is Hiroshima?* she thought. *It can't be.*

She stood there stunned for several minutes. Many others from her train stood nearby, all staring out into the void. But Motoko was determined. She had no choice but to walk.

She had to reach her mother, who was being cared for by a relative, Sumiko Ogi, at her home in the ward of Takasu, in the western end of the city.

Under the blazing sun, Motoko started to walk, as if in a dream. The stench of death and decay filled the air. The first landmark of any kind she recognized was Hijiyama, the city's famous hill about a mile southeast of her father's mayoral residence, close to Field Marshal Hata's destroyed military headquarters. The many trees that had decorated the top of the two-hundred-foot-high hill had all been destroyed by the bomb blast. However, amid the burned ruins, the only thing that could be seen from Hiroshima Station in that direction was this small hill. Motoko estimated the location of Ujina Port and the sea from the position of Mount Hiji. Figuring out her bearings, she drew a mind map of a route from the center of the city to Takasu. It would not be easy, but she set off.

Although ten days had already passed since the atomic bombing, the authorities were clearly struggling to restore anything. She now encountered lines of civilian and military rescuers, their faces covered in scarves, surgical masks, or even bandages. The scorching sun shone down on her relentlessly. Buildings were crumbling, burning, and reduced to mere rubble. Here and there, water pipes had burst and were leaking out. People in rags, some semi-naked, waited their turn to fill their pots and buckets. No one spoke. She could easily hear the sound of the water filling each container. She waited in line to drink some. Quenching her thirst, she continued walking. Over the next few hours, she zigzagged through the city, getting lost several times. Her path forced her to cross the five tributaries that fed into the wider Ota River: the Makuma, the Kyobashi, the Motoyasu, the Honkawa, and the Tenma. A few still had some sort of bridge or causeway. At one crossing, survivors had constructed a makeshift bridge by lashing boats together. Flies were everywhere. The bodies left behind were still here and there, maggots were sprouting, and flies were swarming in black. The horrendous smell made her stop several times to retch.

She finally reached the home of Sumiko Ogi by late afternoon. She was exhausted, physically and emotionally. She had walked through hell, the journey easing only slightly as she got close to Ogi's ward, where the bomb damage was minimal. As she came up to the door of the traditional Japanese single-story wooden house, she drew in her breath to prepare herself. Despite bringing nothing with her, her guilt evaporated as she was greeted with warmth by the Ogi family. Mrs. Ogi herself bore the wounds of the attack. She had been out walking that morning, though not too close to Ground Zero, yet had still suffered some burns. Her dark clothes had protected her from the blast. Before she led Motoko to her mother's room, she described how she had made her way to the old mayoral residence the day after the attack but could not find anyone alive. She had been directed to the Red Cross Hospital in the north of the city, where she had found Motoko's mother. Given a wheelchair, she had loaded her into it as a makeshift ambulance and taken her back to her house.

Motoko was surprised at how well her mother looked. Her wounds seemed to be healing, although the injury to her mouth was severe, needing many stitches and dressings. She was fortunately not burned a great deal thanks to being in the house when the blast occurred. The women fell into each other's arms, Mrs. Awaya pleading for forgiveness for the death of Motoko's daughter, Ayako. There was nothing to be done. Mrs. Ogi then told Motoko of a visit from her father's chief secretary, Kazumasa Maruyama. He had located all three of the burned bodies at the destroyed residence and had taken them for cremation close to City Hall. The ashes were in boxes, now stored in the house.

Motoko would spend the next three days caring for her mother, scavenging for supplies amid chaos and power shortages. She tried her best to console her mother during the waking hours, while praying at night by candlelight for the souls of her dead father, younger brother, and her own infant daughter. She knew she had to return to be with her husband soon and share the news of Ayuko's fate. She had written to her younger sister Yasuko to quickly travel down from Tokyo and take her place by August 30. There was no need for Yasuko to remain in her job at the munitions factory where she had been inspecting and cleaning fuses for antiaircraft shells. Always the brightest and bubbliest of the Awaya brood, Yasuko wrote a farewell to her younger sister, nine-year-old Chikako:

> Mother is alive, how happy and grateful I am. Your father did not die a dog's death. As mayor of Hiroshima, he died together with the citizens of Hiroshima. . . . How painful it would have been for our father if he had miraculously survived. He was a righteous, strong, and honorable man. He was also a kind and gentle father. My sisters and I are very proud to be the children of such an honorable father. . . .

The words that our father used to say to us all live on in our hearts. Even though our bodies may be separated, our hearts will always be with him. . . . Shinobu went all the way to Hiroshima to accompany his father, didn't he? He loved his father very much. He was a really kind and good boy. I am sure that both of them are standing beside God right now, smiling and looking down.

I am going to Hiroshima now to pick up my mother. I will go to Hiroshima to pick up my father's [ashes]. After I return home, I will visit you. Until then, I want you to study hard. If you are upset every day because you lost your father, you will be disobedient to his heart. Please fulfil your heavy responsibility as a person in a higher position.

Take care of yourself. Be strong. Let's not be so gloomy.

Let's do our best!
Yasuko[6]

Yasuko arrived in Hiroshima to the same scenes her elder sister had encountered and made her way quickly to Mrs. Ogi's residence. By this time, Mrs. Awaya had been recovering, or seemed to be, though both elderly women still suffered from diarrhea. The effects of radiation poisoning, however, were quietly destroying her body. Her hair began to fall out in lumps, and she was struck by high fevers that left her delirious. By September 1, she fell into unconsciousness. A desperate Yasuko urged Motoko to return from her husband's hospital bed to be with them. Both daughters watched over their mother until she passed away on September 7.

The city was still not functioning, so an official burial was out of the question. Motoko recalled: "We asked strangers for firewood and, together with my sister and aunts, I borrowed a large cart and transported my mother's body to a nearby field. Long trenches had been dug for the many corpses that were brought in daily. We arranged the firewood inside a hole, gently put my mother's body there, and built a fire. I wonder how many times we hesitated to do so. 'Is there anything as miserable as this?' I recall saying in tears to my sister that day. We reserved some of her remains for a proper funeral ceremony."[7]

In a haunting scene, both surviving sisters boarded a train amid the ruins of Hiroshima Station a few days later. In their baggage, they carried four boxes: the ashes of their parents, younger brother, and Motoko's son. They would take them home to Tokyo. Feelings of national defeat, and the fear of foreign occupation, meant nothing now. Bigger disasters were about to befall them. They arrived back in the capital on September 10 to the family home, where their surviving siblings, Tadashi and Chikako, joined them. The family would be welcomed by their Christian community as the city and the country came to terms with their total defeat. The suffering of the Awayas was a metaphor for the country.

With the Allied press corps and thousands of US Army, Navy, and Marine personnel looking on, Japanese envoys Foreign Minister Mamoru Shigemitsu and General Yoshijiro Umezu came aboard the USS *Missouri* in Tokyo Bay on September 2. Their humiliation would be overseen by the two American adversaries who had made it happen (in their eyes), Admiral Nimitz and General MacArthur, with the official seal of approval from President Truman back in Washington. Though eight short paragraphs in length, the second paragraph laid out Japan's thorough capitulation:

We hereby proclaim the unconditional surrender to the Allied Powers of the Japanese Imperial General Headquarters and of all Japanese armed forces and all armed forces under Japanese control wherever situated.[8]

To cement the omnipotent power of the victor, four hundred B-29s, together with another fifteen hundred carrier aircraft, flew overhead in the biggest show of air strength in history. MacArthur announced to the watching throng as the Japanese delegation made their way off the *Missouri*:

"Today the guns are silent. A great tragedy has ended. A great victory has been won. These proceedings are now closed."

The war in the Pacific, and World War II itself, was now over. MacArthur would embark on arguably the most important appointment of his career—the resurrection of a democratic Japan from the ruins of military totalitarianism. For that to work, the horrors inflicted upon Hiroshima and Nagasaki had to be spun in a positive light for both sides to move forward as one.

Within two months of MacArthur's speech, Motoko would be mourning the loss of her sister. Yasuko died in a Tokyo hospital from radiation sickness on November 24, 1945. She had unwittingly spent too many days close to the center of Hiroshima caring for her mother. Motoko, with her husband Hiroshi, arranged for a farewell ceremony on December 6 for Yasuko, together with her siblings Shinobu and Chikako, her daughter Ayako, and her parents. The Christian ceremony was conducted by her father's longtime mentor, Doctor Toraji Tsukamoto, and attended by a great many friends of the family and colleagues of her father he had worked with over the years.

"Praying and crying, they consoled us. Mr. Tsukamoto's words to encourage us at the time still remain in my ears: 'I have no words of condolence, but please endure quietly until after the storm has gone.'

"Peace was restored after Japan was defeated in the war, but the sacrifice forced on us immediately before the end of the war was truly difficult to bear."[9]

The words of comfort spoken by one of the members of his Bible class would remain with her for the rest of her life: "Truly, the death of the Father finally ended the atrocious Greater East Asia War. I firmly believe that. Peace has come to Japan, the Orient, and the world because of your father's death. With this in mind, I am grateful for your father's death."[10]

Chapter Twenty-Five

CONTROLLING THE STORY

I knew what I was doing when I stopped the war
that would have killed a half million youngsters on both
sides if those bombs had not been dropped. I have no regrets,
and, under the same circumstances, I would do it again—
and this letter is not confidential.

LETTER WRITTEN BY PRESIDENT TRUMAN, AUGUST 5, 1963

Midori Naka knew she was seriously ill. The thirty-six-year-old actress quickly got off the Hiroshima train as soon as it pulled into Tokyo Central Station on August 16. She had called in a few favors from admirers in the capital who had gotten her on one of the rare connections since the atomic attack. Now that the war was over, there seemed to be more freedom of movement, or at least the outside world had managed to get into Hiroshima, despite the devastation. She had been fortunate to be inside her dormitory, seven hundred yards away from Ground Zero, that she rented with her acting troupe—the Sakura-tai ("Cherry Blossom Unit"), which belonged to the Japanese Federation of Movement Theater. She was cooking food in their kitchen when the bomb detonated, she recalled to a friend:

"I immediately lost consciousness. When I came to, I was in darkness, and I gradually became aware that I was pinned beneath the ruins of the house. When I tried to work my way free, I realized that apart from my small panties, I was entirely naked. I ran my hand over my face and back: I was uninjured! Only my hands and legs were slightly scratched. I ran just as I was to the river, where everything was in flames. I jumped into the water and floated downstream. After a few hundred yards, some soldiers fished me out."[1]

Seventeen actors including Naka had been in the house; only four survived the initial blast.

Within a week, she was coming down with a fever, her hair was falling out in clumps, and she suffered terrible diarrhea. Hospital treatment, or any kind of good medical assessment, was impossible in a city destroyed and thousands of its health staff dead or dying themselves. A telephone call had gotten her to the relative safety of her mother's house in Tokyo, now that the Americans were not terror bombing. She staggered out of the station and managed to get a taxi to Tokyo University Hospital. A small team of doctors was waiting for her, including expert radiation and oncologist Professor Masao Tsuzuki, who had taught in the United States before the war. They now attempted to save her life. Tests showed her white blood cell count was dropping alarmingly from eight thousand to just four hundred. Over the next five days as Tsuzuki's team fought to save her, Naka's body temperature soared to 105.8 degrees, her heart rate accelerated to 158 beats per minute, and dark, purple patches appeared all over her body as she writhed in agony. She died on August 24. She would be the first recorded victim of radiation poisoning from the Hiroshima attack.

Twenty-four hours after Naka had tottered into Tokyo University Hospital, another train from Hiroshima had brought back Army physician Koyishi Yamashina from his arduous duties. On August 8, he had been ordered to the stricken city with eight other doctors to care for the sick and wounded. While there, he had performed a variety of autopsies on the deceased. Both he and his fellow doctors noticed strange similarities to those corpses they were dissecting: low white blood cell counts, unexplained internal bleeding, rotting gums, dramatic hair loss, and damaged vital organs. The medical team began to keep a record of what they were discovering, preserving samples in slides displaying bone marrow with a faint yellow color and blackened lung tissue showing extensive bleeding. All these were brought back with them to Tokyo. The surrender signed and MacArthur's occupation government formally set up, American medical teams soon arrived, many working alongside the Japanese medical units. But when more and more victims of the atomic attacks began to arrive in Tokyo, as well as in newly set-up medical centers in both Hiroshima and Nagasaki, the attitude of the US authorities hardened.

As they did so, a Gallup poll of August 26, 1945, proclaimed that 85 percent of the American public endorsed the atomic bombs' use on Japanese cities, while 10 percent disapproved and 5 percent expressed no opinion.[2] With the celebrations of VJ Day still a recent memory, the people of the United States seemed still to agree with the government and military line that the use of atomic bombs was simply an escalation of conventional ordnance already used on the enemy—as had been shown a few months previously with the devastating attacks on Dresden and the later, deadlier, fire raids on Tokyo. The headline comment in *The Chicago Sun* mirrored the common opinion: "There is no scale of values which makes a TNT explosion right and a uranium explosion wrong."[3]

Groves was masterminding the release to the public of the work the Manhattan Project had been doing, with authorized stories allowed to be published of the "hidden cities" in the United States that had perfected the new bombs. The line of celebrating American and Allied scientific ingenuity while burying any sentiment toward the Japanese had been tacitly agreed to by American newspaper proprietors. The first trickle of public concern, however, came from *The Washington Post* just two days after the atomic attack on Hiroshima. In an article headlined "Area Struck by Atomic Bomb Is Saturated with Death for 70 Years, Scientist Declares," a New York–based physicist, Dr. Harold Jacobson, with only a passing association with the Manhattan Project, outlined his concerns. "Tests have shown that the radiation in an area exposed to the force of an atomic bomb will not dissipate for approximately 70 years."

Groves acted quickly, immediately refuting the statement the following day through government channels and enlisting Robert Oppenheimer to refute Jacobson's theories in *The New York Times*. "There is no evidence to show measurable radiation remains on the ground in Hiroshima, and what little there was decayed very rapidly."

One of Groves's key scientists, Arthur H. Compton, the head of the Chicago Met Laboratory for the Manhattan Project, would look back on that moment: "By war's end in August 1945, most Americans agreed that the conduct of total war required Allied obliteration bombing of enemy cities. Accepting the necessity (however regrettable) for such attacks, many Americans saw no fundamental difference between atomic bombing and the use of conventional explosives and incendiaries on urban areas. Atomic bombing was simply a more efficient (and cost effective in lives) form of obliteration bombing."[4]

American mass media could not seriously challenge the storyline being given by Groves and the Truman administration, who played down the risk of radiation poisoning, attempted to water down potential casualties and deaths from the atomic strike compared to a traditional one, and limited the descriptions of what an atomic bomb had done to both Hiroshima and Nagasaki. This at a time when the US government, as well as Great Britain, were focusing on the postwar issues of demobilization, dealing with inflation, a national workforce now feeling confident of going on strike for better pay and conditions, and the looming threat of communism spreading in Europe and Asia. The underlying message was that no good could come from questioning the use of the atomic bombs. Even the scientific community had generally accepted their use, whether because their success justified their own theories, or because the new energy source could place America on a stronger footing, militarily and economically.

The first critical US coverage about Hiroshima came from Japanese American reporter Leslie Nakashima. Through ill fortune, he had been trapped in Japan after Pearl Harbor and lived out his war in the capital. The Hawaiian-born journalist was now a "stringer," busy filing news stories for the United Press (UP). He had ventured down to the city on August 22 to find his mother, whom by a miracle he discovered to be alive. What he then witnessed, he cabled back to the UP office five days later, describing a destroyed city, devoid of life. His horrific scoop made its way into *The New York Times* on August 31 (hidden on page four), but it had suffered at the hands of US censors. His descriptions of potential radiation sickness had been erased, with an editor's note inserted: "United States scientists say the atomic bomb will not have any lingering after-effects in the devastated area."

In the States, Groves was alarmed to read an article in late August, by science editor Howard W. Blakeslee in the Associated Press, which argued that "[t]he Japanese who were reported today by Tokyo radio to have died mysteriously a few days after the atomic bomb blast probably were victims of a phenomenon which is well known in the great radiation laboratories of America."[5] Blakeslee went on to suggest that American scientists were aware of this before the Hiroshima attack. The political impact of a story like this was clear to Groves, and it only sharpened his focus to deal with what he termed these "Japanese horror stories." He wanted his right-hand man, Brigadier General Farrell, on the ground in Japan to assess the situation for himself.

The real breakthrough came when Australian reporter Wilfred Burchett, working for *The Daily Express*, covering the US Marines on Okinawa, heard the radio broadcast of a new type of bomb dropped on Hiroshima. While everyone around him celebrated that the war might be over, Burchett instinctively smelled a story. He arrived in Japan on August 14 with the Marines, armed with a typewriter, a Japanese phrase book, and a Colt .45 service pistol. He then discreetly made his way down south by train to the city. Befriending the local police chief and head of the city's news bureau, Burchett got what he needed in terms of what the bomb had done to the city and its people. The core of the story was a hidden disease that seemed to be killing healthy survivors by the hundreds every day—the majority of whom displayed the same symptoms. His story for the *Express* would appear on September 5, under the title "The Atomic Plague."

"In Hiroshima, 30 days after the first atomic bomb destroyed the city and shook the world, people are still dying, mysteriously and horribly—people who were uninjured by the cataclysm—from an unknown something which I can only describe as atomic plague. Hiroshima does not look like a bombed city. It looks as if a monster steamroller had passed over it and squashed it out of existence."

It was, as Burchett told colleagues, the "scoop of the century," which embarrassed US military authorities and finally exposed to the world that the official storyline was heavily sugarcoated.[6] Unbeknownst to General MacArthur (yet to officially take up his new position in Tokyo), a US government–organized press junket was flown into the city, led by Lieutenant Colonel John Reagan "Tex" McCary, a reporter turned public relations officer for the US Army Air Force. Dozens of journalists were flown from Europe to Asia aboard two purpose-built B-17s, with bespoke seating, writing desks, lamps, and a long-range transmitter for articles to be cabled back to news desks in America.[7] Whereas Burchett had spent days among the ruins and survivors, the reporters of the Associated Press, United Press, *The New York Times*, NBC, CBS, and ABC were given only a few hours on the ground to see the destruction for themselves. Though clearly shocked, their reports were not filed until Lieutenant Colonel McCary had emphasized to them the need to water down their description for an American public back home who "were not yet ready for it."

Despite the official request, the story broke just as big in the States as Burchett's had in Great Britain. The official response was to shut down access to both the cities, corral the foreign press around the American base at Yokohama, restrict access from there into Tokyo, and increase monitoring of the domestic press. As this was happening, Brigadier General Farrell had finally landed in Hiroshima with the Manhattan District investigation team to measure the residual radiation and visit Hiroshima's Red Cross Hospital and other sites of interest. He would report back his findings to Groves, who was busy handling media and political inquiries. They were accompanied by Dr. Marcel Junod, head of the delegation of the International Committee of the Red Cross (ICRC) to Japan (who brought fifteen tons of medical supplies), and Professor Masao Tsuzuki, who had tried valiantly to save Midori Naka a few days earlier.

Shocked by what he encountered, Tsuzuki would clash with Farrell on what was killing the victims on September 9. In response to Professor Tsuzuki's comment to local city authorities that "the press has said that the effects of the toxins from the atomic bomb will last for seventy-five years," Farrell attempted to shut him down, repeating the policy line that there would be no effects two or three days after the detonation. The following day, in the Japanese daily *Chugoku Shimbun*, a four-line headline stated that the theory of seventy-five years was a lie. When he returned to Tokyo two days later, Farrell arrived back in Tokyo to announce that the explosive power of the secret weapon was greater than what its inventors had envisaged and that there was no danger living in this area at present. More bad headlines kept appearing in the domestic press, *Chugoku Shimbun* running: "Losses surpass 110,000: the power of the atomic bomb is still wreaking havoc." And the next day: "Even far removed from the hypocenter, people cannot escape atomic bomb sickness."[8]

The dam holding back the full story was breaking. On September 15, another newspaper, *Asahi Shimbun*, ran a damning article that concluded, "The use of atomic bombs and the murder of innocent civilians is undeniably a greater violation of the international law, and a war crime, than attacking hospital ships or poisonous gas." MacArthur's office ordered a forty-eight-hour suspension of the newspaper, but the article had already circulated nationally. MacArthur's Newspaper and News Agency Department now enforced a new domestic press code. From October 8, all newspaper reports, editorials, advertisements, publications, radio broadcasts, and movies would be monitored for content "inimical to the objectives of the occupation." Anything connected to the bombings of Nagasaki or Hiroshima was to be shut down.

The authorities wanted the concern to dissipate, for the Japanese people to come on board with the occupation, and for Groves, back home in Washington, and the Manhattan Project to continue their work as the debate continued about what role this newfound energy source and military hardware would play in the future. The findings of Farrell's team from both Japanese cities gave good and bad news. Tests showed that they would not quickly become inhabitable again, certainly not for decades. However, the delayed symptoms patients were now dying from by the hundreds each day were linked to the burst of radiation they had received from the blasts. The Japanese and foreign press seized upon the story for now, but Groves still attempted to play it down. In a Senate committee hearing in November, he attempted to water down the number of post-attack deaths, and as for the theory on radiation poisoning, his reply would go down in history: "As I understand it from the doctors, it is a very pleasant way to die."9

Chapter Twenty-Six

"SO FAR FROM HOME, ALMOST BEYOND RETURN."

If any human being is capable of writing one work
of lasting value, they've done something extraordinary–
absolutely extraordinary.

DAVID REMNICK, EDITOR OF *THE NEW YORKER* [1]

Despite becoming an acclaimed Pulitzer Prize–winning novelist for
A Bell for Adano and an adaptation playing on Broadway, John Hersey
was restless. He was thirty-two years old, and the world seemed to be
heading toward a new postwar era. His time spent in Eastern Europe
had proven enjoyable in terms of the characters he had met—such as
the legendary raconteur and British ambassador Archie Kerr—but he
was frustrated by the lack of access to real stories. As with all Western journalists based in the Metropol Hotel in Moscow, a repressive
regime such as Stalin's was not going to allow freedom of travel unless within strict boundaries of supervision. Hersey, like every other
correspondent, reported what the Soviet authorities wanted him to
see, whether that was witnessing the rebuilding of the liberated port
city of Leningrad, the aftermath of the capture of the Polish capital,
Warsaw, or meeting Jewish survivors of a liberated camp. The term
"Holocaust" had yet to be defined.

    This lack of freedom had been compounded by Hersey decid-
ing his independence within the *Time-Life* organization back home
in New York was becoming equally restrictive. By the time he was

back in New York in the spring of 1945, he had become weary of the editorial shackles he believed were being placed on some of his submissions by Henry Luce. In a letter he wrote to his wife Frances Ann in February 1945, he grumbled to her about how a long piece he had penned on Nazi atrocities in the Polish city of Lodz might be doctored in house: "Three careful days to exterminate human beings . . . after *Life* gets through dressing it up with those lurid drawings, I'll bet it will seem as if that Hersey had been writing fiction again."[2]

The previous November, while still in Moscow, he had turned down Luce's offer of a role as senior editor with *Time*. As he had proven countless times during the war, recording ordinary human experiences was at the core of his articles. Accepting a more administrative role, running a team of writers, did not have the same appeal. In Hersey's opinion, Luce had still to fulfill a long-standing agreement that he would be allowed to return to China to report on the civil war once again bubbling up now that the war against Japan was coming to its climax. By July, as talk in the American media turned to US forces invading mainland Japan, he had resigned from his full-time position on Luce's editorial staff. It would be a turning point in their relationship. He was now a freelance for hire, still basking in the limelight of winning the Pulitzer, his article on John. F. Kennedy, and evaluating what was his next step. And then the atomic bombs were dropped on Hiroshima and Nagasaki. The war was suddenly over.

What Hersey thought about the dropping of the atomic bombs is not known. Perhaps he was relieved, as most Americans were, that the fighting was at last at an end and the invasion of Japan would not take place. The boys were coming home. The defeat of Japan and the damage the US air campaign had inflicted were still seen through the prism of the surprise attack on Pearl Harbor four years earlier. The American public, it seemed, were not yet ready to feel any compassion for the "Jap," and an air of triumphalism permeated all aspects of the country's media—whether in newsprint, radio, or in Hollywood. The "Tribute to Victory" national celebration the previous October, three months after the Japanese surrender, was the culmination of this victory fever that gripped the United States. The General Groves–led PR campaign to micromanage early reports of radiation fallout and destruction had seemingly worked. The country had moved on to storylines of a devastated Europe and Asia being rebuilt, its millions of war refugees rehomed, and the punishments being meted out to both Nazi and Japanese war criminals.

Hersey had enjoyed the experience of working with William Shawn at *The New Yorker* for the John F. Kennedy piece. The upmarket magazine had switched its tone since Pearl Harbor, from one of consumerism mixed with intellectual, witty stories to publishing a series of hard-hitting, war-related stories. Hersey's story about John F. Kennedy was no flash in the pan. Its success was due in no small measure to the positive communication and editorial advice he had received from Shawn and the magazine's founder, Harold Ross, two different characters and temperaments as could be, but together editorially, a creative powerhouse. The journalist Lesley Blume, author of *Fallout*, summarized them well enough: "Ross was an extravagant personality with a talent for profanity. He occasionally brandished a knitting needle during editorial meetings. . . . William Shawn on the other hand was introverted to the point of near invisibility."[3]

By the late fall of 1945, Hersey wanted the opportunity Luce was reluctant to give him—a commission to travel. His friend and rival William Laurence at *The New York Times* was in Groves's "circle of trust" and as such had already scooped several big stories in the past eighteen months. Laurence had already been on the government press junket to Hiroshima and Tokyo and believed he had already broken the main story there was to tell from Hiroshima. Perhaps invigorated, possibly envious, Hersey longed to get back to Asia, visit China, the country of his birth, and attempt to then get into Japan, despite the apparent censorship General MacArthur's News Department was operating. A sit-down working lunch at the Algonquin Hotel with Harold Ross would hopefully achieve it.

As the lunchtime traffic buzzed throughout the restaurant, the

New Yorker editor was all ears as Hersey pitched his ideas. They discussed the eyewitness accounts of Hiroshima already published, the work of Wilfred Burchett at *The Daily Express* and Laurence at *The New York Times*. Both centred on the power of the atomic explosions and the devastation they had wreaked upon the city. As Hersey pointed out to Ross, months after the event the actual human angle had so far been overlooked. Perhaps the question posed by fellow novelist George Orwell for the *Tribune* the previous October needed to be further developed. Truman's government and the US military were still loath to reveal their ambitions for this new technology:

"Had the atomic bomb turned out to be something as cheap and easily manufactured as a bicycle or an alarm clock, it might well have plunged us back into barbarism, but it might, on the other hand, have meant the end of national sovereignty and of the highly centralised police State. If, as seems to be the case, it is a rare and costly object as difficult to produce as a battleship, it is likelier to put an end to large-scale wars at the cost of prolonging indefinitely a 'peace that is no peace.'"[4]

As he had achieved with "Into the Valley" at Guadalcanal and, a year later, "Survival" with John F. Kennedy, he intended to find and then humanize the destruction of Hiroshima, if—a big if—he could gain access to Japan and then the city itself. Both men were cognizant that the US military and Truman's administration were intent on playing it down. Ross encouraged Hersey to get out there, dig deep, and find the stories. As a freelancer, he had to keep both his masters happy, so to keep *Life* magazine onside, he pitched a sort of photographic-style travelogue: a tour of China, including a photo shoot along the Yangtze River. But it would be Ross at *The New Yorker* who would be his constant support, cabling him throughout the trip and sending encouragement when events and logistical and visa issues cast doubts in his mind.

As his trip progressed through the early spring of 1946, Hersey fed back a variety of articles as the journey to China developed. Some, as agreed, were for *Life*, while many others were for *The New Yorker*.

At one point he was producing an article a week for Ross, much to the chagrin of Henry Luce. The publishing magnates had loathed each other since the late 1920s. By May 1946, based in Shanghai, Hersey finally received authorization from the US military authorities in Tokyo to travel to Japan. He was anxious that his work should chime in with the mood of the country as the US military prepared to test more atomic weapons.[5] Shawn cabled to discourage him: "The more time passes the more convinced we are that [the] piece has wonderful possibilities. No one has even touched it. Think best to write it back here and time it for anniversary."[6] Both men agreed that whatever Hersey brought back should be published for the anniversary of the Hiroshima attack.

With Shawn's support, he was keen to get moving, for he now had the angle his writer's instinct told him was the best approach to the project. Whilst sailing aboard a US Navy destroyer to Shanghai, he had succumbed to flu and been placed in the ship's infirmary. To pass the time, a member of the crew had given him his copy of a book by the Pulitzer-winning novelist Thornton Wilder, *The Bridge of San Luis Rey*.[7] In it, Wilder described a disaster set in Peru during the eighteenth century told through the eyes of a handful of protagonists. Hersey was convinced the structure of this narrative would fit perfectly for what he intended as he packed his bag and began his long journey to Tokyo.

Via the Twentieth Air Force's base on Guam, he now took a naval flight to Tokyo, setting up residence at the Tokyo Correspondents' Club, a run-down, five-story building, close to General MacArthur's fortress-like headquarters that had been created from the Dai-ichi Life Insurance Company building. Ironically, or perhaps intentionally, MacArthur now ruled over Japan from a desk looking out across Emperor Hirohito's Imperial Palace. The significance was clear to Allied occupier and defeated Japanese alike.

Everywhere he walked in his first day of arriving in the ruined capital, Hersey recorded a scale of destruction that he had never witnessed. The destroyed towns and cities he had traveled through,

from Sicily to the Soviet Union to the Baltics and Poland, were nothing compared to this. His instinct for the story Hiroshima might
provide was strengthened by a meeting with a young US Army filmmaker, Lieutenant Herbert Sussan. Over drinks at the Correspondents' Club, Sussan described the devastation that he had filmed at
Hiroshima. Within twenty-four hours, the Supreme Commander of
Allied Powers had issued a fourteen-day pass for Hersey to travel to
the atomic city. It wasn't a great deal of time, so he would have to be
quick and ruthless in what material he could harvest. Sussan provided
a few contacts to call upon when he arrived. His help would turn out
to be crucial. Hersey was set to hunt out a group of Jesuit priests he
had read about in a *Time* article who had survived the attack and had
continued to provide care for the thousands of survivors. Sussman
confirmed they were still in the city.

As Senkichi Awaya had experienced many months before, Hersey
navigated his way through Tokyo's Central Station to scramble on
board a packed train. The journey of 420 miles to Hiroshima seemed
to last an eternity as they passed through a succession of military and
civil checkpoints. He was lucky to be in the carriage reserved for Allied occupation troops—many of whom were war tourists heading to
the atomic city to see it for themselves—compared to standing room
only in the Japanese sections.

Things now fell into place for a journalist who knew how to
track down a lead and build a story. Within hours of his arrival, he
was unpacking his belongings in a US military police–run boarding-
house close to the city port of Ujina, which had escaped most of the
atomic blast. Despite the rebuilding taking place, he was shocked at
the level of destruction caused by just a single bomb. It was on a scale
far bigger even than Tokyo. He felt a sense of dread. If one bomb
did this to bricks and mortar, what must it have done to the people?
Though the authorities and Allied occupiers had set up a cleanup
program, the survivors and those refugees who had returned from
their safe havens in the surrounding mountains were struggling. Everywhere he went, people were living in shanties, lean-tos, or holes

in the ground covered with corrugated-metal sheets. People walked slowly with the characteristics of those who had little energy because they were starving.

In the summer heat, there was the all-pervading stench of death. You couldn't escape it. The civic burial parties were bringing back hundreds of bodies a day in every ward of the city. Hersey spied American troops driving through the center of town in jeeps and trucks, some with their faces covered in hankies. Some younger Japanese were now cycling, and a few of the city's trams had been put back to work. Several times, his exploration of a particular street was cut short by official tape cordoning off what looked like ruins. Every now and again, despite the signs, he watched American and Australian troops going past the cordons to pick up rubble, which they placed in their knapsacks: war tourism. He wasn't going to raise any objections. He needed to keep onside with the US military if he was going to get a story. They had already agreed to supply him a jeep and gasoline.

Hersey struck lucky almost immediately. He tracked down the Jesuit priest he had read about in *Time*, a German, Father Hugo Lassalle. The Catholic mission he and his fellow priests and local worshippers had belonged to, though only thirteen hundred yards from where the bomb had detonated, had miraculously survived the blast. Some of the mission had died, and many had been injured. They had then spent the next frantic hours and days attempting to rescue as many as possible, setting up their ruined compound as a makeshift medical center. Without any medicines or doctors, dozens of survivors had turned up at their door, many succumbing to their injuries or what would later be called radiation sickness.

Lassalle took Hersey to meet a fellow German priest, Father Wilhelm Kleinsorge. He was a classic example of this mysterious illness that was a plague on the survivors. Over the many weeks after the explosion, his injuries had refused to heal properly, he developed a fever and debilitating diarrhea, and then his teeth and hair began to fall out. He was constantly retching, with or without eating food, until he was skeletal in appearance. Close to death, he had been saved only with hospitalization as the Allies brought in medical teams. Thousands of others had not been so lucky. Hersey listened for hours, gradually winning the priest's confidence as Kleinsorge poured out his experiences. Once he had done so, he felt confident enough to recommend Hersey go see a local Methodist pastor, the Reverend Kiyoshi Tanimoto. He had traveled extensively through the United States before the war, spoke good enough English, and warmed to Hersey, perhaps due to learning of the American's own family background as Christian missionaries. Hersey recalled he was "a small man, quick to talk, laugh, and cry. . . . He moves nervously and fast, but with a restraint which suggests that he is a cautious, thoughtful man."[8]

Indeed he was, but his memories of encountering survivors would shock the American public: "On some undressed bodies, the burns had made patterns. . . . On the skin of some women (since white repelled heat from the bomb and dark clothes absorbed it and conducted it onto the skin), the shapes of flowers that had been on their kimonos."[9] The interview with Tanimoto went well and quickly established Hersey as a trusted American with whom others could talk to share their horrific experiences. Over the next days, he would interview over thirty Japanese men and women who covered the spectrum of Hiroshima's society. From this large cache of testimonies, he would give himself the best chance of weaving together the article he believed would work in the form he had discovered reading the novel of Thornton Wilder.

He had spent two weeks in the baking heat of the city. He was ready to leave and return to the States to file his work, his instincts telling him he was onto a strong story. He set out on his long journey on June 12, cabling Shawn to expect him in the *New Yorker* offices in five days' time. As he traveled back, he gathered his notes and isolated the six main characters from which he intended to tell his story. Along with the testimonies of Father Kleinsorge and the Reverend Tanimoto, Hersey weaved in the stories of four other survivors: twenty-year-old Toshiko Sasaki, a personnel department clerk, who had been only sixteen hundred yards from the center of the blast and suffered severe leg injuries; a widow, Hatsuyo Nakamura, who had managed to save her three young children amid the destruction; and finally, to add expert medical analysis, two doctors to fact-check everything he was being told by the eyewitnesses, Masakazu Fujii and Terufumi Sasaki. What they told him would prove a valuable added layer of detail to explain the trauma the protagonists had suffered.

These six would provide the evidence, from different perspectives, of what the atomic bomb had done to the city. Ironically, as he arrived back in America, the United States military was basking in the country's admiration of a successful nuclear test. The postwar era would be one of American ingenuity and advances in science. Henry Luce's prewar proclamations were ringing true—it really was the "American Century." Hersey would hide himself away to craft what he hoped would be the definitive storyline in thirty thousand words. For ten consecutive days, all three newsmen would be locked away with the magazine's production manager and layout designer, both Ross and Shawn working 10 a.m. to 2 a.m., crafting the final piece. Across several drafts Hersey supplied, as he was prone to do, Ross offered Hersey copious notes, changes, and bombastic commentary throughout the neat, typed-up prose. Studying the original draft in Hersey's papers stored at the Yale University library archives, one can see how much of a collaborative effort it was. Resembling a school essay, each page is littered with Ross's edits, comments, and requested changes.

Two factors dominated: the importance of the event itself and explaining the terrible aftermath without incurring the official wrath of government censors. To discuss the technical consequences of the atomic bomb was still illegal. Hersey suggested he would describe the injuries and symptoms of the six characters, especially Father Kleinsorge. In that way, readers would understand what kind of toxic weapon the US military had used. Ross was anxious that Hersey strike the correct tone in the first few opening lines, describing the exact time when the bomb struck the city. As Ben Yagoda concluded in *About Town: The New Yorker and the World It Made*, doing so "helped give an almost biblical power to the finished piece."[10] Unleashing such biblical power had consequences. Hersey took note of what officials on the ground had said about the casualties in Hiroshima. For the article he would quote them, stating at least one hundred thousand Japanese had died in the attack.

As his staff unknowingly worked on a "shadow" issue, ensuring Hersey's work would be hidden until publication, William Shawn suggested to Ross an unprecedented idea. Hersey was always meant to write this article for serial publication in the magazine's "Reporter at Large" section, with the scope to serialize it across several consecutive editions. Shawn was having none of it. He lobbied Ross hard. Hersey's piece should not be serialized, he declared; it was far too significant for what was going on in the world. With the anniversary of dropping the bomb on Hiroshima approaching, they should devote the whole magazine to it. Concern about scaring off the magazine's loyal readership, or sponsors, was a poor argument. *The New Yorker*'s original declaration in the 1920s had been to "publish the facts that it will have to go behind the scenes to get" and "try conscientiously to keep its readers informed." Ross was won over: thirty-six pages of the August 31 issue would be set aside for the story, titled "Hiroshima."

Through the first two weeks of August, Shawn worked with the magazine's lawyers to oversee the legal changes he thought must come from the War Department. Current world events played into their favor. General Groves, keen to promote the country's forward atomic program and keep Britain onside amid growing Soviet intransigence in Europe, received the final draft. Unaware of how *The New Yorker* planned to publish, he asked for a few cosmetic changes and gave it the green light on August 16. His commitment to the Manhattan Project echoed in the cover note he sent back to Ross: "As I look at the pictures of our men coming home from Japanese prisons and hear second-hand accounts and first-hand accounts of the experiences of the men who made the march from Bataan. I am not particularly worried about how hard this weapon hit the Japanese."

As the "Tribute to Victory" celebrations the previous autumn had shown, a great many of his fellow Americans shared his sentiment. That was soon about to change.

The full-color illustration by Charles E. Martin[11] that decorated the issue that hit the newsstands on August 31 gave no clue as to the shocking content. A summer picnic, possibly in Central Park, reflected exactly what New Yorkers themselves were possibly planning for the weekend: sailing on the Hudson, a game of tennis in Central Park, horse riding, or stretching out to catch some sunshine on the beach on Long Island. Everyone was smiling. The juxtaposition of serenity on the surface with the violent final act of World War II beneath was to prove an ingenious vehicle. It launched Hersey's feature, "Hiroshima—A Noiseless Flash," to an unsuspecting American public. According to the current editor of *The New Yorker*, David Remnick, "The idea that John Hersey, in a popular magazine read by the upper, upper-middle, and middle classes of the United States that's by now quite accustomed to coverage of the war, but also accustomed to gag cartoons, and is a magazine of delight as much as anything else—to encounter the devastation of *Hiroshima*, was a shock."[12]

Spread out between traditional consumer advertisement pages for perfume, clothes, and washing machines, Harold Ross paved the way for what Hersey was about to tell them:

> To our readers,
>
> The *New Yorker* this week devotes its entire editorial space to an article on the almost complete obliteration of a city. It does so in the conviction that few of us have yet comprehended the all but incredible destructive power of this weapon and that everyone might well take time to consider the terrible implications of its use.[13]

The storyline the government had carefully constructed over the past twelve months was about to be obliterated. To stoke the hype,

Harold Ross ensured key media outlets received their own copies twelve hours before the magazine reached newsstands. The immediate editorial for *The New York Times* praised the author and soberly predicted how it would be received by the country:

> Every American who has permitted himself to make jokes about atom bombs, or who has come to regard them as one sensational phenomenon that can now be accepted as part of civilization like the aero plane and gasoline engine. Or, has allowed himself to speculate as to what we might do with that if we were forced into another war, ought to read Mr. Hersey.

Albert Einstein publicly announced he had purchased a thousand copies to send out to science faculties and physicists, stating: "Mr. Hersey has given a true picture of the appalling effect on human beings . . . subjected to the unprecedented destruction achieved by the explosion in their midst of one atomic bomb. . . . This picture has implications for the future of mankind which must deeply concern all responsible men and women."

On the back of such endorsements, Hersey's story caught fire, rapidly selling out its original three-hundred-thousand print run. Within a month, these prized first editions, each with a distinctive white bellyband that had stated, "Hiroshima: This entire issue is devoted to the story of how an atomic bomb destroyed a city," were selling at auction for over a hundred times their face value.[14] Both Ross and Shawn were ecstatic. It was not only a personal triumph, but also, they calculated within days, *The New Yorker*'s bestselling edition for decades.

For Hersey himself, it was not about the money. It was the American public's reaction to what he discovered that both pleased and relieved him. Celebrations had continued throughout the months after the defeat of Japan: imagery of American troops, sailors, and airmen coming home to their loved ones, Hollywood movies of famous battles such as Iwo Jima, and the jingoistic display of patriotism witnessed at the Los Angeles Colosseum months before. Hersey's words had taken a sledgehammer to the dam. Beneath their celebrations, Americans wanted to understand the impact a weapon their own government had used might have on their own lives. As William Shawn noted in his diary:

> No one is talking about anything else but the Hersey article over the last two days. Either in trains, restaurants or at home.

It wasn't all plain sailing. Henry Luce, perhaps in a fit of rage that the story and the writer no longer belonged to him, ordered Hersey's portrait be taken down from *Time-Life*'s "Wall of Honor." *The New Yorker* itself received complaints as well as cancellations of subscriptions. Other commentators offered a different viewpoint: "I read Hersey's report, it was marvelous. Now, let us drop a handful on Moscow!"

Like the bomb itself, the fallout from the story was growing and durable. The article quickly swept across the country on the airwaves as the ABC network adapted (not dramatized) it for national radio broadcast across four nights. An international edition of the magazine sold out on the streets of Europe, particularly in France and Britain. Producer Joel O'Brien at the BBC, after winning a heated debate, followed ABC's example and broadcast Hiroshima across four episodes. The reviewer in *The Daily Express* exclaimed to its readers:

> The most terrifying series of broadcasts I have ever heard! The listening figures are substantial. It is difficult to exaggerate the impression which the broadcast made upon the hearers.

This reaction would be repeated across Europe as Hersey's story was translated into multiple languages. Back in New York, Harold

Ross confessed, "I don't think I've ever got as much satisfaction out of anything else in my life."[15]

The leap of imagination that Truman's administration feared most was of the American public, up until then rock-solid behind the atomic program, reshaping its opinion. Instead of heroic victors of the war, with a mandate to ensure world peace, the government and military would now be placed on par with Nazi Germany, purely from the use of an atomic bomb and developing more. Henry L. Stimson, now retired from the War Department, was tasked with offering a rebuttal. With the assistance of a team including General Groves, a reluctant Stimson's heart wasn't really in it.

Within six months, as Hersey's book version of the article was selling hundreds of thousands of copies worldwide, the more conservative *Harper's* magazine published Stimson's thoughts, titled "The Decision to Use the Atomic Bomb"—the official explanation as to why the bomb had been created and why it had been used on Japan. Within it were the logical and well-used official facts that focused on the cost in American casualties of invading the Home Islands. He concluded: "All of the evidence I have seen indicates that the controlling factor in the final Japanese decision to accept terms of surrender was the atomic bomb."

Though it received wide publicity and gained further admiration for the leaders of the Manhattan Project, especially Groves and Oppenheimer, the genie was out of the bottle. The American public, and people across the Western world, measured Stimson's statistics and science against the imagery of human suffering that Hersey had conjured up in thirty thousand words. It could not be unread.[16] And it would resonate over the decades as the atomic age evolved and the Cold War developed.

Epilogue

LOST LEGACIES AND RECONSTRUCTION

General Groves had welcomed John Hersey's article. In numerous talks at military colleges and foundations, he advocated to his audiences that they should read it. The destruction so vividly described in *The New Yorker* could only support his argument, he believed, that the United States needed to be taking the lead, and that the military should continue its stewardship. Otherwise, he argued, it invited destruction of a similar level on its own cities and people. The end of the war would see his career suffer as he fought hard for the military to retain control of the military weapon he had helped create. The end of hostilities would see the atomic program transferred across to a new civilian agency—the Atomic Energy Commission (AEC)—which would oversee the Manhattan Project as well as the development of nuclear power in the United States. Groves worked hard within the corridors of power in Washington to fight the decision. Once the political battle was lost, he did his best to delay the handover of power to the AEC until January 1947.

Though appointed by the Truman administration to head up a new body, the Armed Forces Special Weapons Project (AFSWP), the power and influence that the general had enjoyed during the war were gone. On January 30, 1948, Groves met with General Dwight D. Eisenhower, now Army chief of staff. In a difficult meeting, Eisenhower presented him with a long list of grievances from civilian members of the AEC, bruised by the high-handed manner that had driven the Manhattan Project to success in wartime. Eisenhower dashed any hopes Groves would continue with the atomic program, or anything else. Groves, he concluded, would not be given the role he coveted, chief of Army engineers. He was too young, Eisenhower argued, and he had not served in combat. A cutting remark for an officer who had yearned for exactly that but had instead obeyed orders and taken on the enormous challenge to manage the atomic program.

Crestfallen, the following month, after almost thirty years of service to the US Army, Groves, at the relatively young age of fifty-one, opted to take early retirement. His friends in Congress attempted to soften the blow by proposing his promotion to the permanent rank of major general, as well as the honorary retired rank of lieutenant general. By June, his military career was over. But his legacy could not be disputed. He had rebuilt America's military infrastructure in record time, which ultimately paved the way for the country's successful rapid expansion of the military forces for war overseas. And of course, he had managed the Manhattan Project to arguably shorten the war. Did he think the latter would bring about lasting peace? He would admit in his memoir, published in 1961, "In answer to the question, 'Was the development of the atomic bomb necessary?' I reply unequivocally, 'Yes.' To the question, 'Is atomic energy a force for good or for evil?' I can only say, 'As mankind wills it.'"[1]

The Manhattan Project would be redesignated on December 31, 1946. Though it had cost approximately $500 million to make each of the four bombs, this was still less than the budget for Hap Arnold's B-29 program. General Groves orchestrated the presentation of Army-Navy "E" Awards,[2] with over twenty key contractors and scientists, including Oppenheimer, being given the prestigious Presidential Medal of Merit. Military personnel would receive the Legion of Merit. Many of Oppenheimer's team—such as Edward Teller— would go on to work for the US government at the highest level.

The secret program had produced a collection of world-class

university laboratories, including Berkeley, Los Alamos, Chicago, and Oak Ridge. Though many brilliant scientists and engineers left Los Alamos, including Oppenheimer, who returned to Berkeley, the site was maintained and restaffed for future use. Under President Truman, the old alliance with the Soviet Union would disintegrate. Joseph Stalin's five-million-strong Red Army remained stubbornly in Central Europe, supressing democratic groups and supporting puppet regimes in the satellite states of Czechoslovakia, Bulgaria, Poland, Romania, and eventually East Germany. To prevent further Soviet incursion westward, Truman's administration would direct the economic might of the United States into the "Marshall Plan," the reconstruction of war-torn Europe.

His government's policy of tackling head-on any communist insurgency around the globe was known as the "Truman Doctrine." It would kick-start an arms race with the Soviet Union, with nuclear technology at its heart. As Oppenheimer and Niels Bohr had predicted, it was now a nuclear race, which we all have been living with over the past eighty years. Winston Churchill realized, too late, that his government had been slow to appreciate the capability of the bomb. British scientists were now directed out of Los Alamos after the war. Henry DeWolf Smyth, who had served on the Uranium Committee, was appointed by Groves to the Postwar Policy Committee, the body that would map out the country's future atomic energy plans. Smyth would write the first official history of the Manhattan Project: *Atomic Energy for Military Purposes*. Within the narrative of the bestseller, Smyth omitted the vital role British science had played in the early years through Tube Alloys.

At the international table, Truman's government played ignorant of Roosevelt's earlier promises to Churchill at the president's home in Hyde Park in September 1944 after the Second Quebec Conference. FDR's verbal promise that the United States would share its nuclear technology with Great Britain was now brushed aside. The new British prime minister, Clement Attlee, had no formal agreement. His own and future British governments would lobby hard through the 1950s and '60s to catch up as the Cold War intensified.

Truman never regretted using the two atomic bombs to end the war. He had a weapon the enemy did not. Using it would tip the scales in the United States' favor. He wanted the war to end and prevent more Americans losing their lives needlessly when the enemy was clearly on its knees. So he ordered its use. As Leslie Blume concludes: "Throughout the remaining years of his presidency, Truman would always keep atomic weapons in 'active consideration' for use in military situations that might arise on his watch. They were no different, he stated, from conventional weapons, just bigger, more efficient, and more effective—a legitimate part of the U.S. arsenal. His successor Dwight D. Eisenhower felt the same."[3]

The rise and fall of J. Robert Oppenheimer was akin to the legend of Icarus. The Trinity Test was perhaps the pinnacle of his career. By war's end, he was a national hero, with his profile adorning the cover of *Time* magazine. For the next half-dozen years, he was arguably the United States', if not the world's, most popular and trusted scientist. He had access to high-level government committees in Washington as well as a key position in the country's debate on how nuclear energy might be controlled and whether the new hydrogen bomb should be banned. For a time, he was the face of the country's scientific future. And then it all fell apart.

Oppenheimer would fall victim to a toxic mixture of envy, old grievances, past political affiliations, and lies, at a time in America when political witch hunts were the rage. McCarthyism was in full bloom when he was called before the Atomic Energy Commission in April 1954, which, after debating a variety of unproven charges laid against his reputation, revoked Oppenheimer's security clearance. Overnight he was humiliated and deemed a national pariah. It would take a decade for the gross error to be partially rectified by the presentation to him by President Lyndon B. Johnson of the Fermi Award[4] in 1963. Retiring to teach at Princeton University, he died of throat cancer in 1967.[5]

Hap Arnold had built the most powerful air force in history by the end of World War Two. His career had spanned the earliest days of manned flight in the twentieth century, through to the United States leading the world in intercontinental flight, the jet fighter, pioneering the widespread use of radar, and of course atomic weaponry. As discussed already, Arnold suffered four heart attacks between 1943 and the end of the war. Continued heart issues forced his retirement on June 30, 1946. He would suffer a fifth heart attack while writing his memoirs. In May 1949, his dream of an independent air force became a reality. He was awarded the rank of general of the Air Force. He is still the only United States officer to hold the five-star rank in two military services.

Curtis LeMay's performance in the Pacific air war was incredibly destructive to the Japanese. His bombers attacked sixty-six of Japan's largest cities, destroying 43 percent of their built-up areas—over 175 square miles. They dehoused more than eight million people, killed as many as nine hundred thousand, and injured up to 1.3 million more. He went on to serve in the highest ranks of the US Air Force after its creation in 1947. He would oversee the Allied efforts to supply by air the blockaded Allied garrisons and residents of West Berlin during the standoff with the Soviet Union (June 1948–May 1949) and continued up the ladder to lead the Strategic Air Command (SAC) until 1957. He would be heavily involved with the administration of John F. Kennedy during the Cuban Missile Crisis, as well as air operations conducted in the Vietnam War. LeMay would retire as chief of staff from the Air Force in 1965. He died of complications from a heart attack in 1990.

By the time of Groves's and Arnold's retirement from the US Army, John Hersey was enjoying celebrity status across the globe. *Hiroshima* was an international bestseller, though not in Japan. General MacArthur's office would give permission for a Japanese translation only in 1949. Hersey's friendship with *Time*'s Henry Luce never recovered fully. The magazine proprietor firmly believed Hersey's article for *The New Yorker* had not only betrayed him personally but politically had undermined public support for President Truman.

During the early 1950s, during the Senator McCarthy witch hunts for suspected communists in public life, Hersey was monitored by the FBI. He and his wife Frances Ann divorced in 1958, having had four children. Hersey retreated from frontline reporting and instead devoted himself to writing fiction, teaching at Yale University, and working for the Authors Guild. Although his later works never reached the heights of *A Bell for Adano* or *Hiroshima*, he would continue to produce novels of high caliber, such as *The Wall* (1950).

The claim that he was the founder of a new form of reporting, "New Journalism," was not a title he wanted or wore in public. His grandson, the documentary filmmaker Cannon Hersey, argued his ethics drove him to reach higher levels in his writing and reporting. "He was, for his time, a moral authority. He was considered a moral authority of the nation, which isn't as sexy as being Ernest Hemingway. He won the Pulitzer for writing about war. . . . I think he was often very concerned with what he had done during the war, in promoting war. So much so, by the time the Vietnam War came, it's my understanding that he said, 'You know, I'm not going to write about the war. I'm going to write about the war at home.' Which was the Civil Rights Movement."[6]

In 1985, on the fortieth anniversary of the attack, Hersey returned to Hiroshima to meet and interview the six survivors he had made famous in his article. The article was published by *The New Yorker* on July 15 and subsequently reproduced in a new edition of the book, Hersey concluding: "What has kept the world safe from the bomb since 1945 has not been deterrence, in the sense of fear of specific weapons, so much as it's been memory. . . . The memory of what happened at Hiroshima."

Just before his death in 1993 while vacationing on Martha's Vineyard, he was recognized by Yale University for his contributions to both journalism and literature. An annual "John Hersey Lecture" was founded, as well as an annual award given to a Yale student intent on pursuing journalism in his style—the "John Hersey Prize." In 2007, Hersey was given the honor of being one of five journalists selected to be featured on a first-class postage stamp. To date, *Hiroshima* has sold over three million copies in the English language. *The New Yorker* publishes the whole article annually on the date of the bombing.

Field Marshal Shunroku Hata survived the war and was later tried as a war criminal, the only Japanese officer of his rank to face charges (the majority had committed suicide). He was sentenced at the International Military Tribunal for the Far East, overseen by General MacArthur, to life imprisonment but paroled in 1955. At his trial, official Japanese government documents showed Hata had argued for clemency for the captured American airmen from the Doolittle Raid, who were executed in 1942. In his postwar memoirs, Hata would state he had no warning of the attack on Pearl Harbor by aircraft of the Imperial Japanese Navy. He would go on to criticize their leadership's conduct in starting the war with the United States and then leaving the Army to defend the empire. He would spend the last years of his life heading up a charitable foundation for war veterans. He died in 1962.

Senkichi Awaya, his eldest son, Shinobu, and his three-year-old granddaughter, Ayako, were all killed instantly when Little Boy detonated several hundred yards away from his mayoral residence along the river. Days later, members of a civilian rescue team would locate their severely burned and disfigured bodies in the destroyed residence. Reports describe Senkichi lying close to Ayako, both grandfather and granddaughter's arms outstretched. His wife, Sachiyo, would survive the blast but die from radiation sickness on September 7, 1945. The couple's second daughter, nineteen-year-old Yasuko, would travel down from the family home in Tokyo to nurse her dying mother. She, too, would succumb to radiation poisoning and die in Tokyo in a local hospital on November 24.

Senkichi Awaya's eldest daughter, twenty-two-year-old Motoko Sakama, had lost her daughter in the blast. Her husband, Hiroshi, survived his illness in Osaka. She was now the head of the Awaya family, or what remained of it. Of her siblings, only her youngest sister, Chikako (ten), and brother Tadashi (twelve), had survived the war. They had lost both their parents, as well as three brothers and a sister. Motoko and her husband would go on to have a second daughter and a son. They would be her younger siblings' adoptive parents, too. Both Chikako and Tadashi would gain university degrees and go on to have productive lives, Tadashi going into his grandfather's profession of the civil service. Motoko captured their resilience in a memory she recalled for an interview with a woman's monthly magazine, *Fujin no Tomo* in 1967, which was subsequently republished in English for the *Christian Science Monitor* in August 1995, the fiftieth anniversary of Hiroshima. Her family and old friends of her parents had gathered in Tokyo to celebrate Tadashi's wedding in 1963:

"On the eve of his wedding, he [Tadashi] expressed his heartfelt thanks to my husband and me for rearing him for eighteen years. He promised that he would make strong efforts so that he wouldn't disgrace his father's name. My husband and I were moved to tears, hand in hand; I will never forget my gratitude and deep emotion on that night, which would have blessed my parents."[7]

At the same time John Hersey traveled to Hiroshima to reunite with survivors in 1995, Awaya's life was also commemorated for the fiftieth anniversary of the Hiroshima attack. The city authorities erected a monument overlooking the Motoyasu River, close to where his mayoral residence had once stood, to where his wife had blindly staggered away from raging fires and intense heat as she tried to find her husband. Tsuneo Kanazawa, the minister of the Independent Church of Sapporo, wrote an epitaph to commemorate his fifty-one-year-long life. I spent an afternoon walking along the banks of the Motoyasu in November 2023, trying to find the memorial after I had spent time in the Hiroshima Peace Memorial Park, which stands approximately a half mile away. The simple stone pillar and sign are thankfully still there, surrounded by trees and shrubs. Most people out for a stroll walk past it without any recognition. An ordinary, plain memorial for a life pretty much forgotten as we come toward commemorating the first atomic bombing in history. People will of course argue that millions of innocent victims of Japan's aggression before and during World War Two, across East Asia and the Pacific, have no epitaph at all. The majority were either worked to death, killed by indiscriminate bombing, murdered in mass killings, or died of starvation and disease. An absolutely fair comment. But I was pleased to find it. Everyone should be remembered if we can discover their story.

Japan had suffered an incredibly high, disproportionate number of casualties—both civilian and military—during the war.[8] Once hostilities ended, and the Home Islands were occupied by the Allies under General MacArthur, the country's reconstruction began in earnest. By 1947, MacArthur pushed through legislation for democratic municipal elections. Shinzo Hamai won the first-ever democratic mayoral election for the city in April 1947.[9] Operational factories that had survived the bombings were turned over from wartime production and back into private ownership, with an emphasis on supporting the recovery. Five-year economic recovery plans raised standards of living and produced enough food and fuel to sustain the population.

The country would become a pivotal ally of the United States as the Cold War developed, with Hiroshima benefiting from both the Korean War (1950–53) and the Allies lifting their previous ban on Japanese shipbuilding. The docks of the city would become as busy as they had ever been. Mayor Hamai would lobby central government in Tokyo for funds to have the central parts of Hiroshima that had been destroyed by the atomic bomb remodeled into a memorial center. A local competition for design ideas would be won by a young poet and peace activist, Sankichi Tōge. His vision was of a green space housing a memorial center (the Peace Plaza), together with a library and a museum. The promotion of peace would be at its core.

The central government agreed to turn over state- and military-owned land free of charge. Now the local authorities needed the money to build it. In 1949, the "Peace Memorial City Construction Law" was passed by the National Diet as Japan's economic resurgence began. By 1958, Hiroshima's population exceeded its prewar total of four hundred thousand as reconstruction and shipping trade combined to launch an employment boom. The city's Peace Memorial Park is now a global center of education, and its "Atomic Bomb Dome" was deemed by UNESCO a World Heritage Site in 1996.

John Hersey's grandson, the documentary filmmaker Cannon Hersey, asked me when we spoke from his home in Millbrook, New York, whether the year 2025 will mark the last official commemoration of the bombing. Though several hundred survivors remain, many are now in their nineties. Like veterans of the fighting in World War Two, they may not be here in another decade. "And what will happen when there are no more survivors left?" Cannon asked me. "It's going to rely on books like my grandfather's and books like yours to keep that alive."

I hope, looking right across the experience of this terrifying and cataclysmic event, that you, the reader, can judge for yourself whether this journey through the experiences of a city mayor, a bomber pilot, an Army general, and an award-winning journalist, who all were intimately connected to Hiroshima, was worth it.

Postscript

THE ENGLISH CHANNEL

On November 1, 2007, and over sixty years since his iconic, somewhat fateful, mission over Hiroshima, Brigadier General (retired) Paul Tibbets Jr. died at his home in Columbus, Ohio, at the age of ninety-two. He had been a public figure to the American people since those first newspaper reports in August 1945 after the surrender of the Imperial Japanese armed forces. With his death, it was assumed he would take his rightful place as a war hero at the country's national military cemetery in Arlington, Virginia. But he didn't. To the surprise of many of his family, close friends, fellow veterans who had served with him, and the US media, once Tibbets was cremated in a private ceremony in Columbus, his ashes were transported days later to France and released over the English Channel by his French-born widow, Andrea.

His grandson, Brigadier General Paul Tibbets IV, graduated from the United States Air Force Academy in 1989. He would go on to command the 509th Bomb Wing, flying the B-2 Spirit stealth bomber. The wing formed part of the Air Force Global Strike Command, Eighth Air Force, based in Whiteman Air Force Base, Missouri. It would be true to say that he was inspired by his grandfather to join the USAAF in the 1980s. Brigadier Tibbets summarized why his grandfather had requested the nondescript ceremony over the English Channel. "On his tire, on the back of his truck, he had a painting of the nose art from his B-17, *The Red Gremlin*, for the rest of his life. The Flying Fortress was his favorite aircraft. He flew it with Sweeney and Van Kirk. So, the English Channel—that whole part of his life and his career—was very meaningful to him. That's where he really proved himself, and where everything happened to him as a young officer.

"He told me, 'Paul, that has a special place in my heart. I loved flying the B-29, but my favorite experiences will always be in the B-17.'"[1]

Acknowledgments

This project would have never gotten off the ground without the support and advice of key people mentioned below. For such an ambitious narrative, at the beginning of my research I started to think I had bitten off more than I could chew. Luckily, when I ventured to Japan in the winter of 2023, I was fortunate to have alongside me two Tokyo-based researcher/translators: Chie Matsumoto and Ken Oka. It was Chie who accompanied me on my first day of interviews to meet and talk with Michiko Kodama, assistant secretary general of the Confederation of A- and H-bomb Sufferers Organizations, the "Nihon Hidankyo." Ken was crucial to discovering and translating the family memoir of Senkichi Awaya, held in the National Diet Library in Tokyo. I will be forever grateful for the advice and hospitality shown to me by Professor Garren Mulloy, who has resided in Japan for thirty years and works in the Faculty of International Relations and Graduate School of Asian Area Studies, Daito Bunka University, Saitama, Japan. I also offer my gratitude to freelance journalist Julian Ryall, a longtime resident of the country, who offered me sound advice when I began my trek across Japan. These men didn't know me to begin with but were so generous with their time and friendship once I was in the country.

When in Hiroshima, I was grateful for the assistance of Steven Leeper and translator Miwako Sawada. I was fortunate to meet, interview, and be guided by the former director of the Hiroshima Peace Memorial Museum, Kenji Shiga. Many thanks to Professor Hidenori Watanave of the University of Tokyo, who oversees the excellent web-based archive of atomic survivors, The Hiroshima Archive, which contains exceptional eyewitness testimonies. To understand the work of John Hersey in Hiroshima, I was grateful for the time given to me by atomic survivor and daughter of the Reverend Tanimoto, Koko Kendo. Our talk of her experiences and the life of her illustrious father when he worked with John Hersey were revelatory.

From my research trips to the United States, I must thank family members of some of the key characters in the book. Firstly, Brigadier General (retired) Paul Tibbets IV, who was generous with his time to be interviewed and discuss the career and life of his grandfather, a man he held in high esteem and whose military career path in the USAAF he emulated through the 1990s and 2000s. His cousin, Mrs. Kia Tibbetts, was equally helpful in discussing the final years of her grandfather's life in Ohio. Richard "Dick" Groves has been a font of all knowledge, not only in the life and career of his grandfather General Leslie Groves, but also the history of the entire Manhattan Project. Our meetings in London were beneficial to the project, as well as a very enjoyable experience finding someone so invested in the subject and willing to share their knowledge of the general, and of key locations such as Los Alamos and the Trinity test site in New Mexico. To try and get under the skin of the great Pulitzer Prize–winning novelist and journalist John Hersey, his grandson Cannon Hersey, himself a long-standing documentary filmmaker of Hiroshima, was both encouraging of my own work, and offered unique insight. I thoroughly enjoyed talking with him.

At the Japanese American National Museum in Los Angeles, curator Dr. Emily Anderson and archivist Jamie Henricks were willing helpers in my education about the experience of those Japanese immigrants who had settled in the United States prior to the outbreak of war in 1941 and who suffered internment as a result. I am also grateful to Dr. Anderson for introducing me to atomic survivor Howard Kakita, whom I interviewed and discuss in the book. My visit to the archives of the National WWII Museum in New Orleans was hugely beneficial to the project. Toni M. Kiser, senior registrar and director of collections, was an ideal guide to the museum's extensive audio archive. Toni introduced me to USMC veteran and survivor of the Battle of Iwo Jima Professor Richard Jessor, who freely gave his time to recall his traumatic experiences. Thanks also to Jeremy Collins, director of conferences and symposia, who read the first draft of this book.

On the East Coast, I am grateful to the staff of the Beinecke Library archive at Yale University who looked after me while I researched John Hersey's personal papers. Holding the very first draft of *The New Yorker*'s "Hiroshima" article, with annotations by Henry Luce, was a privilege. I must pay special thanks to the magazine's current editor, David Remnick, for giving me his time to discuss Hersey's legacy. I am grateful to Dr. Jeremy R. Kinney, associate director for research and curatorial affairs at the National Air and Space Museum who assisted my research on the B-29 bomber program. Advice and details of the Pacific War from scholar and author Mark Stille were crucial to the final draft of the book. He was literally a font of knowledge. Many thanks also to Robert Krauss, whose body of work to record the testimonies of the men who served with the 509th Composite Group in the Pacific is second to none. His kindness to allow me to reproduce a fraction of their memories is much appreciated.

In the United Kingdom, I need to extend my immense gratitude to Peter Johnston, director of narrative and content, and Phil Sawford, head of commercial services, at the Imperial War Museum for their assistance, and curator Dr. Hattie Hearn at the American Air Museum at IWM Duxford. Both she and Peter Johnston accompanied me to climb into the museum's sole B-29 bomber "Hawg Wild" to allow me to understand how the crew operated, and just how revolutionary the plane was for its time. My old friend and colleague,

Marcus Cowper, publisher at Osprey Military Publishing, was always on hand to offer advice on what titles would help with my research of the Pacific War, as well as the bombing campaigns described in this narrative. Historian and author Joshua Levine was kind enough to read my first draft and offer advice. I am also grateful to Fergal Kean, Giles Milton, James Holland, Dan Snow, Joe Greenaway, and Tony Pastor for their support and kind words during the research and writing of this book. I owe multiple lunches also to Karen Farrington and Humphrey Price for advice, friendship, and keen eyes.

This project was inspired by a conversation with my longtime publisher in New York, Colin Harrison of Scribner, who immediately offered me his support and guidance. His team, Emily Polson and Jason Chappell, have been their usual professional best. Back home in Britain I am pleased to have similarly brilliant people in place: my publisher Andreas Campomar and talented editor Holly Blood. To my new agent, Anna Power of Johnson and Alcock, I am glad to join you and look what we have done!

Finally, to my family, who allowed me to travel around the world to make this book possible. I couldn't do this without your love and support.

Iain MacGregor
London, December 2024

Notes

PROLOGUE

1. Hidankyo was founded on August 10, 1956, and is the only nationwide organization of atomic bomb survivors of Hiroshima and Nagasaki. Its main objectives are prevention of nuclear war; state compensation for atomic bomb damage; and improved support for all atomic bomb survivors.

2. Japan used this title as decreed by a cabinet decision on December 10, 1941, thus referring to the new conflict with Western Allies and the ongoing war with China since 1931.

3. Japan is divided into prefectures—a local system of government resulting from the breakup of the country's ancient feudal system in July 1871. This reduced larger provinces into more manageable urban and rural administrations. Before the end of World War II, all forty-seven prefectures were centrally controlled by the Tokyo government.

4. Japan comprises 14,125 islands, of which 260 are inhabited. The four main islands are, north to south: Hokkaido, Honshu, Kyushu, and Shikoku.

5. This will be discussed in detail from page 278 onward.

6. A confidant of Emperor Hirohito, Field Marshal Shunroku Hata was in command of the Second General Army (essentially a home guard formation) based in Hiroshima since mid-

1944, preparing for the expected Allied invasion of the Japanese Home Islands. They would defend Honshu, Kyushu, and Shikoku.

7. Created on March 23, 1945, as a national organization, the authorities of the Hiroshima Prefecture set up its own on May 7, 1945. Source: Kakogawa Village Office's document, "Single File of Volunteer Citizen Corps' Collection of Hiroshima Municipal Archives."

8. Stephen Walker, *Shockwave: Countdown to Hiroshima* (London: William Collins, 2020), pp. 224–25.

9. Interview with Michiko Kodama, interpreter Chie Matsumoto, Tokyo, November 8, 2024.

10. Little Boy missed the intended aiming point, the Aioi Bridge, by several hundred feet and instead detonated directly over the Shima Surgical Clinic. See Map 4 on page 306.

11. To appreciate the power of this single bomb, the British and American carpet bombing of the German city of Dresden on February 13, 1945, unleashed just 2,700 tons, which reduced it to rubble. Little Boy had five times the power.

12. Statistics taken from the Manhattan Project Interactive History on the US Department of Energy page.

13. Hiroshima Prefectural Office, located a thousand yards from Ground Zero, was completely destroyed—of its seven hundred officers, 609 were reported dead by September. Taken from *Atomic Bomb Damage and Administration*, by Dr. Fukuhei Ado, School of Letters, Kyoto University, Japan Society for Archival Science, Hiroshima Municipal Archives.

14. Closest to Ground Zero, 218 students were killed instantly. The three-story concrete building's frame remained intact, however, and the school would reopen in February 1946.

15. Chiba is the capital of Chiba Prefecture, situated twenty-five miles to the east of Tokyo, overlooking Tokyo Bay, with a population of just under a million residents.

INTRODUCTION: THE GOOD WAR

1. The Coliseum was commissioned in 1921 as a memorial to military veterans based in Los Angeles, opening in 1923 with a capacity of over seventy-five thousand. It was then extended upward in 1930 to increase seating to over one hundred thousand people. It would go on to host the 1984 summer Olympic Games.

2. Referred to as the "Infamy Speech," delivered by President Franklin D. Roosevelt to a joint session of Congress on December 8. His words had a long-lasting impact throughout the conflict, appealing to American patriotism, and attracted one of the biggest audiences in radio history (81 percent of the nation).

3. Edward G. Robinson was an American actor of the stage and screen, best known for his portrayals of gangsters and criminals. In the 1930s to the end of World War II, he had been a strong critical voice against fascism, personally donating over $250,000 to eighty-five organizations involved in war relief.

4. Incendiary bombs were used extensively in World War II with a range of filling materials, such as isobutyl methacrylate (IM) polymer and, most famously, napalm. Many of these were developed by the US Chemical Warfare Service.

5. The mass aerial firebombing campaigns against Germany and Japan were deemed huge successes during the conflict in disrupting the enemy's industrial output as well as severely denting overall morale. These campaigns will be discussed in detail later in the book.

6. The B-29 *Bockscar*, piloted by Major Charles W. Sweeney, dropped a plutonium bomb, Fat Man. Over forty thousand people were killed by the initial detonation. By the beginning of 1946, thirty thousand more people were dead. Within the next five years, well over one hundred thousand deaths were directly attributable to the bombing.

7. This figure represented 3 percent of the global population re-
    corded at the 1940 level of 2.3 billion people. International Pro-
    grams, Historical Estimates of World Population, US Census
    Bureau.

8. *The Road to War*, "Japan," season 1, episode 6. Television series
    narrated by Charles Wheeler.

9. Approximately 150,000 square miles.

10. John W. Dower, *War Without Mercy: Race & Power in the Pacific
    War* (New York: Pantheon Books, 1986), p.278.

11. Iris Chang, *The Rape of Nanking* (New York: Basic Books, 1998).

12. Battle of Khalkhin Gol (May 11–September 16, 1939).

13. Despite advances in rebuilding the shattered American econ-
    omy and infrastructure, by the attack on Pearl Harbor, out of
    a population of 132,164,569 the United States still had three
    million unemployed. 1940 United States Census.

14. David M. Kennedy, *The American People in World War II: Free-
    dom from Fear Volume Two* (New York, Oxford University Press,
    1999), p.192.

15. The first year of the German invasion of the Soviet Union on
    June 22, 1941, had cost the country over six million dead or
    captured on the battlefield, but also the collapse of its industrial
    base in territories in Ukraine and Belorussia, and a drop in its
    workforce of thirteen million people.

16. The Lend-Lease Act was signed into law on March 11, 1941,
    and ended on September 20, 1945. A total of $50.1 billion of
    supplies was shipped to Great Britain, France, China, and the
    Soviet Union (the equivalent today would be $801 billion).
    "Lend-Lease Act (1941)," in Milestone Documents, National
    Archives of the United States, Washington, DC.

17. Kennedy, *American People in World War II: Freedom from Fear*,
    p.194.

18. A total of 1,966 locomotives, 7,669 miles of track, 350,000
    trucks, 32,000 motorcycles, 77,900 jeeps, and 956,000 miles of
    telephone cable.

19. R. G. D. Allen, "Mutual Aid Between the U.S. and The British Empire, 1941–45," *Journal of the Royal Statistical Society* (1946).

20. Lawrence S. Wittner, *Rebels Against War: The American Peace Movement, 1941–60* (New York, 1969), pp. 17-124.

21. Dower, *War Without Mercy*.

22. The United States referred to itself in these plans as "Blue." Portugal's Azores was "Gray"; Germany was "Black"; Britain was "Red"; Canada was "Crimson," India was "Ruby"; New Zealand was "Garnet"; and Ireland was "Emerald." Clearly, many of these plans were less likely to occur.

23. Interview with Tami Davis Biddle, associate professor of national security at the United States War College, July 17, 2024.

24. Donald Nijboer, *B-29 Superfortress vs. Ki-44 "Tojo" Pacific Theatre, 1944–45* (Oxford: Osprey Publishing, 2017), p. 35.

25. Horatio Bond, *Fire and the Air War* (Boston: National Fire Protection Association, 1946).

26. The overall cost to the taxpayer would be $45 billion, nearly a quarter of the United States' $183 billion munitions bill in World War II.

27. Jacob Vander Meulen, *Building the B-29* (New York: Smithsonian Institution Press, 1996), p. 100.

28. The United States Army conducted many more amphibious landings than the US Marines and had many more troops committed to the Pacific.

29. "Fortune Survey: Use of the Atomic Bomb," 309; *Fortune* poll, November 30, 1945, *Public Opinion Quarterly* IX (Winter 1945–46): p. 533.

30. A 1943 poll commissioned by senior US Army leaders reflected that 50 percent of all GIs believed it necessary to kill all Japanese before peace could be achieved.

31. FDR was given the macabre present by US congressman Francis E. Walter in 1944. The president later ordered it be returned and given a proper burial.

32. The mission statement of United States Marines about to go into combat from senior officers was a typically worded slogan: "Every Japanese has been told it is his duty to die for the emperor. It is your duty to see that he does so." Dower, *War Without Mercy*, p. 53.

33. In a speech to a joint session of Congress in May 1943, Winston Churchill spoke of "the process, so necessary and desirable, of laying the cities and other munition centers of Japan in ashes, for in ashes they must surely lie before peace comes back to the world."

CHAPTER ONE: FISSION

1. At the end of the war, Hahn was astonished to hear that he had won the Nobel Prize in Chemistry in 1944 and that nuclear bombs had been developed from his basic discovery.

2. Margaret Gowing, *Britain and Atomic Energy, 1935–1945* (London: Macmillan Publishing, 1964), pp. 34–36.

CHAPTER TWO: CONVINCING THE COMMANDER IN CHIEF

1. Franklin D. Roosevelt, "An Appeal to Great Britain, France, Italy, Germany, and Poland to Refrain from Air Bombing of Civilians," Online by Gerhard Peters and John T. Woolley, American Presidency Project, https://www.presidency.ucsb.edu/node /209957.

2. September 3, 1939.

3. French physicist Jacques Allier informed them of the German desire to acquire heavy water from the only place it was created in the world—Norway. He had led a daring raid to capture four hundred pounds of it and store it in London—first at Wormwood Scrubs and then, finally, Windsor Castle.

4. MAUD was not a secret acronym, but rather the name of the governess to the children of Danish physicist Niels Bohr.

5. Both Peierls and Frisch would eventually relocate to the United States to work on the Manhattan Project.

CHAPTER THREE: THE WRITER FROM CHINA

1. His father never fully recovered from his bout of encephalitis and would be physically unable to continue missionary work.
2. Founded in 1891, Hotchkiss was one of the first English-style boarding schools to be established in the United States. Fortunately for scholars such as John Hersey, the school was an early proponent of supplying financial aid to less-well-off students, awarding scholarships since its founding.
3. The *Yale Daily News* was the oldest college daily paper in the United States.
4. It even produced a code breaker who would go on to work at Bletchley Park during World War II.
5. Letter to Hersey's parents, October 4, 1936, Hersey Family Papers, MSS 723, Box 2, Beinecke Rare Book and Manuscript Archive, Yale University.
6. Hersey letter to his mother, October 18, 1936, Hersey Family Papers, MSS 723, Box 2, Beinecke Rare Book and Manuscript Archive, Yale University.
7. Hersey letter to his parents, May 2, 1937, Hersey Family Papers, MSS 723, Box 2, Beinecke Rare Book and Manuscript Archive, Yale University.
8. Ben Yagoda, *About Town: The New Yorker and the World It Made* (New York: Scribner, 2000), pp. 27–28.
9. Lecture, "Henry Luce and the American Century," with David McKean, Jill Lepore, and Alan Brinkley, John F. Kennedy Presidential Library and Museum, Columbia Point, Boston.
10. The Imperial Hotel—a central location in Tokyo—had been destroyed by the Great Earthquake of 1923, and was redesigned and built by American architect Frank Lloyd Wright.
11. Hugh Byas (1875–1945) spent twenty-three years as a journalist in Japan between the wars. He was a Tokyo correspondent of *The New York Times* and was the author of *The Japanese Enemy*.

12. Hersey cable to *Time*, May 30, 1940, Hersey Family Papers, MSS 723, Box 2, Beinecke Rare Book and Manuscript Archive, Yale University.

13. The distinctive approach Luce's editorial team espoused in use of a house style created a *Time*-style adjective—they coined *World War II*.

14. There was no love lost between Luce and Franklin Roosevelt. Luce declared shortly after Roosevelt's death that "It is my duty to go on hating him."

CHAPTER FOUR: THE EMERGENCE OF AMERICAN AIRPOWER: THE B-29 PROGRAM

1. Comment made in a postwar interrogation, 1945.

2. Founded in 1920, and the first such school in the world, the Air Corps Tactical School, also known as ACTS and "the Tactical School," was a military professional development school for officers of the United States Army Air Service and United States Army Air Corps. Their motto was *Proficimus More Irretenti*—"We Make Progress Unhindered by Custom."

3. See Malcolm Gladwell, *The Bomber Mafia*.

4. Would command the United States Eighth Air Force in Europe during World War II from 1942 to 1943.

5. Hansell was a gifted staff officer who served both in Europe and the Pacific and would advance theories such as bombers flying in a defensive "box" formation.

6. One of the US Army's first pilots in 1916, he would command Air Force Combat Command in Europe and then North Africa. After VE Day, he transferred to the Pacific theater to oversee the air campaign against Japan.

7. By war's end, American factories were producing a ship every day and a fully operational plane every five minutes.

8. Roosevelt's Democratic Party lost seventy-two seats, mostly to the Republican Party, in the House of Representatives, and eight seats to the Republicans in the US Senate.

9. In May 1938, France placed an order for one hundred Curtiss-

Wright P-36 fighters, even though only three such planes served in the US Army Air Corps.

10. In attendance was FDR; Secretary of the Treasury Morgenthau; Harry L. Hopkins, the President's principal adviser; Robert H. Jackson, the solicitor general; Louis Johnson, assistant secretary of war; Herman Oliphant, general counsel of the Treasury; General Malin Craig, the chief of staff, and his deputy, Brigadier General George C. Marshall; Major General Henry H. Arnold, chief of the Air Corps; Colonel James H. Burns, executive assistant to the assistant secretary of war; and the president's military and naval aides.

11. Carl Berger, *B-29: the Superfortress, Purnell's History of the Second World War, Weapons Book, No. 17* (London: MacDonald & Co. Publishers Ltd. 1971), p. 21.

12. $10 million in today's money.

13. Berger, *B-29: the Superfortress*, p.27.

14. Though the company had previously created and built a fleet of B-17 Fortresses for the Army Air Corps, it would almost drive it toward bankruptcy in 1940—staved off only by an emergency government loan.

15. This sum equates to $65 million in today's money.

16. XB-29 was short for "experimental bomber number 29."

17. On February 19, 1942, Roosevelt signed "Executive Order 9066," authorizing the forced relocation of over 120,000 Japanese American citizens into internment camps for the war's duration.

18. Passed in March 1941, the act allowed Roosevelt to send aid to any nation whose defense he believed vital to the United States and to accept repayment "in kind or property, or any other direct or indirect benefit"—whether financial or supplies of tanks, planes, aircraft, food, and raw materials to the tune of almost $50 billion by war's end.

19. Wolfe had bluntly called the B-29 program a "$3 million gamble." But Arnold respected his ability as an aviation commander

and trusted his judgment. Wolfe would eventually lead the XX Bomber Command in China in 1944, to be later replaced by Curtis LeMay.

20. One of the biggest problems for pilots, crews, and maintenance crews of the B-29 were overheated engines causing fatal fires. In 1944, as the Twentieth Air Force began operations, seven out of ten instances of fires came from an overheated engine in flight.

21. From January to June 1944, the virtual certainty of fires caused aircrews to bail out quickly in times of engine trouble.

22. Jacob Vander Meulen, *Building the B-29* (New York: Smithsonian Institution Press, 1996), p. 53.

CHAPTER FIVE: COMMITTEES

1. Graham Farmelo, *Churchill's Bomb: A Hidden History of Britain's Nuclear Weapons Programme* (London: Faber & Faber, 2013), p. 136.

2. British physicist Ralph Fowler, who ran the British Central Scientific Office in Washington, DC, would later describe the Tizard meeting as a flow of information going largely one way.

3. Richard Rhodes, *The Making of the Atomic Bomb* (London: Simon & Schuster UK Limited, 2012), p. 373.

4. Mark Oliphant would resign and return with his family to Australia, before taking up a position alongside Ernest Lawrence at Berkeley once the United States was in the war.

CHAPTER SIX: "IF YOU DO THE JOB RIGHT, IT WILL WIN THE WAR!"

1. Leslie R. Groves, *Now It Can be Told: The Story of the Manhattan Project* (New York: Da Capo Press, 1983), p. 4.

2. Rhodes, *The Making of the Atomic Bomb*, pp. 424–25.

3. Groves, *Now It Can be Told*, pp. 3–4.

4. Groves met with the president only once, during the surprise German offensive (the Battle of the Bulge) in the winter of 1944. Worried by American losses, Roosevelt requested atomic bombs be dropped on Germany. Groves informed him the first

workable bomb was months away. The idea was shelved as the Allies successfully counterattacked.

5. Construction would account for approximately 90 percent of the Manhattan Project's total budget.

6. Seaborg would be the principal co-discoverer of ten elements on the periodic table: plutonium, americium, curium, berkelium, californium, einsteinium, fermium, mendelevium, nobelium, and element 106.

CHAPTER SEVEN: THE MAN IN THE HAT

1. Widely considered to be one of the greatest American passenger trains of all time, the *20th Century Limited* was the flagship train of the New York Central, running between New York City and Chicago, primarily for upper-class passengers.

2. Ray Monk, *Robert Oppenheimer: A Life Inside the Center* (New York; Toronto: Doubleday, 2012), p. 90.

3. Algis Valiunas, "The Agony of Atomic Genius," *New Atlantis 14 (Fall 2006): pp. 85–104.*

4. Katherine Puening Harrison had previously married a communist labor organizer who had died in the Spanish Civil War.

5. David Hawkins, *Manhattan District History: Project Y, The Los Alamos Project, Volume I, Inception Until August 1945 (Los Alamos Scientific Laboratory, LAMS-2352 [Vol. I], 1961).*

6. Oppenheimer had himself measured up for a lieutenant colonel's uniform, but then failed the physical.

CHAPTER EIGHT: "FIGHTING FOR APPLE PIE": JOHN HERSEY ON GUADALCANAL

1. Guadalcanal, October 1942.

2. The plan to capture Port Moresby and ultimately take possession of New Guinea, therefore isolating Australia and New Zealand from Hawaii. It would be abandoned after the loss of carriers at both the battles of Coral Sea and Midway.

3. The USS *Hornet* was a Yorktown-class carrier. From its deck had been launched the Doolittle Raid on April 18, 1942. Once

John Hersey had left her, the carrier fought at the Battle of the Santa Cruz Islands (October 25–27), where she was irreparably damaged by enemy torpedoes and dive-bombers. Faced with an approaching Japanese surface force, the *Hornet* was abandoned and later torpedoed and sunk by approaching Japanese destroyers. She was the last US fleet carrier ever sunk by enemy fire.

4. The surrender of seventy-six thousand American and Filipino forces on the Bataan Peninsula on April 9, 1942, was the largest American surrender in military history. They would be marched sixty miles to POW camps on the Bataan Death March, which would claim approximately 600–650 American and five to ten thousand Filipino lives.

5. This is a direct quote from Hersey. Obviously, if one studies the map, the distance is far shorter.

6. John Hersey, *Into the Valley: Marines at Guadalcanal* (New York: Penguin Random House, 1989), p. ix.

7. Cable from John Hersey in Honolulu to David Hulburd at *Life*, New York City, August 25, 1942, Hersey Family Papers, MSS 723, Box 2, Beinecke Rare Book and Manuscript Archive, Yale University.

8. Vice Admiral Ghormley was the choice of both Admiral Nimitz and Admiral King to lead the South Pacific Force, but he had not commanded a warship since 1938. His indecisiveness and inability to lead from the front would see him replaced by Vice Admiral William Halsey in October 1942.

9. Henderson Field was named in honor of Major Lofton Russell Henderson, a US Marine Corps aviator who had been killed in action leading his squadron of Douglas SBD Dauntless dive-bombers against a Japanese aircraft carrier at the Battle of Midway on June 4.

10. The Imperial Japanese Eighth Fleet in Rabaul.

11. The Type 93 (later nicknamed "Long Lance") had a maximum range of twenty-five miles and a speed of forty-four mph, with an 1,100-pound, high-explosive warhead. Its long range, high

speed, and heavy warheads provided a formidable punch in surface battles.

12. The majority of naval engagements that occurred around Guadalcanal took place in the Sealark Channel, a stretch of water between Guadalcanal, Savo Island, and Florida Island. At least forty ships, Japanese, American, and Australian, would be sunk within this confined stretch of water before the campaign ended.

13. Leaders such as Lieutenant Colonel Lewis B. "Chesty" Fuller and Gunnery Sergeant John Basilone, from the First Battalion, Seventh Marines Regiment, would be awarded the Navy Cross and Congressional Medal of Honor, respectively, for defending Henderson Field.

14. Of the thousands of Japanese soldiers killed on Guadalcanal, the most common cause would be from Marine Corps 75mm howitzers and 105mm artillery.

15. "The Slot" was the nickname given to the space of water marked on the map as the New Georgia Sound. Guadalcanal from Savo and Florida Islands to its north.

16. Kiyonao Ichiki was an officer in the Japanese Imperial Army in World War Two. Ichiki commanded the Twenty-Eighth Infantry Regiment, the "Ichiki detachment," in the Battle of the Alligator Creek.

17. Lea would make his reputation later in the Pacific war, with the Marines' First Division in Peleliu in 1944, his painting *The Two-Thousand Yard Stare* capturing the horror of the conflict.

18. John Hersey, "From San Francisco California to David Hulburd, October 18, 1942," Hersey Family Papers, MSS 723, Box 2, Beinecke Rare Book and Manuscript Archive, Yale University.

19. Halsey would become infamous for his public remarks about the Japanese during World War Two. His favorite phrase was "yellow bastards!"

20. John Hersey, *Into the Valley: Marines at Guadalcanal* (New York: Penguin Random House, 1989), p. xiii.

21. Ibid., p. 6.

22. Ibid., p. 26.

23. Ibid., p. 29.

24. Ibid., p. 35.

25. Ibid., p. 48.

26. Ibid., p. 66.

27. Ibid., p. 74.

28. The British Solomon Islands Protectorate was first established in June 1893. Following the attack on Pearl Harbor, an intelligence-gathering network of local informants and messengers was established to carry out the role of "coast watchers" to monitor Japanese activity and rescue downed Allied airmen.

29. Bill Lansford would continue serving with the Fifth Marines as they assaulted Iwo Jima three years later. See Chapter 20.

30. It was during this time that the division took the traditional Australian folk song "Waltzing Matilda" as its battle hymn. To this day, First Division Marines still ship out to this song being played.

31. Jeremy Treglown, *Mr. Straight Arrow: The Career of John Hersey, Author of* Hiroshima (New York: Farrar, Straus and Giroux, 2019), p. 75.

CHAPTER NINE: THE ROLE OF A LIFETIME

1. Paul W. Tibbets Jr., *Mission: Hiroshima—Commander of the Enola Gay* (New York: Stein and Day, 1981), p. 21.

2. Under an agreement with Denmark, the United States had established two bases on Greenland: Bluie West One and Bluie West Eight.

3. Robert O. Harder, *The Three Musketeers of the Army Air Forces: From Hitler's Fortress Europa to Hiroshima and Nagasaki* (Annapolis, MD: Naval Institute Press, 2015), pp .45–46.

4. Tibbets, *Mission*, p. 133.

5. Tibbets, *Mission*, p. 139.

6. Harder, *Three Musketeers*, p. 92.

7. Tibbets would find out after the war that was not in fact the definitive choice. Two other men had also been interviewed for the role: Brigadier General Frank Armstrong and Colonel Roscoe "Bim" Wilson. Like Tibbets, both men had seen air combat in Europe.

CHAPTER TEN: THE GOOD MAYOR

1. Senkichi Awaya, *The Person and Faith of Senkichi Awaya* (Tokyo: Taishindo, 1966).

2. Driven through by the United States' first ambassador to Japan, Townsend Harris. It would open Japanese ports to American exporters, who were in control of what duties they would pay, and with provisions that protected Western trading agents from prosecution. No bilateral clauses were agreed for the Japanese to export themselves. Many civilian and military nationalists would come to see these agreements as "unequal treaties."

3. Townsend Harris (1804–1878) was an American merchant and politician who served as the first United States consul general to Japan. The treaty bearing his name opened up Shogunate Japan to foreign trade and culture.

4. A false rumor spread that Koreans had committed acts of arson, poisoned drinking wells, and robbed amid the disaster. Mobs attacked their businesses and homes in Tokyo and Yokohama. Official reports detailed only 231 deaths, whereas independent reports state over six thousand were murdered.

5. Kanzō could speak English fluently by age thirteen and had been influenced by American missionaries, which would lead to his conversion to a Quaker-style faith. Uchimura would spend the next decades traveling to the United States, developing his religious beliefs that curtailed his teaching career, and espousing his pacifist philosophy in print, which led to political pressure.

CHAPTER ELEVEN: A LUCKY ESCAPE: JOHN HERSEY IN EUROPE

1. In the 110,000 sorties that comprised the Allied Rome air campaign (May 16 1943–June 5, 1944) that dropped over sixty thousand tons of bombs on the capital, six hundred aircraft would be lost and 3,600 aircrew killed. Over forty thousand civilians would be killed or injured.

2. John Hersey Cable, No. 65, "From Algiers to David Hulburd," August 3, 1943, Hersey Family Papers, MSS 723, Box 2, Beinecke Rare Book and Manuscript Archive, Yale University.

3. Patton had publicly slapped a traumatized American soldier in a field hospital, claiming the man was a coward. The attending press had ensured the story went back to the United States. Though a valued, aggressive commander to Eisenhower, the reaction back home meant he had to remove Patton.

4. Jeremy Treglown, *Mr. Straight Arrow: The Career of John Hersey, Author of* Hiroshima (New York: Farrar, Straus and Giroux, 2019), pp. 74–75.

5. Joe Kennedy Sr. would take the story and offer it to *Readers Digest*, which would reprint it. The cunning patriarch would then purchase thousands of copies that he would later use to promote his second son's run for Congress after the war.

CHAPTER TWELVE: FIRE AND BRIMSTONE: IWO JIMA

1. Upon seeing Commodore Perry's small fleet sailing into their harbor, the Japanese called them the "black ships of evil men." Much to the dismay of many Japanese government officials, in 1854 a treaty was signed between the United States and Japan that allowed trade at two ports.

2. Gordon L. Rottman and Derrick Wright, *Hell in the Pacific: The Battle of Iwo Jima* (Oxford: Osprey Publishing, 2008).

3. Max Hastings, *Nemesis: The Battle for Japan, 1944–45* (London: William Collins, 2007), pp. 267–68.

4. Robert Leckie, *The Battle of Iwo Jima* (New York: Penguin Random House, 1967), p. 21.

5. Interview, Professor Richard Jessor, March 17, 2024.

6. Ibid.

7. Rupert Wingfield-Hayes, "Return to Iwo Jima 70 Years On," BBC News, March 24, 2015.

8. The Fifth Amphibious Marine Corps would comprise 2,650 replacements and 250 new second lieutenants. Over eight thousand men had never seen frontline combat before Iwo Jima. Bill D. Ross, *Iwo Jima: Legacy of Valor* (New York: Penguin Random House, 1986), p. 34.

9. The LVT-4 was designed in 1943 and was an improvement on previous models, as its number suggests. It could accommodate twice as many men (from sixteen to thirty) and crucially featured a stern ramp for unloading personnel and cargo. Previous models had suffered heavy casualties as occupants were subjected to more fire in the open as they landed. More than 8,300 LVT-4s were produced.

10. Interview with Richard Jessor.

11. Interview (OH1471) with William "Bill" Lansford, USMC (2015), National WWII Museum, New Orleans.

12. Interview with Mike "Iron Mike" Mervosh, USMC, National WWII Museum, New Orleans.

13. Ibid.

14. Interview with Richard Jessor.

15. The photograph of the iconic moment the Stars and Stripes was raised over the mountain was taken by Associated Press photographer Joe Rosenthal. It is arguably the most famous photograph of the Second World War. A one-hundred-ton bronze statue of this moment was created by Felix de Weldon after the war and stands near the northern end of Arlington National Cemetery in Washington, DC. Three of the six flag bearers in the photograph would be killed in the battle.

16. Of this number, 278 were officers.

17. Walter Sandberg, *The Battle of Iwo Jima: A Resource Bibliography and Documentary Anthology* (Jefferson, NC: McFarland & Company, Inc., 2005), p. 114.

18. Bill D. Ross, *Iwo Jima: Legacy of Valor* (New York: Penguin Random House, 1986), p. 315.

19. Interview with Mike Mervosh.

20. Wingfield-Hayes, "Return to Iwo Jima 70 Years On."

21. Ross, *Iwo Jima: Legacy of Valor*, p. 331.

22. Privates Yamakage Kufuku and Matsudo Linsoki lasted four years without being caught, and finally surrendered on January 6, 1949.

23. Navy Department Library, September 25, 2020, "Battle for Iwo Jima, 1945," Washington, DC, Naval History and Heritage Command. Archived from the original on July 8, 2020. Retrieved July 9, 2020.

CHAPTER THIRTEEN: WELCOME TO "LEFT OVER"

1. The entertainer visited the air base to entertain Tibbett's unit in November 1944. This was his opening line.

2. The crews participated in the strategic bombing of Germany, flew in support of D-Day, and conducted combat operations around the world, including China and India.

3. Though a morale booster, the gesture would net quite a few miscreants for Uanna's agents, who would catch men doing exactly what Tibbets had warned them not to do.

4. Tibbetts would later say the airplane was the best-made, most trouble-free B-29 he ever flew.

5. Paul W. Tibbets, *Mission Hiroshima* (New York: Stein and Day, 1978), p. 180.

6. Gordon Thomas and Max Morgan Witts, *Ruin From the Air: The Atomic Mission to Hiroshima* (London: Hamish Hamilton, 1977), p. 131.

CHAPTER FOURTEEN: A CHANGING OF THE GUARD

1. American intelligence broke the Japanese military codes to target Yamamoto's movements over the Solomon Islands. Operation Vengeance would succeed in shooting down his plane into the dense jungle. Yamamoto was a revered figure, and the regime gave him a state funeral.

2. October 23–26, 1944. The largest naval battle of World War II, with over two hundred thousand combatants involved. Once the Philippines was in American hands, Japan would be cut off from its land forces and access to much-needed oil and natural resources in Southeast Asia.

3. Herman S. Wolk, *Cataclysm: General Hap Arnold and the Defeat of Japan* (North Texas University Press, 2010), p. 97.

4. One of the fastest-climbing Japanese fighters of the war. Like the B-29, it was armor plated, with self-sealing rubber fuel tanks, a maximum speed of 372 mph, a range of 746 miles, and four 12.7mm Ho-103 machine guns, or sometimes two 12.7mm guns and two 20mm cannons.

5. Donald Nijboer, *B-29 Superfortress vs Ki-44 "Tojo" Pacific Theatre, 1944–45* (Oxford: Osprey Publishing, 2017), p. 36.

6. Wolk, *Cataclysm*, pp. 96–97.

7. Chester Williams, *Sky Giants Over Japan: A Diary of a B-29 Combat Crew in WWII* (Winona, MN: Apollo Books, 1984), pp. 116–17.

8. Lee Kennet, *A History of Strategic Bombing* (New York, Charles Scribner's Sons, 1982).

9. Leo P. Brophy, Wyndham D. Miles, and Rexmond C. Cochrane, *The Chemical Warfare Service: From Laboratory to Field. United States Army in World War II: The Technical Services, Volume 2*, (Office of the Chief of Military History, 1959).

10. Warren Kozak, *Curtis LeMay: Strategist and Tactician* (Washington, DC: Regnery History, 2014).

11. It was the largest military campaign of the Second Sino-Japanese War which mobilized five hundred thousand Japanese troops (approximately 80 percent of its China Expeditionary Army), one hundred thousand horses, fifteen hundred artillery pieces, and eight hundred tanks.

12. Nijboer, *B-29 Superfortress vs Ki-44*, p.7.

13. The attack comprised 231 B-29s with aircraft from all three wings, of which 172 found their target. One square mile of the capital was burned and 27,970 buildings destroyed. American losses were minimal.

14. Interview with Tami Davis Biddle, associate professor of national security at the United States War College, July 17, 2024.

15. Months later, when Tibbets met LeMay again at his XX headquarters, he showed him post-op photographs of the destruction of the Tokyo raid. "You were right, Paul." Paul W. Tibbets, *Mission: Hiroshima—Commander of the* Enola Gay (New York: Stein and Day, 1981), pp. 188–89.

CHAPTER FIFTEEN: CROSSING THE RUBICON: THE FIREBOMBING OF TOKYO

1. *Time*, March 19, 1945.

2 James M. Scoot, *Black Snow: Curtis LeMay, the Firebombing of Tokyo and the Road to the Atomic Bomb* (New York: W. W. Norton & Company, Inc., 2022), pp. 186–87.

3. Chester Williams, *Sky Giants Over Japan: A Diary of a B-29 Combat Crew in WWII* (Winona, MN: Apollo Books, 1984), p. 144.

4. LeMay said of Norstad after the war, "[He] would never go out on a limb for anybody in his life. I got no direction from him."

5. Mission Folder, no. 20, XXI Bomber Command, Record Group 18, National Archives; Hansell, *Strategic Air War against Japan*, pp. 52, 58; and Craven and Cate, p. 314.

6. Oral history Interview with Garvin Kowalke, January 23, 2001, text, Fredericksburg, Texas, https://texashistory.unt.edu/ark: /67531/metapth1603452/, accessed May 22, 2024, University

of North Texas Libraries, Portal to Texas History, https://texas-history.unt.edu; crediting National Museum of the Pacific War/ Admiral Nimitz Foundation.

7. Gordon Bennet Robertson Jr., Bringing the Thunder: The Missions of a World War II B-29 Pilot in the Pacific (Stackpole Books, 2006).

8. Max Hastings, *Nemesis: The Battle for Japan 1944–45* (London: William Collins, 2016), pp. 313–14.

9. Williams, *Sky Giants*, p. 146.

10. A uniquely Japanese item, the *imon-bukuro* were hand-assembled comfort packages for the troops sent by a supportive home front from the youngest citizens. They often contained sweets, canned food, toiletries, and letters or cards.

11. Interview with author, Toshiko Kameya, Tokyo, February 10, 2024.

12. The USS *Arizona* was a battleship in the United States Navy that was attacked and sunk during the Japanese attack on Pearl Harbor on December 7, 1941, killing 1,177 officers and men. It is now part of a permanent memorial.

13. "Wartime memories still vivid for B-29 pilot." Interview with Keith Rogers, *Las Vegas Review Journal*, November 11, 2010.

14. Interview Toshiko Kameya. To this day she regrets ever leaving her mother and siblings to their fate.

15. Williams, *Sky Giants*, p. 147.

16. Ibid, p. 147.

17. Interview with Toshiko Kameya.

18. Ibid.

19. Donald W. Kearney, *The Crew of the Reamatroid* (privately published, 1988).

20. Ibid.

21. Interview with Toshiko Kameya.

22. Ibid.

23. Ibid.

24. Ibid.

25. Francis Pike, *Hirohito's War: The Pacific War, 1941–1945* (London: Bloomsbury Publishing, 2016).

26. Casualty lists for the shelter later reported over five hundred people had died, mainly of asphyxiation.

27. Despite the scale of the destruction, the city authorities still held a major military parade in downtown Tokyo for Armed Forces Day the day after LeMay's raid.

28. Bartlett E. Kerr, *Flames Over Tokyo: The U.S. Army Air Forces' Incendiary Campaign Against Japan 1944–45* (New York: Donald I. Fine, Inc., 1991), pp. 212–13.

29. Interview with Toshiko Kameya.

30. Ibid.

31. Samuel Hideo Yamashita, *Daily Life in Wartime Japan, 1940–1945* (University Press of Kansas, 2015), p. 171.

32. Edoin Hoito, *The Night Tokyo Burned* (New York: St. Martin's Press, 1987), p. 158.

33. Three hundred and twenty-seven B-29s attacked Tokyo's arsenal district on April 13, reducing 11.4 square miles to ashes.

34. Wolk, *Cataclysm*, p. 127.

35. "Air Power Now Seen in Proper Perspective," *Washington Star*, March 14, 1945. In RG18, Records of the HQs, Twentieth Air Force, Decimal File 1944-1945, File Media, Box 115, NA II.

36. John W. Dower, *War Without Mercy: Race & Power in the Pacific War* (New York: Pantheon Books, 1986), p. 40.

CHAPTER SIXTEEN: PREPARE FOR THE WORST

1. Gordon Thomas & Max Morgan Witts, *Ruin From the Air: The Atomic Mission to Hiroshima*. (London: Hamish Hamilton, 1977), p. 109.

2. Senkichi Awaya, *The Person and Faith of Senkichi Awaya* (Tokyo: Taishindo, 1966).

3. Ibid.

4. From the spring of 1945, children, in their home cities and towns, as well as those evacuated, would be expected to attend

military education classes: hand-to-hand combat with wooden swords, grenade throwing with small balls, and lunging with spears, all to become "splendid little citizens." Yamashita, *Daily Life in Wartime Japan, 1940–1945* .

5. *Chronicle of A-Bomb Damage to the Prefectural Office*, p. 177.
6. Instruction from the Mayor's Office on May 10. *Chronicle of A-Bomb Damage to the Prefectural Office*, pp. 34–35.

CHAPTER SEVENTEEN: MANHATTAN IN THE MARIANAS: THE ATOMIC WING COMES TO TINIAN

1. Al Christman, *Target Hiroshima: Deak Parsons and the Creation of the Atomic Bomb* (Naval Institute Press, Inc., 1998).
2. A close friend and confidant of the new president, Byrnes would become Truman's secretary of state on July 3, 1945. As there was no vice president at the time, he would have succeeded him.
3. A. J. Baime, *The Accidental President: Harry S. Truman, the Bomb and the Four Months That Changed the World* (London: Transworld Publishers, 2018), p. 230.
4. Ibid., p. 282.
5. Paul W. Tibbets, *Mission—Hiroshima* (New York: Stein and Day, 1978), p. 182.
6. The Imperial Japanese Navy lost three fleet carriers and 480 aircraft and pilots.
7. The statistic of one American being killed and several wounded for every seven Japanese killed shocked US military planners and influenced their thinking on how costly future operations might be as they got closer to Japan.
8. David M. Kennedy, *The American People in World War Two* (Vol. 2), p. 393.
9. In addition, there were three senior officers on Tinian who were part of the Manhattan Project but not formally part of Project Alberta: Rear Admiral William R. Purnell, the representative of the Military Liaison Committee; Brigadier General Thomas F. Farrell, Groves's deputy for operations; and Colonel Elmer E.

Kirkpatrick, who was responsible for base development and was Farrell's alternate. Purnell, Farrell, and Parsons became informally known as the "Tinian Joint Chiefs." They had decision-making authority over the nuclear mission.

10. Russell E. Gackenbach, Interview OH.4269, National WWII Museum, New Orleans, 29:03:2016.

11. Ibid.

12. Robert and Amelia Krauss, *The 509th Remembered: A History of the 509th Composite Group as Told by the Veterans that Dropped the Atomic Bombs on Japan* (Michigan, privately published, 2017), p. 76.

13. Ibid., pp. 92–93.

14. Ibid.

15. Ibid., p. 143.

16. Interview with Russell E. Gackenbach.

17. Tibbets, *Mission Hiroshima*, p. 190.

CHAPTER EIGHTEEN: ENDGAME: OKINAWA

1. MacArthur and Nimitz constantly cooperated over the amount of naval power deployed from the Pacific Fleet to MacArthur's Southwest Pacific Area Command. The US Navy rendered significant support to MacArthur during the later stages of the New Guinea campaign and deployed two fleets to support the Philippine landings.

2. Nimitz would receive at least 90 percent of naval resources by 1945.

3. Interview with Professor Sam Hynes, *The War*, Florentine Production for PBS, 2010.

4. Weeks before Operation Iceberg commenced, the Japanese government made plans to evacuate over eighty thousand Okinawans from the island back to Kyushu and twenty thousand to Taiwan to work in the armaments industry. This was of limited success.

5. Four-fifths of the land in the south of the island was cultivated for sweet potatoes, sugar cane, rice, and soybean production.

6. Beginning on December 13, 1937, after the Battle of Nanking, the Republic of China's capital was looted and burned. Across the following six weeks, Imperial Japanese troops committed other war crimes, raping between twenty and forty thousand women and children, as well as executing between two and four hundred thousand people.

7. David M. Kennedy, *The American People in World War Two*, Vol. 2 (New York: Oxford University Press, 2003), p. 407.

8. A combination of three sixteen-inch, five fourteen-inch, and one twelve-inch battleships, supported by seven eight-inch and three six-inch cruisers, thirty-two destroyers, and 177 gunboats, fired 45,000 shells, 33,000 rockets and 22,500 heavy mortar rounds. It was the heaviest bombardment in support of an amphibious invasion.

9. Kinjo Shigeaki, interviewed by Michael Bradley, "'Banzai!' The Compulsory Mass Suicide of Kerama Islanders in the Battle of Okinawa," *Asia-Pacific Journal* vol. 11, issue 22, no. 3 (June 2, 2014).

10. Kinjo Shigeaki would survive the war, convert to Christianity, and be ordained as a minister before relocating to the United States in 1958 to study theology.

11. James Tobin, *Ernie Pyle's War: America's Eyewitness to World War II* (New York: Free Press, Simon & Schuster, Inc., 1997); "Unopposed Okinawa invasion," column, April 4, 1945.

12. Robert M. Neer, *Napalm: An American Biography* (Cambridge, MA, 2013), p. 60.

13. George Feifer, *The Battle of Okinawa: The Blood and the Bomb* (Globe Pequot, 2001), p. 260.

14. In a single twenty-four-hour period, Japanese artillery fired over fourteen thousand rounds against US XXIV Corps.

15. The use of the term "divine wind" originated in the thirteenth century, when a wild storm destroyed a Mongol invasion fleet bound for Japan and saved the country.

16. Comprising four aircraft carriers, two battleships, and five

cruisers and escorts, in the theater only at the insistence of Winston Churchill and to the consternation of Admiral King.

17. Max Hastings, *Nemesis: The Battle for Japan, 1944–45* (London: William Collins, 2007), p. 425.

18. Bombers sank one ship and damaged sixty-four vessels.

19. A. J. Baime, *The Accidental President: Harry Truman, the Bomb and the Four Months That Changed the World* (London: Transworld Publishers, 2018), p. 280.

20. It was not until September 2 that the head of the remaining Japanese forces on the island signed the formal surrender.

21. At Okinawa, the rate of combat losses caused by battle fatigue, as a percentage of those caused by combat wounds, was a staggering 48 percent.

CHAPTER NINETEEN: THE CITY OF WATER

1. James Broderick, *The Life of Saint Francis Xavier (1506–1552)* (New York: Doubleday Inc., 1957).

2. Scott O'Bryan, *Hiroshima: History, City, Event* (New York: Japan Society, 2009).

3. "The History of Hiroshima City," taken from the City of Hiroshima official website, article ID: 0000005491.

4. Tôyô Industries was also founded in the city in 1920, later renamed the Mazda Corporation and famous in the postwar period as a global manufacturer of automobiles.

5. O'Bryan, *Hiroshima: History, City, Event*. Interview with Kenji Shiga (ex-director of the Hiroshima Peace Memorial Museum), December 2023.

6. It is still the Officer Candidate School of the Japanese Maritime Self-Defense Force and is also the location of the Museum of Naval History.

7. Post–atomic strike on August 6, 1945, and the destruction of the bulk of the city's hospitals, the quarantine center on Ninojima would be used by medical rescue teams as a hospital, morgue, and graveyard. Over ten thousand injured victims were taken

there in the days and weeks after the attack, and their remains were buried there.

8. Because of the Great Earthquake of 1923, many modern buildings in Hiroshima were constructed far more strongly than was required by normal building codes in America, to resist earthquakes. Japanese construction regulations specified that the roof had to safely carry a minimum load of seventy pounds per square foot. Though the regulation was not always followed, this extra-strong construction of buildings near Ground Zero at Hiroshima arguably explains their ability to withstand atomic bomb pressures without structural failures.

9. Horatio Bond, *Fire and the Air War* (Boston: National Fire Protection Association, 1946).

10. Gordon Thomas & Max Morgan Witts, *Ruin From the Air: The Atomic Mission to Hiroshima* (London: Hamish Hamilton, 1977), p. 138.

CHAPTER TWENTY: NATIONAL SUICIDE

1. Henry Stimson, secretary of war to President Harry S. Truman, April 24, 1945.

2. Located in central Honshu Island and facing the Pacific Ocean, the Kantō Plain is geographically the most extensive lowland in Japan, measuring 6,244 square miles. Economically, politically, and culturally, Tokyo is at its heart. It contains the most productive and populous area and thus was a major target for bombing raids during World War Two.

3. United States Strategic Bombing Survey Morale Division, "Resident Interviews by City," December 1, 1945, National Archives at College Park, Maryland, Microfilm Locator M1655, Roll 105; United States Strategic Bombing Survey Morale Division, "Resident Interviews by City," December 1, 1945, National Archives at College Park, Maryland, Microfilm Locator M1655, Roll 115.

4. Nearly 7 percent of the residential housing had thus far been torn down to make firebreaks.

5. See the work of Captain Ellis M. Zacharias, US Navy, whose wartime work for US naval intelligence had him broadcast in fluent Japanese to the country from Washington after May 8, 1945, calling for peace.
6. Senkichi Awaya, *The Person and Faith of Senkichi Awaya* (Tokyo: Taishindo, 1966).

CHAPTER TWENTY-ONE: THE DETONATION DEBATE

1. The Interim Committee, the Pentagon, Washington, DC, June 23, 1945.
2. Philipps P. O'Brien, *The Second Most Powerful Man in the World: The Life of Admiral William D. Leahy, Roosevelt's Chief of Staff* (London: E. P. Dutton, 2019), p. 346.
3. A. J. Baime, *The Accidental President: Harry Truman, the Bomb and the Four Months That Changed the World* (London: Transworld Publishers, 2018), p. 322.
4. Ibid., p.356

CHAPTER TWENTY-TWO: SPECIAL BOMBING MISSION NO. 13

1. Interview with William Lowther, *Glasgow Herald*, 1995.
2. Known as the Tinian "Joint Chiefs": General Thomas F. Farrell, the Manhattan Project's senior officer on the island and General Groves's eyes and ears, Admiral R. Purnell, Commander Frederick L. Ashworth, Professor Norman F. Ramsey, and Professor Robert Brode.
3. He had little idea that by the time the *Enola Gay* was ready to fly, the *Indianapolis* had been sunk by a Japanese submarine (I-58), and its crew decimated in shark-infested waters before help arrived. Of 1,195 crew aboard, only 316 survived the disaster.
4. Paul, W. Tibbets, *Mission: Hiroshima*, (New York: Stein and Day, 1978), p. 200.
5. Interview with Theodore Van Kirk (USAAF), OH2672, 2017, National WWII Museum, New Orleans.
6. Tibbets. *Mission: Hiroshima*, p.203.

7. Interview with Theodore Van Kirk.

8. Ibid.

9. Russell E. Gackenbach, Interview OH.4269, National WWII Museum, New Orleans, 29:03:2016.

10. Shiyakusho Genbakushi, *Chronicle of A-Bomb Damage to Hiroshima City Hall*, p. 33.

11. Interview with Theodore Van Kirk.

12. Interview with Russell E. Gackenbach.

13. Howard Kakita, interview with author, August 23, 2023.

14. Interview with Russell E. Gackenbach.

15. Ibid., Theodore Van Kirk

16. Ibid.

17. Interview with Russell E. Gackenbach.

18. Interview with Theodore Van Kirk.

19. Interview with Russell E. Gackenbach.

20. Tibbets, *Mission: Hiroshima*, p. 227.

CHAPTER TWENTY-THREE: THE SHIMMERING LEAVES

1. Evan Thomas, *Road to Surrender: Three Men and the Countdown to the End of World War II* (London: Elliott & Thompson, 2023), p. 142.

2. Howard Kakita, interview with author, August 23, 2023.

3. The family would shelter that night before finding relatives out in the countryside who would look after them. All four of them would develop high fevers, with Sumiko's aunt dying from radiation exposure within three weeks.

4. Fortunately for Setuko, her father was out of town that morning and was uninjured. Her mother dug herself out of the ruins of their home before it caught fire. Her sister and her four-year-old nephew had been crossing a bridge at the moment of the explosion, and both were badly burned, blackened and swollen beyond recognition. Her parents would later recognize her sister only by her voice and a unique hairpin she wore.

5. Two days later, Mitsuko left for her home in Iwakuni on foot

and then by train. Her family, believing she was dead, had put lit candles outside their home.

6. Fusako would reach safety that day, and she would then travel by train to Yoshida-cho of Takata-gun to an arranged meeting point the family used in case of emergencies. She would find all her family alive and well.

7. The vital water pumps to feed the survivors, as well as eradicate fires, were repaired four days after the bombing. The few survivors from the city's Bank of Japan managed to salvage what materials and equipment they could find and reopened for business within three days. By August 12, what remained of Awaya's office had repaired the telephone exchange, connecting the ruined city to Tokyo.

8. Gordon Thomas and Max Morgan Witts, *Ruin from the Air: The Atomic Mission to Hiroshima* (London: Hamish-Hamilton, 1977), p. 331.

9. Ibid., Interview with Theodore Van Kirk.

10. A. J. Baime, *The Accidental President: Harry S. Truman, the Bomb and the Four Months That Changed the World* (London: Transworld Publishers, 2018), pp. 408–9.

11. Leahy would conclude in his personal diary, perhaps with an eye on how history might judge his part in the act: "The lethal possibilities of such atomic action in the future is frightening, and while we are the first to have it in our possession, there is a certainty that it will in the future be developed by potential enemies and that it will probably be used against us."

CHAPTER TWENTY-FOUR: A DISHONORABLE DEFEAT

1. Samuel Hideo Yamashita, *Daily Life in Wartime Japan, 1940–1945* (University Press of Kansas, 2015), p. 179.

2. It had actually been only lightly bombed five times, mainly with high explosives.

3. According to a Nagasaki Prefectural report, "men and animals died almost instantly" within a half mile of the point of det-

onation. Almost all homes within a mile and a half were destroyed. Of the fifty-two thousand homes in Nagasaki, fourteen thousand were destroyed and 5,400 more seriously damaged. By January 1946, approximately seventy thousand were dead from injuries and radiation exposure. Twice that figure would die within the next five years.

4. Richard Rhodes, *The Making of the Atomic Bomb* (London: Simon & Schuster UK Limited, 2012) p. 745.

5. Richard B. Frank, *Downfall: The End of the Imperial Japanese Empire* (New York: Random House, 1999), p. 315.

6. Takasamata Kadota. *Yasuko, 19 Years Old: Diary of War Damage*, Chapter 12.

7. Motoko Sakama, "Hiroshima's Legacy: The Story of One Japanese Family," *Christian Science Monitor*, August 2, 1995.

8. "Instrument of Surrender," September 2, 1945; Records of the US Joint Chiefs of Staff, Record Group 218, National Archives.

9. Sakama, "Hiroshima's Legacy."

10. Senkichi Awaya, *The Person and Faith of Senkichi Awaya* (Tokyo: Taishindo, 1966).

CHAPTER TWENTY-FIVE: CONTROLLING THE STORY

1. Robert Jungk, *Children of the Ashes: The Story of Rebirth* (New York: Harcourt Brace & World, 1961), p. 28.

2. "American Institute of Public Opinion" (AIPO) poll, August 25, *Public Opinion Quarterly* IX (Fall 1945): p. 385.

3. *The Chicago Sun*, August 9, 1945.

4. Arthur H. Compton, "The Moral Meaning of the Atomic Bomb," *Toward a Better World*, ed. William Scarlett (Philadelphia and Toronto, 1946).

5. *Los Angeles Times*, August 23, 1945.

6. Burchett would pay a price for his scoop. His press credentials, and photographic evidence of his trip were taken by US authorities, and he was threatened with deportation.

7. The purpose of the junket was that, guided by military liaison

officers, the journalists would see for themselves the damage inflicted on German and Japanese cities by aerial bombing, and weigh up the power of the new ordnance used.

8. On September 11, 1945, the results of thirty-seven autopsies of bomb victims conducted by the scientific team of Kyoto University were confiscated on the orders of General Farrell. Many more would be collected by US doctors and shipped back to the United States for analysis.

9. US Congress, Senate Special Committee on Atomic Energy, Seventy-Ninth Congress, 1945–1946, Hearings (Washington, DC, 1946), p. 37. Taken from Sean L. Malloy, "'A Very Pleasant Way to Die': Radiation Effects and the Decision to Use the Atomic Bomb against Japan," *Diplomatic History* 36, no. 3 (June 2012).

CHAPTER TWENTY-SIX: "SO FAR FROM HOME, ALMOST BEYOND RETURN."

1. Interview with David Remnick, September 1, 2023.
2. Letter to Frances Ann Hersey, February 9, 1945, Hersey Family Papers, MSS 723, Box 2, Beinecke Rare Book and Manuscript Archive, Yale University.
3. Lesley Blume, *Fallout: The Hiroshima Cover-Up and the Reporter Who Revealed It to the World* (London: Scribe, 2020), p. 38.
4. George Orwell, *Tribune*, October 19, 1945.
5. On July 1, 1946, nuclear weapons tests occurred near the Marshall Islands, the most famous being the Bikini Atoll detonation.
6. Ben Yagoda, *About Town: The New Yorker and the World It Made* (New York: Scribner, 2000), p. 186.
7. Winner of the 1928 Pulitzer Prize for fiction.
8. John Hersey, *Hiroshima* (London: Penguin Books, 2001), p. 5.
9. Ibid., pp. 39–40.
10. Yagoda, *About Town*, p. 189.
11. Charles E. Martin had worked during the war for the Office of War Information, creating leaflets to be dropped behind enemy lines. Lesley Blume, *Fallout*, p. 122

12. Interview with David Remnick, September 1, 2023.

13. Taken from the author's own copy of the August 31, 1946, edition.

14. In today's market, as this author discovered, a good-quality edition will cost over $1,000.

15. Yagoda, *About Town*, p. 193.

16. As Stimson's article was published, in Great Britain Hersey's publisher, Penguin, announced their first print run of 250,000 copies had sold out within a week. They would be printing a further million. Before the end of 1947, the book had been translated into Czech, Danish, Dutch, Finnish, French, German, Hungarian, Italian, Norwegian, and Swedish.

EPILOGUE

1. General Leslie R. Groves, *Now It Can Be Told: The Story of the Manhattan Project* (New York: Da Capo Press, 1961), p. 415.

2. This was an honor presented to companies and organizations during the war whose production facilities achieved "Excellence in Production" ("E") of war equipment. By war's end, the award had been earned by only 5 percent of the more than eighty-five thousand companies involved in producing materials for the US military's war effort.

3. Lesley Blume, *Fallout: The Hiroshima Cover-Up and the Reporter Who Revealed It to the World* (London: Scribe, 2020), p. 171.

4. The Fermi Award was accompanied by a $50,000 prize ($500,000 today), awarded for "especially meritorious contribution to the development, use or control of atomic energy."

5. After relentless campaigning, his security clearance was posthumously restored by President Biden's administration in 2022.

6. Interview with Cannon Hersey, Millbrook, New York, June 27, 2022.

7. Motoko Sakama, "Hiroshima's Legacy: The Story of One Japanese Family," *Christian Science Monitor*, August 2, 1995.

8. At least 393,400 civilian deaths and another 275,000 wounded.

Japanese military casualties from 1937 to 1945 have been estimated at 1,834,000, of whom 1,740,000 were killed or missing.

9. He would govern the city until 1955, and again between 1959
and 1967. His terms in office would oversee a dramatic rebuilding of Hiroshima into the modern city that we know today.

POSTSCRIPT

1. Interview with Paul Tibbets IV, May 24, 2022.

Bibliography

BOOKS

Antonin, Raymond. *An Autobiography*. Vermont: Charles E. Tuttle Company, 1973.

Awaya, Senkichi. *The Person and Faith of Senkichi Awaya*. Tokyo: Taishindo, 1966.

Baime, A. J. *The Accidental President: Harry Truman, the Bomb and the Four Months That Changed the World*. London: Transworld Publishers, 2018.

Berger, Carl. *B-29: the Superfortress: Purnell's History of the Second World War, Weapons Book, No.17*. London: MacDonald & Co. Publishers Ltd., 1971.

Bird, Kai and Martin J. Sherwin. *American Prometheus: The Triumph and Tragedy of J. Robert Oppenheimer*. New York: Alfred A. Knopf, 2005.

Bix, Herbert P. *Hirohito and the Making of Modern Japan*. New York: Harper Perennial, 2016.

Blume, Lesley. *Fallout: The Hiroshima Cover-Up and the Reporter Who Revealed It to the World*. London, Scribe, 2020.

Bowman, Martin. *Combat Aircraft Series No. 18. B-17 Flying Fortress Units of the Eighth Air Force: Part 1*. Oxford: Osprey Publishing, 2000.

Boyer, Paul. *By the Bomb's Early Light: American Thought and Culture at the Dawn of the Atomic Age*. New York: Pantheon Books, 1985.

Broderick, James. *Saint Francis Xavier (1506–1552)*. New York: Doubleday Inc., 1957.

Chun, Clayton K. S. *Campaign Series No. 200 Japan 1945: From Operation Downfall to Hiroshima and Nagasaki*. Oxford: Osprey Publishing, 2008.

Coffey, Patrick. *American Arsenal: A Century of Waging War*. New York: Oxford University, 2014.

Constandelis, Nicholas, T. *8,000 Feet Over Hell: A Memoir*. Private publication, 2008.

David, Saul. *Crucible of Hell: The Heroism and the Tragedy of Okinawa 1945*. London: William Collins, 2020.

Dorr, Robert, F. *Combat Aircraft Series No. 33. B-29 Superfortress Units of World War 2*. Oxford: Osprey Publishing, 2002.

Dower, John. *Embracing Defeat: Japan in the Aftermath of World War II*. New York: W. W. Norton & Company, Inc., 1999.

Dower, John, W. *War Without Mercy: Race & Power in the Pacific War*. New York: Pantheon Books, 1986.

Farmelo, Graham. *Churchill's Bomb: A Hidden History of Britain's Nuclear Weapons Programme*. London: Faber & Faber, 2013.

Feifer, George. *The Battle of Okinawa: The Blood and the Bomb*. Globe Pequot, 2001.

Fort, Adrian. *Prof: The Life of Frederick Lindemann*. London: Jonathan Cape, 2003.

Fussell, Paul. *Thank God for the Bomb and Other Essays*. New York: Ballantine Books, 1988.

Frank, Richard B. *Downfall: The End of the Imperial Japanese Empire*. New York: Random House, 1999.

Fuller, Richard. *Shokan: Hirohito's Samurai, Leaders of the Japanese Armed Forces, 1926–1945*. London: Cassell, 1992.

Gladwell, Malcolm. *The Bomber Mafia: A Tale of Innovation and Obsession*. London: Penguin Books, 2021.

Groueff, Stephane. *Manhattan Project: The Untold Story of the Making of the Atomic Bomb*. Boston: Little, Brown, 1967.

Groves, Leslie, R. *Now It Can be Told: The Story of the Manhattan Project*. New York: Da Capo Press, 1962.

Hachiya, Michihiko. Translated and edited by Warner Wells MD. *Hiroshima Diary: The Journal of a Japanese Physician, August 6– September 30, 1945*, reissued in paperback 1995. Chapel Hill: University of North Carolina Press, 1955.

Harder, Robert O. *The Three Musketeers of the Army Air Forces: From Hitler's Fortress Europa to Hiroshima and Nagasaki*. Annapolis, Md.: Naval Institute Press, 2015.

Hasegawa, Tsuyoshi. *Racing the Enemy: Stalin, Truman, and the Surrender of Japan*. Cambridge, Mass.: Harvard University Press, 2005.

Hastings, Max. *Nemesis: The Battle for Japan, 1944–45*. London: William Collins, 2007.

Hersey, John. *Hiroshima*, reissued in paperback. London: Penguin Books, 2001.

Hersey, John. *Into the Valley: Marines at Guadalcanal*. New York: Penguin Random House, 1989.

Herzenberg, Caroline L. and Ruth H. *Their Day in the Sun: Women of the Manhattan Project*. Philadelphia: Temple University Press, 1999.

Kadota, Takasamata. *Yasuko, 19 Years Old: Diary of War Damage*, Bungeishunju Ltd., 2009.

Kennedy, David, M. *The American People in World War II: Freedom from Fear Part Two*. New York: Oxford University Press, 1999.

Kerr, E. Bartlett. *Flames over Tokyo: The U.S. Army Air Forces' Incendiary Campaign Against Japan 1944–45*. New York: Donald I. Fine, Inc., 1991.

Kloda, Samuel S. *The Atomic Bomb in Images and Documents*. North Carolina: McFarland & Company, Inc., 2022.

Krauss, Robert, and Amelia Krauss. *The 509th Remembered: A History of the 509th Composite Group as Told by the Veterans that Dropped the Atomic Bombs on Japan*. Michigan, privately published, 2017.

Kunetka, James. *The General and the Genius: Groves and Oppenheimer—The Unlikely Partnership That Built the Atom Bomb*, Washington, DC: Regnery History, 2015.

Lardas, Mark. *Air Campaign Series No. 9, Japan 1944–45: LeMay's B-29 Strategic Bombing Campaign*. Oxford: Osprey Publishing, 2019.

Lindbergh, Charles, A. *The Wartime Journals of Charles A. Lindbergh*. New York: Harcourt Brace Jovanovich, Inc., 1970.

Marshall, Chester. *Sky Giants over Japan: A Diary of a B-29 Combat Crew in WWII*. Minnesota: Apollo Books, 1984.

McMillan, Elsie Blumer. *The Atom and Eve*. New York: Vantage Press, 1995.

Mitsuru, Yoshida. *Requiem for Battleship Yamato*. London: Constable, 1999.

Mitter, Rana. *China's War with Japan 1937–1945: The Struggle for Survival*. London: Penguin Books, 2013.

Monk, Ray. *Robert Oppenheimer: A Life Inside the Center*. New York: Doubleday, 2012.

Neer, Robert M. *Napalm: An American Biography*. Cambridge, Mass.: Harvard University Press, 1964.

Nijboer, Donald. *The Mighty Eighth: Masters of the Air Over Europe 1942–45*. Oxford: Osprey Publishing, 2022.

O'Brien, Phillipps, P. *The Second Most Powerful Man in the World: The Life of Admiral William D. Leahy, Roosevelt's Chief of Staff*. London: E. P. Dutton, 2019.

Olson, Steve. *The Apocalypse Factory: Plutonium and the Making of the Atomic Age*. New York: W. W. Norton & Company, Inc., 2020.

Rhodes, Richard. *The Making of the Atomic Bomb*. London: Simon & Schuster UK Ltd., 2012.

Ross, Bill D. *Iwo Jima: Legacy of Valor*. London: Vintage, Random House, 1986.

Rottmann, Gordon and Mike Chappell. *Elite Series No. 59 US Marine Corps 1941–45*. Oxford: Osprey Publishing, 1995.

Rottman, Gordon and Howard Gerrard. *Campaign Series No. 146*

The Marshall Islands 1944: Operation Flintlock, the Capture of Kwajalein and Eniwetok. Oxford: Osprey Publishing, 2004.

Scott, James M. *Black Snow: Curtis LeMay, the Firebombing of Tokyo, and the Road to the Atomic Bomb*. New York, W. W. Norton & Company, Inc., 2022.

Simons, Graham M. *B-29 Superfortress: Giant Bomber of World War Two and Korea*. Barnsley: Pen & Sword Books Ltd., 2012.

Steinberg, Rafael. *Postscript from Hiroshima*. London: Hamish Hamilton, 1966.

Stille, Mark. *Campaign Series No. 284 Guadalcanal 1942–43: America's First Victory on the Road to Tokyo*. Oxford: Osprey Publishing, 2015.

Thomas, Evan. *Road to Surrender: Three Men and the Countdown to the End of World War II*. London: Elliott & Thompson, 2023.

Thomas, Gordon and Max Morgan-Witts. *Ruin from the Air: The Atomic Mission to Hiroshima*. London: Hamish-Hamilton, 1977.

Tibbets, Paul W. *Mission: Hiroshima*. New York: Stein and Day, 1981.

Treglown, Jeremy. *Mr. Straight Arrow: The Career of John Hersey, Author of* Hiroshima. New York: Farrar, Straus and Giroux, 2019.

Vanderbilt, Tom. *Survival City: Adventures among the Ruins of Atomic America*. New Haven, Conn.: Yale University Press, 2002.

Vander Meulen, Jacob. *Building the B-29*. New York: Smithsonian Institution Press, 1996.

Walker, Stephen. *Shockwave: Countdown to Hiroshima*. London: William Collins, 2020.

Webb, Pauline D. *Letters from Tinian 1945*. Private publication, 2009.

Weller, George. Edited with a new essay by Anthony Weller. *First Into Nagasaki: The Censored Eyewitness Dispatches on Post-Atomic Japan and Its Prisoners of War*. New York: Crown Publishers, 2006.

Wittner, Lawrence S. *Rebels Against War: The American Peace Movement, 1941-60* (New York, Columbia University Press, 1969)

Wolk, Herman S. *Cataclysm: General Hap Arnold and the Defeat of Japan*. Denton, Tex.: University of North Texas Press, 2010.

Yamashita, Samuel H. *Daily Life in Wartime Japan, 1940–45*. Lawrence, Kans.: University Press of Kansas, 2015.

Yagoda, Ben. *About Town: The New Yorker and the World It Made*. New York: Scribner, 2000.

Zinn, Howard. *A People's History of the United States*. New York: HarperCollins, 2015.

ARTICLES, PERIODICALS, AND REPORTS

Selden, Mark. "A Forgotten Holocaust: US Bombing Strategy, the Destruction of Japanese Cities and the American Way of War from World War II to Iraq." *Asia Pacific Journal* 5, no. 5 (May 2, 2007).

Winnacker, Rudolph A. "The Debate About Hiroshima." *Military Affairs* 11, no. 1 (Spring 1947): pp. 25–30.

Yavenditti, Michael, J. "The American People and the Use of Atomic Bombs on Japan: The 1940s." *The Historian* 36, no. 2 (February 1974): pp. 224–47.

PRIMARY INTERVIEWS

Japanese

Howard Kakita, Los Angeles, August 23, 2023

Toshiko Kameya, Tokyo, February 10, 2024

Michiko Kodama, Tokyo, November 17, 2023

Koko Kondo, Hiroshima, November 20, 2023

Haruo Okubo, Tokyo, February 3, 2024

Kenji Shiga, Hiroshima, December 21, 2023

Shizuyo Takeuchi, Tokyo, February 7, 2024

American

Richard Groves, Amsterdam, July 18, 2023

Cannon Hersey, Brooklyn, June 27, 2023

Professor Richard Jessor, Colorado, March 20, 2024

David Remnick, New York, September 4, 2023

Kia Tibbets, Cleveland, Ohio, July 13, 2023

Paul Tibbets IV, Missouri, May 24, 2023

Secondary Archived Interviews

Yoko Morishima, April 2020, from the Imperial War Museum Audio Archives (T17.37)

Sergeant William "Bill" Lansford, (USMC), OH1471, National WWII Museum, New Orleans

Hannah Dailey, (USAAF), OH5455, 2019, National WWII Museum, New Orleans

Eugene Di Sabatino, (Los Alamos), OH0609, 2012, National WWII Museum, New Orleans,

Harry Fukuhara, 2001, National, Japanese American Museum, Los Angeles

Russell Gackenbach (USAAF), OH4269, 2016, National WWII Museum, New Orleans

Lawrence Johnston, (Los Alamos) OH1335, National WWII Museum, New Orleans

Theordore Van Kirk (USAAF), OH2672, 2017, National WWII Museum, New Orleans

Charles Kneflin, (USAAF), OH5455, 2019, National WWII Museum, New Orleans

Masato Eddy Kurushima, 2002, Japanese American National Museum, Los Angeles

Tommy Lofton (physicist at Los Alamos), OH0609, 2012, National WWII Museum, New Orleans

James Molitor (US Army), OH5686, 2021, National WWII Museum, New Orleans

Hiroshima Digital Archive

Fusako Nobe, Hiroshima Digital Archive, Hiroshima

Junko Yoshinari, Hiroshima Digital Archive, Hiroshima

Mitsuko Koshimuzu, Hiroshima Digital Archive, Hiroshima

Setuko Thurlow, Hiroshima Digital Archive, Hiroshima

Sumiko Ogata, Hiroshima Digital Archive, Hiroshima

Index

About the Author

Iain MacGregor is the author of the acclaimed history of Cold War Berlin *Checkpoint Charlie* and *The Lighthouse of Stalingrad: The Hidden Truth at the Heart of the Greatest Battle of World War II*, winner of the Military History Matters Gold Award. He is a Fellow of the Royal Historical Society, has spoken at many literary festivals and conferences in the UK and abroad, and has appeared on podcasts such as *The Rest Is History* and in television documentaries. His writing has appeared in *The Washington Post*, *The Spectator*, *BBC History Magazine*, and *The Guardian*. He lives in London.